WHO IS CHRIST?
A THEOLOGY OF THE INCARNATION

by
JEAN GALOT, S.J.

FRANCISCAN HERALD PRESS
1434 WEST 51st STREET • CHICAGO, 60609

Library of Congress Cataloging in Publication Data

Galot, Jean.
  Who is Christ?
    Translated from the author's unpublished French ms.
    Includes index.
    1. Jesus Christ—Person and offices.
2. Jesus Christ—History of doctrines
3. Incarnation. : Title
BT202.G2413   232   0-20140
ISBN 0-8199-0183-4

Grateful acknowledgment is made to Doubleday and Company, Inc., New York, and Darton, Longman & Todd, London, for permission to quote from The Jerusalem Bible *(1968 edition), as well as to the American Bible Society of New York, for permission to quote from* The Bible, Revised Standard Version, *Second Edition, 1971.*

All Scriptural quotations are taken from The Jerusalem Bible, *with the exception of Philippians 2:6-8, Ephesians 5:25, and Luke 2:49, which are taken from* The Bible, Revised Standard Version.

CONTENTS

PART ONE

THE ORIENTATION OF CHRISTOLOGICAL RESEARCH

V

PART TWO

THE ESSENTIAL FEATURES OF
THE SCRIPTURAL SOURCES

PART THREE

THE FUNDAMENTAL AFFIRMATIONS OF THE
FAITH OF THE CHURCH

PART FIVE

THE PSYCHOLOGY OF CHRIST

Translation by M. Angeline Bouchard

This translation is dedicated to
SAINT JOSEPH,
PROTECTOR OF THE UNIVERSAL CHURCH
Faithful Witness to the Incarnation of the Son of God,
and His Gentle Defender as our Infant Savior
December 10, 1979

ABBREVIATIONS

AAS	Acta Apostolicae Sedis
Bi	Biblica
BLE	Bulletin de littérature ecclésiastique
BTB	Biblical Theology Bulletin
CBQ	Catholic Biblical Quarterly
CCL	Corpus christianorum, series latina
CSEL	Corpus scriptorum ecclesiasticorum latinorum
DBS	Dictionnaire de la Bible — Supplément
DS	H. Denzinger - A. Schönmetzer, *Enchiridion Symbolorum*, 32nd ed., 1963
DTC	Dictionnaire de théologie catholique
ETL	Ephemerides Theologicae Lovanienses
Exp T	Expository Times
Fr F	France Franciscaine
Gr	Gregorianum
LV	Lumière et Vie
MSR	Mélanges de Science Religieuse
NRT	Nouvelle Revue Théologique
NT	Novum Testamentum
NTS	New Testament Studies
PL	Patrologia latina
PG	Patrologia graeca
RB	Revue Biblique
RSPT	Revue des Sciences Philosophiques et Théologiques
RSR	Recherches de Science Religieuse
RT	Revue Thomiste
SC	Sources chrétiennes
SE	Science et Esprit
VT	Vetus Testamentum
ZNW	Zeitschrift für die Neutestamentliche Wissenschaft

INTRODUCTION

"Who is Jesus?" The present study seeks to offer new insights into this question within the context of salvation, but without dealing expressly with the Redemption and its problems which the author has discussed elsewhere. [1]

The task of speculative Christology has become more arduous with the growing number of exegetical works and historical studies of the doctrinal development of Tradition. The theologian, confronted with a vast array of publications, must try to retain all valid contributions to the state of the art, while seeking to clarify his own thinking on the Scriptural sources and on their interpretation within the Church. He may be strongly tempted to limit his perspective to the views presented in a few specialized studies, while neglecting the others. But Christological thought cannot be reduced to a one-sided or less than complete approach. It must embrace all that has been revealed of Christ. While relying on the results of solid research, it can never renounce its own efforts toward a more perfect synthesis.

Now, it is such a synthesis we are striving for here. After pointing out the general orientation and methodological problems of Christology, we shall consider the Scriptural sources, then give a brief overview of Patristical thought together with the Christological formulations of the Councils, and finally discuss the various speculative problems posed by the ontology and psychology of Christ.

---

[1] Cf. Jean Galot, S.J.,*La Rédemption, mystère d'alliance*, Bruges, Belgium, 1965; *Jesus, Our Liberator, a Theology of Redemption*, Rome, Gregorian University Press, 1982, Chicago, Franciscan Herald Press, 1989.

PART ONE

THE ORIENTATION OF CHRISTOLOGICAL RESEARCH

CHAPTER I

CHRISTOLOGY IN JESUS' PRIMORDIAL INTENTION

A. ESSENTIAL ORIENTATIONS OF CHRISTOLOGY

1. *The Person of Jesus in a Dynamic Christology*

Christology is dynamic by reason of its object. It seeks to know the person and the work of Christ in such a way that the person is never separated from his work. In considering Jesus, Christology cannot limit itself to investigations of what he once was in himself. Its objective must always be to express the dynamism of the divine action that willed to effect the salvation of the human race. Christological thought is born of an effort to grasp the even more fundamental dynamism which introduced the Savior into the world and called forth the unfolding of his redemptive mission. It has not yet completely succeeded in grasping this dynamism, and the considerable distance it still has to cover indicates how far human thinking has to progress in order to coincide more faithfully with the reality of God's plan.

Is this to say that the study of the person of Christ might be less important than the study of his work? Or that the ontological problem posed by Jesus should be absorbed by the soteriological problem? Certain theologians have made it their goal to develop a purely or principally functional Christology. They strive to define Jesus in terms of function. In so doing they reduce to a functional signification the various titles given him in the Gospel texts, even those which have received a more ontological interpretation in Tradition, such as Son of God, Word, Lord.

Oscar Cullmann, in seeking to discern the crux of the Christological problem in the New Testament, reacts against the tradition that gave a privileged place to the study of the person of Christ rather than to his work. Even before turning to the Scriptural texts he chooses an orientation based on function: "When it is asked in the New Testament 'Who is Christ?', the question never means exclusively, or even primarily, 'What is his nature?' but first of all, 'What is his function?'" [1]

To judge the soundness of this affirmation, one would have to examine the texts in their totality. Yet an essential guideline is provided us in the question Jesus asked of his disciples: "But you, who do you say I am?" (Mt 16:15; Mk 8:29; Lk 9:20). Jesus did not ask: "What do you say that I have come to do?" or "What is the work to which I am dedicating myself?" Yet he showed by his preaching what this work was. He made clear wherein his mission lay. He could have focussed the question on his mission, to determine whether the disciples had understood the significance of his activity and whether they acknowledged the value of his work. On the contrary, he limited himself to asking them who he was.

Such a question shows the importance Jesus attached to his disciples' understanding of his personal identity. It demonstrates that he wanted their faith to consist first of all in adherence to his person. Obviously, he allowed them to discover him in his actions, but he did not want them to be satisfied to know him only through his works. The question presupposes that the true significance of his achievement can be grasped only through the recognition of his personal identity. It has been stated that "Jesus coincided totally with his mission." [2] The essential event is seen to consist in the presence of his person among men.

---

[1] *The Christology of the New Testament,* London, SCM 1959, 3-4. Cullmann softens the impact of his affirmation by specifying that he does not conceive "the function of Christ in Bultmann's sense as only an event in the 'Kerygma', but as a real Christological event" (footnote 1). According to Bultmann, pronouncements about the divinity of Jesus in the New Testament "do not in fact claim to express his nature, but the place we are to assign to him" (*Das christologische Bekenntnis des oekumenischen Rates,* in *Glauben und Verstehen,* II, Tübingen, 1951-1952, 246).

[2] J. Guillet, *Jésus devant sa vie et sa mort,* Paris, 1971, 125. In rejecting the view that sets Christological function in opposition to the Chris-

With regard to the alternative formulated by Cullmann: "What is his nature?" as against "What is his function?", we must admit that while Jesus did not ask outright what his function was, neither did he ask what his nature was. His question concerned his person. From the answer to this question were to flow in later times clarifications concerning the nature or natures of Christ.

But Jesus did not want to involve his disciples in considerations of this sort. In this connection we can say with P. Bonnard that he "did not pose the question of his intemporal essence to his disciples." However, we cannot agree with him that "the being of Christ consists in what he is charged with accomplishing on earth in the service of God and men."[3] The question "Who am I?", while it does not concern his being in the philosophical sense of the word, cannot be reduced to an interrogation as to what Jesus was destined to accomplish. It refers to his personal identity.

It is significant that Cullmann himself, even though he posited the principle that the Christology of the New Testament is concerned with the functions of Christ, carried on research which in fact concerned the personal identity of the Savior, as is evident in his study of the titles relating to the preexistence of Jesus.

Moreover, the opinions expressed by the crowd and mentioned to Jesus by the disciples confirm that for them the problem was essentially one of identity. Was he John the Baptist, Elijah, Jeremiah, or one of the prophets?[4] They were trying to identify Jesus with a known personality. Jesus, whose mysterious personality was the origin of these diverse assumptions, clearly indicated that the crowd was indeed trying to answer the crucial question.

An understanding of Jesus' work is certainly linked to a

---

tology of the natures, M. de Jonge has stressed that the Fourth Gospel does not dissociate nature and function: *Stranger from Heaven and Son of God. Jesus Christ and the Christians in Johannine Perspective,* Missoula, Montana, Scholars Press, 1977.

[3] *L'Evangile selon saint Matthieu,* Neuchâtel, 1963, p. 143.

[4] Vincent Taylor remarks in this connection that "popular opinion does not hold Jesus to be the Messiah" (*The Gospel according to St. Mark,* London, 1969, 376). What is most evident in these identifications is the desire to give Jesus a name rather than to express his mission.

knowledge of his person. When Jesus received his disciples' profession of faith in his person, he began to explain to them how he would accomplish his mission. Yet, he did not pose the question of his identity merely so that his work might be more clearly understood. He demanded loyalty to his person before seeking collaboration in his work. He invited his followers to share in his close friendship before he sent them out on mission. He brought the world more than his activity, he brought a personal presence.

2. A Dialogic Christology

Jesus wanted Christology to be situated in a context of dialogic dynamism. The question he asked was not merely speculative, such as one concerning the meaning of a doctrine. The emphasis was on interpersonal relations: "But *you*, who do you say I am?" (Mt 16:15). The *you* stands out all the more, as it sets the disciples apart from the crowd. The "*you*" spoken by Peter has the same deliberate emphasis as Christ's "*you*." [5]

Here we can see Jesus' intention to bring Christology into being by way of questions and answers. It is he who initiates the dialogue. The way he assumes the initiative is brought out in Mark's text: "'But you,' he asked, 'who do you say I am?'" (Mk 8:29) where one might have expected a less emphatic statement.

Jesus' initiative is likewise emphasized by the context. For this was not a question provoked by circumstances. It did not arise in response to an event. It sprang from a deliberate intent on Jesus' part, who had chosen this moment to call forth his disciples' response of faith.

The likelihood that Jesus really asked this question concerning the crowd's opinion has been challenged, especialy by R. Bultmann, who finds it strange that Jesus should question his disciples on a matter about which he must have been as well informed as they. [6] But the objection is not very convincing. For while Jesus must indeed have heard echoes of

---

[5] Several commentators note the emphatic tone of the "you," and of Peter's as well. Cf. Taylor (*Mark*, 376).

[6] *Die Geschichte der Synoptischen Tradition*, Göttingen, 1967, p. 276.

8

what people thought of him, the disciples, by reason of their many contacts with the people, had certainly gleaned still more reports. They had heard the various hypotheses on the identity of their master, especially as the people must have spoken more freely to them about this problem than to Jesus himself. It was therefore Jesus' intent to make a point of these opinions concerning him when he questioned his disciples.

This first question was asked only in view of the second, whose authenticity has likewise been contested.[7] Why do some consider it suspect? It is said the question presupposed that Jesus had not yet told his disciples who he was, and that the disciples had not yet recognized him as the Messiah. Now, according to Mark himself (2:10,28), Jesus had presented himself as the Son of Man. According to John (1:41), the disciples had previously professed their faith in the Messiah. Moreover, there could have been no pedagogical intention, for even after Jesus posed the question the disciples remained as opaque to the truth as before. The view is expressed, therefore, that this question was formulated by the Evangelist, and not by Jesus himself.[8]

The two objections, which are in no way decisive, draw our attention to the real significance of Jesus' question. This query cannot be reduced to the level of a simple pedagogical procedure, but it implies a pedagogy that consists in calling for a personal commitment. Jesus obtained what he sought, since the response was a profession of faith. Pedagogy played its part; for before trying to make the disciples understand the nature of his messianism, he had to be sure they were convinced he was the Messiah. He proceeded by stages, so as to enlighten their minds gradually.

---

[7] The argument invoked by E. Haenchen in favor of an interpolation by the Evangelist appears to defeat itself. He relies on the fact that the question of Jesus' identity had already been treated in Mk 6:14, with the mention of opinions similar to the ones in our passage ("Die Komposition von Mk VII 27 - IX 1 und Par.", NT 6 (1963) 85). But since Mark had already recorded these opinions, he had no need to refer to them any more. Why would he have repeated himself? The only reason for returning to these opinions was that Jesus had really asked a certain question which provoked a response by the disciples on this point.

[8] Haenchen, art. cit., 85-86; G. Minette de Tillesse, Le secret messianique dans l'évangile de Marc, Paris, 1968, 299-301, 303-314.

And indeed this was not a superfluous question. Jesus had never yet told his disciples explicitly who he was. The expression "Son of Man," which he had applied to himself, remained mysterious. If it was to become part of a profession of faith it would have to be translated into more mundane language. Besides, the disciples as a group had not yet had the opportunity to profess their faith in a carefully thought-out and deliberate way. The proclamations of faith related in the First Chapter of John were made by individuals. In addition, we may wonder whether these do not reflect a later stage in the development of faith. What Jesus was seeking here was the commitment of the group as a whole, in short, a collective profession of faith.

Thus, there is no valid reason to deny the authenticity of Jesus' question. On the other hand, there are reasons that confirm this authenticity. Jesus liked to proceed by way of interrogation in eliciting acceptance of his revelation. The question he now asked for the first time concerning his identity grew out of all he had said and done before, as an explicit consequence.

We recall that the question had arisen in the minds of the disciples after he had calmed the storm: "Who can this be? Even the wind and the sea obey him" (Mk 4:41). The miracles of Jesus inevitably raised the problem of his identity. The same is true of his claim to have the power to forgive sins (Mk 2:10) and to be the master of the sabbath (Mk 2:29). In Mark's Gospel Jesus' question appears as the conclusion of the first stage of his public life. His teaching, together with the extraordinary "signs" that accompanied it, provided the disciples with the information they needed for their answer.

Obviously Jesus could have proclaimed his identity himself, instead of asking others to formulate it. But that was not his way of doing. He avoided defining himself. He wanted others to discover him and express the result of their discovery.

This means that he did not want to reveal his identity by way of a formula. That would have been too easy and entailed the risk of rallying only superficial commitments or evoking parrotlike repetitions. He wanted a profession of faith that stemmed from a personal effort to understand and not from the passive acceptance of a formula.

Jesus wanted Christology to be dialogic, so that its affirmations might result from the essential questioning of the evangelical facts, and so that it might consist in a confrontation not only between the human intellect and revealed truth, but between the whole human person and a person who had introduced himself by saying "Who am I?"

3. A Christology that Springs from Jesus' Earthly Life

It was not by chance that Jesus asked this question during his earthly life. More than anyone else, he knew that the revelation of his person would attain its plenitude only through the Resurrection. Besides, it was immediately after he had obtained Peter's profession of faith that he told his disciples of his forthcoming Passion, death, and Resurrection (Mk 8:31). Yet even though he attributed the greatest importance to this drama and to its triumphal finale, he did not wait for this glorious fulfillment to call for a declaration concerning his identity.

We may therefore assume that he had given enough signs by his words and actions to elicit a valid response from his disciples. His public life already sufficed in itself to pose the problem of faith and to give a basis for a clear understanding of his identity.

The moment Jesus chose to ask the question throws light on certain present-day debates over the origins of Christology. The faith of the disciples grew to maturity after the Resurrection, but it had already begun to take shape during Jesus' earthly life. And so we cannot consider the Resurrection or the glorious Christ as the point of departure of faith and of Christology, and even less as their sole foundation.

That Jesus intended to obtain a commitment of faith even before his Resurrection was again confirmed shortly before his Passion, in his prayer for the perseverance of Peter in the faith (cf. Lk 22:32). By his Resurrection Jesus was to restore the vigor of this faith. But his intention was specifically to reawaken a faith that had persisted through the Passion, rather than to create entirely new faith. Faith in the risen Lord

11

was meant to develop the faith that had germinated during his earthly life.

Such an intention can be explained only if Jesus' earthly life presented to faith certain aspects that could not be obviated by the Resurrection. A Christology that stemmed exclusively from the risen Jesus would disregard certain irreplaceable aspects of the revelation of the person of Jesus. It is necessary to understand the humble condition of a servant that characterized Jesus' earthly life, in contrast to his glorious life. Only then can we realize what this Jesus has been and what he will continue to be for the men and women involved in this same earthly life.

W. Pannenberg has stressed the revelatory value of Jesus' risen life at the expense of the value of his public life on earth. To his mind, the earthly life was a prolepsis, that is, a preamble that had value only by reason of the Paschal event. Thus, in its proleptic structure, Pannenberg says the claim to authority of the pre-Paschal Jesus was "analogous to that of the Old Testament prophetic sayings." [9] In actual fact, the words of the prophets were only an announcement to be fulfilled later, whereas the teaching and activity of Jesus were a fulfillment in their own right. The Resurrection, in completing this fulfillment, brings confirmation to the earlier revelation of the person of Jesus, a revelation so compellingly offered to the disciples as to elicit their commitment of faith.

If the essentials of Jesus' revelation had been transmitted by him in his risen state, that would have indicated that God could or would reveal himself only in circumstances superior to human life, not subject to the ordinary laws of matter and of the physical world. To the contrary, Jesus showed that this revelation could find perfect expression in a passible human life, one that was fundamentally like that of other men.

4. A Christology Immersed in Mystery

Jesus' first question shows that the problem exists for all men to the extent that they make contact with him. What do "some" or what do "people" (Mt 16:13; Mk 8:27), or what do "the crowds" (Lk 9:18) think of his identity? This

---

[9] *Jesus, God and Man*, London, SCM 1968, 66.

is the question everyone who will ever receive the Gospel message must ask. In this sense Christology concerns every human being, whoever he or she may be.

But there is a superficial approach to the problem. Jesus wanted a deeper response from his disciples which would involve them personally in the mystery.

The question itself suggests the mystery, for it is outside the ordinary run of human dialogues. Normally, a man does not ask others: "Who do you say I am?" The strangeness of this question makes us sense its underlying depth.

The circumstances in which the question was asked are also suggestive. Jesus questioned his disciples on the road to Caesarea Philippi. He was going toward a pagan region where it would be easier for him to speak in confidence to those who accompanied him. Lagrange concludes that Jesus wanted to deal with the supreme question "far from the envious eyes of the scribes and from the irksome eagerness of the Galilean crowds." [10]

According to Luke's account (9:18), Jesus asked the question after "praying alone," which implies he had meditated on it in advance and prayed to the Father for the hoped-for answer. We should not minimize the fact that Jesus prayed before this first Christological declaration. Not only does it suggest the necessity of prayer for all Christology, but it helps us to guess the reason for it. For here is a mystery we can penetrate only with the help of light from a higher source.

The way the question was formulated also confirms its import of mystery. In Matthew's version, the first question is expressed in this way: "Who do people say the Son of Man is?" (Mt 16:13). Jesus' hearers could have had little understanding of the term "Son of Man." It drew their attention to a personal secret. [11]

---

[10] *Evangile selon saint Marc*, Paris 1920, 203.

[11] O. Cullmann considers Mark's formulation: "Who do people say I am?" (Mk 8:27) to be unquestionably more primitive (*Saint Pierre disciple-apôtre-martyr*, Neuchâtel, 1952, 158). But he does not give the precise reason why. It seems more probable in our view that this formulation is a very natural simplification of the formula recorded by Matthew. The question: "Who is the Son of Man?" is strange, and we can understand that attempts have been made to render it in more ordinary language. It most probably reproduces the exact words spoken by Jesus.

Finally, the question presupposes that Jesus' identity was superior to his human origin. His human antecedents were well known and presented no problem. Jesus was a Nazarene whose mother had been seen several times during his public life. It was not in this sense of his origin that Jesus could ask: "Who do you say I am?" The question was an invitation to go beyond what was known of him in simple human terms and what was known of his family origins.

B. THE FIRST CHRISTOLOGICAL DECLARATION

1. *Peter's Answer*

Peter's answer is recorded for us in different terms in the three Synoptics: "You are the Christ" (Mk 8:29); "The Christ of God" (Lk 9:20); "You are the Christ, the Son of the living God" (Mt 16:16).

The earliest version was probably Mark's. [12] We cannot determine precisely what Peter meant by "the Christ." According to Taylor, this confession certainly signifies that Peter was saluting in Jesus "the One in whom the hopes of Israel would be fulfilled." [13] It would seem that Peter included in this name the sovereignty that Jesus had exercised in his miracles. The one whom the wind and the sea obey (cf. Mk 4:41) is a Messiah who exceeds everything that had been announced about the ideal Messianic king. The expression "the Christ", used in referring to the events of Jesus' public life, could thus take on a more ample meaning than that of the Jewish tradition, and express the transcendence that had often impressed the disciples.

In this first answer we sense the inadequacy of formulas to express the mystery of Jesus. The Jewish conceptions of the Messiah were deficient, yet there was no choice but to use terminology inherited from tradition.

This is perhaps the justification for the more complex term used by Luke: "The Christ of God," in which an insight into the origins of Jesus surfaces. This becomes more ap-

---

[12] Cf. R. Vögtle, "Messias-bekennitnis und Petrusverheissung," *Biblische Zeitschrift*, N.F. 1 (1957) 252-272; 2 (1958) 85-103.
[13] *Mark*, 376.

parent in the use of two titles in Matthew's version: "the Christ, the Son of the living God."

It would seem that Matthew, according to his custom, inserted into the simpler account as set down by Mark, another passage that came to him from a special tradition and that recounted the promise made to Peter. Such an insertion does not signify it was a tradition of lesser value.

The coherence and naturalness of the dialogue recorded by Matthew make its authenticity difficult to challenge. Jesus' words correspond to Peter's answer: "You are the Christ, the Son of the living God." He responds: "Simon son of Jonah, you are a happy man! Because it was not flesh and blood that revealed this to you but my Father in heaven" (Mt 16:17). These words are the fulfillment of his earlier statement: "... no one knows the Son except the Father, just as no one knows the Father except the Son and those to whom the Son chooses to reveal him" (Mt 11:27). [14]

Let us note in particular the probable authenticity of Peter's answer. It finds confirmation in the solemn questioning of Jesus by the high priest during his trial: "I put you on oath by the living God to tell us if you are the Christ, the Son of God" (Mt 26:63). This supreme indictment makes it clear that Jesus, by his teaching and demeanor, claimed to be not only the Messiah but also the very Son of God. [15] If Jesus' enemies had grasped that he was making such a claim, his disciples must certainly have discerned it too, and much sooner. It is therefore most probable that at least on one occasion, either on the road to Caesarea Philippi or in other circumstances, [16] Peter expressed his faith in the Messiah Son of God in answer to Jesus' questioning.

---

[14] Guillet remarks: "Jesus' answer is so appropriate that it is hard to separate it from the preceding question, and this is the strongest argument in favor of Matthew's version of the episode" (*Jésus devant sa vie et sa mort*, 133).

[15] Concerning Mark 14:61, P. Carrington writes: "And the form of this question suggests that the association [of the two titles 'Christ' and 'Son of God'] was a perfectly natural one, or (more likely) that it was known to be current among the disciples of Jesus" (*According to Mark*, Cambridge University Press, 1960, 176).

[16] O. Cullmann thought he had discovered the true context of Mt 16:17-19 in an episode of the Passion recorded in Lk 22:31-32 (*Peter, Disciple,*

What Peter meant by " Son of the living God" we have no way of determining with certainty. This mention of the divine sonship which harmonizes with the quality of Messiah and enhances its value [17] can be explained by the filial attitude that Jesus, to his disciples' amazement, had manifested by addressing God as "Abba." It points to a higher relationship of origin and of intimacy with God, a sonship of a unique kind. The disciples would have been hard put to define its significance. They accepted whatever meaning Jesus wanted to give it without being able to grasp everything their master intended to signify. [18]

Here we see an essential characteristic of Christology emerge. Faith seeks to express what Jesus manifested of himself, within a dynamism that tends to coincide as completely as possible with Revelation, but still cannot exhaust its great richness of meaning.

When we seek to understand the underlying reason for the power of this dynamism, we realize that God is the being who exercises the most powerful attraction on man. It is God who, in Jesus, draws the intellect into an effort of discovery and expression. If Jesus himself avoids defining himself by a name or a formula, it is because in him God is present, and God cannot be completely contained within any human expression. However, such expression is necessary for

---

Apostle, Martyr, London, SCM, 1962, 188-181). Such an identification can be contested, but the dialogue recorded by Matthew may have come from a context other than the one where it was inserted.

[17] For Cullmann, on the contrary, the amplification of Matthew "appears to be in fact a weakening of the Marcan text" and "is not merely an edifying liturgical paraphrase" but the joining of "two entirely different narratives" (*op. cit.,* 177). But this interpretation, expressed with "the prudence needed in judgments of this sort, based on impressions" is difficult to justify. For the expression "Son of the living God" is not a diminished synonym for "Messiah." It adds a new dimension of a special relationship of sonship toward God.

[18] In particular, we find it hard to attribute to Peter an understanding of the expression which, according to Cullmann, stems from the witness of the Synoptics. He writes: "Jesus is the Son of God not because he is a miracle-worker, but because he carries out his mission in obedience and above all because he accepts suffering" (*Christologie du Nouveau Testament,* 241). It would be paradoxical to attribute such a view to the disciple who vigorously rebelled against the announcement of the Passion.

the development of faith. The task of Christology is to seek the best possible formulation of the God revealed in Jesus.

2. A Definitive and Unique Profession of Faith

Imperfect as Peter's profession of faith may be, it has an undeniable ring of truth. It expresses clearly who Jesus is, as can be seen by Jesus' tacit assent according to Mark and Luke, and, according to Matthew, by the suggestion of a revelation coming from the Father. Human formulations are thus capable of bringing to light real aspects of the person of Jesus. While we cannot overlook the dynamism of a faith that always exceeds the limits of any specific formula, neither can we disregard the objective value of affirmations of faith for Christology.

Peter's profession of faith has enduring value, [19] even if the man who expressed it did not as yet have as complete an understanding of the identity of Jesus as he would have after the Resurrection. This definitive value appears in particular in the fact that Jesus was to vouch for the truth of his positive answer to the high priest by the witness of his life. He was to be sentenced to death for proclaiming he was the Christ, the Son of God. Peter's declaration could not have received a more valid confirmation.

This declaration of Peter, made in the name of the Twelve, manifests the unity of their profession of faith. Although divergent opinions circulated among the populace, the profession of faith made by those who might be called the original nucleus of the Church expresses a single, undivided belief. The reason, as Jesus points out elsewhere, is that there is a distinction between "those who are outside" for whom everything is expressed in parables, and the Twelve to whom "the secret of the kingdom of God is given" (Mk 4:11).

Such a Gospel context throws light on the future. A great diversity of opinions would indeed arise in subsequent history concerning Jesus among "those who are outside." Yet for those who were to accept the mystery there would be a

---

[19] His words "are the embryo of the creed" to quote Carrington (*According to Mark*, 176).

single Christology, the one that developed along the lines of Peter's answer and that would seek to explore more completely the meaning of the affirmation: "You are the Christ, the Son of the living God" (Mt 16:16).

There has been talk recently of the diverse Christologies of the New Testament. There is diversity in the manner the person and the work of Jesus are considered and expressed. Each author has his own way of seeing Jesus or of telling about him. But this pluralism excludes any incompatibility and remains within limits that do not jeopardize the essentials of faith. The diverse Christologies are harmonized into a single Christology that is the continuation of the Christology of the primitive Church and that professes faith in Christ, the Son of God.

CHAPTER II

THE DYNAMISM OF FAITH
AND THE METHODOLOGICAL OPTIONS

A. A CHRISTOLOGY FROM ABOVE AND A CHRISTOLOGY
FROM BELOW

The divergences in method have found expression in the
opposition between a Christology from above and a Christology
from below. The two categories are used to distinguish the
works of Protestant theologians who write in the German
language.[1] The Christology of R. Bultmann is considered by
many as an example of a Christology from above, as is also
the very different theology of Karl Barth. The reason is that
both seek their foundation in God's Word. The Christology
of Pannenberg, on the other hand, is seen as specifically "from
below," because his approach consists in starting out with the
historical Jesus and concluding to his divine sonship.

However, the designations "from above" and "from below" can take on diverse significations or aspects. In the
debate between the two approaches, two methodological problems should be clearly discerned.

The first concerns the mode of knowledge that must serve
as the basis for Christology. Should Christology be founded
on the affirmation of faith and on the message of preaching,
considered to be essentially superior and irreducible to any
historical demonstration, or should Christology be founded on
the Jesus of history? The second problem concerns the reality
under consideration: should we start out from the divinity

---

[1] A presentation of these two contrary points of view in Christology is
given by R. Slenczka, *Geschichtlichkeit und Personsein Jesu Christi*, Göttingen 1967.

of Christ in order to arrive at his humanity, or should we ascend from his humanity to his divinity?

The two problems are interrelated, for when faith is the foundation of Christology, we tend to look toward God as the primordial object of our quest and to take the divinity of Christ as our starting point, or at least the divinity that is revealed in Jesus. On the other hand, when we opt in favor of the historical foundation, we normally start out from the humanity of Christ in order to arrive at his divinity. But the two problems remain distinct. Faith addresses itself to the humanity no less than to the divinity of Christ, and in the way of faith some can begin by considering the man Jesus before turning to what is divine about him. These two problems must therefore be approached successively, the former relating to the subject who knows and the latter relating to the object of study.

B. The Christ of Faith and the Historical Jesus

There are those who have emphasized the distinction between Christ and Jesus, to the point of setting up a "Jesusology" in opposition to a "Christology." For them Christ is the object of our faith, whereas Jesus is the man who lived in Palestine in historical fact.

How can we clarify the relationship between the knowledge of faith and historic knowledge? Which of these two knowledges holds primacy in Christology? How are we to conceive of the influence of the one over the other?

The answer is complex, and from this point of view we cannot opt solely and exclusively either for a Christology from above or for a Christology from below.

1. *The Objective Priority of the Historical Event*

Objectively, Christology is concerned with recognizing the Jesus of history. In fact, Christianity began as an historical fact, and the partisans of the Christology from below justifiably affirm that it is an historical religion. It did not grow out of an idea that took shape in the mind of an individual or of a community, then became organized and codified in a message of evangelization. Christianity came into being through a person who, while living the life of a man, accomplished the divine work of salvation. The event that consisted in the coming of this person into the history of mankind was the point of departure of the Church's development and has retained its fundamental importance. Therefore we cannot disregard this historical event or cut Christian evangelization off from its origins. We cannot admit, as Bultmann does, a rupture between a historical Jesus, a rather colorless and nonmessianic personality, and the kerygmatic Christ, clothed in the images of the Jewish apocalypse and the Gnostic myth of redemption. [2] Indeed, it was against this rupture that the post-Bultmannian theologians reacted, affirming the continuity between the Jesus of history and the Christ of faith. [3]

Besides, from an objective point of view we cannot claim that the Christian religion is first of all dogmatic, consisting primarily of a dogma that demands a commitment of faith. It was the historical Jesus who called for faith in his person. It was he who asked the question that is at the origin of the Church's profession of faith and of Christology: "Who do you say I am?" The fundamental direction of faith as it is recorded in the Gospels is prolonged in the faith of our own day.

Authentic faith remains faith in Christ himself and not only in his message. And it is faith not in an abstract or imaginary Christ, but in a Savior who was born, lived, and died in Palestine, where he afterwards manifested the victory of his Resurrection. Therefore Christology can develop only along these lines. It must seek to delineate as accurately as possible the Jesus who lived in concrete reality; it must show not only what he means here and now for Christian life or the life of faith, but what he was in his historical existence.

Fidelity to the Jesus of history expresses a fundamental

---

[2] Cf. R. Bultmann, *Theologie des Neuen Testaments*, Tübingen 1953; *L'intreprétation du Nouveau Testament*, Paris 1955; *Histoire et eschatologie*, Neuchâtel 1959; *Foi et compréhension*, Paris 1969-1970; A. Malet, *La pensée de Rudolf Bultmann*, Geneva, 1962; L. Malevez, *Le message chrétien et le mythe*, Brussels, 1954; *Histoire du salut et Philosophie*, Paris 1971.
[3] The author has given a brief summary of this reaction in "L'attuale problema cristologico," in *Correnti teologiche postconciliari* (A. Marranzini) Rome (Città Nuova) 1974, 191-195.

dimension of faith. It does not allow any separation between a "Jesusology" and a "Christology." To believe is to believe in Christ Jesus. Every "Jesusology" that conforms to the truth is a Christology, and vice versa.

Let us note that from the very beginning, Christian evangelization claimed to announce the historical Jesus. The Gospels were likewise written to witness to a faith founded on events that really happened, a faith that presented, to legitimize its origins, accounts by witnesses to these events.

2. The Subjective Priority of the Knowledge of Faith

Subjectively, the disposition of faith is essential to anyone who undertakes Christological investigation. Faith in Christ is the starting point for all such research. Christology has developed through the Christian community's efforts to attain a deeper understanding of the object of its faith. Today, as in the past, Christology must stem from a Christian faith that is continually seeking more light, firmer foundations, and greater depth.

In actual fact, those who study the authentic historical content of the Gospel most intensely are not historians but exegetes and theologians. Jesus cannot be taken as the object of historical research in the same way as other historical personalities. The interest of the historical Jesus comes from what he signifies for faith. And faith, as we understand it here, cannot be considered to be an attitude of mind arrived at simply as a conclusion based on historical research. Rather, faith is the principle of such research. It is believers who devote themselves to this research, impelled by a faith that seeks greater understanding. While unbelievers sometimes take an interest in the story of Jesus, their interest is religious in nature, and seems to indicate that for them a problem of faith is either remotely or proximately involved.

These facts corroborate the principle of the primordial value of faith in Christology. The only authentic Christology is one which addresses itself to a deeper understanding of the meaning of the deposit of faith. That being so, method in Christology cannot presuppose a priority of historical research over faith. We cannot proceed as if faith, for the ordinary

Christian or the theologian of our day, can result from an investigation carried out according to the laws of history; nor as if the "dogmatic" image of Christ were provided in the first place by an historical inquiry.

It is the dynamism of faith [4] that commands the entire doctrinal effort of Christology.

This faith is not simply the faith of an individual, as we have pointed out with respect to Peter's answer made in the name of the Twelve. It is the faith of the Church. And by the ecclesial dimension of faith we must understand not only that the believer belongs to the Church, but that the content of his faith is truly the same as the Christian community's. We are talking about a faith that has developed and matured through the centuries, continually enriched by many varied perspectives and doctrinal clarifications. Faith engages in Christological reflection at the particular stage of development it has already attained. It must never proceed in this effort by stripping itself of its own riches.

Since the dynamism of faith that impels the growth of

---

[4] Msgr. A. L. Descamps reacted against the position taken by E. Käsemann, for whom Jesus is not reached through pure history, since the object of Christological inquiry is indissolubly the man Jesus of history and the Christ of faith. In opposition to this point of view, Descamps wants Christology first of all to develop a life of Jesus, purely historical in nature, then to build on a careful analysis of the post-Paschal faith. To his mind, the Jesus of history is a Jesus whom his disciples apprehended to be the Messiah, but whom it would be anachronistic to call the Christ of faith. It is this Jesus who would be discovered by every open-minded historian who followed a rigorously historical method, independently of faith. According to Descamps, Christological faith must be rooted in a "scientific" and "preliminary" knowledge of the Jesus of Nazareth ("*Portée christologique de la recherche historique sur Jésus,*" in *Jésus aux origines de la christologie* (J. Dupont), Louvain, 1975, 23-46; cf. E. Käsemann, *Die neue Jesus-Frage,* ibid., 47-57).

Nevertheless, Käsemann's position seems sound to us. An inquiry into the Jesus of history cannot totally abstract from faith, on the one hand because this Jesus addressed himself to faith, and on the other because anyone interested in the historical Jesus is necessarily influenced by his own dispositions in the realm of faith. Would it not be to minimize the commitment of the disciples to Jesus during his earthly life if it were defined as a "certain human hope in a Jesus of history" who would not be the Christ of faith? The Gospel texts stress the importance Jesus attached to the attitude of faith, and this cannot be attributed simply to a reinterpretation by the post-Paschal community.

Christology is essentially that of the Christian community, no individual theologian can set forth all its aspects or orientations. The dynamism that inspires him is beyond his capacities. The Christological views he expresses always retain an aspect of incompleteness and need to be complemented by the views of other theologians. From this standpoint there is necessarily a Christological pluralism. The diversity of Christologies involves debates, intellectual conflicts that may at times reach great intensity. Notwithstanding, it would be a mistake to draw unduly relativistic conclusions from this fact and renounce efforts toward synthesis.

Finally the diversity is integrated in a broader and richer unity, one that is postulated by the dynamism of faith. For this dynamism leads to the search, among the divergent opinions, for those valid contributions that point the way to an overall vision of the person and work of Jesus. As we have already indicated, the diversity of Christologies does not eliminate the more fundamental unity of Christology. It simply nurtures it and gives it a more ample base providing, of course, these Christologies do not stray from the authentic tenets of faith in Christ and from its essential content.

The fact that we possess a traditional doctrine that expresses this essential content in professions of faith or in dogmatic formulas should never be an obstacle to free inquiry. For however true a formulation may be, it cannot absorb or condense the entire dynamism of faith. It calls for a subsequent deepening, and its signification as well as its limitations make the need for new research felt. The mystery of Christ is above and beyond any and all of its expressions. These presentations cannot petrify Christology, or put a stop to its onward movement. No formula can immobilize this trend.

Besides, we should note that the goal of Christology is not simply to render all the riches hidden in a dogma, but to explicate ever more clearly what is implied in the mystery of salvation, whose aim goes beyond any particular dogma. The definition of dogmas is a necessary expression of the dynamism of faith, which is impelled to clarify its intellectual content. Dogmatic definition cannot take the place of this dynamism and should instead be a stimulus to constant progress.

3. Faith and Historical Research

How can we come to a clearer understanding of the relationship between faith and historical research The urgency of the problem of method is evident here. Can our objective be to give a complete historical verification of our faith in Christ, a demonstration through history of the soundness of the belief in the divine sonship of Jesus?

This is the goal Pannenberg has set for himself. He applies the principle in the most radical way: "The task of Christology is to establish the true understanding of Jesus' significance from his history, which can be described comprehensively by saying that in this man God is revealed." [5] In Pannenberg's view, all the affirmations of primitive Christianity were born of this history, as were all the Christological theses formulated in the Church in later times. These theses must be verified in the light of the history of Jesus. Using this history as a foundation, and especially the event of the Resurrection which signified for Jesus the end of his history, Pannenberg establishes the unity of Jesus with God, an identity of being within the distinction between the persons of the Father and the Son. He wants to show by this that history provides us with the proof of the divinity of Jesus, and particularly of his divine sonship.

Some fault him for having developed an overly ambitious Christology, for "wanting to prove too much, and for having given too much importance to the desire for firsthand evidence." [6] This criticism should not cause us to forget the great merit of a Christology that stresses the value of the historical Jesus who is identical to the Son of God professed by faith. It was a legitimate reaction in favor of the Jesus of history that led to this extreme point of view.

There can be no doubt that historical investigation is necessary. Yet we cannot speak of an historical verification or demonstration in the strict sense of the affirmations of faith. A verification would presuppose that everything that is affirmed by faith is subject to historical inquiry in every respect, and can find its certitude in such inquiry. A demonstration would

---

5 *Jesus, God and Man,* London SCM 1968, 5.
6 I. Berten, "Bulletin de christologie protestante," *RSPT* 54 (1970) 163.

imply a proof developed according to historical methods. It would follow from this that historical inquiry would ultimately determine the object of faith, and that the degree of certitude of faith would depend directly on the certainty of the conclusions of history.

Now, faith involves a certitude that is far stronger than the certainty of historical science. Pannenberg holds the view that historical demonstration can at best attain a very high probability. [7] But faith is a commitment based on a certitude that a probability, however high, can never satisfy. The person who believes in Jesus the Son of God cannot hope that historical inquiry into New Testament writings will of itself bring him a certitude equal to that of his faith.

Faith possesses a superior certitude because it adheres to God's word, to a Revelation which — even while being actualized in history — surpasses history by the truth it proposes. In the case of Christ, this utterance of God was presented concretely in the Word made flesh. The Incarnation of the Son of God is a reality that goes far beyond all historical findings, even though it is manifested in the historical life of Jesus. In itself, the Incarnation can never be justified by a verification or demonstration governed strictly by the laws of history.

On the other hand, faith invites historical investigation because it seeks greater knowledge of its own object. Faith in Christ, we have already said, is a faith in the historical Jesus. We cannot, as Bultmann has suggested, separate the Christ of evangelization from the Christ of the history. When faith is emptied of almost all its historical content, it is stripped of its substance. In contrast to other religions that are founded on myths, Christianity rests on an event of salvation that has been fulfilled in history. The Incarnation signifies that God personally entered into the history of mankind.

Bultmann retained of Christ only what fitted into his existential analysis; that is to say, he wanted to reduce Christ

---

[7] Thus, concerning the question of the historicity of the Resurrection of Jesus, which is of capital importance, Pannenberg concludes from an examination of the traditions on Jesus' apparitions and on the empty tomb that the affirmation of the reality of the Resurrection is "historically very probable," "and that always means in historical inquiry, that it is to be presupposed until contrary evidence appears" (*Jesus, God and Man*, 195).

to human experience as he conceived it. To his mind, the event of salvation is produced only within the subjective experience of each individual. Salvation is announced by Christ but not objectively realized by him. Indeed, according to Bultmann there is no objective intervention by God in the human world, or sensible manifestation of a divine person. The only thing that matters is to live authentically in faith, faith in the salvation made known by God in Christ.

Karl Barth comments: "This is the theology of the solitary who reflects on himself (this time on his authenticity or his lack of authenticity), who expresses himself and in so doing expresses what a believing individual is." [8] Now, Christ tends to save man from his subjectivism. Being the Word made flesh, he has an objective impact on faith. He makes of this faith not simply an interior relationship with God, but one that focuses on the historical revelation of God in person.

It is the entrance of the Son of God into human history that works the real demythologization. Myth does not designate every representation of God in his relations with men, but more specifically a representation outside of all historical manifestation, exclusively produced by human thinking and imagination. The myth may reveal certain aspects of God and of his salvific work, but it is situated outside of history and cannot express the authentic revelation of God in this world, his intervention in our history in order to save us. This authentic manifestation, inaugurated in Judaism, occurs in its fullness in the Incarnation. Thus it is Christ who delivers mankind form its prison of mythology.

The personal involvement of the Son of God in the realities of history clears away all pseudo-history. It shows by contrast the fiction of mythical representations. That is why Christianity has not absorbed pagan religions, but eliminated them. History cannot feed on myths; it excludes them. The Incarnation makes known whatever hidden truth the myths contained. But only the Incarnation encompasses the historic truth of the intervention of God in the world for its salvation and presents the authentic face of God in a human face.

Barth says that Bultmann, in his refusal to accept that the Word became man, did not in fact demythologize but

---

[8] *L'humanité de Dieu*, Geneva 1956, 39.

returned to a "much more subtle myth," the "anthropocentric myth."[9] This myth is born not of popular and primitive imagination, but of philosophical "gnosis." It is a myth of an existential message that is the subjective representation of the divine and of its relationship to us.

If theology is to continue Christ's work of demythologizing it must strive unremittingly to understand who the Jesus of history was, what he said and what he did. Faith inspires this effort to achieve historical objectivity. At first sight, this might seem to orientate research toward subjective views, but, says Barth, it really aims at objectivity. For the sincerity of faith's commitment implies objectivity. The person who believes in Christ aspires to discover the real, objective countenance of Jesus.

Let us explain what is meant by the orientation of faith toward historical research. First of all, faith implies a *predisposition* to Christological inquiry. This predisposition includes a strong intellectual interest in this research and the willingness to accept its results. Besides, it gives a *pre-understanding* of the inquiry by illumining the goals of exegetical and historical research and nurturing a general approach that will make it possible to grasp the meaning and importance of the elements studied.[10] This pre-understanding is not a prejudgment, for it does not predetermine what is to ensue from the inquiry and it does not orientate research in a direction contrary to scientific objectivity.

The positive role of faith in Christological inquiry makes us see that there is no ideal method that would abstract from the faith of the exegete or theologian in his research. There can be no presupposed universal doubt as a methodological procedure to better assure objectivity. To expect to approach the study of the texts with a mind that is a "tabula rasa" can only be an illusion, for despite his attempts to abstract

---

9 Barth, *L'humanité de Dieu,* 40.

10 The pre-understanding of which we speak is in no sense identifiable with the precomprehension affirmed by Bultmann in the acceptance and interpretation of the Christian message (cf. on this subject Malevez, *Histoire du salut et Philosophie,* 9-49). This precomprehension consists in an existential anthropology and is prior to the acceptance of God's word. Here we are speaking of a pre-understanding that stems from faith, where exegetical and historical inquiry are concerned.

from his own convictions of faith, the theologian is inevitably influenced in his investigations by his own personal mode of thinking. Besides, such abstraction would rob research of the support it needs. For the best guarantee of objectivity still remains the disposition of faith, insofar as it implies a total openness to truth and the desire to proceed according to the norms of the exegetical and historical sciences. Faith owes it to itself, as a matter of honesty and sincerity, to respect the autonomy of exegesis and of history.

If we were called upon to state the ultimate reason for this principle, we would have to say that faith in Christ implies a faith in God which is a commitment to absolute truth. Such a commitment implies the acceptance of everything that reflects this truth in the world, everything that is a finite participation of the infinitely true. Faith nurtures a primordial concern for truth wherever it may be found. In historical inquiry, it must therefore provide the best conditions to arrive at truth, while conforming to the scientific demands that will permit the reaching of correct conclusions.

The reason for the trend toward a Christ seen "from below" has been the hope of keeping historical inquiry free of undue infiltration by dogmatic convictions. When one starts "from above," one cannot predetermine what the historical Jesus will be. Thus, for example, from the historical point of view, faith in the risen Christ could not be a reason for admitting or stressing the veracity of the Gospel accounts concerning the discovery of the empty tomb. This veracity can be established only by virtue of reasons provided by an exegetical analysis of the various testimonies. We can understand the opposition to all attempts to introduce a Christ "from above" into history. Such an approach cannot conform to the fundamental orientation of faith, which essentially implies respect for truth and the use of the historical method to establish the facts of history.

If we were to think of "Christology from above" as one in which faith would dictate the conclusions of historical research, it would be impossible to admit its coundness. Faith cannot claim to replace history, or to govern historical science, any more, for that matter, than history can provide conclusions that would supersede faith, or a certitude identical to that of faith. From this point of view Christological method cannot consist either in a dogmatization of history or in an historicization of dogma.

What, then, can faith expect from historical research if it cannot obtain from it any verification or demonstration in the strict sense? It asks research to provide it with more facts about the Christ in whom it believes. Historical and exegetical investigation permit faith to emerge from an overly generalized view of its object, and to delineate the historical countenance of Jesus even in many of its details.

Besides, this investigation gives the believer a better understanding of why he believes. It illumines not only the object of faith but also its reasons. Of itself, as we have already said, research cannot inspire the commitment of faith, but it can show that in the order of historical knowledge there are solid reasons for admitting the existence and the work of Jesus as the Church professes them in her faith.

Thanks to historical research, faith can therefore deepen its knowledge of Jesus and grasp more lucidly why it cleaves to him.

4. Historical Research and Doctrinal Systematization

Now, while the dynamism of faith impels to historical research, it also calls for doctrinal systematization. An analysis of Scriptural testimonies, such as practical exegesis, does not suffice. There is need of a synthesis, for faith wants to delve more deeply into what it must think by studying not only a certain number of texts but the person and the work of Christ himself.

That is what warrants the pursuit of speculative Christology. And this poses a new methodological problem: how are we to understand the relationship of Christology to exegesis, and on what principle must it base its work of synthesis?

Today the problem arises with greater cogency, because exegetical works have been multiplied and diversified to the point that a synthesis of their conclusions is difficult to arrive at and requires continual revision. Besides, we cannot abstract from the divergences of interpretation which are often considerable among the various exegetes. These divergencies demand a certain critical sense on the part of anyone seeking to evaluate the Scriptural sources. How, then, is it possible to assure an adequately reliable foundation for the development of speculative Christology?

The problem would easily be solved by the transcendental method proposed by K. Rahner. [11] "Transcendental Christology" actually poses a basic principle that removes Christology from the fluctuations of exegetical research. It claims to be a "Christology from below" and adopts an anthropological point of departure, namely, man considered in his transcendental necessity, in an existential situation characterized by constant and ineluctable circumstances. This man is defined by his thirst for the absolute that can be called a natural desire for the beatific vision, or more specifically he is defined by his hope of a free self-communication on the part of God.

From this hope Rahner deduces the essentials of Christology. God's self-communication can be realized only within history by a man who, in death, renounces any future within the world and is accepted by God in the total gift of himself. Historically, such an acceptation must be seen as a resurrection. This man can be called the absolute Savior. His being and his destiny can be expressed in the formulations of the classical Chalcedonian Christology and a genuine soteriological causality can be attributed to him.

However, Rahner stresses, transcendental Christology is not prepared to say that this absolute Savior, who is the object of human hope, is already a reality, or that he is identified with Jesus of Nazareth. These two affirmations can result only from the experience of history, which cannot be deduced. And yet we would have to be blind to this history if we failed to make the identification. Transcendental Christology, says Rahner, makes us seek what we have already found in Jesus of Nazareth. [12]

After he has sketched the ideal portrait of the absolute Savior through a transcendental deduction, Rahner attempts to specify the historical minimum that should be retained of the Gospel texts so that the Christology or Christologies of the

---

[11] K. Rahner - W. Thüsing, *Christologie — systematisch und exegetisch,* Freiburg, 1972.
[12] *Ibid.,* 22-24.

New Testament may sufficiently verify the Christology implied in the fundamental hope of man. For example, he thinks that it was not necessary that Jesus be aware, during his earthly life, of the redemptive value of his death. [13] Thus, transcendental Christology would make it possible to determine, within the Biblical message, the most essential facts about Christ, those that must have been historically realized and that must therefore be found in the texts. The transcendental necessity in question, moreover, remains subject to the supreme freedom of divine action.

Can this transcendental method be accepted in Christology? Obviously it has the advantage of setting forth doctrinal affirmations prior to historical inquiry, abstracting from all exegetical interference. But its deductive nature leaves us perplexed.

First of all, does deduction have the power of conviction that it ought to have? Starting from human hope, it seems very difficult to conclude that salvation can be given to man by a Savior who is God in person and who accomplishes the Redemption by his own death. It would be hard to deny that other ways might be possible. And a fact causes us to pause and reflect: the coming of the incarnate Son of God considerably exceeded the human hope that was best prepared to accept the advent of the Savior, that is to say, the hope of the Jews.

This leads us to ask a question regarding the point of departure of the deduction: Are we to seek the essentials of the divine plan of salvation within the heart of man, prior to any consideration of the Biblical texts? In order to grasp these essentials, must we not first of all listen to God's word as it has been delivered to us in Scripture? Could we discover in human life a kind of preliminary revelation of the salvific action and person of the Savior, and afterwards verify its fulfillment in the Gospel, instead of starting out from the Gospel in search of the authentic revelation of Christ, and thereby clarifying the meaning of human existence?

Even in man's transcendental existence we cannot discover

---

[13] *Ibid.*, 33-34. On this point, in the critical notes he formulates from the point of view of exegesis, W. Thüsing remarks that we would have to take into account the words Jesus spoke at the Last Supper (*ibid.* 132).

everything involved in the divine transcendence of the plan of salvation. [14] Otherwise there would be danger of transferring this transcendence back to man himself, and thus transforming anthropology into theology.

The essential lines of Christological development must stem from the witness of Scripture. The task of Christology consists specifically in going from the traditional affirmations of the Catholic faith in Christ made by the Church today back to the source of these affirmations, and in exploring the continuity of the historical development from the event of Jesus through the dogmatic pronouncements.

The theologian cannot refuse to gather the fruit of exegetical research, at least on the fundamental points that must serve as a basis for doctrinal systematization. This is as much his task as it ever was, for he cannot limit himself to accepting the conclusions of exegesis. In the light of patristic and theological tradition, and prolonging it, he turns his thinking to the Scriptural sources and seeks to explore their underlying meaning. He establishes connections between the various elements, in order to bring out the articulation of the divine plan of salvation. In the development of doctrine, he strives to make use of the contributions of the most recent human thinking, and thus translate a Christological synthesis into more modern language.

We must not confuse the development of Christology with exegesis. The systematic effort of the theologian, or more specifically of the dogmatist, is very important in its own right. While Christology cannot be built on a deductive foundation, neither can it dispense with reflection and argumentation. Yet the theologian must remain aware that the doctrinal structure involves a fundamental continuity with Biblical research, and he must vigilantly maintain its essential reference to the Scriptural sources.

The dynamism of faith involves commitment to the initial Gospel representation of Christ. It calls for speculative inquiry enriched by all that, in human thinking, can throw greater light on the mystery of the figure of Christ. It there-

---

[14] Thüsing asks critically if the Christology of Rahner is sufficiently theocentric, with respect to the Christological conceptions of the New Testament (*ibid.*, 135).

fore involves exegesis, and something beyond exegesis. Systematic Christology has its own method, the method of reflection that discerns the essential elements of the Biblical sources, that studies their interrelations, and organizes them into a synthetic view. It asks itself all the philosophical and psychological questions that can help elucidate Christ in his ontological constitution and in his consciousness. It strives to determine the meaning of the Incarnation, its reasons, and its value to mankind, within the context of the work of salvation and of the redemptive action of Jesus.

In the picture Christology gives of Christ, based on Scripture, it must seek to show how Christ answers man's essential aspirations, and in what sense he is the desired one of all mankind. What we must retain of Rahner's hypothesis is the importance of the answer Jesus brings to human hope. The human heart has a secret aspiration for the "absolute Savior" that Jesus is in all perfection. But this aspiration can be revealed only in the presence of the Savior described for us in the Gospels. It is Christ who reveals the human heart to itself. And when the human heart reveals Christ, it is because the eye of faith has already grasped him in a more fundamental revelation given to the Church and transmitted by the testimony of the Gospels.

C. From Man to God and from God to Man

Once we have clarified the relationships between faith, historical research, and doctrinal systematization, we face a second problem: Must Christology start from the divinity or from the humanity of Christ? Should it assume a downward direction, going from God to man, or an ascending direction, rising from man to God?

1. *The Christology from Below*

The trend toward a Christology from below stems from a reaction against undue emphasis on the divinity of Christ. Just as we cannot accept the invasion of historical research by dogmatizing principles, similarly we cannot tolerate the encroachment of Jesus' divinity on his humanity. We must

34

recognize the legitimacy of this reaction, as well as of the need experienced by the Christians and theologians of our own day to find in Christ someone who is completely a man, like us in all things except sin. One of the most urgent tasks of contemporary Christology consists in exploring all the aspects and implications of Christ's human existence.

Christology from below is right in stressing that it is in Christ's humanity that his divinity is revealed. The revelation is not addressed to us directly by a simple interior illumination that would make us cleave to the Son of God. It is produced in the man Jesus, and all that we can know of the Son of God is transmitted to us by the words, actions, and events of the human life of Jesus of Nazareth. Consequently, we must constantly scrutinize this human figure to discover the Savior's identity.

This does not mean that we can know only what is human about Jesus. In fact, while he is fully a man, he exceeds human dimensions, and manifests a divine transcendence. But it is always through the human that he reveals what is superior to the human.

Since we must go back to the origins of Christology in order to explain the formation of faith in the divinity of Christ, it is indipensable to base our thinking on Jesus the man. Christological investigation necessarily starts out from the humanity of Jesus.

From this point of view, there is a priority of the human in Christology. This priority should not be understood to mean we must first recognize the purely human in Jesus, then proceed to discern in this man a manifestation of God. There is no first stage at which we might consider only Christ the man, and a second where we would strive to ascend to the Christ who is God. In fact, the whole of Jesus' humanity is a revelation of the divine, [15] and must be approached with this in mind.

The completely human life that Jesus lived forms a whole that cannot be separated from his divine identity or from his

---

[15] It is this revelatory function of the human in Jesus that Barth misunderstood, at least before his doctrinal turnabout in his conference on the humanity of God. And Bultmann recognizes this function far less clearly even than Barth.

intention to reveal this identity. When we say that Christ's identity is like our own, we are not denying its transcendental dimension. We must not seek to make it more commonplace, poorer, more "insignificant," disregarding in our analysis of his human attitudes the mystery of his divine person. We would then be depriving this mystery of its true value as revelation. Christ is man, but a man who expresses God, who reveals him.

2. The Christology from Above

Now, while Christological investigation must address itself to the man Jesus, it cannot disregard a complementary perspective which implies a point of departure from above and a downward movement.

In the faith of the Jews which historically preceded the Christian faith in Jesus, the essential revelation was of the one God. The manifestation of God in his covenant with the Jewish people prepared the way for the coming of Christ. For the work of salvation, strict Jewish monotheism provided a single point of departure, namely God himself. Therefore, there was a progression from God to the man Jesus. Christology cannot ignore this truth.

In the New Testament, it is necessary to think in a downward direction about the origin of Jesus. From the fact that Jesus revealed himself as the Son of God, we are obliged to ask ourselves about the trajectory from divine life to human life that the coming of the Son of Man presupposes.

Christological investigation is ineluctably led to consider the act by which the preexisting Son of God entered the human race. John does this in the Prologue of his Gospel when he starts out by evoking the eternal existence of the Word and asserting that the Word became man and lived among us. Even before that, the Christological hymn of the Letter to the Philippians (2:6-11) had considered the descending movement that proceeds from the divine condition to the condition of a servant, before stressing the elevation of the glorious Christ to the level of the divine. Any Christology that considered only a movement originating from below and directed upward would be fundamentally incomplete.

36

Christology cannot refuse to explore the deepest mystery that consists in the very act of the Incarnation. Here we must go back to God's initiative and to the intention which commanded the action by which the Son of God launched into the adventure of human life. The meaning of the whole economy of salvation is involved in this exploration, and we can understand the bitter arguments among the theological schools regarding the motive for the Incarnation. This also brings into question the whole metaphysics of God and of his relations with man. The descending movement manifests a strictly divine dynamism and obliges theology to discard unduly immobilistic conceptions of God.

Thus, the descending direction in Christology remains fundamental. From the point of view of Biblical research, it is primordial by reason of God's own revelation of himself to the Jewish people. The man Jesus did not spring up in an indeterminate human milieu; he was born within the bosom of the people who had contracted a covenant with the true God. Jesus appeared on earth as the fruit and the fulfillment of God's promises of salvation.

From the point of view of speculative theology we can penetrate the true depth of the mystery of Christ only if we see him to be the Word made flesh. Jesus' declaration on his identity as the Son of God and the manifestation of his divinity in the Resurrection are only a point of departure for the intellect seeking to understand the primordial origin of the Savior. They are an invitation to explore what the coming of the Son of Man signifies. Theology always tends to focus all of its light on the process of the Incarnation, the passage of the Son of God from eternal existence to temporal existence. It is only in this process that the divine love that brought salvation to mankind can appear in its full force.

The love of the man Jesus for men is the most poignant mark of his earthly life. But it takes on all its value only when we see in it the expression and the revelation of divine love, specifically of the love of the Father reaching out to sinners, just as Jesus himself went out to them. The love of God, which, through Christ descends toward men by putting itself on a par with them, constitutes the essence of the message, and we can perceive it only in a descending movement.

Only this movement can make us grasp the sense of the ascending movement which complements it, the movement of the divinization of the human in Christ.

Only by striving to grasp the descending movement of the Incarnation can the dynamism of faith tend to coincide with the divine dynamism manifested in Jesus. That is the purpose of the Incarnation. Divine dynamism descends from God to man in order afterwards to rise again from man to God.

PART TWO

ESSENTIAL FEATURES OF THE SCRIPTURAL SOURCES

CHAPTER III

THE DYNAMISM OF INCARNATION
IN THE OLD COVENANT

In the Old Testament we find a dynamism of incarnation
that inspires not merely a few isolated texts, but that can be
said to mold the whole structure of the Jewish religion. We
must consider this general structure before going on to the
more individualized oracles. By the term "dynamism of incarnation" we mean the movement by which God enters into
the world of human relations and participates in the life of
mankind.

A. THE STRUCTURE OF INCARNATION IN THE JEWISH RELIGION

1. *The Covenant, as an Incarnation of the Relations between
God and his people*

   a. The Treaty

The most fundamental and characteristic structural element
of the Jewish religion is the covenant. While it is indeed true
that we have not yet attained "an adequate theology of covenant" [1] many studies of this matter have been made that throw
light on various aspects of the Jewish covenant and manifest
a certain pluralism of traditions and conceptions within a single
essential framework.

It is interesting that the relations between Yahweh and
his people were conceived on the model of a treaty. A treaty
presupposes a certain equality among the partners, since there
is a reciprocity of obligation. This would have seemed in-

---

[1] This is the conclusion of D. J. McCarthy, *Old Testament Covenant:
A Survey of Current Opinions,* Richmond, Virginia, John Knox Press, 1972, 88.

compatible with the superiority of Yahweh over his people, a superiority which has been so clearly affirmed in the Jewish religion. We can see why certain exegetes draw back before the bilateral thrust of the covenant, and prefer to hold to more unilateral conceptions of the divine action of salvation. [2] Yet, while we can argue over the diverse forms of treaty that served as models, there can be no doubt that the covenant between Yahweh and his people is really an alliance, that is to say, a pact that involves mutual obligations.

More particularly, in the matter of the ratification of the covenant by Moses (Ex 24), we must admit that the spirit of this covenant — whether sealed in blood or in a common meal — is the spirit of a "reciprocal commitment that establishes an indissoluble bond between the two contracting parties, and is conceived and described after the manner of human covenants." [3]

Now, this reciprocal commitment implies a certain incarnation. From God's point of view, to become a partner to a treaty is to choose to enter a relationship such as men establish among themselves, and consequently to place himself on a level of equality with mankind. On God's part, the element of incarnation consists in "acting after the manner of a man." The One who could have dealt with men as a sovereign being deals with lesser creatures chose to deal with mankind in a human fashion. He did not thrust himself upon men unilaterally, as he had the power to do. Instead, he established religion on a basis of mutual agreement rather than on a decree promulgated by his divine will.

A treaty could have taken on a purely juridical form and established purely external reciprocal relations. In that case

---

[2] One of the last efforts in this direction was made by E. Kutsch, for whom *berît* would never signify covenant or treaty, but only unilateral obligations (*Der Begriff berît in vordeuteronomischer Zeit, Rost Festschrift*, 133-143; *Gesetz und Gnade. Probleme des alttestamentlichen Bundesbegriff, Zeitschrift für die Alttestamentliche Wissenschaft*, 79 (1967) 18-35. Mc Carthy does not find the demonstration convincing (*op. cit.*, 60).

[3] A. Jaubert, *La notion d'alliance dans le judaïsme aux abords de l'ère chrétienne*, Paris, 1963, 45. The author moreover notes the astonishing aspect of this reciprocity: "At the worst, it might involve a certain irreverence... toward this God, the partner to a contract, dealing with his people on a footing of equality..." (46).

the dynamism of incarnation would have remained superficial. God's commitment would have been limited to the stipulation of certain promises or obligations. Actually, the development of the theology of covenanting among the Jewish people proceeded by way of interiorization. The need for a new covenant that would consist in the people's belonging to God and of God's belonging to the people was more clearly understood soon after the Exile.[4] This new covenant has been customarily defined by the formula: "They will be my people; I will be their God"[5]

b. Fatherhood and Sonship

God's intention to establish the most intimate human contacts is manifested by his entering into a father-son relationship.

The bond established in the Covenant involves the exercise of fatherhood by God[6]: "Israel is my first-born son" (Ex 4:22). It is sometimes presented as an adoption (Dt 32:10), but above all it implies a fatherly love that presides over the origin and the life of Israel as a people: "When Israel was a child I loved him, and I called my son out of Egypt" (Ho 11:1). There is question therefore of a sonship not of the physical but of the moral order, resulting from God's free election. That is the meaning also of Yahweh's declaration: "For I am a father to Israel, and Ephraim is my first-born son" (Jr 31:9). This fatherhood is manifested above all in God's mercy: "Is Ephraim, then, so dear a son to me, a child so favoured, that after each threat of mine I must still remember him, still be deeply moved for him, and let my tenderness yearn over him?" (Jr 31:20). According to the Book of Wisdom Egypt had been forced to acknowledge "this people to be son of God" (Ws 18:13).

This sonship is sometimes seen less as an existing reality than as an ideal to be pursued, as God's own hope:

---

[4] Cf. P. Buis, "La nouvelle alliance," *VT* 18 (1968) 3-4.

[5] Cf. Gn 17:7; Ex 6:7; 20:2; Lv 26:12; Dt 26:17; 29:12, etc.

[6] McCarthy stresses that the father-son relationship is essentially a contractual idea, inasmuch as there is question here of an adopted sonship (*Old Testament Covenant*, 33).

"And I was thinking:
How I wanted to rank you with my sons,
and give you a country of delights,
the fairest heritage of all the nations!
I had thought you would call me: My father,
and would never cease to follow me" (Jr 3:19).

The goal of God's great plan is to establish father-son relations with his people.

Fatherhood expresses the human relationship God willed to establish with his people. It is an incarnation of these relations that is more substantial than the juridical ratification of a pact. It reveals God's innermost sentiments that explain his exterior attitude of protection. While it is situated on the level of affection, it is not entirely without allusion to generation. For when God called his son from Egypt it was to form with the Hebrews a nation that would have an existence of its own, distinct from all others.

God's loving choice was the determining factor in the birth of the people as an autonomous entity. Besides, fatherhood was affirmed with reference to Creation: "Yahweh, you are our Father; we the clay, you the potter" (Is 64:7; cf. 45:10). God's fatherhood is also linked to the Redemption: "... you, Yahweh, yourself are our Father, Our Redeemer is your ancient name" (Is 63:16).

Fatherhood signifies a superiority and is joined to the mention of the divine sovereignty: "he is our Master and he is our God and he is our Father and he is God for ever and ever" (Tb 13:4)[7] And yet we should not underestimate the fact that God's fatherhood also implies a progress toward more horizontal relations, for it demands a reciprocity of affection and implies a certain claim of the sons on the Father's compassionate and merciful heart.

---

[7] It should be noted that in Is 63:16 the fatherhood of God is affirmed to be superior to all human fatherhood: "a fatherhood without limitations" "in contrast to the limited fatherhood of ancestors." "As for God, he has been Father from the very beginning, the Father of fathers, ineffably a Father; fully alive, he is constantly present to all his sons in all generations: he sees, he knows, he hears, he understands from eternity to eternity; he can exercise his role of "gô'êl", of a parent devoted to his family, of a redeemer" (P. E. Bonnard, Le second Isaïe, Paris, 1972, 452).

c. The Matrimonial Union

Still another image is used to describe the affective relations between Yahweh and his people, one that bespeaks a more strikingly horizontal relationship between himself and mankind: the image of the matrimonial union. Sometimes the two images — of father and spouse — are used in succession, so that they may both elucidate the power of the bond of love. Thus Israel is compared to a rebellious son and to an unfaithful wife (cf. Jr 3: 19-22). The image of the spouse accentuates the intention of equality, and manifests the incarnational intention of God's love which assumes the form of the most intense human love. We must not forget that the union between man and woman was considered by the Jews as the most complete human commitment, one that was to take precedence over all other family affections (Gn 2: 24).

However, the divine Spouse does not lose his transcendence. Just as the role of Father is attributed to the Creator and to the Redeemer, so is the role of husband: "For now your creator will be your spouse .....; with everlasting love I have taken pity on you, says Yahweh, your redeemer" (Is 54: 5,8).

In The Book of Ezekiel, Israel is presented as a husband whose beauty was created by Yahweh (cf. Ez 16: 1-14). Already, in Hosea, God had been considered as the author of betrothal: "I will betroth you to myself for ever, betroth you with integrity and justice, with tenderness and love; I will betroth you to myself with faithfulness, and you will come to know Yahweh" (Ho 2: 21-22). Everything that constitutes a betrothal, one might say — justice, integrity, grace, tenderness, fidelity — are the work and the gift of Yahweh.

But the reciprocity of love is not lost sight of. In proof of this are the words: "you will come to know Yahweh." The Song of Songs lays even greater stress on this reciprocity in the words attributed to the bride: "I am my Beloved's, and my Beloved is mine" (Sg 6: 3). These words translate in terms of affection the typical formula of the Covenant: "I will be their God and they shall be my people" (Jr 31: 33). Mutual belonging shows how completely God's gift is placed on a par with man's gift, so as to make a true exchange possible. This divine gift even makes use of the love poetry of betrothed lovers. God became the greatest poet of love, in order to incarnate to the fullest his own way of making contact with mankind.

d. The New Covenant

The failure of the Old Covenant led to the prophetic announcement of a new covenant. Since Israel had failed to carry out its obligations as son or as spouse, the ideal image of the loving son and of the faithful spouse came into being. The New Covenant could result only from a more powerful action on God's part to remedy human weakness. Did this more powerful action signify greater emphasis on divine transcendence in God's relations with mankind? Since God had not succeeded in what might be called his first attempts at incarnation and at achieving a horizontal love relationship, would he return to a stance of superiority to more surely attain his goals? If this had been the case, the New Covenant would have involved a lesser incarnation.

In actual fact, that is not the way things happened. Divine power was to manifest itself in a more striking way, accentuating the process of incarnation still more. In the coming covenant God would no longer be content to propose his law to his people for their loyal acceptance. He would choose to place his law within man himself: "Deep within them I will plant my Law, writing it on their hearts" (Jr 31:33). The law which expresses God's will would no longer be presented to men merely from the outside. It would become incarnate, as it were, in the human, so that man's will might truly coincide with God's.

To put it more explicitly, God's action creates new dispositions in man: "I shall give you a new heart, and put a new spirit in you; I shall remove the heart of stone from your bodies and give you a heart of flesh instead. I shall put my spirit in you ..." (Ez 36:26-27). This communication of the divine spirit to man gives us an insight into the depth of this incarnation. The spirit of God enters into the depths of man to inspire and guide his actions. God no longer limits himself to being the partner to a covenant, to look upon his people as a son or a spouse. He now wants his own divine

46

dispositions to enter into the heart and mind of his people.[8]
The structure of the covenant which characterized Yahweh's relations with the Jewish people from the beginning evolved in the direction of a more intimate penetration by God into human life, that is to say, in the direction of a deeper incarnation.

2. Incarnation of the word, the action, and the presence of God

a. Revelation, the Incarnation of God's Word

Revelation is an aspect of the dynamism of incarnation.[9] God presents his message in human language. His words are never communicated in their pure state. They take shape in human words, thereby assuming the limitations and imperfections of humanity. There is more involved here than a phenomenon of expression and of "translation," for God's thought makes itself known by flowing into human thoughts. The men who transmit Revelation impress the mark of their opinions, their reflections, on God's message. In this sense they contribute not only to its transmission but also to its formation. The prophets each had their own way of proclaiming God's Word. They were striving to transmit their innermost thoughts in this communication.

We therefore see a kind of identification between God's thought and human thoughts. God's thoughts were so completely incorporated into man's thinking that the two could not be dissociated. To grasp the message of Revelation we must accept the integral thought of the prophet or writer and discover God's intention within it.

God's Word successfully achieves its incarnation by being transmitted in human language that preserves its own qualities and is not constrained to become less human in order to express God's thought. Very often exegetes might be tempted

---

[8] W. Zimmerli remarks that in the Old Testament "spirit" means not only to acknowledge, to understand, but is also a power that makes one capable of attaining a new attitude (*Ezechiel,* Neukirchen, 1969, II, 879).

[9] The importance of God's Word as a progression toward Christology has been stressed in a special way by L. Bouyer: "The notion and above all the reality of God's Word, as they are revealed in the Old Testament, must be studied as the first and most basic preamble to all Christology" (*Le Fils éternel. Théologie de la Parole de Dieu et Christologie,* Paris 1974, 39).

to retain only the human, without sufficiently grasping the divine thought hidden within it, because the divine has so completely permeated a spontaneously human expression.

b. History, the Incarnation of God's Action

The history of the chosen people manifests the incarnation of God's action. According to the commitments made in the Covenant, God's power acted in the people by guiding their destiny. This power was placed at the service of the Jews to save them and direct them toward the promised land, as is clearly seen in Exodus, the wonderful unfolding of God's protection and intervention, and as is evident in the unfolding of subsequent events.

So complete was this service that it involved a kind of identification between God's plan and the destiny of his people. The sovereign power that is God's alone became incarnate in the victories and the expansion of Israel. To clarify the meaning of this incarnation, it is helpful to distinguish two essential aspects of God's action. On the one hand there was an action that reproved and punished the people because of their erring ways. This is the story of the trials inflicted on Israel in view of its conversion and forgiveness. On the other hand there was the action that preserved the people from dangers and assured them life, triumph, and prosperity: "A large army will not keep a king safe, nor does the hero escape by his great strength; it is delusion to rely on the horse for safety, for all its power, it cannot save. But see how the eye of Yahweh is on those who fear him, on those who rely on his love, to rescue their souls from death and keep them alive in famine ..." (Ps 33:16-19). It is in this second mode of action that Yahweh realized the greatest identification with his people. Here we see the ultimate incarnation of God's action in the actions of men.

The history of the people thus became God's own work. Divine power engaged in human activities in order to carry out its plans.

c. The Incarnation of God's Presence

God was present among his people not simply by a moral

48

presence that lent support and brought help. In other words, God's presence did not merely signify his intention to protect and help Israel. It was a real presence. Yahweh was truly within his people, in a mysterious, invisible yet authentic way. From this point of view we must indeed speak of the incarnation of God's presence. God accompanied his people in their Exodus, he was with them in their nomadic wanderings and in their sedentary settlement.

This incarnation was of great importance, for it manifested how intimately God was giving himself. He did not merely take on the obligations of a covenant, he did not merely proffer his help and his Word. He gave his very Being. In the incarnation of God's presence, his gift to his people attained a measure of fullness.

The incarnation was made even more emphatic in the more specific local form that God's presence assumed. To reserve a tent for Yahweh, the "Tent of Meeting" where he could receive those who sought him, was to recognize in the divine presence an aspect very much like that of a human presence. In the Book of Exodus we read that within this tent "Yahweh would speak with Moses face to face" (Ex 33:11). Here we can see the horizontalism that is the mark of God's incarnation. God came down to man's level to enter into friendly dialogue with him. There were still limits to God's accessibility, since the tent was located outside the camp, and a climate of fear was provoked by extraordinary manifestations such as the pillar of cloud. But the principle of a friendly presence, with the invitation to the "Meeting," clearly expressed and made known how much God wanted to dwell among men.

In the Temple this presence was established in a more cultic way. It was the soul of official Jewish worship. The place where the Jews venerated the divine presence was the center around which all ritual activities were organized. It was the divine presence that conferred meaning on the Temple. Without that presence, the Temple would have been nothing but a deserted building.

The fact that Yahweh possessed his house shows to what extent — while he exceeded the boundaries of every individual locality (cf. I Kgs 8:27; Is 66:1) [10] — he wanted to make himself present in a human way.

B. The Presages of a Divine Messianic Figure

The dynamism of incarnation does not merely bespeak a collective plan. Certain texts of the Old Testament tend to show the joining of man and God in a more individualized messianic perspective.

This orientation finds expression in two directions, one ascending and the other descending. In the ascending way, a human being tends to accede to the rank of the divine. He separates himself from the people in order to be given some of God's attributes, either by receiving a divine name or the attribution of a divine sonship. In the descending way, a person tends to separate himself from God or from the divine sphere in order to join mankind. This way is found in the personification of divine wisdom that comes on a mission among men, and in the announcement of the coming of the Son of Man, a heavenly personage who receives supreme power.

1. *The Ascending Way*

a. Giving a divine name to the king or to the Messiah

In addressing the king, Psalm 45:6 declares: "Your throne, O God [Elohim], shall last for ever and ever." [11] Some exegetes had seen in the term "Elohim" the idea of a Messiah-God which would supersede the idea of a purely human messiah. Feuillet has chosen to adopt this view, affirming

---

[10] "The Creator of the universe cannot be imprisoned within four walls. He exceeds the bounds of any localization so completely that one can say in a figurative way: the heavens are his throne and the earth is his footstool" (Bonnard, *Le Second Isaïe*, 483, concerning Is 66:1). But this transcendence with respect to any localization brings out more vividly the importance of God's dwelling in a specific place.

[11] Other exegetes adopt another version of the text. M. Dahood translates: "The eternal and everlasting God has enthroned you!" (*Psalms 1-50*, The Anchor Bible, N.Y./Doubleday & Co., 1966, 269). This version avoids the problem the text presents when the name of Elohim is applied to the king. Here we are considering the more difficult version, which is also the more traditional.

that the title must be understood in the strong sense.[12] It is in this sense that the Epistle to the Hebrews (1:8) cites the text, in order to show that Jesus is the Son of God, incomparably superior to the angels. The patristic tradition had followed this interpretation.

However, when considered in itself the text does not go that far. The title of Elohim is applied elsewhere to great personages without intending thereby to attribute a strictly divine character to them: Moses, Samuel, the leaders and the judges, the house of David.[13] J. Calès defines the term as "a superior being, supernatural in a certain respect."[14] A. Gelin translates it "*divine.*"[15]

Even though the Psalmist did not want to affirm the divinity of the king, he nevertheless showed, by the use of the title "Elohim" a tendency to recognize a certain divine greatness in a man, a tendency that we find in various other passages of the Bible. It seems as though there was a religious need that strict Jewish monotheism was unable to completely dissimulate, a need to find something divine, or more specifically divine power, in those who exercised power over men. It is this deep-seated tendency that we must keep in mind.

Isaiah 9:5 gives the Messiah a very long name, proportionate to his dignity: "Wonder-Counsellor, Mighty-God, Eternal-Father, Prince-of-Peace." Ceuppens, following the view of other exegetes, has felt the need to admit the literal sense of "Mighty-God," because in other passages of the Old Testament (Dt 19:17; Is 10:21; Jr 32:18; Ne 9:32) the same expression appears and is always applied to Yahweh: the prophet would therefore be announcing a Messiah who would be the true God.[16] On the other hand, Gelin thinks the

---

[12] *Cantique des cantiques,* Paris, 1963, 219. For this author the divine character attributed to the king helps to prove that the psalmist was not speaking purely and simply of an historical king but of the Messiah.
[13] Ps 5:11; 82:1,6; Ex 4:10; 7:1; 21:6; 22:7; 1 S 28:13; Zc 12:8; cf. 2 S 14:17. Cf. R. Tournay, *Les Psaumes,* Paris, 1950, 186.
[14] *Le livre des Psaumes,* Paris, 1936, I, 470.
[15] "L'attente de Dieu dans l'Ancien Testament," *LV* 9 (1953), 12. *Id.* in H. J. Kraus, *Psalmen,* I, Neukirchen 1960, 330: "O. Göttlicher."
[16] *Theologia biblica,* III, *De Incarnatione,* Rome 1950, 28.

title "could have been accepted by the hearers only in the sense of "divine valiant warrior." [17]

Not only did the hearers accept the words in this sense, but the author himself could not have intended to affirm the divinity of the messianic child. In the prophecy, Yahweh is completely distinct from the child, even though his divine power is manifested in him. The Messiah was to be the one in whom the Mighty-God would reveal himself. This title can be compared to the theophoric names. Thus, the name of Jesus, which was quite common among the Jews, does not of itself signify that the one who bears it is the "God-Savior," but that God the Savior reveals himself in him. To have the word "God" as part of one's name did not mean one was identified with God himself.

It is unthinkable that Isaiah should have identified the messianic child with Yahweh. Nevertheless, the fact that the title "Mighty-God" was expressly included in the child's name implies the intention to elevate the Messiah's role very high, as high as possible, and to discern in him the most characteristic revelation of God's power. One might say there was tendency toward a dynamic identification, not by an identification of nature but by an identification of energy, inasmuch as the child was to put divine power to work in a singular fashion.

Jeremiah 23:6 calls the Messiah "Yahweh-our-integrity" or "our justice." We cannot find the affirmation of the Messiah's divinity here either. Zedekiah signifies "Yahweh is my justice," but there is no thought of identifying him in some way with Yahweh. By the name Jeremiah attributes to the Messiah he presents him as the one in whom Yahweh will establish his "justice" in the people in a real way, and not falsely as in the case of Zedekiah. The name signifies "true revelation of the justice of Yahweh." In this sense we might still speak of a tendency toward a dynamic identification, insofar as the Messiah was to personify in some way the action of divine justice, the work of divine salvation. He "will reign as true king and be wise, practising honesty and integrity in the land. In his days Judah will be saved and Israel dwell in confidence" (Jr 23:5-6).

---

[17] "L'attente," LV 9 (1953), 13. This is the translation adopted for El Gibber, by J. Steinmann, Le Prophète Isaïe, Paris, 1950, 124.

The Importance of the Name

Giving a divine name to the Messiah might seem an unimportant indication of the mystery, more symbolic than real. However we must remember the importance the Hebraic mentality attached to the name that designates a person. For the Jew, the name encompassed within it the reality of the person. To give the Messiah a title such as "Mighty-God" or "Yahweh-our-integrity" was to affirm the reality of God's power and justice, which would be deployed in a unique manner in this personage. It meant getting used to seeing God's action in his actions. In this person, as in no one else, God was to be present in order to reveal himself.

b. The Attribution of Divine Sonship

The texts that attribute divine sonship to the king must be considered throughout a traditional trend that associates the king with Yahweh. [18] One might say they give extreme emphasis to this association.

1 - The Prophecy of Nathan

In Nathan's prophecy (2 S 7:1-16), where we discern the origin of royal messianism, Yahweh promises to act like a father toward David's descendant. "I will be like a father to him and he a son to me" (7:14). This is the reciprocity of the covenant. From the point of view of incarnation, the promise is particularly interesting because it shows how this fatherhood enables God to act in a human way: "if he does evil I will punish him with the rod such as men use, with strokes such as mankind gives. Yet I will not withdraw my favor from him ..." (7:14-15). In his role as father, God places himself on a par with the one whom he considers his son.

This prophecy is echoed in Psalm 89: [19] "He will invoke me, 'My father, my God and rock of my safety,' and I shall make him my first-born, the Most High for kings on earth" (26-27). We should note that there is greater emphasis here

---

[18] Cf. J. Coppens, "Le messianisme royal dynastique," *NRT* 100 (1968) 225-251.

[19] On the problem of the connection between the two texts, cf. Coppens, *art. cit.*, 235 ff.

on the elevation granted the Davidic king: as a son, he receives the likeness of the one who is his father, and becomes the Most High among kings.

2 - Psalm 2:7

The king reportedly declares at the time of his enthronement: "Let me proclaim Yahweh's decree; he has told me, 'You are my son, today I have begotten you.'" Here we recognize an act of covenant. By proclaiming the divine decree the king is understood to accept Yahweh's covenant.[20]

The Psalm concerns an historic king, but he has been given an ideal, messianic quality in Jewish tradition. This process of messianic idealization, moreover, has its point of departure in the perspectives evoked by the Psalm itself.

What is the meaning of the sonship proclaimed by Yahweh? There are some who understand it as a purely juridical sort of sonship, an adoption. Its juridical character is undeniable. There is question here of a decree that guarantees the legitimacy of the king's power. This power results from the adoption, from the attitude of God who — beginning as of "today" — looks upon the new king as his son.

However there is more to it than that.[21] It appears that the sonship proclaimed does not consist simply in a juridical act, for it is presented as a "generation." Besides, the affirmation "I have begotten you" could not be justified merely as an attitude of paternal affection on God's part. There is more involved here than the promise of paternal sentiments.

For the Assyro-Babylonian kings, there was mention of a *mystical birth.*[22] In certain respects these kings shared in

---

[20] Cf. G. H. Jones, "The Decree of Yahweh (Ps 2:7)," *VT* 15 (1965) 336-344. The author recognizes the psalm contains above all God's promises, whereas the demands of God are less clearly expressed. R. Press ("Jahwe und sein Gesalbter," *Theologische Zeitschrift* 13, 1957, 321-334) sees the foundation of Psalm 2, as well as of Psalms 110 and 132, in God's covenant with the house of David, in 2 S 7. We find the same opinion expressed by Gelin, *LV* 9,12.

[21] "The affirmations of Psalm 2 by far exceed what Nathan's prophecy expresses concerning the relations that would exist in the future between Yahweh and the son of David," according to Coppens (*art. cit.*, 245).

[22] R. Labat, *Le caractère religieux de la royauté assyro-babylonienne,* Paris, 1939, 53.

the divinity of the god or goddess from whom they received a share of power. The Egyptian parallels also indicate a mystical kind of sonship. This is seen for instance in an inscription in Memphis concerning King Horemheb (1329-1306 B.C.): "Then Amon said to Horemheb: you are my son and my heir, who came forth from my loins." [23]

The words of Psalm 2 — "You are my son, today I have begotten you" (2:7) — suggest a sonship that is an authentic generation by God, involving a certain communication of divinity. There is an attribution of divine power described at greater length by the Psalm in the context of domination over enemies. Likewise, there is the communication of a certain divine character that invests the person of the king from the moment of his accession.

3 - Psalm 110:3

The authenticity of the first text is not certain, and has given rise to many hypotheses. [24] And yet, as Gelin has pointed out, the comparative method makes it possible to pinpoint the meaning in a more satisfactory manner. "Royal dignity was yours from the day you were born; on the holy mountains, from the womb of the dawn, as the dew, I begot you." [25]

In the Greek version of the Septuagint a rereading has brought about a transposition in the direction of transcendence: a heavenly enthronement, the preexistence of the Messiah:

"With you is sovereignty on the day of your power
in the splendor of the saints;
From the womb, before the star that bears
the dawn, I begot you." [26]

---

[23] Cited by E. Lipinski, *La royauté de Yahwé dans la poésie et le culte de l'ancien Israël*, Brussels 1965, 346.

[24] For bibliographical references, the reader can turn to Coppens, 245, footnote 73. Coppens considers as more probable the version that mentions the generation: "As to verses 1-3, we still think a textual reading that discerns the mention of the monarch's generation should be accepted as valid" (245).

[25] This is also J. Bonsirven's translation in the Crampon Bible. It is used almost literally by A. Gelin, "La question des 'relectures' bibliques à l'intérieur d'une tradition vivante," in *Sacra Pagina, Miscellanea biblica Congressus internationalis catholici de re biblica*, Paris 1959, I, 313.

[26] On the other hand, the Masoretic text produces another transposition

The primitive text is clarified by Phoenician and especially by Egyptian parallels. For vs 1: "Sit at my right hand" the representation of the pharaohs is cited, sitting next to a divinity seated on a throne.[27] Verse 3 could stem from the colorful representation in which the sun god begets the dew from the womb of the dawn. According to the hymns of Tel el Amarna, Aton "begets the king each morning with his rays, with his body, and even with his mouth," according to the theories of the creative word ... This creative act makes the king an image of Aton, like to him in all things: "He makes him the image of what he has made of himself." "He grants him the power to seize every foreign land on which he shines ..."[28]

However certain exegetes prefer to use Ugaritic parallels.[29] In any case, these parallels from other religions help to explain how the affirmation that the king was generated by God may have found its way into the psalms.

This divine generation involves the granting of divine power. It seems less embedded in a juridical context than in Psalm 2. It has a more clearly poetic value that suggests mystical sonship.

The Septuagint version sees this generation as occurring in heaven and tends to suggest a Messiah begotten of God in eternity, before the creation of the stars. In a rather surprising way it comes close to the idea of an eternal sonship. It witnesses to a trend of thought that, during the last centuries of Judaism before Christ, situated the Messiah in a heavenly and transcendental sphere.

---

in the more earthly and mundane perspective of a preparation for battle: "Your people hastens to you on the day when you gather your army, with sacred ornaments; from the womb of the dawn the dew of your young warriors comes to you."

[27] Cf. J. de Savignac, "Essai d'interprétation du psaume CX à l'aide de la littérature égyptienne," *Oudtestamentische Studiën*, IX, Leiden 1951, 107-135; "Théologie pharaonique et messianisme d'Israël," *VT* 7 (1957) 82-90.

[28] A. Barucq, *L'expression de la louange divine et de la prière dans la Bible et en Egypte,* Cairo, 1962, 234 ff.

[29] Coppens, *Le messianisme royal,* 246.

4 - Psalm 87:6

Usually, only Psalms 2 and 110 are cited as supporting the divine sonship of the messianic king. Without taking sides in exegetical controversies, we might point to the version of Psalm 87:6 that has been adopted by some exegetes: "My Prince, he was born in her." According to R. Sorg, the reference here is not to a post-exilic Messiah but, as in Psalm 110, to a king who is the son of Yahweh. God is represented as the spouse of Zion and the father of the Prince.[30] As this psalm belongs to the era of Solomon, an Egyptian influence is not impossible, in view of the fact that David's and Solomon's courts were organized after the model of the Egyptian court. The idea of a sacred marriage, that we find in Canaan, Egypt, and in Mesopotamia, was purified according to the demands of Jewish monotheism, and Yahweh's spouse became the people.[31]

2. The Descending Way

a. The Coming of Divine Wisdom Among Men

Divine wisdom is represented as a person distinct from Yahweh, but sprung from him: "Yahweh created me ..." or "acquired me through generation" (Pr 8:22).[32] "I came forth from the mouth of the Most High ..." (Si 24:3). But even while detaching herself from God, she remains divine: "She is a breath of the power of God, pure emanation of the glory of the Alminghty; ... She is a reflection of the eternal light, untarnished mirror of God's active power, image of his goodness" (Ws 7:25-26).

This wisdom has played the role of an "architect" or "artist" in creation (cf. Pr 8:30), performing her work in the

---

[30] *Ecumenic Psalm 87*, Fifield, Wisconsin, 1969, XIV.

[31] *Ibid.* XV.

[32] A. Barucq (*Le livre des Proverbes*, Paris, 1964, 93) opts for "acquired me," as being more faithful to the Hebrew text, whereas the Septuaginr translates "created me."

[33] Cf. J. de Savignac, "La Sagesse en Proverbes VIII 22-31," *VT* 12 (1962) 211-215.

[34] A. Robert, "Les attaches littéraires de Proverbes I-IX," *RB* 44 (1935) 523; A. Feuillet, "Le Fils de l'homme de Daniel et la tradition biblique," *RB* 60 (1953) 323.

manner of a game or of a dance that charmed the Creator. [33]

She comes among men: "delighting to be with the sons of men" (Pr 8:30), and she is given to them as their heritage: "Happy the man who listens to me,... For the man who finds me finds life" (Pr 8:34-35). God has given her to Jacob and to Israel: "so causing her to appear on earth and move among men" (Ba 3:38). "Over ... the whole earth ... I have held sway" (Si 24:6). But she has been established in a special way on Zion (cf. Si 24:10) where she grew "like a vine" (Si 24:17). "In each generation she passes into holy souls" (Wi 7:27). She invites men to her banquet (cf. Pr 9:1-12) and gives herself as food and drink (cf. Si 24:19/26).

Wisdom is clothed with certain messianic attributes. Robert and Feuillet have shown the messianic role of wisdom. She claims gifts which are strictly the Messiah's (cf. Pr 8:14). She is invested with the Messiah's Davidic kingship (cf. Pr 8:15). She exercises messianic functions such as the teaching of true doctrine (Pr 8:6), judging the wicked, offering a meal like to the messianic banquet. [34] Here we have a "messianism without a Messiah, dependent upon eternal Wisdom." [35]

In this a purely literary personification, or is it a real personification, i.e., the affirmation of a distinct divine hypostasis? That is to put the question too bluntly. The authors who spoke of wisdom did not intend to affirm a divine person distinct from Yahweh. On the other hand, wisdom, was not merely a literary personification. For her role was a real one, and her self-communication to men not pure allegory. [36]

There was an evolution of thought, probably inspired by ideas stemming from other religions. For the monotheism of Israel could not turn in this direction of itself. We cannot establish an equivalence between the role of Wisdom in creation and the Egyptian representations. Yet there is considerable similarity between them. "We know that in Egypt Maât, the order of the world, the divine and royal order, or that Heu and Sia, the two creative principles in certain cosmogonies

---

[35] F. M. Braun, "Messie. Logos et Fils de l'homme," in *La venue du Messie, Recherches Bibliques*, VI, Louvain 1962, 138.

[36] Wisdom, like Providence, could be understood "as an attribute of God *ad extra*," according to M. Gilbert (*La critique des dieux dans le livre de la Sagesse* (Sg 13-15), Rome, 1973, 271.

(originally Memphis, it seems) gradually acquired a divine personality (anthropomorphic representations with divine insignias, names accompanied by the divine determinative. Yet this does not allow us to affirm that Israel orientated its thinking in the same direction and came to the same conclusion." [37] But this fact suggests what must have occurred. Pagan speculations on a divinity representing wisdom were assimilated by Judaism and residuated in the framework of the one God, who is the principle of all things. The assimilation even went to the point of identifying Wisdom with the Law, with the Torah (Si 24:23; Ba 4:1).

Thus, foreign influences made it possible to span the growing distance between mankind and a God conceived in a constantly more transcendent manner. It also made possible, within the context of a messianism without a Messiah, to confer a messianic mission on divine Wisdom. This Wisdom was very close to men and communicated herself to them. She appeared in their midst in order to give herself to them, to live in them.

It is worth our while to note the paradox in all this: Wisdom is transcendent and by far exceeds everything that can be said about a human messianic king, inasmuch as she is divine and has participated in the work of creation. And yet she enters more deeply into the lives of men than the Messiah as traditionally conceived, for the mission of this Messiah tends to be external to man. In divine Wisdom, transcendence and immanence go hand in hand.

b. The Announcement of the Coming of a "Son of Man"

1 - In Daniel's Prophecy

"I gazed into the visions of the night. And I saw, coming on the clouds of heaven, one like a son of man. He came to the one of great age and was led into his presence. On him was conferred sovereignty, glory and kingship, and men of all peoples, nations and languages became his servants. His sovereignty is an eternal sovereignty which shall never pass away, nor will his empire ever be destroyed" (Dn 7:13-14).

This prophecy does not refer to a coming to earth, but

---

[37] Barucq, *Proverbes*, 96.

to an eschatological coming within a heavenly setting, contemplated in an apocalyptic vision. In this sense we are far from the earthly realism of the mystery of the Incarnation. Even so, the idea of the *coming* should be retained.

Who is this person who comes "like a son of man"? It is hard to interpret these words, for the origin of the expression has remained mysterious, and the context must be invoked prudently because of rereadings and editorial changes.

Is this a human being? He seems rather to be a heavenly being, superior in nature, angelic in the broadest sense. This being belongs to the sphere of divinity, as is indicated by his coming "on the clouds of heaven." [38] In fact, as Feuillet observes, [39] in Biblical language clouds are the characteristic sign of theophanies. In every instance where the word does not refer to a simple natural phenomenon but takes on a religious significance, it accompanies the apparition or the intervention of God. For instance, the pillar of cloud of the march through the desert, the cloud of the revelations of Sinai or of the Tent of Meeting, the cloud of the Temple (1 K 8: 10-11; 2 Ch 5: 14-6: 1; 2 M 2: 8); the cloud of Ezekiel's visions (1: 4; 10: 3-4); the cloud of the eschatological visions (Is 4: 5; Ps 97: 2; Na 1: 3), etc. We must conclude from this that the personage who comes with the clouds possesses a certain divine quality.

From this we see that "like a son of man" expresses only an appearance. We must note the parallel with Ezekiel's initial vision, a vision dominated by a throne on which sat "a being that looked like a man" (1: 26). This human figure was simply the manifestation of God, "It was something that looked like the glory of Yahweh" (1: 28). In Daniel's vision the one who comes like a son of man is distinct from the one of great age, that is to say, God. But he assumes the appearance of a son of man, just as God had taken on the appearance of a man.

In this context, the human form is an indication of supe-

---

[38] "With the clouds (Masoretic text; Theodotion; Mk 14: 62; Rv 1: 7): "on the clouds" (Septuagint; Mt 24: 30; 26: 64; Rv 14: 16). This second version also stresses the transcendent nature of the personage, a tendency that is noticeable in the Septuagint.

[39] "Le Fils de l'homme de Daniel et la tradition biblique," *RB* 1953, 187.

riority.[40] The description of the four animals has been given earlier, just as in Ezekiel the vision of the four living beings precedes that of the figure of a man. Here we find an application, as it were, of the principle that man bears the likeness of the Creator. The figure of a man is worthy of manifesting God, and the appearance of a son of man is worthy of revealing the advent of a divine being.

This personage receives all power from God, as described in the scene of the eschatological enthronement. He possesses divine dominion over the universe in a definitive, perpetual way.

According to the second part of the vision, this power likewise belongs to "the people of the saints of the Most High (Dn 7:27). Some exegetes have concluded that "the saints of the Most High" were the angels.[41] However, the majority agree in seeing it as a reference to the chosen people, or at least admit that the text evokes "devout men of the messianic kingdom admitted into the society of the angels."[42]

Should we consider the one described as a son of man to be the collective designation of the messianic people? Obviously the mysterious personage represents this people in a certain manner, but should we deny him any individual existence? Some exegetes think so, but others opt for the existence of an individual person joined to a collective significance. In support of the individual quality of the son of man, the exegetes point to the heavenly and more or less divine nature of the personage who comes with the clouds, an image that does not apply very well to a designation of a whole people. Moreover, the angel who explains the vision and who declares: "these four great beasts are four kings" (Dn 7:17) is careful

---

[40] Cf. A. Caquot, "Les quatre bêtes et le 'Fils d'homme' (Daniel 7)," *Semitica* 18 (1968) 37-71; J. Coppens, "La vision daniélique du Fils d'homme," *VT* 19 (1969) 171-182.

[41] Cf. J. Coppens and L. Dequeker, *Le Fils de l'homme et les Saints du Très-Haut en Daniel, VII, dans les Apocryphes et dans le Nouveau Testament*, Louvain, 1961. L. Dequeker nevertheless admits (p. 52) that the last author of Daniel identified the saints of the Most High with the Jews. This interpretation, supported even more recently by L. Dequeker ("'The Saints of the Most High' in Qumram and Daniel," *Old Testament Studies* 18, 1973, 108-187) was strongly criticized by G. F. Hasel, "The Identity of 'The Saints of the Most High' in Daniel 7," *Bi* 56 (1975) 173-192.

[42] H. Kruse, "Compositio Libri Danielis et ideo Filii Hominis," *Verbum Domini* 37 (1959) 198.

not to say: "The son of man is the people of the saints of the Most High." In his interpretation he disregards the one of great age and the son of man. [43]

Perhaps the relationship between the chosen people and the heavenly being who comes like a son of man should be explained by the notion of the heavenly *šar*. This is a kind of angel who guides and protects every people, a conception that was manifested in the biblical passages that refer to the angel of Yahweh. For the other peoples, these *šarim* or angels were really pagan gods that the Jews transformed into creatures of Yahweh. [44] From this would stem the idea of a heavenly being who guides the destiny of the messianic people.

In conclusion, the personage who comes like a son of man does not appear to be a man but a divine being, distinct from God and inferior to him, who receives from him a universal and eternal power which is shared by the chosen people.

Why does this divine being appear as a man? Because in the apocalyptic context which presents animals as symbols, man is the best symbol to represent a divine being. What ultimately justifies the use of this symbol is man's resemblance to God. Why "son of man"? The context of Daniel and the parables of Enoch suggests an answer: The mysterious, divine personage appears in the presence of the one of great age. If the one who unquestionably represents God has the face of a man, of an old man, we can understand that the divine being subordinate to him and who seems to inherit everything from him has the face of a son of man. He fulfills a certain role as the son of God.

2 - In the Parables of Enoch

Judaism after Daniel emphasized the transcendent aspects of the Son of Man. In the *Book of Parables* of the Ethiopian *Book of Enoch* (1st century B.C.), [45] a mysterious personage with messianic functions is called the Son of Man, or the Chosen One. He is identified with the Messiah, the Anointed One.

The reference is most certainly to an *individual*. The

---

[43] Cf. Feuillet, *RB* 1953, 191 ff.

[44] Kruse, *VD* 1959, 210.

[45] Coppens cites the date as "before 63 B.C." (*Le Fils de l'homme*, 76).

title of Son of Man is reserved for him alone, in contrast to the title of Chosen One shared with the just (thus the day of the Chosen One is also the day of the chosen ones: 51:2). It is never extended to the community. The role of the Son of Man is his alone.

This Son of Man is clearly presented as a divine personage. His transcendence results from the following qualities:

He is *preexistent*: "Before the sun and the signs were made, his name was named before the Lord of spirits" (48:3). His preexistence is expressed in terms that recall the origin of Wisdom in Proverbs 8:22-31.

He is *presented in the company of the one of great age,* that is to say, of God, as if he were on a level of equality with him, associated to his supremacy over the universe (46:1: "There I saw someone who had a 'head of days,' and his head was like white snow, and with him another whose face had the appearance of a man .... It is the Son of Man ....")

He has a capital role in the economy of salvation, analogous to God's: "It is by his name that they will be saved" (48:7). "It is the Son of Man who possesses justice and with whom justice dwells" (46:3). "His fate has conquered by righteousness before the Lord of the spirits for eternity" (46:3). The Son of Man is a judge "sitting on the throne of his glory," precisely like "the Lord of the spirits," that is to say, God (comp. 62:2 and 5; cf. 69:27). The Son of Man is the one who reveals the mysteries: "He will reveal all the treasures of the secrets" (46:3). He is the "light of the peoples" (48:4). All men will hope in him and will pray to him; all will worship him (62:9; 48:2).

The life to come will be spent with the Son of Man as well as with God: "And the Lord of the spirits will dwell on them, and with this Son of Man, they will eat, they will sleep and arise for ever and ever" (62:14; cf. 71:17).

These qualities of the person of the Son of Man are so close to the Christ of the Gospel that certain authors have assigned a Judaeo-Christian origin to the book or invoked Christian interpolations. [46] But no quality involves a specific allu-

---

[46] The composition of the *Book of the Parables* is situated in the 2nd

sion to the Gospel language, and the vocabulary remains that of the Jewish apocalypses. Indeed, it would have been strange for a Christian to have passed over in silence the death and the Resurrection,[47] so important in the life of Christ and so characteristic of his declarations on the Son of Man. Besides, the Son of Man of the *Parables of Enoch* is not presented as a man. He remains a being of a superior, angelic, and divine nature. In this heavenly and glorious personage, there is no indication of an authentic Incarnation, or any evocation of a redemptive drama.

3 - Conclusion

The ascending and the descending approaches have both been used in the progress of Jewish revelation toward the Incarnation. First, the ascending way, which is clearly set forth in the most ancient texts of the royal Psalms and that has the messiah-king accede to a divine sonship. Then there is the descending way of divine Wisdom which tends to detach itself from God to come close to men, and of the Son of Man, an angelic and divine being who receives messianic power. These two ways are developed not in parallel fashion but successively. The succession results from an evolution in the thinking of the Jewish people who saw the hope of a savior-king stymied and thus came to understand that their salvation was to come from above, from God himself. The descending way implies awareness of man's powerlessness to realize the work of salvation.

Moreover we should note that even in the ascending way there is a descending aspect: the divine name signifies qualities communicated by God to man, and the divine sonship implies the paternal attitude or the generative action of God. The idea of a man who, by his human capabilities, could raise himself to a divine level would be totally foreign to Biblical thinking. As the Bible announces him, the Messiah is not simply the product of a human evolution, albeit a religious evolution of the Jewish people.

---

century by J. T. Milik, *Dix ans de découvertes dans le désert de Juda,* Paris, 1957, p. 30. Cf. J. Coppens, *Le Fils de l'homme,* 74, No. 48.

[47] Cf. E. Dhanis, "De Filio hominis in V.T. et in judaismo," (*Gr* 45. 1964, 17).

Neither of these two paths reaches its culmination in Judaism: the dynamism of incarnation is far from being totally accomplished. By virtue of divine names or better still through divine sonship, the Messiah accedes to a certain divine rank, but not to the point of possessing the nature of God. As for Wisdom, she is not a human being, it would seem, any more than the Son of Man, who remains a heavenly being. Thus man does not completely accede to God, and God does not unite himself completely to mankind.

However, even if the conjunction of God and man is a long way off, a large part of the journey has been completed on the part of both. In this progression, we must stress the role played by foreign religions. Some scholars have tended to minimize this role, in order to safeguard the originality of the Jewish religious thought. But the influence of these religions mut be acknowledged and appreciated: their conceptions of divinized kings or of divinities closer to men orientated Jewish thinking toward representations that their strict monotheism would have tended to discourage. We see here a symbol and a testimony of the participation of the whole of mankind, Jewish and non-Jewish, in the preparation for the mystery of the Incarnation.

Chapter IV

THE FAITH OF THE PRIMITIVE CHRISTIAN COMMUNITY

If we want to follow the chronological order leading from the Old to the New Testament, we must consider how Jesus presented himself to men according to the Gospel record. It is in Jesus that the dynamism of incarnation already present in Judaism reached its fulfillment. In him the descending way, by which a person detached himself from God to join mankind, reached its culmination. And likewise the ascending way, that of a man raised to the rank of God. In Jesus the true covenant was established, involving the perfect mutual belonging of God and man as well as new bonds of fatherhood and sonship. In Jesus the Word of God became man, the action of God in the history of salvation became human activity, and the divine presence among men was concretized in a human presence. Everything that had been "planned," announced, concerning a coming together of God and man was perfectly fulfilled in him.

We might be tempted to turn at once to what Jesus said about himself and what he did in order to explain this fulfillment. But we know that these words and actions have not come down to us directly, in their pure state. They were transmitted to us through the testimony of men, and this occurred precisely by virtue of the dynamism of incarnation that instituted a human mode of presence, revelation, and action.

That is why we first consider the faith of the primitive Christian community. For this will help us to appreciate the conditions under which this testimony took shape and to more clearly discern the original Jesus through it. To get a truer grasp of the Christology Jesus himself offered, we shall start by studying the Christology of the first believers.

A. The First Christology in Apostolic Preaching

The *Acts of the Apostles* recount the earliest apostolic preaching. While this preaching bears the mark of Luke's composition, there are signs of archaism not only in its form but in its doctrine.[1] This helps us to identify the earliest proclamations of the faith. One of these signs is precisely a rather vague way of expressing the divinity of Jesus.

In this preaching Jesus is presented as the one in whom the salvation offered by God to mankind is concentrated exclusively and totally. Pentecost is its primordial demonstration, perpetuated in the development of the Christian community. The risen Christ, raised up to the right hand of God, pours forth the Holy Spirit. This is the essential fact that governs the earliest Christology, as we see from the conclusion of Peter's discourse: "For this reason the whole House of Israel can be certain that God has made this Jesus whom you crucified both Lord and Christ " (Ac 2:36). Other comparable affirmations are made concerning Jesus in his glorious state: "By his own right hand God has now raised him up to be leader and saviour" (Ac 5:31); "God has appointed him to judge everyone, alive or dead" (Ac 10:42; cf. 17:31).

These affirmations acknowledge Jesus to be the Messiah; and yet we cannot limit the meaning of this messianism to what had been announced in the Old Testament.[2] The prophetic announcements are fulfilled, but it is essentially the experience of Jesus' efficacious action in the emergence of the Church that explains the affirmations of faith concerning him, and the qualities attributed to his person. The messianism

---

[1] Cf. J. Schmitt, *Jésus ressuscité dans la prédication apostolique*, Paris, 1949, 22 ff.; V. Taylor, *The Person of Christ in New Testament Teaching*, London, 1958, 24-31; S. S. Smalley, "The Christology of Acts," *Exp T* 73 (1961-1962) 358-362; "The Christology of Acts again," in *Christ and Spirit in the New Testament* (B. Lindars - S. S. Smalley, Cambridge, 1973, 79-93; C .F. Moule, "The Christology of Acts," in *Studies in Luke-Acts* (L. E. Keck · J. L. Martyn), Nashville-New York, 1966, 159-185.

[2] Concerning the minimalist interpretation of the Christology of Acts adopted by J. A. T. Robinson ("The most primitive Christology of all?" in *Journal of Theological Studies*, n.s. 7, 1956, 177-189; *Twelve New Testament Studies*, London 1962, 139 ff.; *Jesus and his Coming*, London 1957, 143 ff.), Moule (*art. cit.*, 167 ff.) and Smalley (*art. cit.*, *Exp T*, 73, 359 ff.) have commented critically on it.

expressed in Peter's discourse, for instance, must be evaluated not in terms of the ancient oracles, but by reference to new and totally unprecedented facts.[3] The first sermon must be understood in the light of the experience to which it refers.

The messianism professed in this preaching is situated on a divine level. It certainly applies to the man Jesus, with its very vivid remembrance of his human existence and especially of his Passion. But it recognizes a divine power in this man, now forever glorified.

Let us point out various instances when the Messiah was given the attribute of divinity.

1 - The term Christ is used a number of times in the Acts of the Apostles, not merely as a name given to Jesus but as a title.[4] When Peter declares that Israel must acknowledge Jesus as "the Christ," he gives the name its full messianic value, understanding it in the light of Pentecost. Jesus is "the Christ," "the Anointed One" in the sense that he is filled with the Holy Spirit to the point of pouring him out upon mankind (cf. Ac 2:33). Now, the power to communicate the Spirit belongs to God. In the Old Tecstament only God pours out his Spirit and only he can pour him out. Jesus therefore possesses a divine power. While he has certainly received the Holy Spirit from the Father, it is he who pours him out, and therefore exercises a power that belongs strictly to God. We need only compare the prophecy cited by Peter in which the Lord promises: "I will pour out my spirit on all mankind" (Ac 2:17; Jl 3:1), with the affirmation that Jesus has poured out the promised Spirit (cf. Ac 2:33).

The Title "Lord" which Peter associates with that of "Christ" also indicates a divine rank in the context in which it is spoken. Psalm 110 is cited in the perspective of a transcendence over David, for the latter "never went up to heaven"

---

[3] J. Dupont, ("Ascension du Christ et don de l'Esprit d'après Actes 2:33" in *Christ and Spirit in the N.T.*, Lindars-Smalley, 219-228) points to the value of the allusion of Ac 2:33-34 to Ps 110:1. The event of Pentecost is interpreted "in the light of the meaning Jewish tradition attributed to the feast by relating it to the theophany of Sinai." But the parallel between Moses' ascent and the Ascension of Jesus serves to show the superiority of the gift of the Spirit over the gift of the Law. The reality of Christ exceeds that of the Old Testament figures.

(Ac 2: 34). According to the testimony of the Gospels, Jesus had cited this Psalm to evoke this transcendence, pointing out to his adversaries that the Messiah was to be the Lord of David rather than his son (cf. Mt 22: 45; Mk 12: 37; Lk 20: 44). Peter sees this transcendence in the light of Jesus' glorious elevation.

Here, we see, the "Lord" is the one who has power even over the Spirit, that is to say, supreme power. He who had been called "my Lord" in Psalm 110 shares the omnipotence of "the Lord."[5] Thus the Psalm is fulfilled at the highest possible level.[6]

---

[4] Concerning the use of "Christ" as a name for Jesus, Smalley has stressed the analogy between the Acts of the Apostles and Peter's First Epistle (*art. cit., Christ and Spirit in the New Testament*, 85-88). Moreover he rejects the opinion that would consider the use of the title of Messiah to be a later development (*art. cit., Exp T* 73, 362). In fact, this use is archaic. It belongs to the period when "Christ" had not yet become an accepted name for Jesus. It is from the use of the title that the designation of Jesus by this name stems.

[5] Smalley makes a distinction here between *dunamis,* i.e., the power that Jesus had manifested by his miracles during his public life, and *exousia,* his authority. He thinks that the term *Kurios* designates Jesus as the one who possesses not only *dunamis,* but also *exousia,* authority, and in particular the authority that guarantees the character and content of the Apostles' ministry (*art. cit., Exp T* 73, 301). The reference to authority seems rather implicit, whereas the power to pour out the Spirit is more explicitly indicated.

[6] J. Dupont contests the opinion that the designation "Lord" applied to Jesus stems from Ps 110. He cites as among those favoring the opinion: H. Hahn (*Christologische Hoheitstitel,* Göttingen 1963, 112 ff., 131); Ch. Dodd (*According to the Scriptures,* London 1953, 129-122); J. Daniélou (*Etudes d'exégèse judéo-chrétienne,* Paris 1966, 46, no. 9); P. Beskov (*Rex Gloriae. The Kingship of Christ in the Early Church,* Uppsala, 1962, 48-49, 54-55). And yet he thinks that an examination of the texts does not favor this hypothesis, and he points to other explanations. Among these is the invocation *Maranatha,* and also Joel's expression: "those who invoke the name of the Lord" ("*'Assis à la droite de Dieu'.* L'interprétation du psaume 110,1, dans le Nouveau Testament," in *Resurrexit* (E. Dhanis), Actes du Symposium International sur la résurrection de Jésus, Rome 1974, 416-417).

Even so, Joel's text seems more remote, and the invocation *Maranatha* needs justification. In Peter's discourse recorded in the Acts the linking of "Lord" with Ps 110 is evident, and it is not easy to seek some other origin of the title given to Jesus by the first Christians. This origin appears to be confirmed by Jesus' application of the psalm to himself, according to the Gospel, in his answer to the high priest. Yet the crucial point for us is that the title cannot be interpreted simply with reference to the psalm.

3 - Jesus clothed with divine prerogatives

When Peter recognizes in Jesus the judge of the living and the dead (cf. Ac 10:42), he attributes to him a power that is God's alone.

When Peter calls Jesus "the prince of life" (Ac 3:15) he proclaims a divine power that has just been manifested in the healing of a helpless cripple. For the master of life is none other than God. The miracle had been worked in the name of Jesus, that is to say, by invoking someone who, of himself alone, has the power to grant health (cf. Ac 3:16; 4:10).

It is above all the quality of "saviour" (Ac 5:31) that witnesses to Jesus' divine power. We must remember that in the Old Testament God was looked upon as the Savior: "Am I not Yahweh? There is no god besides me, a God of integrity and a saviour; there is none apart from me" (Is 45:21). In the Septuagint version the Greek term "saviour" (*Soter*) was habitually a predicate of God.[7] This predicate is now transferred to Jesus, with the same exclusivism as one was shown for the God of Israel: "For of all the names in the world given to men, this is the only one by which we can be saved" (Ac 4:12).

Thus, Jesus also has a role that is God's own. J. Schmitt comments: "Just as in earlier times Israel was saved 'by the name' of Yahweh, so, too, the believer henceforth owes his salvation to 'the name of Christ.'"[8] All "who believe in Jesus will have their sins forgiven through his name" (Ac 10:43). The power to save, to demand a commitment of faith, to obtain the remission of sins, belonged strictly to God. To these was added the power to sanctify in baptism, for it was in the name of Jesus that baptism was administered (cf. Ac 2:38; 8:16).

It takes on a new meaning through the power of the glorious Christ who pours out the Holy Spirit, a power far superior to that visualized in the psalm.

[7] Cf. G. Voss, *Die Christologie der lukanischen Schriften in Grundzügen,* Paris-Brugge 1965, 47-51.

[8] *Op. cit.,* 222. "Through his exaltation Jesus possesses the 'name', i.e., the very condition of God" (221). "The divine name in a certain manner actualizes the salvific power of God. The same holds true for the name of Jesus" (J. Dupont, *Nom de Jésus,* D B S 6, 516).

4 - In the account of Stephen's death, faith in the divinity of Jesus takes on striking proportions. First, we must consider Stephen's declaration which provoked the stoning. His long discourse before the Sanhedrin, with its very harsh words for those who had put "the Just One" to death, had roused his hearers' anger. Yet, for all their rage and gnashing of teeth, they still did not have sufficient grounds to condemn him to death. Their chance was provided by Stephen's words: "I can see heaven thrown open and the Son of Man standing at the right hand of God" (Ac 7:56).

The reason they rushed upon Stephen to stone him was that they had interpreted his words as blasphemy. In themselves, none of the words Stephen had used expressly attributed to Jesus the mark of divinity. But his hearers understood them in that light. Were they mistaken? First of all, Stephen spoke these words at the very place where Jesus had answered Caiaphas' question by affirming his identity as the Son of God and announcing the elevation of the Son of Man to the right hand of God (cf. Mt 26:64; Mk 14:62; Lk 22:69). So now Jesus' "blasphemy" was being confirmed by his own disciple's words. It was Stephen's intention to witness that what Jesus had said to the Sanhedrin was being confirmed as true. In his declaration he deliberately repeated what Jesus had said of himself.

Moreover, the intention to witness to the divinity of Jesus appears in his invocation: "Lord Jesus, receive my spirit" (Ac 7:59). Here again Stephen was inspired by Jesus' own words: "Father, into your hands I commit my spirit" (Lk 23:46); but instead of addressing them to the Father he addressed them directly to Jesus: Thus, by his death Stephen showed that for him Jesus was equal to God. The same holds true of his prayer: "Lord, do not hold this sin against them" (Ac 7:60), in which he asked of Jesus the forgiveness that Jesus had asked of his Father for his enemies (cf. Lk 23:24).

This episode shows faith in the divinity of Jesus being lived rather than stated in so many words. In those early days of Christianity there was no concern as yet to define the position of Jesus with respect to the God of the Jews. Nor was there any attempt to reconcile professed monotheism with the recognition of divine power and divine attributes in a man who had lived a very real human life.

What the faith of the early Christian community grasped first of all was the divine dynamism acting in Jesus and that was his personal possession. Over the centuries, this starting point of faith has retained its cogency. The divinity of Christ has continued to manifest itself through the effusion of the Holy Spirit. It can be perceived in its ever-acting power in the Church today. This action, with its countless manifestations, makes us look to its source, namely, Christ risen and raised up to heaven. For the truth of the event of the Resurrection has been guaranteed by the witness of the Apostles. The task remains to discern in this glorious Christ the complete meaning of the divinity affirmed. Inevitably, the first Christians asked questions concerning the origin and existence of Jesus, seeking to determine more clearly what this Jesus had been before his Resurrection in his innermost reality.

The divine dynamism of Christ strains forward toward the unfolding future of the Church. The dynamism of faith tends to join in this movement to better understand where it leads. But the dynamism of faith also looks in the opposite direction, reaching back to the earliest origins, to fathom everything implied in the affirmation of the divinity of the glorious Christ.

We should note that at the outset the dynamism of faith focussed on the glorious elevation of Christ, without trying to discern at once everything that this Jesus had been before. Although Jesus was described as a man whose earthly life was remembered by those who had witnessed it, we cannot conclude that he was thought of as only a man. His human existence was remembered and reflected upon, but there was no attempt to make a pronouncement as to his true identity.

There was a kind of indetermination, therefore, in this primitive Christology. We would be wrong to describe it as Adoptionist, for that would imply the first Christians thought Jesus to be simply a man adopted by God as his son and divinized. Adoptionism involves more than the affirmation of a link between the glorification of Jesus and the manifestation of the divine sonship. This link appears, for instance, in one of Paul's discourses when he applies Psalm 2 to the risen

72

Christ: "You are my son: today I have become your father" ((Ac 13:33). Adoptionism would imply that before that "today" Jesus was not truly the Son of God and was considered exclusively as a human being. In actual fact, the earliest Christology did not inquire into what manner of being Jesus had been before his death and Resurrection. Later, when it set about solving the problem, it expressly acknowledged his preexisting divine state.

B. In the Teaching of Saint Paul

1. The Son of God

St. Paul calls Jesus "the Son of God" (2 Co 1:19; Ga 2:20; Ep 4:13), or categorically "the Son" (1 Co 15:28). On a number of occasions he evokes the relationship between God and "his Son." God sent "his own Son" (Rm 8:3; Ga 4:4); "God did not spare his own Son" (Rm 8:32); he has intended us "to become true images of his Son" (Rm 8:29); "he has ... created a place for us in the kingdom of the Son that he loves" (Col 1:13), etc.

Now, we have a precious sign pointing to the origin of this designation. According to the Acts of the Apostles (9:20), this was the essential truth Paul preached immediately after his conversion: "After he had spent only a few days with the disciples ..., he began preaching in the synagogues, 'Jesus is the Son of God.'" And yet when Jesus had appeared to Paul on the road to Damascus, he had not presented himself explicitly as the Son of God. Paul must have become convinced of it in the light of the very meaning of his encounter. As the persecutor of the Christians, Paul had looked upon Jesus as an imposter who had set himself up as the Son of God and claimed a certain equality with God; and it was for this blasphemy that Jesus had been convicted. Saul had considered Jesus' death on the cross as a sign of divine reprobation, as the proof that Jesus was not indeed the Son of God he had claimed to be.

When Paul was thrown to the ground on his way to persecute Christians, he understood that this Jesus was alive and endowed with divine power. He must therefore really be what he had affirmed, that is to say, the Son of God. It was in the glorious Christ that Saul recognized this divine title, and more specifically in Christ as he had manifested himself to him personally. Paul affirmed the divine sonship in its strongest, transcendent sense, that Jesus had defended and the Sanhedrin condemned.

Above all we must stress that Paul conceives the divine sonship not as acquired or the result of adoption. Christ's preexistence is implied in Paul's affirmation that God sent his Son: "God dealt with sin by sending his own Son in a body as physical as any sinful body, and in that body God condemned sin" (Rm 8:3). "... when the appointed time came, God sent his Son, born of a woman, born a subject of the Law" (Ga 4:4).

This preexistence is not lost sight of when Paul attributes an effect of sonship to the Resurrection: "The Gospel of God is about his Son who, in the order of the spirit of holiness, was established Son of God in all his power through his resurrection from the dead" (Rm 1:3-4); he was already, before that resurrection, "the Son of God." [9]

That is why it has been said that Pauline theology proceeded "from the notion of the Son of God revealing himself in the glory and power of his Parousia toward the idea of an eternal sonship." For Paul, it is claimed, "this was the only possible solution of the theological problem." [10]

And yet the affirmation of Christ's eternal sonship did not come to Paul solely as the solution of a problem. The Christ who victoriously thrust himself upon him was the one who had declared he was the Son of God even before his Resurrection. Jesus possessed divine sonship, a sonship that put him on a par with God, because he had proved it to Paul by the power of his Resurrection.

Paul's discreet affirmation of Christ's preexistent sonship moreover corresponds to the way Jesus had revealed his iden-

---

[9] It is possible that Paul used an ancient creed here, which would explain his use of language not customary for him. But the idea of a sonship stemming from the Resurrection occurs in Ac 13:33.

[10] L. Cerfaux, Le Christ dans la théologie de saint Paul, Paris, 1954, 385. Cerfaux adds in a footnote: "We 'reason', whereas Paul obviously had inspired intuitions." (Footnote 1).

tity. Paul does not dissert on this preexistence. He is content to declare that "God sent his Son," in the same veiled way that Jesus said he was sent by the Father, that he had come in the name of the Father.

2. Divine Preexistence

Does Paul go directly from the affirmation of the transcendent sonship to the specific affirmation of Jesus' divinity? Paul is not much inclined to speculate on the mystery of Jesus' origin, but he transcribes two hymns that evoke more clearly Jesus' condition before his earthly life. These two hymns emphasize the fullness of divinity possessed by the glorious Christ, while also affirming his divine preexistence.

a - The hymn of the Epistle to the Colossians [11]

This hymn describes Jesus as "first to be born from the dead" (Col 1:18), the one in whom "God wanted all perfection to be found" (Col 1:18-19), since "in his body lives the fullness of divinity" (Col 2:9). [12] But in the "first to be born from the dead," Christian reflection discerned "the first-born of all creation" (Col 1:15). Before affirming the sonship that stems from the Resurrection, the hymn affirms a primordial sonship antedating creation. Before pointing to him as the principle of the Church, he shows him existing "before anything was created" (Col 1:17). In itself, the expression "first-born of all creation" might seem ambiguous, for it could be interpreted as a priority among creatures. But it is sufficiently clarified by what follows. Christ holds priority not as a creature, but as the Creator. For it is in him that all things were created: "all things were created through him and for him. Before anything was created, he existed, and he holds all things in unity" (Col 1:16-17).

---

[11] N. Kehl has shown that the primitive form of the hymn is not Gnostic but Christian (Der Christus-hymnus - Kol 1:12-20, Stuttgart, 1967).

[12] A. Feuillet considers it quite probable that Paul thought of the first-born from the dead before thinking of "the first-born of all creation." He points out that in 1 Co 15:20 Paul already calls Christ "the first-fruits of all who have fallen asleep" (Le Christ Sagesse de Dieu d'après les épitres pauliniennes, Paris, 1966, 186).

75

Seen in this light, if the fullness of divinity is really in Christ for the sake of reconciling all creatures with God, this means that before Christ became the universal Redeemer, he was the universal Creator. Now, the power to create is a divine attribute. [13]

In this same passage we see the outline of a rudimentary theology on the relationship of Christ with God. He is "the first-born," and also the Son begotten by the Father, "the image of the unseen God" (Col 1:15). He bears the resemblance of the Father in a way that calls to mind what is said about divine Wisdom in the Old Testament: "She is a reflection of the eternal light, untarnished mirror of God's active power, image of his goodness" (Ws 7:26). [14]

It is because of these two characteristics — generation and resemblance — that the Son has his own role to play in creation, distinct from the Father's. The Father is the one who creates, the Son the one through whom and in whom creation occurs. For creation is accomplished after the model of the Son's generation and is rooted in his likeness to the Father. That explains the logical link between the characteristics of Christ as image and first-born on the one hand, and the affirmation that all things have been created in him.

Here we see the first intimations of the idea of a distinction of persons in God: Christ possesses divinity after the manner of a son who resembles his father, and his divine activity is not purely and simply identified with the Father's. It has its own distinctive mark. This is really an explication of the affirmation that Jesus is the Son of God.

b - The hymn of the Epistle to the Philippians (2:6-11)

This hymn forcefully expresses the divinity of the glorious Christ: "God raised him high and gave him the name which is above all other names" (Ph 2:9). The expression

---

[13] This divine attribute is confirmed by the reference to Wisdom implicit in "the first-born of all creation," as has been shown by F. M. Burney ("Christ as the APXH of Creation" in the *Journal of Theological Studies* 276, 1926, 160-177; and A. Feuillet, *op. cit.*, 185-202).

[14] Cerfaux writes: "We can say that what constitutes Christ in the reality of his person is the fact that he is an image" (*op. cit.*, 387). Feuillet speaks even more affirmatively (*op. cit.*, 172).

reflects the Biblical mentality from two points of view. The name signifies the reality of the person. And, as is the custom where the name of God is concerned, it is not spoken. Even so, the words "name which is above all other names" are clear enough.[15] The closing of the hynm brings us to the conclusion that Jesus received the divine name and must be acknowledged as God: "so that all beings ... should bend the knee at the name of Jesus and that every tongue should acclaim Jesus Christ as Lord, to the glory of God the Father" (Ph 2:10-11). It calls to mind Isaiah (45:23) in which Yahweh says: "before me every knee shall bend, by me every tongue shall swear, saying, 'From Yahweh alone come victory and strength'." So the adoration won for Christ by his name above all other names is the same that Yahweh rightfully claimed.

This state of the glorious Christ is also expressed by "equality with God." There has been much confusion as to the meaning of the text because "equality with God" was thought to refer to the Son's divine preexisting condition, whereas it really designates his state of glorious elevation. Christ chose not to grasp at this state of eminence by an act that would have been comparable to Adam's, but instead obtained it from his Father through his sacrifice.[16]

However, even before he lived a human life, Jesus was "in the form of God" (Ph 2:6).[17] This "form" certainly indicates an appearance or manner of presenting himself, but one that corresponds to reality.[18] Before Christ lived the life of a man, he lived the life of God. He lived after the manner of God

---

[15] Cerfaux writes: "Two points appear to be beyond doubt: 1) The name is a personification; it reaches to the depths of a being, indicating its power, its role, its nature. 2) The name par excellence, the name above all other names, designates the mysterious name that is the innermost reality of the divine being" (*op. cit.*, 321).

[16] Cf. P. Grelot, "La valeur de *ouk ... alla* dans Philippiens 2:6-7," *Bi* 54, 1973, 25-42.

[17] This is the English translation given in *The Bible, Revised Standard Version*, New York, American Bible Society, 1971. In view of its greater accuracy, this translation will be used in quotations from Ph 2:6-8, in preference to *The Jerusalem Bible*, from which all other quotations are taken.

[18] Cf. Cerfaux, *op. cit.*, 290; P. Grelot, "Deux expressions difficiles de Philippiens 2,6-7," *Bi* 53 (1972) 503-507.

because he was God. Without saying so explicitly, this is the implication of the words "being in the form of God."

In the hymn there is even a deliberate insistence on this initial divine state because it indicates the extent of the self-emptying that accompanied his passage to the condition of a servant.

Nothing was lacking to him in his initial state. His was not an inferior or diminished divine nature to be completed when he attained the fullness of divine being at the instant of his glorious elevation. For "equality with God" and the attribution to him of the name above all other names apply to Christ as man. Before he became man, he was "in the form of God," but he still had to be fully divinized in his human condition. That is what occurred through the glory granted him in consequence of his sacrifice.

Thus, the divine power Christ received in his glorification, a power to be invoked and worshipped as God, was in accord with his innermost being which was "in the form of God."

And so this hymn manifests in the most remarkable way an ontological inquiry seeking to determine what Christ was at the origin of his existence, and does not hesitate to discover him to be divine.

3. The Name of God reserved for the Father

While conceiving of Jesus' divine sonship as transcendent and preexisting, Paul never says that Christ is God. He reserves the use of the name of God for the Father.

Now, this manner of speaking is intentional on Paul's part. He restates the monotheistic affirmation of the Old Testament: "Yahweh our God is the one Yahweh" (Dt 6:4), applying it to the Father. "we know ... that there is no god but the One ... for us there is one God, the Father, from whom all things come and for whom we exist; and there is one Lord, Jesus Christ, through whom all things come and through whom we exist" (I Co 8:4-6). Clearly Paul makes a clear distinction between the "one God," the Father, and Jesus Christ, the "one Lord."

Two texts have been cited as exceptions to this rule. One, in the Epistle to Titus (2:13), reads: "... the Appearing of the glory of our great God and saviour Christ Jesus." However it is not certain that the use of the word "God" here refers to Jesus Christ; [19] and the Pauline origin of the Epistle is seriously debatable.

The other text, in the Epistle to the Romans (9:5) has been bitterly disputed with regard to its grammatical structure. Speaking of the privileges of the Israelites, Paul declares: "Theirs are the patriarchs and from them came Christ according to flesh who is above all, God for ever blessed!" The expression "God for ever blessed" seems to apply to Christ, but the punctuation has provoked many arguments because of the efforts to place a separation between "Christ" and "God for ever blessed." [20] None of these efforts seem convincing. However, it is hard to admit that Paul could have applied the title of "God" to Christ in such a resounding way, when he ordinarily takes great care to avoid this identification. [21] The most likely solution is to admit an omission or a transposition in the copying of the text. The end of the sentence would be more coherent with what precedes if it read: "from them came Christ according to flesh, to them belongs the God who is above all, for ever blessed." [22]

---

[19] This is the most probable sense, considering the expression in itself (Cf. R. E. Brown, *Jesus God and Man*, Milwaukee 1967, 16-18). However, in favor of a distinction between God and Jesus, we can invoke the use of the term "God" in closely related texts to designate the God distinct from Jesus (Tt 2:10; 2:11; 3:4).

[20] It has been suggested that a period be placed either after *sarka* ("from them came Christ according to flesh,") or after *pantôn* ("who is above all"). But these interruptions do not seem very plausible (cf. Brown, *op. cit.*, 20-22; W. Sanday - A. C. Headlam, *The Epistle to the Romans*, Edinburgh 1968, 233-238).

[21] Paul's use seems decisive to Cerfaux, who wants to avoid "the great disadvantage of changing the Pauline vocabulary" and prefers to "allow God his usual doxology" (*op. cit.*, 391).

[22] In the hypothesis of the omission, the text would originally have been *hôn ho ôn* (ὧν ὁ ὤν) instead of *ho ón*; in the more probable hypothesis of the transposition, *hôn ho* (ὧν ὁ) instead of *ho ôn* (ὁ ὤν). This second correction had been proposed by Samuel Crell, under the pseudonym of L. M. Artemonius (*Initium Evangelii S. Johannis restitutum*, Amsterdam, 1726, 223-238). It was adopted by various commentators, including K. Barth; C. H. Dodd (*The Epistle to the Romans*, London 1949, 152) leans toward admitting it, and C. K. Barrett finds it intriguing (*A Commentary to the Epistle to the Romans*, London 1957, 179). Recently it has been proposed

In conclusion, let us keep in mind that Paul probably never applied the name of "God" to Jesus. This name is linked to the monotheistic vocabulary of the Old Testament that affirmed a single God in the way one affirms a single person. To have said that Jesus was God would have been to face the danger of identifying the Father and the Son as being a single person, or implying that Jesus was identified purely and simply with the God of the Old Testament. To avoid such errors in affirming the divinity of Jesus would have required recourse to a terminology similar to the one John used, which distinguishes "*o Theos*," "the God," with the article to designate the Father, and "*Theos*," without the article, to signify the divine being — which can refer to the Word as well as to the Father. As Paul did not know this distinction, he did not use the term "God" directly to express the divinity of Jesus.

4. *The Lord*

The title that Paul usually attributes to Jesus is that of "Lord." It is a title that he obviously borrows from the language of the first Christian communities, for he himself records the formula of faith that was then in common use: "Jesus is Lord" (Rm 10:9; 1 Co 12:3).

Paul attests above all to the antiquity of the title by

---

again by W. L. Lorimer ("Romans IX, 3-5," *New Testament Studies* 13, 1966-67, 385-386), which cites accidental cases of inversion on the part of copyists. B. M. Metzger ("The Punctuation of Rom. 9:5" in *Christ and Spirit in the New Testament*, 99-100) rejects this view, but without advancing any decisive reasons. He concludes that Paul cannot be speaking of the God of the Jews here since he calls him elsewhere the God of the Gentiles (Rm 3:29). But in fact the two names are not mutually exclusive, since the God of the Jews, in this text, is likewise the God of the Gentiles. On the other hand it would have been strange if in citing the privileges of the Israelites Paul had not mentioned the supreme privilege, of their adherence to the true God. These privileges which are expressed in the sentence by the *hôn* possessive which is repeated, had to conclude by a *hôn* with the mention of God. Grammatically, the sentence is well constructed on parallel *hôn*'s, even to the ultimate privilege which inspires a doxological exclamation: "Theirs is the adoption as sons; theirs the divine glory, the covenants; the receiving of the Law, the temple worship and the promises. Theirs are the patriarchs and from them came Christ according to flesh; theirs is God who is above all, forever blessed!. Amen" (Rm 9:4-5).

reproducing the Aramaic formula, Maranatha (1 Co 16:22).[23] This liturgical formula can be interpreted in the sense of a profession of faith: "Our Lord is coming" (*maran atha*), or of a prayer: "Our Lord, come!" (*marana tha*).[24] In all probability it is a prayer, for this interpretation best explains the preservation of the Aramaic formula (as in the case of "Abba"), and it is confirmed by the invocation of Revelation (22:20): "Come, Lord Jesus."[25] The presence of this formula in Paul's writings attests to the Aramaic origin of the name "Lord" applied to Jesus, as against those who, like W. Bousset, have sought to root it in Hellenistic cultic conceptions.[26] It points to the Palestinian community as the original locus where the expression "Lord Jesus" developed.

We should call to mind that according to the testimony of *Acts* Stephen died invoking the "Lord Jesus" (7:59), and that Peter had explicitly applied the title of "Lord" to Jesus from the day of Pentecost, by calling him "Lord" and "Christ," two qualities in which Christians were expected to profess their faith (2:36). There is, therefore, a continuity with the origins of Christian preaching.

In itself the title "Lord" signifies power, and more particularly royal power. And it is particularly applicable to the glorious Christ, in full possession of his royal messianic power, as indicated by the affirmation: "This explains why Christ both died and came to life, it was so that he might be Lord both of the dead and of the living" (Rm 14:9).

Besides, the term "Lord" had been used in the Septuagint version to designate God himself. It had become a proper

---

[23] Concerning *Maranatha,* there are many studies, such as: Cullmann, *Christologie du N. T.,* 181 ff.; P. E. Langevin, *Jésus Seigneur et l'Eschatologie, Exégèse de textes prépauliniens,* Bruges-Paris 1967, 168-208, which sees the formula as indicating a current lordship but even more one that is eschatological, "already inaugurated at the Pasch of Christ and that would be exercised in its fullness at the judgment of the Parousia" (208).

[24] According to M. Black, the meaning could be one of supplication or of a profession according to the context. See "The Maranatha Invocation and Jude 14:15 (1 Enoch 1:9)" in *Christ and Spirit in the N.T.,* Lindars-Smalley, 189-196.

[25] Langevin analyzes this invocation as a pre-Pauline text (*op. cit.,* 209-235).

[26] Cullmann (*op. cit.,* 185) refers to A. E. Rawlinson's remark (*The New Testament Doctrine of the Christ,* London 1926, 235) which calls the formula *Maranatha* the Achilles' heel of Bousset's thesis.

name of God. Jewish theology, as exemplified in Philo, distinguished two divine names: "God" and "Lord." [27] When Paul affirms "one God, the Father" and "one Lord, Jesus Christ" (1 Co 8:6) he applies one divine name to the Father and the other to Jesus Christ. He clearly wants to teach the divinity of Christ, but under another name than the Father's. [28] The distinction between the two names permits him to express the distinction between two divine persons. We have seen how the use of the term "God" only would have entailed the danger of confusing the Father with the Son.

Paul's intention to attribute the value of a divine name to the term "Lord" can be seen in the way he applies to Jesus what had been said of God in the Old Testament. Thus, he repeats Joel's promise: "... all who call on the name of the Lord will be saved" (Jl 3:5), but uses the name Lord to mean Christ (Rm 10:13). Here again Paul accepts a usage of the Christian community, whose religious attitude was defined by the invocation of the name of the Lord Jesus (cf. Ac 9:13-19).

Other expressions like "the table of the Lord" (1 Co 10:21), "the fear of the Lord (2 Co 5:11), "the word of the Lord" (1 Th 1:8; 4:15; 2 Th 3:1), "the day of the Lord" (1 Co 1:8; 4:17, etc.), [29] transfer to Jesus what concerned Yahweh. We can point even more to "the glory of the Lord" that Christians reflect, unveiled, as in a mirror, by his allusion to Moses, who was permitted to look upon Yahweh unveiled (2 Co 3:19). As "Lord," Jesus thus holds the place that the Old Covenant had acknowledged to be God's.

---

[27] Cf. on this matter Cerfaux, *op. cit.*, 355-357.

[28] Concerning the origin of the title *Kyrios* in the N.T., J.A. Fitzmyer reacted against the theory of the pagan Hellenistic origin admitted by W. Bousset, R. Bultmann, P. Vielhauer, H. Conzelmann and others, and showed that there are serious indications of a religious Palestinian-Semitic origin. Against Bultmann, he shows that the title "Lord" had been used in its absolute sense to designate Yahweh. He notes that the title applied to Jesus implies a transcendence that places Jesus on a level of equality with Yahweh without identifying Jesus with him inasmuch as he is not the Father ("Der semitische Hintergrund des neutestamentlichen Kyriostitels," in G. Strecker, *Jesus Christus in Historie und Theologie*, Tübingen 1975, 267-298).

[29] Cf. Langevin, *op. cit.*, 153, which notes the identity between "day of the Lord Yahweh" and "day of the Lord Jesus" (Parousia). He considers the expression to be pre-Pauline (112-118).

Not only did the use of the title of "Lord" allow Paul to attribute divinity to Jesus without running the risk of confusing him with the Father. It also reflected the experience of Christ's divine power which was being deployed in the primitive Church. Paul must have constantly experienced it in his apostolic mission, and he never ceased professing his faith in Jesus' victorious power. The title of "Son" or "Son of God" tends to inspire thought of the relationship between Christ and the Father, whereas the title of "Lord" addresses itself more directly to the relations between Christ and ourselves. We can understand that since Paul was more conscious than anyone else of the relationship that bound him to Jesus, he saw him above all as "the Lord," and used this title much more often than the title of Son (222 as against 27).

There is scarcely any need to point out that Paul's frequent use of the name "Lord" reveals the dynamism of his Christology. For him Jesus is the one who, possessing divine omnipotence, acts sovereignly in the world and in each human life. The "Lord" is the one who deploys his energy in the Christian, to the point that the latter, as Paul well understood, lives in Christ.[30]

C. IN THE EPISTLE TO THE HEBREWS

The *Epistle to the Hebrews* focuses on the sacrifice of Christ, with the glorification that resulted from it and conferred upon him the supreme power of priestly intercession.

In the hymn that forms a prologue to the Epistle, the author stresses the preexistence of the Son: "At various times in the past and in various different ways, God spoke to our ancestors through the prophets; but in our own time, the last days, he has spoken to us through his Son, the Son that he has appointed to inherit everything and through whom he made everything there is. He is the radiant light of God's glory and the perfect copy of his nature, sustaining the universe by his powerful command; and now that he has destroyed

---

[30] Cf. V. Taylor (*The Person of Christ in New Testament Teaching,* London, 1958, 43), who repeats Bousset's comment: "Thus, he observes that the living experience of the Lord Christ, present in the worship and life of the community, stands behind the Pauline mysticism of 'being in Christ'."

the defilement of sin, he has gone to take his place in heaven at the right hand of divine Majesty. So he is now as far above the angels as the title which he has inherited is higher than their own name" (Heb 1:1-4).

The revelation transmitted by the prophets contrasts with the revelation brought by Jesus because of his attribute as the Son. God has spoken many times through men, such as the prophets, but he could speak only once through his Son, in a unique manner that transcends all prophetic words and that constitutes the definitive, eschatological Revelation. [31]

To conceive of Jesus as a prophet who distinguished himself among the others but did not exceed the level of a man through whom God utters his words, would be to misunderstand the fundamental distinction established by the Epistle. Between the Revelation of the Old Covenant and that of the New, the difference is not one of degree, but of nature. The former is prophetic, the latter is filial.

Was the Son divine from the beginning? It cannot be held that he possessed the attribute of a Son only from the time of his glorification; he was already the Son at the time he was bringing God's words to us, since God "has spoken to us through his Son." [32] Moreover, the Son took part in the work of creation. Through him God "made everything there is" (Heb 1:2). Now, this participation in the creation implies the Son's preexistent divine power. Besides, the Son's creative activity is described as continuing here and now, "sustaining the universe by his powerful command" (Heb 1:3). Finally, the Son is endowed with qualities that had been attributed to divine Wisdom (Ws 7:26): "the radiant light of God's glory and the perfect copy of his nature." We can discern the author's effort to pinpoint the distinctive mark of the eternal Person of the Son. In the Christological hymn of the Epistle to the Colossians, two such marks had already been mentioned, the qualities of image and of firstborn, that is to

---

[31] G. W. Buchanan has noted that the authority of a son and heir, by comparison with the other messengers, appears in the parable of the homicidal husbandmen: Mt 21:33-41. (*To the Hebrews*, New York, 1972, 5). The contrast seems to have been suggested to the author of the Epistle by Jesus' own words.

[32] The Son is characterized by being, not by becoming (cf. A. Van Hoye, *Situation du Christ, Hébreux 1-2*, Paris 1969, 71).

84

say, the likeness and the generation. Here, only the likeness is stressed, but the title of "Son" implies the mark of generation as well.

The choice of citations from the Old Testament in the following verses (1:6, 8, 9, 10, 12) tends to confirm Christ's divinity, and manifests the author's intention more clearly. [33] But the Prologue already presents a picture of Christ's divine preexistence which is, as it were, an outline of the one that will be developed in different terms in the Prologue to John's Gospel.

D. IN THE TESTIMONY OF THE EVANGELISTS

The Evangelists, of course, record traditions that sprang up in the Christian community and through the preaching of the Gospel. At the same time, they witness to their own personal faith by their choice and ordering of these traditional elements, by the way they present or interpret them, and sometimes also by certain affirmations which form a framework for these accounts or go beyond them.

It has been said that each of the Evangelists has his own "Christology." This can refer only to the orientation of their thinking, for none of the Evangelists developed a systematic Christology. And yet it is important to explain these orientations at least in a summary and synthesizing way, in order to better understand the individual approaches of each author and thus get a better grasp of the authentic Christ expressed through them.

1. The Presentation from Above, Common to the Synoptics

All of the Synoptics transmit to us a presentation of Jesus by the Father in the theophanies of the baptism and of the Transfiguration. In both accounts, a voice from heaven proclaims the divine sonship of Jesus. At the time of his baptism the declaration is addressed to Jesus, according to Mark (1:11) and Luke (3:22): "You are my Son, the Beloved; my favour rests on you." And according to Matthew (3:17), it is ad-

---

[33] T. F. Glasson, "'Plurality of Divine Persons' and the Quotations in Hebrew 1:6 ff." in *NTS* 12 (1966) 270-272.

dressed to the witnesses: "This is my Son, the Beloved; my favour rests on him." At the Transfiguration, the words are addressed to the disciples: "This is my Son, the Beloved. Listen to him" (Mk 9:7; cf. Mt 17:5; Lk 9:35).

a - The Voice

Whose voice is it? According to Jewish usage, God is not named, but there is no doubt that this is indeed God's voice.

Several exegetes have identified the voice heard at Jesus' baptism with the "Bath qol" often mentioned in rabbinical literature. [34] This "Bath qol," literally translated "daughter of the voice," designates the echo made by God's voice when it makes itself heard on earth. It is only a reverberation, a "sound proceeding from another," according to its interpreters who, after the end of the era of prophetism, limited their efforts to commenting on the prophets. Judaism considered the phenomenon as a remnant of revelation. In prophecy the voice came directly from God, whereas in the "Bath qol" God spoke to Israel only through an intermediary. The "daughter of the voice" had a lesser value than the voice itself. [35]

In the accounts of the baptism and the Transfiguration the reference is definitely not to "the daughter of the voice." The voice that resounds from the heavens can only be the voice of God himself. [36] There is no question in either instance of a remnant of revelation or of a "sound proceeding from another." What is involved here is a theophany involving a declaration by the Father himself. [37]

---

[34] Taylor cites the "Bath qol" as "the nearest analogue to the divine voice at the Baptism," adding however: "It is another question whether this interesting analogue adequately explains the experience of Jesus Himself" (*Mark*, 161).

[35] Cf. Strack-Billerbeck, I, 125-134.

[36] E. Haenchen, (*Der Weg Jesu*, Berlin 1966, 54) refuses to identify the voice from heaven with the "Bath qol," for "here God himself speaks." Others who have refused to identify the two include J. Kosnetter, *Die Taufe Jesu - Exegetische und religionsgeschichtliche Studien*, Vienna, 1936, 142-144), C. Spicq (*Agapè dans le Nouveau Testament*, Paris 1958, I, 55 No. 4), A. Feuillet ("Le baptême de Jésus d'après l'évangile de saint Marc," CBQ 21, 1959, 478).

[37] E. Lohmeyer has stressed the fact that the Bath-Qol, in Judaism,

Clearly, we are beyond prophetism. It is God the Father in person who speaks. In beginning his account of the baptism, Mark says: "It was at this time that Jesus came" (1:9). Eschatological fulfillment is beginning, and God makes his own voice heard. It is the ultimate and definitive revelation. If only because of the voice coming from heaven, the revelation inaugurated at Jesus' baptism is different in nature from earlier revelations.

b - The Designation of Jesus

In the designation of the identity of Jesus we discern the fusion of three prophetic figures: that of the messianic king (Ps 2:7), of the servant (Is 42:1), and of Isaac (Gn 22:2, 12-16). The interaction of the citations or allusions culminates in a synthesis that is far superior to all its component elements.

The reference to the messianic king: "You are my son" or "This is my son" corrects and complements the allusion to the servant: "my favour rests on you." The one who is presented is not a servant, in contrast to the oracle: "Here is my servant" (Is 42:1). He is a son. The emphasis is on the quality of being a son.

Moreover the words "my favour rests on you" replace those of Ps 2:7: "today I have begotten you." There is no question here of a generation that might take place on this day, as in the case of a royal enthronement. Jesus is presented as a son on whom the Father's "favour" already rests. [38] His sonship is anterior.

The evocation of Isaac, "the beloved son," [39] confirms that there is no question here merely of an adoptive sonship.

---

never accompanies a divine epiphany (*Das Evangelium des Markus*, Göttingen 1963, 22).

[38] M. Black notes that here the Greek aorist translates a Semitic perfect tense (*An Aramaic Approach to the Gospels and Acts*, Oxford 1954, 93). Cf. likewise P. Joüon, *L'évangile de Notre-Seigneur Jésus-Christ*, Paris 1930, 14. The "favour" thus expresses a permanent relationship between the Father and his "Son, the Beloved."

[39] The expression used in the account of the baptism is a "clear echo" of the account of the sacrifice of Isaac, according to A. Richardson, *An Introduction to the Theology of the New Testament*, London 1958, 180. The allusion is even more applicable to the account of the Transfiguration, which is more directly orientated toward the Passion. On the significance of the sacrifice of Isaac, cf. H. Riesenfeld, *Jésus transfiguré*, Lund 1947, 86-96.

The relationship between Jesus and God parallels the one that exists between Isaac and Abraham, that is to say, a sonship based on natural generation and involving equality of nature. Moreover, this sonship is unique, for that is the meaning of the expression "my Son, the Beloved."

The confluence of the various prophetic images therefore suggests a sonship in the strict sense, anterior to Jesus' baptism, a unique sonship, which implies a likeness of nature.

c - The Value of the Declarations

The two declarations appear so similar as to give the impression of a doublet. Yet, it seems quite unlikely that there should have been two almost identical declarations, one at the beginning and the other toward the end of Jesus' public life. This is not the place to determine the historical authenticity of the two accounts. We would simply point out that the account of the Transfiguration can rely on the witness of the three disciples, [40] whereas the account of the baptism cites no witness at all. It is possible that facts relating to the episode of the Transfiguration have been transferred to Jesus' baptism.

What really concerns us is the intention of the Evangelists who report these two declarations to us. They want to show that the Father, in person, presented his Son to mankind. We find this intention even in the accounts of the baptism given by Mark and Luke. In these latter the words "You are my Son ...," reproduced literally in accordance with the text of the Psalm, are addressed to Jesus, but are meant to be heard by everyone.

Thus the Evangelists show a fundamental agreement in their way of conceiving the public life of Jesus. From the start, this life is revealed to be the Father's gift of his Son to men, and as it were the decisive revelation of which he himself is the supreme custodian. Here we have the very vigorous expression of a Christology from above. The his-

---

[40] We might call to mind the confirmation in 2 P 1:18: "We heard this ourselves from heaven, when we were with him on the holy mountain." The confirmation remains hypothetical, since Peter is not the author. Yet the author may be reporting some of Peter's words here, to give the attribution of the Epistle to Peter greater authenticity.

torical era that is dawning has its point of departure in God.
And before the voice of Jesus is heard, the Father speaks out.
This Christology is first of all a theology.

2. Mark: The Gospel of Mystery

From the beginning of his Gospel Mark expresses his
faith in the divine sonship of Jesus: "The beginning of the
Good News about Jesus Christ, the Son of God" (1:1). It is
a faith in the transcendent sonship, for the citations of the
prophetic oracles in the following verses apply to Jesus what
had been said of God himself.

In a general way, the Evangelist stresses human situations
and the human sentiments of Jesus. He delights in bringing
out concrete features of his physiognomy. But through these
human features the mystery of the person comes through.

a - The Human Features

Let us point out a few examples of the revelation of the
mystery of Jesus within the human.

(1). A characteristic *human situation* is that of his leaving Capernaum. Jesus rises very early in the morning and
goes out to a lonely place to pray. Simon and his companions
search for him, find him and urge him to return. He answers:
"Let us go elsewhere, to the neighboring country town, so
that I can preach there too, because that is why I came"
(1:38). Jesus does not specify where he has come from, and
this vagueness opens the possibility of a deeper meaning. The
obvious conclusion would have been: "that is why I went out
from Capernaum." But his mission to preach in the other
towns came from the Father. And do we not have an intimation of the name of God in his silence on this point? [41]
The underlying sense: "I went out from God" is confirmed
by Luke's version: "that is what I was sent to do" (Lk 4:43).
Mark's less explicit version has the advantage of keeping the

---

[41] We can point to Mark's agreement with the more explicit references
of Jn 8:14,42; 13:3; 16:27,30. Meaningful is the observation of Lagrange
speaking of the "mysterious parallelistic contrast" between the going out
from Capernaum and the coming from his Father: "The explanation would
be unchallengeable if this were John's text" (*Evangile selon S. Marc*, Paris
1920, 26).

human event in the foreground, while suggesting the underlying level of mystery.

(2). Jesus' *human sentiments* likewise have a value of
revelation, especially his reaction to the hostility of those who
seek to condemn him: "Then,he looked angrily round at them,
grieved for the hardening of their hearts" (Mk 3:5). This
anger surprises us. Matthew and Luke avoid mentioning it.
Mark does not hesitate to describe it, and invites us to discover the mystery hidden within it. At this moment of anger,
Jesus is about to exercise his divine power on the sabbath by
healing the man with the withered hand. Indeed, his anger
surges as a human expression of divine anger. As we know,
the Old Testament frequently relates instances of God's wrath
provoked by the hardening of men's hearts.

No less surprising is the mention of a compassionate sadness, associated with this anger. But it, too, evokes the mystery of the divine wrath that is accompanied by even greater
mercy.

Two scenes reveal one of Jesus' very special loves. Mark
alone of the Synoptics tells us that Jesus embraced little children
(Mk 10:16). [42] Matthew limits himself to saying that "he laid
his hands on them" (Mt 19:15). The gesture which Matthew
probably considered inappropriate to Jesus' dignity reminds us
of God's predilection for little ones, and shows the warmth
of this love. This reference to the mystery of God results from
the account of the episode. For Jesus has just declared: "Let
the little children come to me; do not stop them; for it is to
such as these that the kingdom of God belongs" (Mk 10:14).
Jesus is identifying himself with this kingdom in a certain way.

When Jesus called the rich man, Mark was also the first
to tell us: "Jesus looked steadily at him and loved him" (Mk
10:21). [43] There were witnesses to this loving gaze, and it
must have made an impression on them since this fact is ex-

---

[42] The same applies to Mk 9:36 where Mark alone says that Jesus "put
his arms around" the child whom he had placed in front of the Twelve.

[43] Taylor points out, but does not share, the opinion that the translation
should be "he caressed him." He stands by Moffatt's interpretation that
there was nothing more than an interior feeling of admiring affection (*Mark*,
429). However, we should note that the verb in its strict sense expresses
not admiration but love.

plicitly reported in the Gospel account. [44] Jesus acts as a person with sovereign power in calling the rich young man to give up everything and follow him, and his love is of such a nature as to reveal the divine love that governs a vocation. (3). Mark tells of one of Jesus' *human actions* in what might be called brutally honest terms. He says that Jesus "made them twelve," that "he made the Twelve" (Mk 3: 14,16). [45] Modern translations strive to tone down the expression. They prefer to say: he "appointed" or "named" the Twelve. But the verb "to make" has its full meaning here, and certain exegetes have recognized in it the verb used in the Greek Bible to recount the creation of the world. What is suggested here is the new creation, the creation that gives birth to the Church. In the human action of choosing the Twelve to entrust a new destiny and a new mission to them, the mystery of God's creative action pierces through, as witnessed by Jesus' changing Simon's name to Peter.

(4). Jesus' *answer* to Caiaphas' solemn question, as recorded in Mark (14:62) is striking in its simplicity: "I am" (*ego eimi*). [46] This is the colloquial expression a man uses to make himself known to those around him. No words could be more human, and they show to what extent Jesus entered the interplay of human relations. Even so, these words give us an insight into the mystery of the name of God "I Am" (Ex 3:14), or of Yahweh's answer: "I, Yahweh ... am" (Is 41:4; 43:10,25, etc.).

(5). Death is the moment when human weakness reaches its omega point. In the case of Jesus it is seen to be a moment of revelation. "The centurion, who was standing in front of him, had seen how he had died, and said, 'In truth this man was a son of God.'" (Mk 15:39). The cogency of Mark's description takes on its full force when it is compared to Matthew's. For, in Matthew's view, the centurion's reaction was

---

[44] "Jesus' look and the insight into Jesus' sentiments are recorded by a witness, and one who is sure of himself as St. Peter can well be" (Lagrange, *Marc,* 250).

[45] Lagrange finds the expression so difficult that he concludes the text was probably altered (cf. *Marc,* 250).

[46] Although V. Taylor prefers this version (*Mark,* 568), there is so little support by witnesses for the lesson "You yourself have said it: I am," and its harmonization with Mt and Lk is so likely that its authenticity is doubtful.

explainable by the experience of the earthquake, and is expressed in this way: "In truth this was a son of God" (Mt 27:54). For Mark, here was a man who was a son of God, and the centurion recognized this sonship by seeing the way he died — for Jesus died in a human way, and yet in a way that was truly filial and that witnessed to a mystery.

b - *The Mystery of the Person*

The mystery of the person of Jesus results from the manifestation of the divine in the human. And it is a mystery that the disciples have personally confronted: "Who can this be? Even the wind and the sea obey him" (Mk 4:41).

The blindness of the disciples, which Mark stresses in a special way, brings out the grandeur of the mystery by contrast. The disciples cannot grope their way to an understanding, because of the limitations of the human mind. In Mark's words, "their minds were closed" (Mk 6:52; cf. 8:17-23).

Nevertheless, the mystery is offered to them: "The secret of the kingdom of God is given to you," Jesus says, distinguishing them from "those who are outside" for whom "everything comes in parables" (Mk 4:11). Matthew and Luke report this statement in a different way: "The mysteries of the kingdom of heaven are revealed to you ..." (Mt 13:11; cf. Lk 8:10). Mark's version goes deeper. He is speaking not only of the mysteries of the kingdom of God, but of the one and only mystery. This mystery is given not only that it may be known; it is given in a far more absolute way in the very person of Jesus.

What Mark has sought to transmit to the readers of the Gospel is this giving of the mystery in Jesus himself. He has a more explicit intention to be faithful to the testimony of tradition on Jesus because of his own keener insight into the mystery.

Some exegetes agreed that Mark witnesses to a faith in the divinity of Jesus as total as the faith witnessed to in John's Gospel. What Mark understood in a more decisive way is the fact that *God reveals himself only as a mystery* through his very transcendence, and that this was indeed Jesus' mode of revelation. As unveiled by Jesus, the mystery implies rather than proclaims his divine identity.

Moreover, Mark realized that there is *no opposition between the divine and the human* in Jesus. Whereas in Matthew we discern the tendency to disregard certain traits which he considers scarcely worthy of Jesus' greatness, Mark does not hesitate to tell everything. For he sees the whole of Jesus' humanity as the bearer of the divine mystery and capable of revealing it, even for example a simple burst of anger or a sign of affection. And so it is that in Mark's Gospel simplicity is joined to depth of understanding.

3. Matthew: The Gospel of the Kingdom

a - Matthew likes to think of Jesus as the *messianic king.* From the start of his Gospel Jesus is presented as the "Son of David," in a genealogy whose fundamental intent is to demonstrate this origin. As the Gospel account unfolds, Jesus is given this title several times (Mt 9:27; 12:23; 15:22; 20:30 ff.; 21:9,15). The Evangelist nevertheless mentions the transcendence that accompanies this kingship. First, the virginal conception points to a superior origin. Moreover, Jesus' power surpasses David's, for he calls himself David's Lord (Mt 22:45).

This transcendence raises Jesus' messianism to a divine level. The mark of divinity in the Messiah is indicated by his name. "Jesus" signifies "Yahweh saves," and this name is interpreted not only in the sense that Yahweh will save through him, but that Jesus himself will save his people from their sins (Mt 1:21). Another name taken from Isaiah's prophecy is cited in confirmation: Emmanuel, "God-is-with-us" (1:23).

The Son of Man will appear as a king who will pass judgment (Mt 25:34-40). Now, this king who has the power to pass universal judgment can be none other than a divine king.

Matthew likes to stress external manifestations of Jesus' divine power. He accentuates the miraculous incidents recorded in Mark (cf. Mt 8:16; 12:15; 14:21; 15:38; 21:19). Actually, he tends to take an external approach to Jesus' kingship, following the most common tradition of Jewish messianism.

b - The divine transcendence of the Messiah is revealed

especially in *the power he exercises over "the kingdom of heaven."* In this kingdom Jesus appears as the initiator and master. Of course, the supreme master is the Father, but the banquet has been initiated by the king for his son's wedding (cf. Mt 22:2). So we see it is the son in whom God is wedded to his people and who brings God's own love to Israel.

Jesus behaves like a sovereign lawgiver, to the point of establishing a law that corrects or complements the Old Law, and in any case surpasses it: "... it was said to our ancestors ..... But I say this to you ..." (Mt 5:22, 28, 32, 34, 39, 44). This claim to legislate is so clear that it brings up a problem: Did he not come to abolish the law? Jesus answers that he came not to abolish it but to fulfill it (cf. Mt 5:17). Here he reaffirms what must have seemed to the Jews an extremely bold claim to divine authority.

We find an even more radical manifestation of this claim in Jesus' institution of the Church. Just as Yahweh had formed the Jewish people, so Jesus founds a new gathering. He builds his Church, and he gives the keys of the kingdom to whomever he chooses (cf. 16:18,19). He behaves like the absolute master of the kingdom.

Matthew's Gospel closes with an affirmation of sovereignty: "All authority in heaven and on earth has been given to me" (Mt 28:18). And Jesus communicates this power to his disciples for the fulfillment of his mission. In addition, he guarantees the covenant by his perpetual presence, similar to the presence Yahweh had promised to his people: "And know that I am with you always ..." (28:20). He will hold God's place among his disciples in a definitive way.

c - In Matthew's perspective, the consideration of the kingdom leads us to the divinity of Jesus. Only someone who is God could establish the kingdom of God with the sovereignty of a founder and legislator manifested by Christ. The ancient Judaic idea that only God in person could establish his kingdom is realized in an unexpected way. Instead of a messianism without a Messiah, whose author is God, there is a messianism in which the messianic king is human, but is God as well.

4. Luke: The Gospel of the Lord and of the Spirit

a. Luke reflects the custom of the primitive Christian community when he calls Jesus "Lord." Among the Synoptic writers he is almost alone to give Jesus this title. [47] In several places, the usage is obviously redactional (7:19; 10:1; etc.), and in other passages it also appears to stem from the Evangelist's own literary style. [48] From the very start of Jesus' public life, Luke attributes to him the divine sovereignty that will reach its fullness of development after the Resurrection. [49]

b - Luke's conception of this divine sovereignty is less external, less institutional than Matthew's. It is Luke who records the words: "Look here! Look there! For, you must know, the kingdom of God is among [i.e., within] you" (Lk 17:21). Jesus is *he who is quickened by the dynamism of the Spirit*. The exercise of his divine power stems from the action within him of the Spirit, and touches others inwardly rather than outwardly.

In Luke's account, the virgin birth appears more clearly, and the intervention of the Holy Spirit is mentioned in terms that stress his link to the divine sonship. [50]

Only Luke relates how, in the synagogue of Nazareth, Jesus applied to himself Isaiah's prophecy: "The Spirit of the Lord has been given to me, for he has anointed me. He has sent me to bring the good news to the poor ..." (Lk 4:18). The Jesus Luke presents to us is aware that his entire public mission springs from the permanent inspiration of the Holy Spirit.

The Evangelist mentions the role of the Holy Spirit in the hymn of praise to the Father. Instead of Matthew's banal sentence: "At that time Jesus exclaimed ..." (Mt 11:25), Luke reads: "It was then that, filled with joy by the Holy Spirit,

---

[47] The following exceptions should be noted: Mk 11:3 and Mt 21:3.

[48] Cf. for an analysis of all the texts, I. de la Potterie, "Le titre Kyrios appliqué à Jésus dans l'évangile de Luc," in *Mélanges B. Rigaux,* Gembloux 1970, 117-146.

[49] Cf. S. Zedda, *Un aspetto della cristologia di Luca: il titolo Kyrios in Lc 1-2 e nel resto del III Vangelo, Rassegna di teologia* 13 (1972) 313.

[50] Referring to the notion of this sonship, A. Voss writes: "There is no moment for Luke when Jesus was not the Son, even if, strictly speaking, the history of this sonship begins only with the proclamation at the time of Jesus' baptism" (*Die Christologie,* 173-174).

he said ..." (Lk 10:21). What comes from the Spirit is not only enthusiasm but the revelation of the intimate relationship between the Son and the Father (Lk 10:22). For the Spirit reveals the divine sonship of Jesus.

Luke loves to describe the mysterious power that emanated from Jesus the miracle-worker: "... and everyone in the crowd was trying to touch him because power came out of him that cured them all" (Lk 6:19; cf. 5:17). Jesus was conscious of possessing and exercising this hidden divine power (cf. Lk 8:46).

Jesus is presented as a prophet, as befits a man possessed by the Spirit: "A great prophet has appeared among us; God has visited his people" (Lk 7:16; cf. 7:39; 24:19).

Luke makes us see Jesus' death in its innermost reality, through his words of surrender to the Father: "Father, into your hands I commit my spirit" (Lk 23:46).

The risen Christ of Luke's account announces the sending of the Holy Spirit who will communicate divine power to the disciples: "And now I am sending to you what the Father has promised. Stay in the city then, until you are clothed with the power from on high" (Lk 24:49).

In his presentation of Jesus Luke was influenced by the experience of the primitive Church, within which Jesus revealed himself as the Lord who pours out the Spirit. [51] This is the picture the Evangelist had gotten from the testimonies of Jesus' earthly life and that he wanted to highlight.

5. John: The Gospel of the Word and of the Son

a - The Gospel of the Word. In the Prologue, John immediately shows how far his faith in the divinity of Jesus goes. He begins his Gospel by a consideration of the eternal Word. [52] To John's mind the origin of Jesus can only be

---

[51] "Luke used ho kurios in his Gospel whenever, to his mind, the event he was relating had a value of anticipation or of prefiguration for the time of the Resurrection, the life of the Church, or eschatology ..... Luke seems to have seen in the Gospel a prefiguration of the history of the Church" (de la Potterie, art. cit., 119).

[52] According to F. M. Braun, in the primitive Church the "Word of God" most probably designated evangelical doctrine. "If we call to mind how forcefully Jesus identified himself with his message, we cannot find it

explained by starting out from eternity. For him Christology from above is indispensable. From the very first words of John's Gospel we hear the affirmation of Jesus' divinity, presented under a twofold aspect. Eternally, the Word "was [turned] toward God" (*ho Theos*, with the article); that is to say, the Word has always had an intimate relationship with the Father. And the Word was God (*Theos* without the article). That is to say, his being is the divine being. What would later be clarified as a distinction between the divine persons and the identity of the divine nature is already set forth in substance here.

In addition, the act of Incarnation is set before us: "The Word was made flesh, he lived among us" (Jn 1:14). Here again, it is good to notice the two aspects of the process. One concerns the nature: to become flesh, that is to say to become man, is to share in the weakness inherent in the human condition. The other concerns personal relationships: for the Word, to become incarnate means to establish permanent relationships with men, by living among them.

Finally, the whole achievement of Jesus is considered from the point of view of the Word made flesh: A manifestation of glory has been placed before our eyes, [53] which has enabled us to know God, in other words, to see the invisible (Jn 1:14-18).

The hymn of the Prologue appears to have been taken from the liturgy of the primitive Christian community, and thereby witnesses to the faith of this community. The poetic description of the existence of the Word "in the beginning" is not merely the fruit of intellectual speculation, but the expression of a living faith that seeks to reach back to the primordial origin of Christ.

b - *The Gospel of the Son.* Even more than it is the

---

surprising that, to signify his creative and revelatory function, John should have begun by affirming that Jesus is the Word of the Father, just as he is the light, the truth, and the life." (*Jean le Théologien*, II, *Les grandes traditions d'Israël. L'accord des Ecritures d'après le quatrième évangile*, Paris 1964, 140-141).

[53] In the writings of St. John the word that comes closest to the meaning of our abstract term "divinity" is the word "glory" (D. Mollat, "La divinité du Christ d'après saint Jean" in *LV* 9 (1953) 101).

Gospel of the Word, John's Gospel is the Gospel of the Son. He speaks of the Word only in the Prologue, in a hymn borrowed from another source, but even here the Word is presented as the only Son of the Father (Jn 1:14-18).

For John, the attribute of Son of God is the essential object of faith. [54] He declares he wrote his Gospel for the purpose of arousing this faith: "These are recorded so that you may believe that Jesus is the Christ, the Son of God, and that believing this you may have life through his name" (Jn 20:31). [55] In his First Epistle he formulates the profession of faith along these lines: "If anyone acknowledges that Jesus is the Son of God, God lives in him, and he in God" (1 Jn 4:15).

This formula differs from the one Paul borrowed from the primitive Christian community: "Jesus is Lord" (Rm 10:9; 1 Co 12:3). The early use of this latter formula is nonetheless confirmed by John when, at the end of his Gospel, he relates Thomas' profession of faith: "My Lord and my God!" (Jn 20:28). [56] This profession combines the two names applied to Jesus. We may however question whether the words "and my God" were not added by the Evangelist to explicate the words "My Lord." In that case, Thomas would simply have said: "My Lord!"

In any event, here was an invitation to adopt as the formula of the Christian faith: "Jesus is Lord." If John pre-

---

[54] "Indeed, John's Christology can be summed up in these two propositions: 1) the Son of God was sent into the world so that he might live his hour; 2) he is now alive and reigning" (F. M. Braun, *Jean le Théologien, 3, Sa Théologie, 3, Le Christ, Notre-Seigneur hier, aujourd'hui, toujours,* Paris, 1972, 8).

[55] S. Sabugal notes the value of the juxtaposition of the two titles: "Christ, the Son of God," which indicates the vertical dimension of Jesus' messianism, his natural divine sonship, and his existential communion with the Father (*Christos, Investigación exegética sobre la cristología joannea,* Barcelona, 1972, 445). He rightly insists on the importance of Jn 20:30,31, "too often neglected by commentators, for an objective interpretation of the Fourth Gospel" (363).

[56] The words that follow: "You believe because you can see me. Happy are those who have not seen and yet believe" (Jn 20:29), "should also be considered, says Cullmann" "as an occasion to admonish all future readers to believe in this Kyrios ..." (*The Christology of the New Testament,* Philadelphia, 1959, 232).

ferred "Jesus is the Son of God", it was because his attention focussed on the personal status of Jesus in God. "Lord" could signify an attribution of divinity in a vague sense, which posed the problem of the relationship to the one God professed in Judaism. This is the problem that is resolved by Jesus' words on the relationship between the Son and the Father, as expressed by John. The Evangelist meditated on these words in order to understand the personal status of Jesus within God. He has recorded for us declarations that bring out the perfect similarity between the action of the Father and of the Son (Jn 5:17,19,26), their total mutual belonging (17:10), their reciprocity of knowledge (10:15), of immanence (10:38), and love (5:20; 15:10), as well as their complete unity: "The Father and I are one" (10:30; cf. 17:21).

John clearly understood that to affirm the divinity of Jesus he had to specify that he was the Son of God, in accordance with Jesus' own testimony as to his identity through his relations with the Father.

John did not limit himself, in describing the act of the Incarnation, to the affirmation of the Prologue on the Word made flesh. He describes this act as the sending of the Son by the Father, an act in which God reveals his deepest reality: "God is love. God's love for us was revealed when God sent into the world his only Son so that we could have life through him" (1 Jn 4:8,9; cf. 4:10,14; Jn 3:16). That Jesus is the Son helps to indicate the value of the Incarnation by revealing the Father's love that presides over it.

c - The Gospel of the Incarnation

In pointing to the vigorous emphasis on a Christology from above in John's thinking, we cannot lose sight of the fact that in the Word made flesh John considers not only the Word but also the flesh. He demonstrates the amplitude of the Incarnation.

In the Prologue, John affirms the incarnation of the divine generation. For the eternal generation of the Word is made manifest in the virginal generation: He "... was born not out of human stock or urge of the flesh or will of man but of God himself" (Jn 1:13). [57]

In the accounts of the public life, the Evangelist mentions Jesus' deeply human traits. He does so even more than the other Evangelists. He describes Jesus' exhaustion (Jn 4:6), his thirst (4:7; 19:28), his sorrow (11:33), his tears (11:35), his anguish (12:27), his emotions in the face of betrayal (13:21). Even more does he reveal Jesus' love, for it is he who speaks of "the other disciple, the one Jesus loved" (20:2). It is also John who tells us: "Jesus loved Martha and her sister and Lazarus" (11:5), and who records the exclamation of witnesses: "See how much he loved him!" (11:36).

The ultimate profession of faith: "My Lord and my God!" occurs in the context of personal relationships that lead Thomas to say "*My* Lord!" and also in the context of a witnessing to the reality of the body of the risen Christ. In short, the context is one of veritable incarnation.

In his own way, John witnesses that the divine and the human are not in opposition. Mark makes us see that nothing human veils the superior identity of Jesus, in other words, that everything about Jesus' humanity evokes the mystery of his divinity. In John, the preliminary presentation of the eternal Word, the only Son of God, in no way hinders the description of his truly human life. When the Word was made flesh, he assumed flesh in its totality.

---

[57] On the version in the singular, cf. the present author's work: "Etre né de Dieu, Jean 1,13," *Analecta Biblica* 27, Rome 1969.

CONCLUSION

1. *The Unity of Primitive Christology*

The faith of the primitive Christian community found expression in various ways, and each of the authors of the New Testament presents Jesus from his own point of view. But this diversity is no obstacle to their fundamental agreement. In truth, the primitive Christologies are ramifications of one and the same essential Christology. Their common foundation is faith in the divinity of Jesus. This faith underwent a development in the sense that it began with the affirmation of the divinity of the glorious Christ who was sending forth the Spirit into his Church. Then came a better understanding of the preexistence of this divinity before Jesus' human life; attention turned increasingly to the divine sonship which determined Jesus' personal status by reason of his relationship to the Father.

The Christological orientations of the Evangelists, far from setting them in opposition, enable them to complement each other. The divinity of Jesus retains its aspect of mystery; it is revealed in the external acts of the Master of the kingdom and in the more hidden action of the Lord who works through the Spirit. It finds expression through his fundamental attributes as Word and Son. It is to be hoped that partial points of view will converge into a fruitful synthesis.

2. *The Point of Departure*

We would be straying from the viewpoint of the primitive Christian community if we were to choose the single fact that Christ is man as the starting point of our Christology. There has never been an "adoptionist" epoch in the history of the Church when Jesus might have been considered to be simply a man who attained to divinization. From the beginning, the Christian community believed in the divinity of Jesus. It discerned the divine power exercised by the glorious Christ when, at the moment of Pentecost, he poured out the Holy Spirit. It acknowledged the divine quality of his person by calling him "Lord."

The expressions of this faith did not take final shape under the influence of isolated individuals such as Paul or John. They appear, together with the most basic affirmations, in the hymns that came out of the early Christian communities, and especially the Christological hymns recorded in the Epistles of Paul or in the Prologue of John's Gospel.

It would not suffice to add certain attributes to complement the human qualities of Jesus the man, taken as the starting point. For instance, it would not be enough to add that this man is utterly unique, to attribute a human transcendence to him, to conceive of him as the eschatological man, the Messiah. The Christian community always believed in a man who was "Lord," that is to say, God. Again we point to Mark's formula: "The beginning of the Good News about Jesus Christ, the Son of God" (Mk 1:1).

At the point of departure of any Christology that conforms to the faith of the earliest days, we encounter the humanity *and* the divinity of Jesus. They are united in his person. Neither can be eliminated in favor of the other. No Christology can disengage itself from this dualism, while acknowledging that Jesus, the man and the Son of God, is, to the depths of his being, one.

CHAPTER V

THE TESTIMONY OF JESUS ON HIS IDENTITY

Even though the words and actions of Jesus have come down to us only through the faith-filled testimony of the earliest Christian community, and above all of the Evangelists, these expressions cannot be seen merely as subjective affirmations of faith. By a study of the testimony we can in great measure arrive at their historical objectivity.

We cannot forget that the faith that inspired the writing of the Gospel texts was a commitment to Jesus the historical figure. Each of the Evangelists claimed he was recording what Jesus had truly been in his earthly life, the Jesus that witnesses had known, drawn close to, and heard. While each of them inevitably left his personal mark on his writings, they have all transmitted to us, at least in substance, the teachings and demeanor of Jesus.

Recent exegesis has sought to determine the role played by variations in individual composition, as well as to delineate the turn of mind and the theology of each sacred author. In so doing, it brought us to a better appreciation of what has come to us directly from Jesus himself. We have briefly examined how Christology was understood and set down by each of the authors of the New Testament, first of all so as to enter into the perspective of the primitive faith, but also to determine, by contrast, wherein lies the true originality of Jesus' words.

Let us point out once more the reaction against the radicalism of Bultmann who accepted very little concerning the Jesus of history. This reaction has tended to restore the value of the historical foundation of the kerygma. A similar reaction may already be occurring in Catholic exegesis. After a period when the emphasis was placed in too unilateral a way on the work of redaction, exegetes are coming to sense more clearly the need to guard against the natural propensity to attribute everything to the human writer, and to proceed to a more objective examination of the historical foundation of the texts.

Exegetical research has sought to establish with greater care the criteria of historical authenticity that are normally demanded of the interpretation of texts. [1] Even more specific criteria are required for the words of Jesus. Certain exegetes have devoted themselves above all to determining which of Jesus' words were authentic. Jeremias distinguishes the *ipsissima vox*, the form of discourse Jesus preferred, and the *ipsissima verba,* words that were spoken exactly as they have been recorded. [2] Moreover, we must not lose sight of the fact that in addition to these literally authentic words there are others, still more numerous, reported in texts in which one senses the additions made by the transmitters, but must nonetheless recognize their essential fidelity to what Jesus intended to say.

On the basis of exegetical research, it is possible to ferret out with greater precision Jesus' own testimony on his identity. We discover that Jesus spoke about himself differently from the way that later prevailed in the Christian community and that is reflected in the Gospel language.

As our focus of interest is the Incarnation, we shall consider the testimony of Jesus in terms of the fulfillment he brought to the structure of incarnation already present before his time in the Jewish religion. The fulfillment goes considerably beyond the announcement or the prefigurement, but it confirms the orientations manifested in the earlier revelation. For this reason we shall not follow the rather easy but superficial order of the titles attributed to Jesus. What interests us here is the manner in which Jesus presents himself in the context of the divine action that preceded him, so as to fulfill its promises in a transcending way. In other words, we want to determine what the primordial process of incarnation under the Old Covenant became in the person of Jesus.

---

[1] Cf. R. Latourelle, "Critères d'authenticité historique des Evangiles," *Gr* 55 (1974) 609-638.

[2] Cf. *Théologie du Nouveau Testament,* I, Paris 1973, 49.

A. THE INCARNATION IN THE COVENANT

1. *The Covenant*

The fundamental structure of the Covenant, which characterized God's relations with his people, takes on a new meaning. The only time that Jesus speaks of a covenant in the Gospel texts is to identify himself with it. This identity is affirmed in the formula of the consecration of the wine recorded by Mark (14:24) and Matthew (26:28): "This is my blood, the blood of the covenant." Literally, we should translate: "This is the blood of me, of the covenant." The strangeness of the grammatical construction [3] makes the intention of stressing the identity more manifest. The "I" of Jesus has been inserted into the formula used by Moses when the covenant was concluded on Sinai: "This is the blood of the Covenant" (Ex 24:8). This insertion, made contrary to linguistic usages, is of capital importance. The covenant is no longer a simple relationship instituted between God and men. It is now a person.

In Paul's version (1 Co 11:25) and Luke's (22:20) the formulation is different, but it also contains a note of strangeness: "This cup is the new covenant in my blood." [4] To affirm the identity between a cup and a covenant is very unusual. It confirms that Jesus must have intended to identify himself personally with the covenant.

This version includes the expression: "new covenant." The specification seems secondary. We can understand the concern of the first Christians to manifest the distinction between the covenant instituted by Christ and the one that had marked the destiny of the Jewish people. Jeremiah's prophecy provided the expression "new covenant." [5] We know that it

---

[3] "A strange expression from the point of view of grammar. The word 'blood' is modified by two genitives joined together. The expression is difficult in Greek, and it is no less so in Aramaic: a determinative complement is not given to a substantive that has a possessive suffix" (J. Dupont, "Ceci est mon corps, ceci est mon sang," *NRT* 90 (1958) 1030-1031).

[4] The formula is grammatically correct, but with J. Dupont (*ibid.* 1032), it seems preferable to grant priority "to the less correct and more difficult expression" of Matthew-Mark.

[5] The expression is found only in Jr 31:31. In other texts (Jr 32:40; Ez 16:60; 37:26; Is 55:3; 61:8, etc.) the promised covenant is characterized

was also used in the vocabulary of the Essene group of Qumran.[6] The expression may therefore have been introduced from either source.[7] The simpler term "the covenant" is probably the one Jesus actually used. Under its apparent indetermination it more adequately expresses the meaning of the covenant personified by Christ. This is *the only real covenant*. The covenants of the Old Law were merely figures. They had value only by reason of the covenant that was now being inaugurated.

This manner of speaking about the significance of his mission shows that Jesus was aware he was fulfilling what had been related in the Old Testament as already accomplished or as a future event. Christ had his own way of understanding and interpreting the history of the Jewish people. He knew that this history had its meaning and fulfillment in him. Behind the appearances of this history he pointed to the reality accomplished in himself. Everything that had been said about the covenant up to that time was present in him. To speak of an "old" and a "new" covenant, of a temporary covenant and a permanent covenant is to think in terms of the chronological succession of events. To speak of a single covenant, of "the covenant," is to view the matter on the ontological level, which is the divine level of salvation. Jesus saw everything not from "the outside," but from "inside" history.

The boldness of Jesus' thinking appears even more strikingly if we compare it with the doctrine of the Epistle to the Hebrews. In that epistle, Christ is called "the mediator" of "a new covenant" (0:15; cf. 8:6). This meaning harmonizes with the more customary context of Jewish thinking. Here is a new covenant that follows, one that is "better" than the old covenant; and the role of mediator was one that Jewish

---

by its definitive value; it is a "definitive and irrevocable covenant, rather than an eternal covenant," according to Buis, "La nouvelle alliance," *VT* 1968, 6.

[6] *L'Ecrit de Damas* speaks of "those who have entered into the new covenant" (6:9; 8:21; 19:34; cf. 20:12). Cf. Jaubert, *La notion d'alliance*, 209-249.

[7] "In the present state of our knowledge, it is hard to say whether Jeremiah's formula resurfaced spontaneously in the primitive Church, or whether a part was played by the influence of the Jewish milieus in which the New Covenant was lived as a contemporary reality" (Jaubert, *op. cit.*, 447).

tradition had attributed to Moses (cf. Ga 3:19).[8] By simply saying "the covenant," Jesus suggested his was a more important role. He was saying he was more than a mediator, for within him lay the very reality of the covenant, and moreover this was not merely a covenant coming after others, but the one authentic covenant.

The identification of a person with the covenant is not an innovation, however. We find it in the hymns of the servant of Yahweh. There it is presented as the result of a new creation by God: "I have ... formed you; I have appointed you as covenant of the people...." (Is 42:6; 49:8).

Jesus probably drew from this declaration. And yet he does not say exactly the same thing. He does not say he was formed or appointed as covenant. He says more simply that he is the covenant. While his affirmation is more discreet, it is also more powerful.

Jesus does not define himself as "the covenant of the people." He speaks only of "the covenant." This might seem to be a very slight difference, but it is important. The expression "covenant of the people" signifies that the servant personifies the people in the covenant established with Yahweh. Jesus is "the covenant," that is to say, he personifies the two covenanters, God and the people. Under the old dispensation the servant represented the people. Jesus represents both parties at once. To personify the covenant signifies, in the fullest sense of the term, to join God and man in oneself.

And thus we see that Jesus' words expand the meaning of the prophecy of the servant in two ways. There is a vertical extension. Since Jesus is the covenant, he is first of all the covenant of God. The covenant was seen as the work and the gift of God. God had called it "my covenant" (Gn 6:18; 9:8, etc.). In addition, there is a horizontal extension: the covenant is no longer limited to "the people." It now extends to all mankind, as is more explicitly indicated in the

---

[8] In his analysis of the theology of the Epistle to the Hebrews, C. Spicq has insisted on the difference between the title of mediator given to Moses and the title applied to "Jesus, Son of Man and Son of God." "Christ is the author, the founder, the preserver ... and the instrument of the new order" (*L'épître aux Hébreux,* Paris, 1952, I, 370, n. 1). This need for rectification helps to show that the term "mediator" must be understood in a superior sense if it is to define Jesus' real status.

words about the shedding of blood "for many," that is to say, for all men. The oracle of the servant had indeed expressed a certain universalism, since the servant had been formed and appointed "as covenant of the people and light of the nations" (Is 42:6). [9] But the universalism professed by Jesus is more far-reaching. The people no longer hold a privileged place in the covenant. In the covenant personified in Jesus, the people are no longer simply a steppingstone to "the nations." "Many," that is, all men are directly included in this covenant.

The twofold extension manifests the fullness of the Incarnation. Before Jesus' time, there had been men who represented the people's covenant with God. The superlative form of this image had been the servant. With the coming of Jesus, it is the whole covenant, God's covenant with mankind and mankind's with God, that is realized. In referring to himself as the covenant, Jesus was implying that he joined in himself both God and mankind. This is logically contained in the term "covenant" when it is considered in its most far-reaching sense. If this affirmation were seen as an isolated fact, we might doubt that Jesus had intended this all-inclusive meaning. But when we consider it in connection with other pronouncements of Jesus in which we discern a similar intimation of divinity on his part, it is easier for us to admit the full density of the term.

2. *The Bridegroom*

On several occasions Jesus intimates that he is the Bridegroom, the one who realizes the matrimonial covenant announced in the Old Testament between Yahweh and his people.

---

[9] This universalism would be accentuated in the translation proposed by P. E. Bonnard, *Le Second Isaïe,* Paris, 1972, 117: "the covenant of the multitude." Still we might fear that this translation may have been influenced by a preconceived notion that interprets the servant as being identical with Israel, and that points to a reluctance to see this servant as the covenant of the people. The term used is not "multitude" ("many") but "people." Others have proposed "covenant of a people" in an indeterminate sense, which would not refer to the people of Israel (J. L. McKenzie, *Second Isaiah,* New York 1968, 39). The absence of any reference to the people of Israel would be quite strange. Normally, the "covenant of the people" concerns Israel, and "light of the nations" adds the dimension of a universal mission.

We find the most explicit affirmation of this in his answer to the disciples of John the Baptist. [10] In this connection we should remember, according to the testimony of the Fourth Gospel, that the Precursor had referred to Jesus as the bridegroom: "The bride is only for the bridegroom; and yet the bridegroom's friend, who stands there and listens, is glad when he hears the bridegroom's voice" (Jn 3:29). This reference gives us an insight into why Jesus in turn uses this image in response to a question on fasting. Speaking to John the Baptist's disciples, he calls to mind what their own teacher had told them: "Surely the bridegroom's attendants would never think of fasting while the bridegroom is still with them? As long as they have the bridegroom with them, they could not think of fasting. But the time will come for the bridegroom to be taken away from them, and then, on that day, they will fast" (Mk 2:19-20). All the argumentation concerning the behavior of the disciples thus rests on the principle that Jesus is "the bridegroom." This is not to be looked upon as a mere parable, [11] as a comparison that would evoke a wedding solely to influence the behavior of the disciples, without a pronouncement on the identity of Jesus. Indeed, Jesus affirms his presence as a bridegroom, then refers to his absence that will sadden his friends.

This is not the only instance when Jesus claims this role. He compares the kingdom of heaven to a banquet organized

---

[10] According to Mark, the question is asked by people who apparently are neither disciples of John nor Pharisees (2:18); but Matthew seems closer to the facts in attributing the questioning to John's disciples (Mt 9:14). Cf. Lagrange, *Evangile selon S. Matthieu*, Paris 1923, 183; A. Feuillet, "La controverse sur le jeûne (Mc 2,18-20; Mt 9,14-15; Lc 5,33-35)", NRT 100 (1968) 119. In addition to the reasons advanced by Lagrange, we should note that Jesus' answer seems to apply in a special way to John's disciples. Feuillet (*ibid.* 126) poses the hypothesis that the mention of the Pharisees may be an editorial addition destined to justify the insertion of the pericope into a series of conflicts between Jesus and the Pharisees.

[11] Among the supporters of a purely parabolic exegesis of Jesus' answer, Feuillet cites C. H. Dodd, J. Jeremias, E. Klostermann, S. E. Johnson. According to this exegesis, there would be no question here of Jesus' personal identity, and his answer would simply signify that the disciples cannot fast when their master brings them the joy of salvation, a joy comparable to that of a wedding. Feuillet shows the inadequacy of this interpretation (*art. cit.*, 132 ff.).

by a king for his son's wedding (cf. Mt 22:2), to bridesmaids (virgins) who are going out to meet the bridegroom (cf. Mt 25:1-13), to servants who await their master's return from his wedding (cf. Lk 12:36). Jesus is to be welcomed and feasted as a bridegroom.

Jesus' presence at the wedding feast of Cana should be interpreted in this sense. The first miracle, intended to save the marriage feast and give it added glamor by offering the guests a better wine, has a symbolic quality. However this symbolism alone would not justify referring to Jesus as a bridegroom. It must be understood in the light of Jesus' remarks about his own wedding when he explicitly identifies himself as the bridegroom.

We are surprised that Jesus speaks only of the bridegroom, and never evokes the presence of the bride. This manner of speaking is all the more surprising since the Old Testament image of Yahweh's matrimonial union with Israel referred to the bride's behavior. She had once been an adulteress, but an ideal future time would come when she would be united to God in fidelity (Ho 2:21-22). Paul would later apply this prophetic oracle to Christ and to the Church, above all when he proposed this union as the model for husbands and wives: "Husbands, love your wives just as Christ loved the Church and sacrificed himself for her" (Ep 5:25). For Paul, the whole of the Christian life is defined in terms of a wife's love for her spouse Christ: "I arranged for you to marry Christ so that I might give you away as a chaste virgin to this one husband" (2 Co 11:2). We surmise that the reason Paul uses this image is that he is drawing from the use Jesus himself had made of it. But Jesus, for his part, refrains from bringing a bride into the picture. He speaks of himself as a bridegroom in an exceptinal way, and does not follow the normal mode available to him by way of the prophetic oracles.

The role of bridegroom, without any mention of a bride, takes on a more total signification. It suggests that the entire matrimonial union is effectuated in the person of Jesus. Here we find the equivalent of the covenant. Jesus is not one of the two parties contracting the covenant. Likewise he is not simply a bridegroom in the presence of a bride. To return to the perspective of the Old Testament, Jesus unites Yahweh and the people in himself. We discover here the characteristic marks of the personification of the covenant: a vertical aspect, a horizontal extension, and the value of a sacrifice. In calling himself the Bridegroom Jesus stresses that he is assuming the role that had been attributed to God in the matrimonial union. In the prophetic oracles, the name of bridegroom had been given to the one who would restore Israel. When Jesus claims this title he is implying that he is fulfilling what had been said about God's action.[12] In the symbolic prefiguration of the Old Testament, God was always the Bridegroom. Jesus is certainly referring to this prefiguration, and hence claims for himself the role of God.

On the other hand, the essential intent of the parable of the wedding feast is to reveal the universal extension of this union. First, the "elect" are invited to the feast, that is, the members of the Jewish people, but afterwards all men are invited, regardless of who they are (Mt 22:9-10). While the elect are few, those who are "called" are very numerous. They are "many" (Mt 22:14). It is no longer a question of the marriage of Yahweh to his people, but of God to all mankind.

The role of sacrifice is affirmed in the reference to the days when the bridegroom will be taken from his friends.[13] Those will be days of fasting, that is, days of sorrow and privation. The complete answer to the question on fasting is given in the announcement that the Bridegroom will disappear. Jesus passes from the notion of material fasting to that of a much deeper fasting, which will consist in his disciples' participation in his Passion. Matthew's version gives

---

[12] After trying to provide an exegetical foundation for calling the Messiah the Bridegroom, Feuillet, who realizes the vulnerability of the argumentation, offers a more solid reason: "It is a fact on which everybody can agree: in the Gospels Jesus often claims titles and functions reserved to Yahweh in the Old Testament. Why would he have made an exception of the title of bridegroom?" (*art. cit.*, 134).

[13] The mention of the taking away of the bridgroom seems to stem from Is 53:8 and relates to the suffering servant (cf. Feuillet, *art. cit.*, 254 ff.). According to the Masoretic text, Is 53:8 expresses the taking away twice "by oppression and by judgment, he was taken away. As for his generation, who has thought he was taken from the land of the living?"

a broader, more spiritual sense to this passage, by using the word "mourning." [14]

Too often the words "on that day, they will fast" have been interpreted in a material sense, as if Jesus had wanted to foretell the observance of fasting in the Church. But apart from the fact that Jesus never wanted to impose upon the life of Christians something from which he had dispensed his disciples during his earthly life, this would reduce the teaching of the Gospel to the doctrine of the Baptizer's disciples. [15] In his answer, Jesus makes it clear that the coming of the Bridegroom completely transformed the relations between men and God. These relations were thenceforth to be dominated by the presence and the sacrifice of the Bridegroom.

But how does the taking away of the bridegroom fit into the context of the matrimonial union? When Jesus refers to himself as the covenant, he mentions the shedding of his blood for many. His sacrifice is destined to seal the covenant. On the other hand, when he evokes the absence of the bridegroom, to come after his presence, he seems to set the wedding and mourning in opposition. In any event, we should note that in Jesus' thinking the taking away of the bridegroom is part of the event of the wedding. According to the Jewish wedding customs, the friends of the bridegroom withdrew,

---

[14] The occasion for Matthew's expression, which Feuillet and others consider more primitive than Mark's, may have been the mourning of John's disciples over their master's death (cf. *art. cit.,* 136). While referring to this experience of mourning, Jesus' answer would have its full meaning by evoking mourning for the death of one who is not only the Master but the Bridegroom.

[15] K. T. Schäfer has stressed Jesus' opposition to the point of view expressed in the question ("*Und dann werden sie fasten an jenem Tage,*" in *Synoptischen Studien A. Wikenhauser ... dargebracht,* Munich 1953, 138-139). On the contrary, Feuillet would like to safeguard an allusion to material fasting by affirming that "other words of the Savior show us that he intended to preserve the practice of fasting, albeit infusing a new spirit into it" (*La controverse sur le jeûne,* 261). But of the only passages he can cite, one is of very doubtful authenticity (Mk 9:29), and the other does not recommend fasting but rather the renouncement of all ostentation on the part of those who practice it (Mt 6:6-18). As for Jesus' fast in the desert, it seems to come from a Jewish interpretation of this experience. Feuillet moreover acknowledges that in the pericope Christ's concern "is not primarily to specify the future cultic practices of the Christian community, but rather to stress the mysterious relationship that unites his disciples' destiny to his own" (*ibid.*).

leaving the bridegroom with the bride. In this instance, the bridegroom is taken away, but the violence done him does not thwart his intention of consummating his marriage. In Jesus' case, the marriage is consummated not by a voluntary departure but through a sacrifice.

We should note that this taking away contrasts not only with Jewish custom, but even more with the behavior of the Bridegroom in the Old Testament. God had abandoned his bride: "I did forsake you for a brief moment, but with great love will I take you back. In excess of anger, for a moment I hid my face from you. But with everlasting love I have taken pity on you, says Yahweh, your redeemer" (Is 54:7-8). The people's distress resulted from this voluntary turning away of the Bridegroom. The disciples' sorrow, on the contrary was to stem from the snatching away of the Bridegroom, and it would have an altogether different meaning. For this snatching away would not interfere with the wedding, but would be its consummation.

If we reflect on the way Jesus presents himself as the Bridegroom, we must admit he reveals himself to be more profoundly a Bridegroom than did the God of the Old Testament. The realization is superior to the prefiguration. In the Old Covenant, the absence of the Bridegroom was the sign of God's anger. Now, this absence becomes the sign of a more complete love that expresses itself in total self-sacrifice. From this point of view Jesus completes the revelation of God. He shows a new countenance of the divine Bridegroom. He can do this because of God's involvement in a human life to the point of total self-giving in suffering and death.

B. The Incarnation of the Divine Sonship

The relationship of fatherhood and sonship that characterized Yahweh's covenant with his people assumes a new form in Jesus.

1. *The Invocation "Abba"*

The Aramaic term *Abba* is used only once in the Gospel accounts, namely, in Jesus' prayer at Gethsemane as recorded

113

by Mark (14:36): "Abba (Father)! ... Everything is possible for you. Take this cup away from me. But let it be as you, not I, would have it." And yet it has been shown that in all of his prayers Jesus invoked the Father by the name of *Abba*, except for the cry: "My God, my God, why have you deserted me?" (Mk 15:34; Mt 27:46).[16] This exception is only apparent, since it is a citation of Psalm 22:2.

The term *Abba* had never been introduced into Jewish religious language. Only rarely was God invoked even as Father, since we know of no such anterior instance in Palestinian Judaism. Even in the Judaism of the diaspora we find only two examples of this (Ws 14:3; Si 23:1-4). To invoke God by calling him *Abba* was something totally unheard-of.[17] The term was used by the Jews — children or adults [18] — in their conversations with their fathers. It was a familiar, intimate way of speaking, equivalent to "papa" or "daddy." It would never have been used in the language of prayer because of the Jews' sense of reverence for God's transcendence. The disciples must have been shocked when they heard Jesus utter this word. It Mark reported it, we must concede that Jesus really spoke it, for no one else would have had the audacity to do so.

Moreover, we surmise that the reason the Evangelist recorded the word was because it must have been spoken by Jesus in an unforgettable way, and with a shade of meaning that the Greek word for "father" could not translate. This word sprang spontaneously from Jesus' deepest consciousness. It brought a revelation to the disciples without being a part of any revelatory discourse. When Jesus prayed he could express what was deepest within him more freely and intimately.

What does the expression *Abba* imply? It signifies that

---

[16] Cf. J. Jeremias, *Théologie du N.T.*, 82; W. Marchel, *Abba, Père! La prière du Christ et des chrétiens*, Rome 1963, 132-138.

[17] Cf. Marchel, *Abba, Père!*, 127.

[18] On this point Jeremias revised his interpretation: "The fact that the word *Abba* was originally a childish word has sometimes led to the view that Jesus used the language of a small child in addressing God as his father. The present author once thought so too. Now the fact is that, even before the New Testament, sons and daughters, even though adolescents or adults, addressed their fathers in this way, thus disallowing this overly narrow interpretation" (*Théologie du N.T.*, 88).

Jesus's relations with God the Father are akin to those of any child with his or her father. Therefore, if the God to whom he speaks is a Father to him in the full force of the term and with all the intimacy it implies, it must mean that Jesus is a Son to this God in the same full meaning of the word. Jesus bears to God the Father the relationship of God the Son. Fatherhood implies a relationship of generation and a similarity of nature. Jesus certainly never gave a formal definition of the word *Abba*. And yet if the Father had not been endowed with fatherhood in the most complete and real sense, the invocation would not have been completely true. It was on this fatherhood that Jesus relied when he addressed his prayer to him and trusted in its efficacy.

In fact, the word *Abba* contains a whole theology, the theology that led the Council of Nicea to proclaim that the Son is consubstantial with the Father. Nonetheless, we should note that this word does not express the divine fatherhood independently of the Incarnation. When Jesus pronounced the word *Abba,* he did so as a man and through his human consciousness. He was living his divine sonship within a human experience. And so the word *Abba* signifies a relationship of divine fatherhood with the Son who has become man. In this sense, we must say it signifies an incarnated divine fatherhood.

Should we hesitate to draw theological conclusions from this single word? We could easily sense a disproportion between a simple word and the importance of a conclusion such as the affirmation of Jesus' divine sonship. J. Jeremias cautions us against an exaggerated interpretation of the invocation that would attribute to Jesus, in all its details, the Christology of the Son of God which developed very early in the Church, including for example, the idea of his preexistence. He points out that such an interpretation would be contrary to the colloquial and intimate tone of the term. [19]

But after all, why would anyone demand solemn affirmations of Christology in Jesus' language? Its colloquial and intimate tone has the advantage of introducing us to Jesus' ordinary mode of thought. It does not prohibit our reflecting

---

[19] *Théologie du N.T.,* 88.

on everything that is included in this thought. The spontaneity of the word *Abba* is a guarantee and not a contraindication of its value as a basis for Christological systematization. [20]

An excessive interpretation, for example, would be one that claimed that Jesus manifested by the use of this word his awareness or remembrance of a divine preexistence. *Abba* is an expression of human consciousness, not the direct manifestation of a divine consciousness. Yet, objectively speaking, the implications of this name remain undeniable. Jesus behaved like a Son, and the divine sonship that was thereby expressed requires that we attribute to him all the traits that belong to the personality of a Son of God.

In Jesus' use of the term *Abba* we discover once again the characteristics we discerned with regard to the titles of covenant and Bridregroom. Of course, there is the difference that here Jesus was not using a term from the Old Testament in a new sense, but was introducing a profane term into the language of religion and giving it a new meaning. In Jesus' use of *Abba* we discern a vertical reference, a universal horizontal extension, and an intimate connection with sacrifice.

The vertical reference stems from the fact that Jesus attributed the name "daddy" to God, thus placing himself at the level of a divine Son. As when he identified himself with the covenant or as the Bridegroom, there was in his use of *Abba* an implicit affirmation of his divine identity. For, as we have already emphasized, this divine identity was not detached from the human reality of Jesus. Rather ,it was perfectly incarnated. Indeed, *Abba* expressed a human experience of divine sonship. There is no more human word than "papa" or "daddy." Here it became a divine name. This was perhaps the most remarkable expression of the Incarnation.

A horizontal extension of the meaning also appears in the fact that the primitive Christian communities used the word *Abba*. This usage is recorded for us by Paul on two occasions (Ga 4:6; Rm 8:15). It does not give Christians a status equal to that of Christ, for it is in his name and not their own that

---

[20] Marchel showed that *Abba* was "a term that revealed the trinitarian life" (*Abba, Père!,* 172-174). He sees in it "the most characteristic expression of the Mystery of the Father" (172-173).

they say *Abba*. "The proof that you are sons is that God has sent the Spirit of his Son into our hearts: the Spirit that cries, 'Abba, Father'" (Ga 4:6). According to the Letter to the Romans (8:15-17) this is a spirit of adopted sonship which attests that we are children of God and coheirs with Christ. The use of the word *Abba* in this sense reveals a boldness that calls to mind how Jesus himself addressed the Father. This audacity had been deliberate on Jesus' part when he recommended a prayer which, according to Luke's version (11:2)[21] began with the word *Abba*. In a still more general way, Jesus presented his Father as the Father of his disciples. He made a distinction within the fatherhood of one and the same Father. He said either "my Father" or "your Father,"[22] "your Father in heaven,"[23] "their Father,"[24] and "your Father" in the singular.[25] Such consistency in making the distinction must have corresponded to a very clear usage on Jesus' part. His most significant distinction is the one in his message to Mary Magdalene after the Resurrection: "I am ascending to my Father and your Father" (Jn 20:17). This message testifies to the fact that he had told the disciples of his own divine sonship, while retaining the distinction. Jesus' sonship remained unique, even when it assumed universal extension.

It is important to point out that Jesus' affirmation of his filial consciousness did not originate with the Jews' awareness that God was their father. Rather, it followed a contrary course. Jesus was aware of his unique filial relationship to the Father, and was impelled to share his sonship with all men.

The connection between the sonship and his sacrifice is suggested by the fact that the name *Abba* has been recorded for us in the Gospels only within the context of Gethsemane, as if this dramatic hour had led Jesus to utter the word in a more poignant way because his full awareness of his sonship was involved in the drama.

The link between Jesus' consciousness of his sonship and

---

[21] Luke's version seems to be the more primitive: cf. Jeremias, *Théologie du N.T.*, 244-246.
[22] Mt 6:8,15; 10:20-29; 23:9; Lk 6:36; 12:30-32; Jn 8:42; 10:17.
[23] Mt 5:16,45,48; 6:1,14; 6:26-32; 7:11.
[24] Mt 13:43.
[25] Mt 6.4,6,18.

his sacrificial mission is revealed in another text that relates Jesus' words in the Temple: "Did you not know that I must be in my Father's house?" (Lk 2:49). It is quite likely that Mary actually said: "See how worried Abba and I are, looking for you," and that Jesus answered: "... I must be in Abba's house."[26] This would explain even more clearly why Mary did not understand the answer. Now, this episode prefigures the Pascal mystery.[27] For Jesus, to be in his Father's "house" * foretold the drama of the Passion when he would be snatched from his mother and be in the Father's house for three days. Jesus' knowledge that he was the Son involved his awareness of belonging to the Father to the point of being committed to a course of sacrifice in which this belonging would be proven in the most absolute way.

There is a very close link between Jesus' consciousness of his filial identity and his awareness of his redemptive mission. His sacrifice was to be the supreme filial act, the one in which *Abba* would assume the utmost fullness of meaning for Jesus' human existence.

2. The Name "Son of Man"

a - Jesus' use of the name

It is characteristic of the name "Son of Man" that only Jesus used it. Although we find it frequently used in the Gospels (30 times in Matthew, 14 times in Mark, 25 times in Luke, and 13 times in John), it is never recorded as being spoken by Jesus' interlocutors or in statements made by the Evangelists themselves. The exceptions are only apparent. For instance: the crowd repeats the name that Jesus has just spoken, to ask its meaning (Jn 12:34); after the Resurrection the angel reminds the women of a prediction made by Jesus (Lk 24:6-7); Stephen repeats the announcement made to the Sanhedrin in witness of its fulfillment (Ac 7:56; cf. Mk 14:62; Lk 22:69). Subsequent tradition did not use this title to designate Jesus,

---

[26] Cf. Marchel, *Abba, Père!*, 133, footnote 22; 138, 142; 144 footnote 60.
[27] Cf. R. Laurentin, *Jésus au Temple. Mystère pascal et foi de Marie*, Paris 1966.
* Translator's note: "in my Father's house" is used in the *New American Bible*.

and in commenting on it did not seem to grasp its significance. This nonuse and incomprehension by the community lead us to the following conclusion: *the name comes to us from Jesus' own words.* The fact that Jesus alone used the name "Son of Man" can be explained only if it was authentically spoken by Jesus as referring to himself personally. [28]

To attribute the expression to a title that might have been in common usage in the primitive community and applied by the community to Jesus is to reject the fundamental conclusions that stem from the texts themselves. The name was used exclusively by Jesus and it remained enigmatic for his contemporaries. [29]

Moreover, as in the case of the name *Abba,* we must ask ourselves if the use of the title "Son of Man" was not more extensive than the Gospel accounts record. Those who transmitted Jesus' words must have tried to substitute a less enigmatic term for it. [30]

In a certain number of cases, they have simply replaced the words "Son of Man" by "me." In fact, Jesus did refer to himself with this expression, so that an "I" or a "me" or a "he" might have seemed a good equivalent, and more comprehensible. The Synoptics offer us several parallel texts in which we notice the substitution. Thus, Luke tells of the happiness of those who are persecuted "on account of the Son of Man" (Lk 6:22). And in Matthew's Gospel Jesus speaks of those who are persecuted "on my account" (Mt 5:11).

---

[28] This conclusion seems solidly established in spite of all efforts to label "Son of Man" as a title in common use in the primitive community. These efforts run up against the undeniable fact that in the Gospel texts this name is always used by Jesus and not by anyone else. For a discussion of the matter, cf. I.H. Marshall, "The Synoptic Son of Man Sayings in Recent Discussion," *NTS* 12 (1966) 327-351; S.S. Malley, "The Johannine Son of Man Sayings," *NTS* 15 (1969) 278-301.

[29] R. Leivestad invokes the fact that the name is spoken *exclusively* by Jesus to refute the opinion of those who, like Bultmann, Tödt, and Hahn, accept only some of the words spoken about the Son of Man as authentic ("Exit the Apocalyptic Son of Man," *NTS* 18, 1971-1972, 254). But this author goes too far in denying that "the Son of Man" can be an apocalyptic title that Jesus has applied to himself.

[30] We have dealt at greater length with this problem in our book, *La conscience de Jésus,* Gembloux-Paris, 1971, 19-29.

Other examples can be cited, [31] but we must note above all the transformation of "The Son of Man has come" into "I have come." We can compare "the Son of Man has come to seek out and save what was lost" (Lk 19:10) with "I did not come to call the virtuous but sinners" (Mt 9:13; Mk 2:17; Lk 5:32). This easy transposition makes us suspect that in texts where we read "I have come ..." the words Jesus really used were more probably: "The Son of Man has come" (Mt 5:17; 10:34; Lk 12:49-51; Jn 10:10).

In the Fourth Gospel Jesus is quoted as sometimes applying the title "Son of God" to himself. But doubts immediately arise concerning the authenticity of this language. In the Synoptics Jesus never uses this title to express his identity. Even in answer to Caiaphas' question as to whether he is the Son of God, he explicitly avoids this title and speaks of himself as the Son of Man. [32] In the few Johannine texts where Jesus uses the name "Son of God" to refer to himself, we have indications that the primitive expression must have been "Son of Man." The context and similar passages would point to such a conjecture. [33] Inasmuch as the Evangelist was writing so that his readers might believe "that Jesus is the Christ, the Son of God" ((Jn 20:31), he must have been predisposed to substitute for "Son of Man" the expression "Son of God" which was clearer and conformed more closely to the language of faith.

Since Jesus deliberately chose a mysterious title to identify himself and even used this name in his solemn profession of his identity, it is unlikely that he called himself "the Son of God" on other occasions. He most probably used only one identifying name when he referred to himself in the third person.

A similar problem arises regarding the title "Son," spoken twice by the Jesus of the Synoptics, and more frequently in the Fourth Gospel.

The two passages in the Synoptics would tend to justify

---

[31] Comp. Mt 16:16 with Mk 8:29 and Lk 9:20; Mk 8:31 and Lk 9:22 with Mt 16:21; Lk 12:8 with Mt 10:32.
[32] Cf. on this subject J. Dupont, *Le Ps 110 dans le N.T.*, 359-362; 368.
[33] Comp. 3:18 with 3:14; 5:25 with 5:27; 11:4 with 12:23 and 13:31.

120

the use of the words "Son of Man" rather than "Son."[34] To go back to a form that would be closer to Jesus' own words, we might render them: "... no one knows who the Son [of Man] is except the Father, and who the Father is except the Son [of Man] and those to whom the Son [of Man] chooses to reveal him" (Lk 10:22; cf. Mt 11:27). Indeed, according to the question Jesus asks, the problem is: Who is the Son of Man? (cf. Mt 16:13). And the mission of revelation belongs to "the Son of Man." It is he who "knows" the Father and makes him known. The knowledge in question here is not specifically an eternal knowledge, but a "recognition" that occurs within the context of earthly life and that is transmitted in a human manner. All these things are fitting for "the Son of Man." Indeed, we may wonder whether the preceding passage was not originally stated in this way: "The Father has given the Son of Man sovereignty over all things," following the thrust of Daniel's oracle (cf. Dn 7:14).

Likewise, one could attribute ignorance as to the date of the end of the world to the Son of Man: "But as for that day or hour, nobody knows it, neither the angels of heaven, nor the Son [of Man]; no one but the Father" (Mk 13:32; cf. Mt 24:36). The eschatological context agrees more closely with a reference to the Son of Man. Besides, there is question here of a human ignorance. Since it is not his mission to reveal this date, the Son of Man does not know it.

The Johannine texts also intimate a transformation of the "Son of Man" into "the Son." For every time the title "Son" is used, we can find other texts, either in John's Gospel or in the Synoptics, where a similar affirmation is made concerning the "Son of Man." Thus, the expression "to believe in the Son" (cf. Jn 6:40) assumes a more primitive form in the question asked of the miraculously healed blind man: "Do you believe in the Son of Man?" (Jn 9:35). [35] The references to the glorification of the Son (Jn 14:13; 17:1) seem to derive

---

[34] The Trinitarian formula of baptism (Mt 28:29) probably derives from a liturgical addition.

[35] In addition, compare Jn 5:19 with Mt 12:8, Mk 2:27, and Lk 6:5; comp. Jn 5:21,26 with Jn 6:27,53; Jn 5:22 with 5:27; Jn 8:34-36 with Mk 2:10, Mt 9:6, and Lk 5:24.

from the theme of the glorious elevation of the Son of Man (Jn 6:62; 8:28; 11:4; 12:23-24, etc.).

In conclusion, Jesus used the name "the Son of Man" to identify himself more often than the Gospel texts would indicate. These texts have replaced the term "Son of Man" either by an "I" or by a more explicit title of divine sonship, "the Son of God" or "the Son." The two substitutes tell us what Jesus' contemporaries grasped of the mysterious title "Son of Man": they saw it as a name identifying Jesus and as an indication of his divine sonship.

b - The Son of Man during his earthly life
(1) - His coming and preexistence

The affirmation "the Son of Man has come," used on several occasions by Jesus, attests to his awareness of having had a certain preexistence. In the first place, we think of a prophetic preexistence: Jesus is the personage announced by the Prophets as the Son of Man. From this point of view a parallel exists with John the Baptist, who fulfills another prophetic figure: "Elijah has come already" (Mt 17:12; cf. Mk 9:13).

However, more is involved in the coming of the Son of Man than the indication of a prophetic preexistence. Even John the Baptist recognized in Jesus a coming of a unique sort: "... and he sent his disciples to ask him, 'Are you the one who is to come, or have we got to wait for someone else?'" (Mt 11:3; Lk 7:19). "The one who is to come" is the one whose coming has a quality of absoluteness, because it manifests the coming of God himself for the final judgment. The Precursor had announced: "Someone is following me, someone who is more powerful than I am..." (Mk 1:7; Mt 3:11; Lk 3:16). These words referred to the one who would come to institute the divine judgment whose imminence he was proclaiming. Under these conditions, "to come" no longer means only the fulfillment of a prophetic figure, but the effective coming of God through a human mediation.

In Jesus' words we find signs that he is alluding to a a real preexistence. The coming of the Son of Man is described *as a journey*, a coming to seek and to save what was

122

lost (cf. Lk 19:10), or a coming to serve and to give his life as a ransom (cf. Mk 10:45; Mt 20:28). This presupposes a change of place, the relinquishing of his status to place himself at the service of mankind and to bring it help. The presence of the Son of Man springs from a generous course of action whose origin antedates his earthly life. The enigmatic words recorded by Mark (1:38): "that is why I came" contain the same implication. And what is merely suggested in the Synoptics is explicated in the Johannine declarations: The Son of Man is "the one who came down from heaven" (Jn 3:13; cf. 8:14; 16:17); and his elevation consists in ascending "to where he was before" (Jn 6:62). To come means to come into the world: "I, the light, have come into the world" (Jn 12:46; cf. 18:37).

Preexistence in the present moment

Jesus' affirmation of his preexistence is not expressed in terms of a backward look into the past, but in the context of his situation in time and space. For the Son of Man, the fact that he is living a human life means that he has come. It signifies that his preexistence is operative in the present moment, that it is experienced as a dynamism.

It is especially worth noting that the coming of the Son of Man is mentioned in relation to the most commonplace actions of human life: "The Son of Man comes, eating and drinking" (Lk 7:34; Mt 11:19). The stress on his coming tends to link the fact of eating and drinking to a mysterious origin. This origin is inseparable from all other aspects of Jesus' human life. It is quite natural for a man to eat and drink, and the behavior of the one who says he is the Son of Man should not cause astonishment. But since this is someone who has come, these commonplace actions take on a new meaning, they are part of a revelation.

The context contains indications that help to reveal the identity of the Son of Man. Let us call to mind the following context: "For John came, neither eating nor drinking, and they say, 'He is possessed'. The Son of Man came, eating and drinking, and they say, 'Look, a glutton and a drunkard, a friend of tax collectors and sinners'. Yet wisdom has been proved right by her actions" (Mt 11:18-19; cf. Lk 7:33-35).

The most obvious sign consists in Jesus' mention of Wisdom. In the face of the accusations that pour down on the Son of Man, Wisdom is justified by her actions (or "by all her children," according to Luke's text). The equivalence between acceptance of the Son of Man and the justification of Wisdom suggests that the Son of Man is the supreme manifestation of divine Wisdom. Jesus' actions bear witness to this Wisdom, so that she is in a certain sense personified in the Son of Man. [36]

Another sign should be pointed out because of its likelihood. To reproach Jesus for being a glutton and a drunkard could be an allusion to the fate of the wayward son, as described in Deuteronomy: "This son of ours is stubborn and rebellious and will not listen to us; he is a wastrel and a drunkard" (Dt 21:20). This son was to be stoned to death by his fellow citizens. [37] Such was the picture of Jesus given by his contemporaries to justify his condemnation to death. In reality, he was just the opposite of the rebellious son. He was the obedient son, for he was the Son of Man who had come and his actions were worthy to be described as those of the Wisdom of God. In Jesus' docility we can recognize the true way to be a son of God. Thus, what is intimated is the authentic divine sonship of Jesus.

So we see there is a way of eating and drinking that is characteristic of the coming of the Son. This coming makes itself known by a total immersion in Jesus' human life. In it the dynamism of the Incarnation reaches its ultimate extension. The Son of Man is more human than John the Baptist. Those who had been rebuffed by the Baptist's austerity, should have been willing to accept the Son of Man in his more human closeness. In other words, those who might not have been satisfied with the very incomplete incarnation in the Old Testament should have been ready to welcome the perfect incarnation realized in the Son of Man.

---

[36] It is especially important to note that the identification to Wisdom occurs in a logion of the Q Source. "The juxtaposition, already attested to in Q, of words concerning the Son of Man and mention of Wisdom shows that in the old tradition the Son of Man was seen as the personification of Wisdom (W. Grundmann, *Das Evangelium nach Matthäus*, Berlin 1971, 312).

[37] The reference is mentioned by Grundmann (*Das Evangelium nach Lukas*, Berlin 1971, 168), following Stauffer.

124

(2) - Divine power

The Son of Man exercised the eschatological power of judgment during his earthly life through *the power to forgive sins.* When Jesus says to the sinful woman who has repented: "Your sins are forgiven," the following question arises in the minds of the witnesses: "Who is this man, that he even forgives sins?" (Lk 7:48-49). In the case of the paralytic, the question is posed even more pointedly, together with Jesus' complete answer. It is not merely a question, but a condemnation: "Now some scribes were sitting there, and they thought to themselves, 'How can this man talk like that? He is blaspheming. Who can forgive sins but God?'" (Mk 2:6). In his answer, Jesus identifies himself as the Son of Man to stress that although he is truly a man, he also possesses this power: In heaven God forgives sins, but on earth it is the Son of Man who forgives them. Jesus proves it by performing a miracle: "'But to prove to you that the Son of Man has authority on earth to forgive sins', — he said to the paralytic — 'I order you: get up, pick up your stretcher, and go off home'" (Mk 2:10; Mt 9:6; Lk 5:24).

Correlative to the power to pass judgment is *the power to give life.* Thus, according to one of John's texts, "the Father, who is the source of life, has made the Son the source of life; and, because he is Son of Man, has appointed him supreme judge" (Jn 5:26-27). The goal of the glorious elevation of the Son of Man will be to communicate eternal life: "...the Son of Man must be lifted up ... so that everyone who believes may have eternal life in him" (Jn 3:14-15). In this context the Eucharist makes its appearance: the Son of Man offers "food that endures to eternal life" (Jn 6:27). "I tell you most solemnly, if you do not eat the flesh of the Son of Man and drink his blood, you will not have life in you" (Jn 6:53). Now, no less than the power to forgive sins, the power to give eternal life is a divine power.

c - The Glorious Son of Man

(1) - The coming on the clouds

Jesus called himself the Son of Man not merely because of the intrinsic meaning of the expression, indicating a man whose dignity or weakness one wants to stress. [38] He also said he was the Son of Man in referring to Daniel's prophecy (Dn 7:13-14). This is the only prophetic text in which the term Son of Man refers to a personage of messianic stature. Jesus clearly alluded to it when he professed his personal identity before the Sanhedrin as the "Christ," and the "Son of God": "...I tell you that from this time onward you will see the *Son of Man seated at the right hand of the Power* and *coming on the clouds of heaven*" (Mt 26:6. It was characteristic of Daniel's "son of man" to come on the clouds of heaven, and to share in God's power.

The reference to Daniel's oracle was not simply a backward glance at an apocalyptic vision. Jesus habitually held to the point of view of contemporary Jewish tradition. He cited the texts of the Bible to confer upon them a new meaning, starting from the understanding of these texts by those around him. We can therefore surmise that the tradition concerning the Son of Man as expressed in the Book of Enoch was present to his mind. We have noted that the individual aspect and the transcendence of the Son of Man were more clearly stated in this book. Now, it is in this direction that Jesus' use of the expression tends.

The coming of the Son of Man "on the clouds of heaven" is of the theophanic order, for clouds are the sign of theophany. [39] When Jesus announces this coming he uses an image that signifies a divine way of coming, a way that will contrast with the one that has until then characterized the coming of the Son of Man. This mode of coming will be such as to demonstrate that he is really the "Christ" and the "Son of God."

(2) - The Son of Man, the universal judge

The picture of the universal judgment is especially indicative of divine authority. The manner in which the Son of Man comes in his glory, "escorted by all the angels" (Mt 25:31) calls to mind Yahweh's coming, according to Zechariah's

---

[38] Cf. on this subject the texts cited by G. Vermes in M. Black, *An Aramaic Approach to the Gospels and Acts,* Oxford, 1967, 310-328; R. Le Déaut, "Le substrat araméen des évangiles" in *Bi* 49 (1968) 399.

[39] Cf. Feuillet, "Le Fils de l'homme de Daniel et la tradition biblique," *RB* 1953, 187.

oracle (Zc 14:5): "Yahweh your God will come, and all the holy ones with him." The power to judge is, strictly speaking, a divine power. What is surprising is that the Son of Man exercises this power with complete sovereignty. He passes judgment as an absolute master.[40] It is in relation to himself that he evaluates the actions of all men. All will be judged on the attitude they have had toward him, for he is mysteriously present in every human being.

The theme of the judgment passed by the Son of Man recurs several times in Jesus' teaching, notably to stress the decisive value of professing faith in him. "For if anyone is ashamed of me and of my words, of him the Son of Man will be ashamed when he comes in his own glory and in the glory of the Father and the holy angels" (Lk 9:26; cf. Mk 8:38). "I tell you, if anyone openly declares himself for me in the presence of men, the Son of Man will declare himself for him in the presence of God's angels" (Lk 12:8).

Certain exegetes have invoked these texts to deny the identity of Jesus as the Son of Man.[41] For these texts reveal a certain distance between the Jesus who speaks and the Son of Man as eschatological judge. Admittedly, they evoke two different situations, one earthly and the other heavenly, the latter involving a function exercised in the world beyond. Nevertheless, they imply the identity of the one of whom one has been ashamed and the one who will be ashamed, between the one who has been proclaimed before men and the one who will declare himself before the angels. Judgment will be passed in the light of a reciprocal relationship. That is the way Matthew understood it in a parallel text: "So if anyone declares himself for me in the presence of men, I will declare myself for him in the presence of my Father in heaven" (Mt

---

[40] Lagrange notes the difference with the Chosen One of Enoch, who acts only in the name of the Lord of spirits: "The Son of Man comes as a sovereign judge, in his own glory and on his throne of glory." He comments: "There is nothing more forceful, especially if we take into account the reserve of Enoch himself, to indicate the divinity of Christ" (*Matthieu*, 486).

[41] Cf. in defense of this view, R. Bultmann, *Die Geschichte der synoptischen Tradition*, 117; G. Bornkamm, *Jesus von Nazareth*, Stuttgart 1959, 161; H. G. Tödt, *Der Menschensohn in der synoptischen Überlieferung*, Gütersloh 1963, 50 ff.; A. J. B. Higgins, *Jesus and the Son of Man*, Philadelphia 1964, 24, 57-60.

10:32). Through the interplay of reciprocity the Son of Man thus appears as the one who judges and the one with reference to whom one is judged.

To be this central point of reference belongs to God. Mankind is judged on to its attitude toward Jesus in the same way it will be judged on its attitude toward God. This is what emerges likewise from the declaration: "... anyone who loses his life for my sake will find it.... For the Son of Man is going to come in the glory of his Father with his angels, and, when he does, he will reward each one according to his behaviour" (Mt 16:25-27). [42] The Son of Man is a judge who possesses, in addition to the divine power to judge, the power to request of men the total sacrifice of their lives; and this, too, is one of God's privileges.

What clinches the demonstration that the Son of Man, as judge, has all the attributes of God is that at the end of the world he will exercise complete power over the forces of evil, for the freedom then to be granted the devil will be temporary: "The Son of Man will send his angels and they will gather out of his kingdom all things that provoke offences and all who do evil, and throw them into the blazing furnace" (Mt 13:41-42). The kingdom belongs to the Son of Man quite as much as to God, and it is the Son of Man who assures its definitive holiness.

d - The Human Quality of the "Son of Man"

While Jesus stresses the divine identity of the "Son of Man" in various ways, he also brings out the reality of his humanness.

When Jesus says the Son of Man has come, he means the man that he himself is, living an authentic human life. Whereas in the oracle of Daniel and in the parables of Enoch

---

[42] The affirmation that the Son of Man is going to come in the glory of his Father clearly shows that in Matthew the terms "Son of God" and "Son of Man" are equivalent, according to W. Grundmann (*Das Evangelium nach Matthäus*, 401), who points out the parallel between 16:13 and 16:17. "Son of Man" is the title by which Jesus presents himself to the public, whereas the title "Son of God" is confessional, according to J.D. Kingsbury, who defines the distinction between the titles in "The Title 'Son of God' in Matthew's Gospel", BTB 5 (1975) 15, footnote 44; and in "The Title 'Son of Man' in Matthew's Gospel", in CBQ 37 (1975) 193-202.

the "son of man" was a heavenly or divine being but not a man, in Jesus the Son of Man is a man living an earthly life. There is a great difference between the two.

When Jesus refers to himself as the Son of Man, he moreover intends to call attention to the importance of his human condition. This condition makes it possible for him to fulfill his mission.

While the power to judge has been given to the Son, according to John's Gospel, "because he is Son of Man" (Jn 5:27), it is not merely by virtue of a title that might imply eschatological judgment. The underlying idea seems to be this: it was necessary that judgment be entrusted to a man, for in this way men are judged by one who is their equal and who understands human situations by reason of his own experience. [43] The power to judge remains a divine power and the Son of Man manifests his divine personality by exercising judgment. But he also judges as man. We can thereby better understand that his judgment is a judgment of salvation rather than of condemnation (cf. 3:17).

When Jesus claims the Son of Man has the power to forgive sins, he specifies that he possesses this power "on earth" (Mk 2:10 and par.). He therefore owes it to his human condition. If the power was to have been exercised only in heaven, God would have sufficed. But the Son of Man, a real man, was needed to forgive sins on earth. According to Matthew (9:8), this is what aroused the crowds' astonishment, and "they praised God for giving such power to men." The forgiveness granted by the Son of Man intimates the communication of this power to other men. [44]

Jesus' mastership over the sabbath, which implies a sovereign power equal to God's, is also linked to the human quality of the Son of Man: "The sabbath was made for man, not man

---

[43] The absence of an article, which is exceptional, since elsewhere the article is customary before Son and before Man, seems to be explained precisely by the intention to stress the human quality of the Son (cf. Barrett, *John*, 118). It is as if John wanted to call to mind that the name "Son of Man" referring to the personage entrusted with judgment takes on its full human value in Jesus, and is not merely a formal title.

[44] The link between Christ and the community is one of the characteristics of Matthew's Gospel. The community shares in Christ's power (cf. 10:7 ff.; 18:18), according to Grundmann (*Matthäus*, 268).

for the sabbath; so the Son of Man is master even of the sabbath" (Mk 2:27). The unstated principle is that it is the right of the one for whose benefit the sabbath exists to determine the meaning of this law. [45] This principle bespeaks God's intention to entrust into human hands what was most sacred in the practice of the Jewish religion. Henceforth religion would have not only the guarantee of God's pure love, but also the guarantee of man to whom this love is addressed. This explains the fundamental role of the Son of Man.

The quality of humanity is also essential to the Son of Man in his mission of communicating eternal life, since he communicates it through his flesh and blood. The power to give this life, while it is a divine power, belongs to him thanks to the Incarnation. [46] Indeed, what is referred to is the flesh and blood of the Son of Man in his spiritual, glorified state, as indicated by Jesus' answer to his hearers who were shocked by his promise: "Does this upset you? What if you should see the Son of Man ascend to where he was before?" (Jn 6: 62). [47] The fact remains nonetheless that it is human flesh and human blood that he gives as food and drink.

The same holds true of the presence of the Son of Man within each human being, and especially within the unfortunate, a presence that allows him to experience personally what makes them happy or causes them suffering. This presence, whose

---

[45] This does not justify Wellhausen's interpretation, adopted by Bultmann, Ed. Meyer and others, according to which "the Son of Man" would originally have designated man in general. Here Jesus is claiming and justifying his personal authority (cf. Taylor, *Mark*, 219-220). This sort of claim is totally in keeping with the habit of healing on the sabbath and thereby showing that the sabbath is made for man.

[46] The twofold value of the expression "the Son of Man" is clearly apparent with respect to the Eucharist. This expression attests to the reality of the flesh and blood, to the point that his hearers think of his body in its mortal state. But it also implies a superior, "spiritual" order of things. As R. Schnackenburg remarks, referring to Jn 6:53, the intention is to make it understood "that believers receive in the Eucharist, not the flesh and blood of the earthly Jesus, but the spiritualized flesh and blood of the heavenly Son of Man" (*Das Johannes-evangelium*, II, Freiburg-Basel-Wien 1971, 92).

[47] The allusion to the Ascension of the Son of Man is intended not only to enhance the scandal, but to show how to overcome it, according to F. Porsch (*Pneuma und Wort. Ein exegetischer Beitrag zur Pneumatologie des Johannesevangeliums*, Frankfurt-am-Main 1974, 210).

universality bears a divine seal, shows how thoroughly human Jesus is in his empathy that makes him sensitive to everything that concerns his brothers.

This makes us understand that faith in the Son of Man embraces both his humanity and his divine identity. The question: "Do you believe in the Son of Man?" (Jn 9:35) was asked of a man born blind who, when he saw Jesus, was seeing a man for the first time. [48] The commitment of faith stems from God's coming so close to men as to demand faith in God through faith in a man.

Finally, the humanity of the Son of Man takes on its greatest universality, in his sacrifice: he came "to serve, and to give his life as a ransom for many" (Mk 10:45; Mt 20:28).

How can the Son of Man's life be a ransom for the whole human race? This requires that his person have a value at least equal to that of all mankind. Yet it is possible if, as the "Son of Man," he has a divine origin and divine power; it also implies a truly human condition that will allow him to represent all men before the Father.

e - The theology implicit in the name "the Son of Man"

It is significant that Jesus chose to identify himself by using a name that in itself signifies "man." He did not introduce himself under a title that would have suggested his divinity more directly, such as "Son of God." And to say he was a man he even adopted an expression which did not seem to make any claim to superiority over the human condition. For "son of man" indicates a man who is included in the sequence of human generations and who in this sense is completely immersed in the lowliness of the human condition.

(1) - The human reality

The first intention of the name is to stress that Jesus is *truly* a man. This emphasis might seem superfluous on the part of someone who is obviously living a human life like other men. But it is precisely by virtue of this concrete human

---

[48] John does not use the words "believe in the Son of Man" anywhere else, but as Barrett notes (*John*, 302), verses 12:34 ff. offer a parallel, since they refer to the elevation of the Son of Man and of faith in the light.

existence that the name "the Son of Man" takes on a new consistency, one it did not have in the apocalyptic images of Daniel or Enoch, which described only the appearance of a man. Besides, the name implies that Jesus is a man *in every sense of the word.* He lacks no human attribute. We know that no one can convict him of sin (cf. Jn 8:46), but this absence of sin is not a deficiency of his human condition, inasmuch as sin degrades man, diminishing him and making him a slave (cf. Jn 8:34). Jesus is more deeply a man precisely because he is untouched by the disfigurement or corruption of humanity that sin involves. He is man as he came forth from the hands of the Creator, without any defect or degradation.

In the perspective of the Bible, the expression inevitably evokes Adam. The best genealogical commentary on the name is to be found in Luke's Gospel. When we go back through the human generations, we finally come to Jesus, "son of Adam, son of God" (Lk 3:38). Just as Adam bore the generic name of man, Jesus adopts the generic name of "Son of Man." He is the replica of Adam, but in the role of a son. The name already suggests the comparison that Paul would make in his Letter to the Romans between Adam and Jesus, between the one man through whom all men became sinners and the one man through whom mankind received grace and justification (cf. Rm 5:12-21). Adam was the figure of Jesus, he "prefigured the One to come" (Rm 5:14), according to a way of speaking that evokes the Son of Man but with a strong contrast underlying the similarity.

Can we say the similarity and the contrast are implied in the name "Son of Man," as Jesus himself used it? They are certainly consonant with the broad meaning of the term. For the "Son of Man" resembles the primordial man, and is man in his integral wholeness, as opposed to the sin that denatures and fragments him. Moreover, we should recall certain affirmations concerning the Son of Man, in particular his coming to serve and to give his life as a ransom for many (cf. Mk 10:45; Mt 20:28), in which we can see him inaugurating a new race of men.

(2) - The Theological Dimension

How does the Son of Man manifest a reaching beyond the merely human? The reference to Daniel's apocalyptic figure gives the name a theological dimension. According to the oracle, the personage who came "like a son of man" was of heavenly origin, and he appeared by God's side as a son. He had been called "son of man" by virtue of man's aptitude to represent a divine being. In Ezekiel's first vision (Ezk 1: 26), God was described as "a being that looked like a man." The best way to describe a son of God, therefore, was to call him a son of man. This image implies a fundamental principle: the being that most closely resembles God in our world is man. The account of the creation of man in the image of God lends essential support to the use of this image.

Besides, Daniel's "son of man" represented the people of the saints of the Most High, so that he was at once a personage of divine rank and the personalization of the Jewish people in their ultimate destiny.

When Jesus calls himself the Son of Man he incorporates all the elements of Daniel's personage into his title: a divine being whose relationship to God is that of a Son and who represents the chosen people, i.e., the new mankind. As in Daniel, the Son of Man has a heavenly origin which is expressed by a mysterious coming, and he possesses divine powers.

However, in contrast to Daniel's son of man, Jesus' Son of Man is really a man and no longer merely the appearance of a man. Therefore the human must not disappear before the divine. It has a real value of its own. Thus, the principle of likeness is given its full efficacy. The divine is expressed in the human, and enhances it. There is no opposition, no disharmony between the two.

The divine origin of the Son of Man does not prevent him from living a human life like other men, for "the Son of Man came, eating and drinking" (Mt 11:19). He exercises his divine power in his human reality. It is both as God and as man that he judges, forgives sins, is master of the sabbath, gives his flesh as food for eternal life, and demands the faith and love of men.

This fact indicates that in him an Incarnation has been perfectly accomplished. In the person of the "Son of Man,"

God and man are inseparably present and inseparably active. Someone who ranks with God acts after the manner of a man and in his humanity. This is possible because of the essential likeness we have already pointed out that permits the human to adequately express the divine.

The very expression "Son of Man" is itself the sign of a completely realized Incarnation. Through the meaning that Jesus gives these words, they are the equivalent of "Son-of-God-made-man." And yet since the term refers only to man, it suggests that the richness of the divine person lies hidden and is revealed through the human nature.

From this point of view, the name Son of Man tends to exclude any conception of a Christ "in two strata," or more exactly of a Christ whose divinity might be manifested apart from or at a level superior to his humanity. Such a dualism is avoided by the very way Jesus identifies himself. On the other hand, the name in no sense reduces Jesus exclusively to the structure of man. It presupposes that the divine person finds expression only in the man and through him, and yet does not justify a negation of this divine person.

(3) - The Ontological and the Functional

The way Jesus uses the name Son of Man points to the relationship between th ontological and the functional aspects of his identity. The importance of the function results from Jesus' insistence on the fact that he "has come" and on his powers. The Son of Man has come to accomplish a mission. He has come "to seek out and to save what was lost" (Lk 19:10); he has come "not to be served but to serve, and to give his life as a ransom for many" (Mt 20:28; Mk 10:45). When Jesus announces his Passion, death, and Resurrection, he sees them as the fulfillment of God's plan for the Son of Man: "The Son of Man is destined to suffer grievously ..." (Lk 9:11; Mk 8:31).

Nevertheless, the choice of the expression "Son of Man" draws attention to the ontological. Jesus does not identify himself by a simple functional title. For example, he never calls himself "the servant," although he likes to emphasize the service implicit in his activities and in his deepest attitudes. By declaring that the Son of Man has come to serve, he incorporates the idea of the servant into the definition of the Son of Man, but the name "Son of Man" is retained. Likewise, in announcing his future glory, Jesus could have called himsef the Messiah or the Christ. Instead, he declares that the Son of Man will sit at the right hand of God. In this, he appropriates the messianic kingship, but without claiming the title of Messiah and while still calling himself the Son of Man.

This indicates that Jesus refuses to be absorbed by a function. He is not merely sent by God. He is the Son, and he comes as the Son. His personal reality as the Son comes first, before any mission, and this reality remains in his glorious triumph. Jesus is not the personification of a mission. What matters first of all is who he is, and that is why he always draws attention to the mystery of his personal identity. It is through this identity that the meaning of what he does becomes clear.

(4) - The Human Sonship

Since the expression "Son of Man" is centered on a mystery of filial origin, it leads us inevitably to the question: in what sense is there a human generation? The name signifies that Jesus is a man and a son. But it says more: he is the son of a human being. It does not suffice to recognize him as the Son of God who is man. We must also consider in what way he is a son of man.

The accounts of the Childhood tell us how the problem was solved. The virginal conception of Jesus, accomplished through the power of the Holy Spirit, resulted in a child who was at once begotten from above and the son of a woman. It manifested the divine sonship within a human sonship.

Jesus himself does not allude explicitly to this origin, which gives the name "Son of Man" its full value and likewise emphasizes its human realism. Nevertheless, we must point out in this connection that on the two occasions during his public life when, according to John, he speaks to Mary, he does not call her "mother" but "woman" (Jn 2:4; 19:26). Now, the reason he refuses to consider her simply as a mother, in the context of their intimate relationship, is because he is carrying out a mission in which he is acting as the Son of Man. The name that befits Mary in relation to the name

"Son of Man" is "woman." She is the woman who has made it possible for Jesus to call himself the Son of Man.

Do we not find this implication echoed in the name used by Paul when he says: "... God sent his Son, born of a woman ..." (Ga 4:4). "Son, born of a woman" explicates the content of the expression "Son of Man."

Thus, the expression "Son of Man" implies an anthropology as well as a theology. Jesus defines himself as Mary's son, the sign that he is the Father's Son. We have spoken of the resemblance between God and man which is the root principle of the image "Son of Man." Concretely, in Jesus' case, it is Mary who in her motherhood bears the resemblance to the Father in his Fatherhood. By reason of this, the female sex plays an essential role in the Incarnation.

C. THE INCARNATION OF THE WORD, THE ACTION, AND THE PRESENCE OF GOD

1. The Incarnation of the Word

a - The Authority of the Word

Among the most significant words Jesus spoke is the word *Amen,* whose use has practically no antecedent in Judaism and no analogy anywhere else in the New Testament. [49] This word meant "certainly," "I solemnly assure you," and had generally been used to express an answer of acquiescence. [50]

---

[49] Cf. Jeremias, *Théologie du N.T.,* 47-48.

[50] Some authors have sought a Hellenistic origin of the term *Amen* used in the Gospel texts, pointing out in particular the quality of a response the term has in Hebrew (V. Hasler, *Amen. Redaktions-geschichtliche Untersuchung zur Einführungsformel der Herrenworte "Wahrlich, ich sage euch".,* Zurich-Stuttgart 1969; K. Berger, *Die Amen-Worte Jesu. Eine Untersuchung zum Problem der Legitimation in apokalyptischer Rede,* Berlin 1970; "Zur Geschichte der Einleitungsformel 'Amen, ich sage euch'", ZNW 63, 1972, 42-75). Against such an interpretation, J. Strugnell has emphasized the discovery of the term *'mn* in a Hebrew ostracon of Yabneh-Yam of the 7th century B.C., with the meaning of "really" (cf. "'Amen, I Say Unto You' in the Sayings of Jesus and in Early Christian Literature", *Harvard Theological Review* 67, 1974, 177-182). This use would prove that the sense Jesus gives the term was not totally unknown in the Hebrew language. It would require us to tone down Jeremias' position that the Gospel use had no antecedent at all.

To the contrary, Jesus uses it as an introduction to his own discourses to stress the truth of his words: "Amen, I say to you ..." In this use, Jesus is expressing his authority in a unique and original way. The only Biblical formula to which it can be compared is the prophets' "This is what the Lord says" (Jr 28:2, 4, 11, 13, 14, etc.). Now, the comparison immediately suggests that from that time onward Jesus has the rank of Lord. He is speaking on his own authority. There is identity between his words and God's.

Jesus' hearers clearly grasped the difference between his teaching and that of the scribes, based exclusively on the Law: "And his teaching made a deep impression on them because, unlike the scribes, he taught them with authority" (Mk 1:22; cf. Mt 7:29; Lk 4:32). Whose authority is meant here? The hearers probably could not have pinpointed it. But the essential remains that they had found in Jesus a mode of teaching unheard-of until then, and one in which personal authority replaced the authority of the Law. A careful analysis of what underlies this claim to authority will show that Jesus attributed to his own teaching the same value the Law had for the Jews. He was presenting his teaching, therefore, as God's, and as given with divine authority.

It is in this vein that he affirmed: "Heaven and earth will pass away, but my words will not pass away" (Mk 13:31; Mt 24:35; Lk 21:33). [51] His own words evoked Yahweh's. [52]

For his part, Jeremias maintains the responsorial sense of the *'mn* of the ostracon ("Zum nicht-responsorischen Amen", *ZNW* 64, 1973, 122-123).

It appears to us that even in the translation of the ostracon proposed by Strugnell the responsorial value is not absent: "And all my brothers will answer for me, those who reap with me in the heat of the sun, all my brothers will answer for me: truly (*'mn*), I am innocent of all sin ..." (178). The man accused of fraud invokes the testimony of his brothers. By saying "truly," they will acquiesce to what he himself says. The "truly" will come like an echo, a confirmation of the protestation of innocence. No doubt, as Strugnell points out, "the *ipsissima vox* does not need to find expression in locutions never heard before" (182). But the originality of the non-responsorial use of *Amen* seems to stand, in addition to the still more unchallengeable uniqueness of the association of "Amen" with "I tell you" (181, foot note 7).

[51] The interpretation of this logion cannot be restricted to the context in which it occurs, for it was introduced by the Evangelist because of its analogy with "this generation" that "has passed away" (Mk 13:30). Lagrange

137

They were not transitory like created things, but brought the eternity of God into this world. [53]

Jesus' words have the transcendence as well as the immanence of the Incarnation. Indeed, while they have divine authority and the quality of eternity, they are in very truth human words. The superiority of Jesus' language is revealed in his human way of speaking with men. The answer of the soldiers who, enthralled by Jesus' teaching, could not carry out the order to arrest him, is recorded for us by the Evangelist of the Word-made-flesh: "There has never been anybody who has spoken like him" (Jn 4:46). *Jesus' teaching comes from above, but its power to convince lies in its human expression.*

The formula setting up the new teaching in opposition to the old is particularly clear-cut: "... it was said ... But I say this to you" (Mt 5:21-22, 27-28, 31-32, 33-34, 38-39, 43-44). Jesus claims an authority superior to the Law. Such a claim is surprising since "it was said" is a passive that signifies divine action. [54] How to explain that Jesus can consider himself superior to God's own words?

The claim is justified by the fact that until then God had spoken through human mediators, and human mediation is fraught with imperfections. Jesus' claim to have authority to correct and complete God's utterances, and thereby bring the Law to its plenitude (cf. Mt 5:17) can stem from one source only. Jesus is not merely a mediator or intermediary.

---

remarks: "Verse 31 is not limited by Verse 30" (*Marc*, 325). The declaration has a general import (comp. Lk 16:17). It applies to all of Jesus' words.

[52] Jeremias shows a relationship between Jesus' affirmation: "Therefore, everyone who listens to these words of mine and acts on them ..." (Mt 7:24 par.) with a typical affirmation of contemporary Judaism: "Whoever hears the words of the Torah and performs good deeds builds on solid ground" (*Théologie du N.T.*, 316).

[53] The opposition between the level of the world that passes and God's level which will not pass had been compellingly expressed in Second Isaiah: In the face of the heavens that disappear and the earth that wears out, Yahweh affirms his eternal salvation, his justice without end (51:6): elsewhere it is his love, his covenant of peace that cannot be shaken (54:10). The prophet does not say "his words," but that is the meaning implied in these declarations.

[54] The "*passivum divinum*" is mentioned by Jeremias as the first of the language forms preferred by Jesus (*Théologie du N.T.*, 16-22).

In him God's words are present in their totality, and are free of all limitations. And this maximal presence implies that he himself is personally the Word of God.

b - Word and Person

Two of Jesus' declarations suggest more directly, although still in veiled terms, the identity betwen word and person. "On Judgment day the men of Nineveh will stand up with this generation and condemn it, because when Jonah preached they repented; and there is something greater than Jonah here" (Mt 12:41; Lk 11:32). Jonah is cited as the type of the prophet. Jesus affirms that he himself is more than a prophet: [55] inasmuch as the prophet speaks in the name of God, only God's word itself can be superior to the prophet. Jesus thus implies that he is the Word of God in person.

There is a similar reference to Solomon: "On Judgment day the Queen of the South will rise up with this generation and condemn it, because she came from the ends of the earth to hear the wisdom of Solomon; and there is something greater than Solomon here" (Mt 12:42; cf. Lk 11:31). The Jews looked upon Solomon as the supreme herald of Wisdom, and so there can be above him only divine Wisdom herself. It is no longer merely a herald or a mouthpiece of Wisdom who is present, it is Wisdom in person. This exegesis finds confirmation elsewhere, when Jesus affirms that "wisdom has been proved right by her actions" (Mt 11:19).

The Word of God and the Wisdom of God are two very closely related realities. The former lays stress on expression, whereas the latter tends to emphasize thought. But in fact the two concepts are more or less congruent. Jesus has given us to understand that he is both the Word and the Wisdom of God.

---

[55] W. Kasper remarks: "This 'more' has an eschatological ring" (*Jesus der Christus*, Mainz 1974, 82). "Jesus is not simply one prophet among many, but the eschatological prophet, the last, the supreme prophet, the one who exceeds everything." We should particularly note that there is a difference in quality in the "more." Jesus not only realizes the figure of Jonah as John the Baptist did the figure of Elijah. He is above Jonah, that is, he is above the model of the prophet. This logically leads to acknowledgment that he is more than an interpreter of the Word, and that he must therefore be the Word itself.

In the Fourth Gospel we find an analogous identification of Jesus with light and truth. The formulation is more explicit than in the Synoptics. In Matthew and Luke Jesus says equivalently, implicitly: "I am the Word of God," "I am the Wisdom of God." John records their identity in more explicit terms: "I am the light of the world" (Jn 8:12; cf. 3:19; 9:5; 12:35-46); and "I am the Truth" (Jn 14:6). In addition to these categorical statements, there are others that explain more clearly how Jesus could say: "... anyone who follows me ... will have the light of life" (Jn 8:12); "all who are on the side of truth listen to my voice" (Jn 18:37). The formulas with the "I am" merely emphasize the identity implied in the more discreet affirmations.

In Second Isaiah we find parallel declarations attributed to Yahweh: "I am Yahweh, ... I form the light" (Is 45:7). "I revealed things beforehand" (Is 48:5). The Gospel affirmations contain what appears to be a superior claim. Jesus is not only the one who gives light and who speaks, he is the light, he is the truth. This superiority stems from the Incarnation: the light and the truth are no longer merely a divine gift communicated to men, but a person who joins the human race in order to give himself as the light and the truth. The spirit of Incarnation is especially indicated by the expression "the light of the world." [56] Here "truth" is the concrete truth that reveals itself, not the abstract truth that belongs solely to a metaphysical universe. [57]

When Jesus said: "Yes, if you do not believe that I am He [I am], you will die in your sins," his adversaries asked him who this mysterious "I" was: "Who are you?" Jesus answered: "[I am] what I have told you from the outset" (Jn 8:24-25). [58]

The explanation of this answer is to be found in his allusion to divine Wisdom which, according to Pr 8:23, "from

---

56 We can compare the expression to the affirmation about God: "God is light" (I Jn 1:5). Jesus is light in this world.

57 This aspect of the "truth" in St. John has been especially emphasized by I. de la Potterie, Gesù Verità. Studi di cristologia giovannea, Turin, 1973.

58 The meaning of the text may be contested. We are using the meaning adopted by C. K. Barrett, The Gospel according to St. John, London 1962, 283, and A. Feuillet, "Les Ego eimi christologiques du quatrième évangile," RSR 54 (1966), 17.

everlasting ... was firmly set, from the beginning, before the earth came into being." It appears in the context of a dialogue that culminates with a more explicit declaration: "I tell you most solemnly, before Abraham came into being, I am" (Jn 8:58). If Jesus has been what he claims from the beginning, he is, in his divine identity, the very words he speaks. We are obliged to recognize in him the divine Word who existed from the beginning.

We are dealing here with the Word Incarnate. "I am what I tell you I am" belongs to human language. "From the beginning" could refer to the beginning of the dialogue or to the beginning of Jesus' preaching. The expression has a human meaning through which the more lofty sense of the absolute beginning pierces through.

The impetus to faith given by Jesus follows the meaning of the incarnation of the Word. *To believe in his words and to believe in him are two inseparable attitudes.* Jesus does not limit himself to demanding faith in his teaching, which, he affirms, originates in the Father. He asks faith in his own person, and that is what he obtains, as the Evangelist records. The words "what the Father has taught me is what I preach" call for a commitment of faith: "As he was saying this, many came to believe in him" (Jn 8:28-30). Faith in the words and faith in the person merge into one. In the last analysis, this identification leads to the acknowledgment of a certain identity between the word and the person. Jesus has a claim to men's belief inasmuch as he is the Word of the Father.

2. *The Incarnation of God's Action*

a - A recapitulation of the great figures of Israel

God had guided the history of Israel through men of his choice. In his mission Jesus retraces this history, while attaining a level that transcends everything the mediators had accomplished, as recorded by Scripture. [59]

Everything Abraham hoped for culminated in Jesus: "Your father Abraham rejoiced to think he would see my Day; he saw it and was glad" (Jn 8:56). The real Isaac, whose name

---

[59] Cf. on this subject the interesting pages of D. Mollat, "La divinité du Christ d'après saint Jean," *LV* (9) 1953, 103-111.

means "God has smiled" and who had been Abraham's joy (Gn 17:17) is indeed Jesus. We find this identification with Isaac in the voice heard at Jesus' baptism and at his Transfiguration.

But this might lead us to assume Jesus was in some way inferior to Abraham. To the contrary, Jesus affirms a decisive superiority over him, for he existed before Abraham (cf. Jn 8:58). Moreover, in the order of the realities that fulfill the figures, Abraham reminds us of the Father who sacrifices his Son: "Yes, God loved the world so much that he gave his only Son ..." (Jn 3:36). [60] Thus, in the definitive history of salvation the image of Abraham and Isaac takes on a transcendent meaning, that of God Father and Son.

We find the same trend toward transcendence confirmed for the patriarch Jacob. When Jesus offers to give the Samaritan woman living water, she challenges his claim: "How could you get this living water? Are you greater than our father Jacob who gave us this well ...?" (Jn 4:11-12). [61] Jesus immediately adopts the image, stressing the higher value of the fountainhead that quenches thirst forever. He does what Jacob once did, but on the divine level of one who gives eternal life.

The mention of Jacob is related to the reference to Moses who made water gush from the rock to quench the people's thirst. On the occasion of the feast of Tabernacles, which commemorated this miracle, Jesus cried out: "If any man is thirsty, let him come to me! Let the man drink who believes in me!" (Jn 7:37-38). Similarly, Moses had given the famished people bread from heaven, manna. Jesus said: "I tell you most solemnly, it was not Moses who gave you bread from heaven, it is my Father who gives you the bread from heaven, the true bread; for the bread of God is that which comes

---

[60] This text probably evokes the sacrifice of Abraham, according to R. Le Déaut, *La nuit pascale,* Rome 1963, 204.

[61] We can make a comparison with the Palestinian Targum for Gn 28:10: "After our father Jacob had removed the stone from the mouth of the spring, the spring rose to the surface, overflowed, and flowed for twenty years, all the days that our father lived in Haran" (J. Ramon Diaz, "Palestinian Targum and New Testament," *N.T.* 6, 1963, 77). The contrast between these twenty years and the eternal wellspring shows the great distance that separates the two personages.

down from heaven and gives life to the world" (Jn 6:32-33).
Jesus' superiority over Moses does not remain within human
limits. The bread Jesus gives is the bread of God, the Father's
bread.

Finally, let us mention David, the messianic personage.
Speaking to the Pharisees who share the traditional view of
the Messiah, son of David, Jesus cites Psalm 110: "The Lord
said to my Lord ...," and asks the question: "If David can
call him Lord, then how can he be his son?" (Mt 22:45;
cf. Mk 12:37; Lk 20:44). The idea of a "Lord of David"
is an innovation that clearly shows a transition from figure
to reality in the direction of transcendent Messiah.

b - The Mission to Establish the Kingdom

(1) - Jesus and the kingdom

All of Jesus' preaching concerns the coming of the kingdom of God. His entire work consists in establishing this
kingdom. This means he is doing God's work.

He speaks equivalently of the kingdom of the Son of Man
and of the kingdom of the Father (Mt 13:41-43). This means
he acts as the master of the kingdom, and not merely in the
name of another, of the Father. To leave everything for the
kingdom of God (Lk 18:29) means to leave everything for
his name (Mt 19:29) or for his sake (Mk 10:29). The kingdom of heaven belongs to those who are persecuted because
of him (Mt 5:11). In his boldest declaration he confers the
kingdom on his apostles, just as the Father has done for him
(cf. Lk 22:29 ff.). To confer the kingdom in this way amounts
to claiming divine sovereignty as the Son of God.

Where the world to come is concerned, Jesus describes
the power of the Son of Man who confers the kingdom as
a heritage upon those who have loved their brothers, and turns
away those who have not demonstrated such love (cf. Mt
25:34). This power to confer the kingdom in eternity is
but one aspect of the power to pass judgment.

Where earthly life is concerned, Jesus sets the conditions
for access to the kingdom and the laws that govern its members.
The formula: "It was said ... but I say this to you" (Mt 5:22,
28, 32, 34, 39, 44) witnesses to Jesus' absolute authority over

the kingdom. The same holds true of his power to forgive sins and to grant eternal life.

(2) - An "I" who acts with the power of God

When Jesus says "I" (*ego*) to stress the worth of his action, we find in it the implication of a divine power or authority.

Speaking to the centurion about his paralyzed servant, he says: "I will come myself and cure him" (Mt 8:7). There is a contrast here with the centurion who also uses "I" to say that he is subject to another, whereas Jesus' "I" is sovereign and commands sickness.

In the incident of the adulterous woman, Jesus opposes his "I" to the men who want to condemn the guilty woman to stoning according to the Law of Moses; and his "I" brings her divine forgiveness: "Neither do I condemn you" (Jn 8:11).

Jesus' insistence on using the word "I" helps to show that he is not merely the instrument of divine action. The mystery of his achievement is first of all the mystery of his person. He personally possesses the power to act after the manner of God.

Miracles can't be forced out of him. When a woman tries to remain unnoticed while she touches the fringe of his cloak from behind, Jesus reacts: "I felt that power had gone out from me" (Lk 8:46).

In healing the epileptic, he drives out "the unclean spirit" with authority: "I command you: come out of him ..." (Mk 9:25). Speaking in a more general way, he affirms: "... I cast out devils ..." (Mt 12:27; Lk 11:19). And he invites those around him to see in this power "the finger of God" or "the Spirit of God."

Jesus stresses the sovereignty of his call to the disciples: "I chose you" (Jn 15:16,19). He performs the action of God who chooses and who sends forth: "Remember, I am sending you out ..." (Mt 10:16). God's action is even more transparent in his declaration: "I am sending you prophets and wise men and scribes" (Mt 23:34). He sounds like the God of the Old Testament.

Jesus promises his help to his apostles when in days to come they are persecuted and dragged before tribunal: "I myself shall give you an eloquence and a wisdom that none of your opponents will be able to resist or contradict" (Lk 21:15).

(3) - The shepherd

The title of "shepherd" expresses an authority that tends to act under the impulsion of love. When he says "I am the good shepherd" (Jn 10:11), Jesus offers himself as the model of a shepherd and calls to mind the way Yahweh had presented himself as the shepherd of his people.

Jesus' claim to the title of "shepherd" has been considered a messianic claim on his part, especially in the light of Ezekiel's oracle: "I mean to raise up one shepherd, my servant David, and to put him in charge of them and he will pasture them ..." (Ez 34:23). This claim is true, but we also know that Jesus intended to fulfill the messianic prophecy in a way that went beyond David, since he declared he was David's Lord. Here again his superiority over David appears. [62] For Jesus fulfills more completely what had been said of Yahweh himself in the oracle. [63] Against the shepherds of Israel who "feed themselves," Yahweh declares: "I am going to look after my flock myself and keep all of it in view" (Ez 34:11). The opposition can also be seen in Jesus' words to the robbers. Against these robbers, his "I" asserts itself, as Yahweh's did in earlier times: "I have come," "I am the good shepherd" (Jn 10:10-11).

Moreover, Jesus takes on two functions assumed by Yahweh, namely gathering the dispersed sheep and providing them with rich pasture. Jesus gives life in all its fullness, and this is one of God's attributes. He also gathers his sheep around himself, the "one shepherd" (cf. Jn 10:16), as though identifying himself with God. On another occasion Jesus applies to himself another distinctive mark of Yahweh the shepherd.

---

[62] Cf. Feuillet, " Les *Ego eimi*," *RSR,* 1966, 220: In Jn 10, Jesus "is the one shepherd, just like Yahweh in Ezekiel, and this is so for the strongly intimated reason that he is one with Yahweh or God the Father."

[63] Cf. R. Brown, *The Gospel according to John,* I, 398: "Basically it would seem that Ezekiel's portrait of God (or the Messiah) as the ideal shepherd, in contrast to the wicked shepherds who plunder the flock and allow sheep to be lost, served as the model for Jesus' portrait of himself as the ideal shepherd, in contrast to the Pharisees, who are thieves who rob the sheep and hirelings who allow the sheep to be scattered."

He is the one who seeks out the lost sheep (cf. Mt 18:12-14; Lk 15:4-7), and justifies his own behavior by reference to God's. Similarly, when, at the time of the final judgment, Jesus acts as a shepherd who separates the sheep from the goats, he acts with divine authority (cf. Mt 25:32-33). In Ezekiel Yahweh says he will "judge between sheep and sheep, between rams and he-goats," and "between fat sheep and lean sheep" (Ez 34:17-20).

The shepherd's knowledge of his sheep had not been explicitly stated in this oracle, but it was presupposed in the judgment. In order to judge between sheep and sheep, Yahweh had to know them. In the Gospel this knowledge is stressed, its model being the very knowledge that the Father has of Jesus: "I know my own and my own know me, just as the Father knows me and I know the Father" (Jn 10:14-15). We note that the two terms of this reciprocal knowledge suggest a certain claim to divine identity by the Son. Not only does Jesus know the way the Father knows, but he is known by the sheep the way the Father is known by him. The value of the Johannine affirmation of this mutual knowledge is confirmed, we should point out, by the affirmation that accompanies the hymn of jubilation: "... no one knows the Son except the Father ..." (Mt 11:27; cf. Lk 10:22). The testimony of the Synoptics does not, strictly speaking, concern the knowledge that Jesus, the good shepherd, has of his sheep. However it brings out his relationship to the Father that is the basis of this knowledge.

It is important to note that the affirmation: "I know my sheep and my sheep know me" indicates a far more intimate knowledge than does Ezekiel's oracle. For all Yahweh's solicitude for his lost, bruised, or sick sheep, he remained more distant. It is significant also that the prophet does not speak of a reciprocal knowledge. By reason of the fact that the good shepherd is living on this earth, he can establish a deeper intimacy with his sheep.

On one essential point, the Gospel description of the good shepherd is also superior to Ezekiel's: "the good shepherd is the one who lays down his life for his sheep" (Jn 10:11). Now this point brings out very clearly the value of the Incarnation: what Yahweh, in his divine transcendence, could

146

not accomplish, Jesus can do because he is man. He can realize the ideal of the shepherd in all perfection through the sacrifice of his life. Here we find the superiority already noted elsewhere: Jesus realizes what had been attributed to the God of the Old Testament, but in a more perfect way because of the fact that he is a man.

c - The Miracles

(1) - The problem of miracles

Miracles are included in the traditional demonstration of Jesus' divinity, but today "the proof provided by miracles" is often challenged.

We need not be surprised that such a proof should be contested by those who are engaged in a "systematic demythologization." [64] However it has also been the object of criticims on the part of those who, without seeking to deny miracles, reject a certain apologetic presentation that has been given of them. If a miracle is accepted as a fact scientifically demonstrated as impossible to explain by natural causes, and therefore produced by God's transcendent action, two difficulties arise. Can there be an absolute scientific demonstration of miracles? The cure of an illness or an extraordinary event can be inexplicable by natural causes as they are known today. This does not mean we can state with absolute certainty there will be no future discovery of as yet unknown natural forces which could account for the phenomenon. On the other hand, science cannot, through its own investigations, identify with God an unknown force that happens to be at work in visible events.

To overcome these difficulties, recent theology has recognized miracles essentially as signs, exceptional signs of the divine action that accomplies salvation. [65] In so doing, it

---

[64] Cf. M. Dibelius, *Die Formgeschichte des Evangeliums,* Tübingen 1919; R. Bultmann, *Die Geschichte des Synoptischen Tradition,* 223-260. For a critique of the theories of Bultmann and Dibelius, the reader can consult L.J. Mc Ginley, *Form-Criticism of the Synoptic Healing Narratives. A Study in the Theories of Martin Dibelius and Rudolf Bultmann,* Woodstock, 1944.

[65] Cf. E. Dhanis, "Quest-ce qu'un miracle?," *Gr* 40 (1959) 201-241; L. Monden, *Le miracle, signe de salut,* Bruges 1960; F. Lepargneur, "La nature fonctionnelle du miracle," *NRT* 84 (1962) 283-294; B. Prete, "Senso

reverses the order of thinking on miracles. Instead of first considering the order of nature which cannot explain the event and then postulating a supernatural cause, its starting point is the supernatural context of salvific activity. In this approach, miracles have no meaning except in this supernatural context, as a call by God to man's faith. Thus, miracles are part of the divine language, of the dialogue initiated by divine love with the human community.

In consequence, the way Jesus conceived of miracles is of particular importance.

(2) - The perspective of Jesus' miracles

When the disciples of John the Baptist question Jesus on his identity, he answers: "Go back and tell John what you hear and see; the blind see again, and the lame walk, lepers are cleansed, and the deaf hear, and the dead are raised to life and the Good News is proclaimed to the poor ..." (Mt 11:5; cf. Lk 7:22). To show that he is truly "the one who is to come" and that another is not to be expected, he invites his hearers to grasp the lesson of the miracles he is performing, using terms by which the Book of Isaiah announced the messianic era (cf. Is 29:18; 26:19; 35:5 ff; 61:1). In Jesus' intention, therefore, miracles are signs of his identity .

By this answer Jesus also situates miracles in their true perspective, which is not one that involves scientific verification of a phenomenon inexplicable by natural forces. He makes it quite clear that the cures he is performing exceed the laws of nature. Then, too, the resurrections he mentions constitute an irrefutable example of works impossible to mere natural forces; for while we can discuss the possibility of certain cures in some future time, the obstacle of death remains insurmountable. [66] But even while Jesus points to facts that merely hu-

---

e valore del miracolo nei vangeli," *Sacra Doctrina* 5 (1960) 317-351; F. Mussner, *Die Wunder Jesu - Eine Hinführung*, Munich 1967; L. Sabourin, "Les miracles de Jésus," *Bulletin de Théologie biblique* 1 (1971) 64-86; "I miracoli di Gesù," *Rassegna di teologia*, suppl. footnote 5 (Sept.-Oct. 1972) 91-99.

[66] The resurrection of the dead, announced in Is 26:19, was considered by Judaism to be exclusively the work of God's power. Thus in his answer to John, Jesus attests that he is a Messiah of the divine order; cf. S. Sabugal, "La embajada mesiánica del Bautista (Mt 16,2-6; Lc 7,18-23). Análisis histó-rico-tradicional," *Augustinianum* 13 (1973) 257-258.

man capacities cannot explain, he asks his hearers to recognize in them the fulfillment of God's plan proclaimed by the prophets. Besides, the ultimate fact that he mentions: "and the Good News is proclaimed to the poor," is not a miracle, but explains the meaning of all the miracles previously enumerated. In fact, it is this last criterion, the one that is not " miraculous," that is the most decisive. It attests to the reality of God's action, one of whose distinctive marks is compassion for the "poor." Miracles can only be considered within the broader context of God's total action in the world, at the level of faith. Since Jesus refers to prophecy, let us briefly summarize the Biblical context of miracles.

In the Old Testament, all of creation, including what we call the order of nature, is considered as the wondrous deed of God. In the description of God's salvific action, all events manifest the extraordinary nature of the interventions of God the Savior, even those that are ostensibly the result of natural or human causes. [67] These events simply express in a modest and limited way a power that transcends them. In order to interpret and understand them we must perceive them in their quality as signs, just as we grasp the language of others by recognizing the superior intention of the person in his words.

When the history set forth in the Biblical accounts becomes extraordinary, it continues to be understood in this general perspective. This context helps us to have a more exact sense of the value of miracles. Miracles belong to the economy of signs. While a miracle is exceptional because it is an abnormal manifestation of transcendence, it is nonetheless a part of God's continuous action which is lavished in the signs of history. And as such, miracles cannot be detached from this much wider array of signs. A miracle is not an interlude, a reversal of the established order. It is a summit, an especially intense moment in the ongoing language of divine signs.

In Jesus' case, there was a concentration of these summits. The intensity of the signs of God's action attained an incomparably higher level than in any other period of human

---

[67] "What makes an event a miracle is less its abnormal nature than its aptness to manifest the providential government of God and the presence of his invisible power" (L. Sabourin, "Les miracles de l'Ancient Testament," *Bulletin de Théologie Biblique* 1, 1971, 239).

history. There was such a multiplicity of extraordinary facts in Jesus' public life that we are obliged to speak of a sudden invasion of miracles. In addition to the thirty or so miracles specifically reported in the Gospels, there were the vast number of cures of the sick referred to in a general way. This abundance witnesses to a unique display of God's power.

(3) - The historicity of the miracles.

In comparison with other periods or other milieus, the miracles performed by Jesus enjoy the guarantee of reliable historical testimony.

In the case of the Old Testament, it is not easy to eliminate doubts regarding the authenticity of the extraordinary events related in the Biblical accounts, or to reject the hypothesis that the actual events were considerably amplified. These accounts are inspired in that they are prophetic announcements and prefigure a future reality. When Jesus refers to the miracles attributed to Elijah and Elisha (cf. Lk 4:25-27), he sees in them the Scriptural prefiguration of the miracles he himself is performing in the historical reality of his time. When he speaks of the sign of Jonah (cf. Mt 12:39-41; Lk 11:29-32), he sees in it only the announcement of his death and Resurrection. In the manna and the water gushing from the rock Paul recognizes "figures" of a spiritual food and drink, the Eucharist (cf. I Co 10:1-5). The historicity of what had been prefigured in the Scriptural miracles of the Old Testament is to be found in Jesus' coming.

As for miracles that might have been performed in other religious contexts, we must ask ourselves if they are based on sufficiently reliable testimony to guarantee their historical truth. In the matter of miracles attributed to rabbis or to personages of the Hellenistic world like Apollonius of Tyana, legitimate doubts remain. [68]

To the contrary, this guarantee of historical authenticity

---

[68] "Quite apart from any polemics or false apologetic concern, we believe we can affirm that none of the extraordinary events of the Hellenistic and rabbinical documentation presents a sufficient guarantee of authenticity for us to recognize in them the marks of a single authentic miracle" (L. Sabourin, "'Miracles' hellénistiques et rabbiniques," *Bulletin de Théologie Biblique* 2, 1972, 806).

is present in the Gospel accounts for a good number of Jesus' miracles. [69] Only the blanket rejection on principle of miracles as such could lead to the challenging of all the miracles recorded in the Gospels. Anyone who approaches the Gospel testimonies with a critical eye but without any prejudice against "the wonderful deeds of God," has to accept at least some of the miraculous events as historical. Obviously, in each individual case the exegete must assume the task of studying the author's input, the possible amplifications, and the doctrinal interpretations that influence the presentation of the facts. And yet while certain accounts or parts of them appear doubtful after a critical examination, the authenticity of the great majority of the miracles attributed to Christ is sufficiently guaranteed by the accounts. The truthful quality of most of the testimonies is truly impressive.

Scepticism has tended to focus above all on the resurrections and on miracles that manifest a power above nature, such as the miraculous draft of fish, the changing of water into wine, the multiplication of the loaves, the calming of the storm, and Jesus' walking on the sea. But an analysis of the texts that relate these miracles tends to confirm their historicity. The miracle that shows Jesus' power over nature most cogently is the raising of Lazarus from the dead. Now, many signs guarantee the truth of this event, which in turn explains other facts of Jesus' public life and is linked in a special way with the Resurrection of Christ himself. [70]

Why should this category of miracles be particularly suspect? The reason for the suspicion may lie in a repugnance to admit demonstrations of the extraordinary that are too theatrical, or that imply a certain pleasure in the use of omnipotence. Jesus, for his part, refuses to make ostentatious demonstrations. The account of the temptations in the desert shows how he avoids making a spectacle of himself and seducing the crowds by jumping off the pinnacle of the Temple. It is during his Passion that his refusal to perform prodigies takes on its full meaning. Jesus refuses to ask for legions of angels

---

[69] Cf. R. Latourelle, "Authenticité historique des miracles de Jésus: Essai de critériologie," *Gr* 54 (1973) 225-262.
[70] Cf. Latourelle, *art. cit.*, 255-258.

to overwhelm his enemies, and he leaves unanswered taunts to come down from the Cross. [71]

Jesus' customary discretion in performing his miracles is especially evident in the most astonishing of them all, the resurrections. Far from wanting to make everyone realize that Jairus' daughter was really dead, so as to prove the truth of her resurrection, he minimizes her death by saying: "The child is not dead, but asleep" (Mk 5:39; Lk 8:52). [72] The same holds true for Lazarus: "Our friend Lazarus is resting, I am going to wake him" (Jn 11:11). This discretion reveals Jesus' determination not to force the human intellect to abdicate before dazzling wonders. His invitation addresses itself to faith, while maintaining a zone of mystery and safeguarding the personal freedom of man's commitment. Jesus never uses a miracle to do violence to the human mind or to compel anyone's assent.

---

[71] An extraordinary event like the earthquake, described only by Matthew as occurring at the moment of Jesus' death (Mt 27:51-52), has little in common with this principle of frugality in miracles. It is a materializing expression of Jesus' passage into the kingdom of death. This seism seems to have been introduced into the narrative to explain the opening of the tombs, that is, the deliverance brought to the dead, which is a reality not of the physical but of the spiritual order. The tendency to materialize spiritual realities is also shown in the description of the darkness "over all the land" from the sixth to the ninth hour (cf. Mt 27:45; Mk 15:33; Lk 23:44). The extension of this phenomenon to the whole earth is proof enough that no single individual could have witnessed it. But it indicates the meaning of the symbol very well, namely, the participation of the whole universe in the death of Jesus. The same holds true of the tearing of the veil of the Temple (Mt 27:51; Mk 15:38; Lk 23:45), the sign of the disappearance of God's presence from the Temple. The two images used to comment on the meaning of Jesus' death, the mourning of the cosmos and the end of the Jewish religion, were interpreted as physical realities, but must be retained solely for the value of the idea they express.

[72] This declaration has led some exegetes to ask themselves whether this was a true resurrection. Taylor remains in doubt, while concluding that Mark probably considered the fact to be a resurrection (*Mark,* 295). But the scoffing at Jesus' words confirms that there was no doubt that the child was dead. When Jesus says she is asleep, he is already announcing that for him this death is only a sleep, because of the power he wields over life. H. Schür-mann remarks: Jesus "has not yet seen the dead child, he does not make any diagnosis," but in these words lies the truth "that now death is no longer death," since it is no longer eternal but only for a time (*Das Lukasevangelium,* Freiburg-Basel-Wien 1969, 495).

Let us stress the difference between extraordinary acts performed for personal glory and the miracles in which Jesus manifests his dominion over the forces of nature. These latter are performed for an altruistic purpose and tend to express, through this dominion, certain aspects of a spiritual mission. The resurrections signify the new life brought to mankind by Christ, as well as his victory over death. The wine of Cana and the multiplication of the loaves announce the Eucharist. The calming of the storm and the walk on the sea witness to his power to help the disciples in difficult situations by enabling them to overcome all dangers. The miraculous draft of fish is a sign of the fruitfulness promised to the Apostles' mission. [73]

These miracles have meaning in their own right. While the miraculous cures reveal the intention to liberate man from his moral and spiritual infirmities, the miracles involving dominion over nature show that the entire material universe is encompassed in the work of the kingdom. Not only can natural forces not pose a threat to this work, but they obey Christ who has the power to make them contribute to the realization of his mission. This is, as it were, an extreme outreach of the Incarnation, for Jesus exercises God's control over the world around him as well as over his own flesh.

If we look at these miracles in the light of the Old Testa-

---

[73] The only exception is when Jesus tells Peter to open the fish's mouth to remove a shekel with which to pay the tax he owes. This command is recorded only by Matthew (17:27), without any account of the miracle. It would be completely contrary to Jesus' way of acting, for he never performed a miracle for his own benefit, even less to obtain money, nor did he ever have recourse to actions resembling magic. When Jesus was asked to pay the tax, he most probably answered by telling Peter he would pay the tax out of the gains from their catch, and this answer was materialized to include the pulling of a shekel from a fish's mouth. Lagrange sensed the incongruity of this: "Several moderns, even some who are believers, express their surprise at a miracle intended to provide for the needs of the Master and of his faithful servant. It was not Jesus' custom to act in this way." But the argument Lagrange offers to defend the miracle does not seem very valid: "But this time it is a question of money. Neither Jesus nor Peter have any" (*Matthieu*, 343). The money was an added reason for not performing any miracle. In fact, everything comes clear if Jesus' words are seen as materialized to satisfy a mentality that hungered too much for miracles. The absence of any description of the miracle confirms that there is question here of a misinterpretation of Jesus' words.

ment, we can better discern the significance of this deployment of divine power. When Jesus walks on the water, he accomplishes specifically and visibly what had been said of Yahweh: "You strode across the sea, you marched across the ocean" (Ps 77:19). When he calms the storm, we recognize in him the sovereignty of Yahweh who calms "the clamour of the ocean, the clamour of its waves" (Ps 65:7; cf. Ps 89:9; Ps 107:29). We must not forget that mastery of the sea had been attributed in a special way to the Creator in the formation of the universe (Gn 1:7; cf. Pr 8:29). Jesus shows that he possesses this power personally. What God had accomplished by intervening in the history of the chosen people and especially in the passage over the Red Sea, Jesus effectuates in his human condition. Divine power resides in him totally, and this power can be deployed in its fullness in his life as a man. What could only be a metaphor when applied to Yahweh becomes a concrete reality in Jesus.

The same holds true of the cures. When, in the Book of Job, Eliphaz declared that the hand of God heals (Jb 5:18), the word "hand" could only be a figure of speech. When Jesus lays hands on the sick and the cripple, [74] the figure becomes a visible reality (Mt 9:18; Mk 5:23; 6:5; 7:32; 8:23-25; 16:18; Lk 4:40; 13:13). In the person of Jesus, God has real human hands with which to heal. When Jesus stretches out his hand and touches the leper (Mk 1:41 and par.), his authoritative gesture (cf. Ex 7:19; 14:16) is a claim to be above the law that forbids contact with lepers (cf. Lv 14). He claims a divine authority that expresses itself in compassionate action. Only the hand of God can touch those who have been cast out of human society.

(4) - The Meaning of the Miracles

We have seen that Jesus intended his miracles to be a proof of his identity, at least of his messianic identity, which was questioned by John the Baptist. From his prison, the

---

[74] "Neither the Old Testament nor rabbinical literature mention healings or exorcisms by the laying on of hands," according to J. Martucci, who sees in this action the expression of "Jesus' Lordship over all things" ("Les récits de miracle: influence des récits de l'Ancien Testament sur ceux du Nouveau," *Science et Esprit* 27, 1975, 145, 143).

Precursor had heard speak of "what Christ was doing" (Mt 11:2), his miracles in particular. [75] How is it that Jesus answered his question by pointing to his miracles? [76] According to the question, the Baptizer did not consider these works sufficient. He was expecting something more, a more explicitly messianic action, involving the display of the redoubtable power he had announced in his preaching (cf. Mt 3:7-12; Lk 3:7-18). Jesus wanted John to understand that in these miracles he was carrying out his mission as the Messiah, but in a different way, not with the show of a vengeful God's power but with miraculous compassion expressed in the gift of the "Gospel" to the poor.

It will be helpful to remember that when Jesus cured the paralytic he explicitly pointed out his purpose in performing this miracle: "to prove to you that the Son of Man has authority on earth to forgive sins" (Mt 9:6; Mk 9:10; Lk 5:24). Therefore miracles are signs of Jesus' identity by revealing the Son of Man and his power. But they are more than apt symbols for making a truth known. Miracles are the exercise of a divine power of liberation. [77] Bodily healing is the sensible manifestation of spiritual salvation, of the forgiveness of sins. The salvific intention of Jesus' miracles is especially highlighted by the fact that Jesus begins by saying to this paralytic who is brought to him for healing: "My child, your sins are forgiven" (Mk 2:5 and par.). Miracles are not their own reason for being. They are commanded by the work of salvation

---

[75] The words "what Christ was doing" are derived from the Old Testament expression "the works of the Lord," which signifies the acts of eschatological salvation accomplished by God (cf. Is 29:23). They suggest that this is a Messiah of divine stature. Such is the view of Sabugal (*art. cit., Augustinianum*, 1973, 233-235).

[76] Lagrange asks the question: "Where is the strength of the argument?" (*Matthieu*, 219), and he answers that in the opinion of that time the gift of miracles in itself was not one of the marks of the Messiah.

[77] For this reason it would be inappropriate to speak of a signification of the juridical order. P. E. Langevin uses this expression only "for lack of a more exact epithet" ("La signification du miracle dans le message du Nouveau Testament," *SE* 27, 1975, 172). Miracles are more than credentials. They are not merely a public guarantee of God's approval, for this would give them a finality founded too much on appearances. Miracles are the exercise of God's salvific power.

and express in a physical sign the reality of the spiritual order that is being actualized.

Jesus' words clearly delineate the demonstrative value of miracles. It is a value that can be understood only in a context of faith. The emphasis is not on exceeding the laws of nature for its own sake, but on the manifestation of a divine power in which the witnesses are invited to believe. On the one hand, it is after "seeing their faith" (Mk 2:5), i.e., the faith of those who have brought the paralytic down from the roof, that Jesus forgives the man's sins. On the other, he performs the cure as an answer to the incredulity of those who accuse him of blaspheming (cf. Mk 2:7-8). Even in this unbelief there is a faith in God, but Jesus wants to show that this faith in God must be extended to faith in himself.

When Jesus reproaches the lake-towns, it is because they have not been converted in spite of the many miracles he has performed under their very eyes (cf. Mt 11:20-24; Mk 10: 13-15).

In the case of the paralytic, we must stress that Jesus performs this miracle in his own name. His way of speaking emphasizes his personal authority: "I order you: get up, pick up your stretcher, and go off home" (Mk 2:11). For the problem his miracles presented to those around him was precisely the extent of his own power: did he personally possess a power that belongs to God alone? Jesus provides the proof that the Son of Man has, on this earth, the power of God.

In other episode, this same personal authority of Jesus is clearly discernible. To the leper, he says: "Be cured!" (Mk 1:41). [78] Speaking to the daughter of Jairus whom he is about to raise from the dead, he commands: "Little girl, I tell you to get up" (Mk 5:41). During the storm he "rebukes" the wind and commands the sea. And they "obey" him (Mk 4:39-41). In the same way, he commands the dead Lazarus to come forth from his tomb. On that occasion, he gives thanks to the Father who always hears him. In this he attests that his authority is that of a Son. But the way he

---

[78] J. Martucci remarks: Such an expression "is unthinkable on the lips of a prophet of the Old Testament. The prophets of the Old Testament have to implore the God of Israel, often at great length, before they finally obtain a miraculous action on his part" (*art. cit.*, *SE*, 1975, 145-146).

performs the miracle shows that, as a Son, he personally possesses divine power over life and death: "Lazarus, here! Come out!" (Jn 11:43). [79] And he precedes this command by asking Martha to make an act of faith in him (cf. Jn 11:25-26).

This claim of personal authority is confirmed by the miracles of the primitive Church. The Apostles perform miracles, not in the name of God himself but in the name of Christ. Peter tells the cripple from birth: "In the name of Jesus Christ the Nazarene, walk!" (Ac 3:6). Likewise, speaking to the paralytic of Lydda: "Aeneas, Jesus Christ cures you: get up ..." (Ac 9:34). Paul wants to proclaim what Christ has done through him, through the power of signs and wonders (cf. Rm 15:18-19).

That is the definitive status of miracles. They are the sensible deployment of divine power, but they are always linked to the person of Jesus. In fact, it is in Jesus that divine power has become incarnate, and this incarnation of power is linked to the Incarnation of the person of the Son of God. This is also an illustration of the dynamism of incarnation in which the ontology of the person and the exercise of the action are inseparably joined.

(5) - Miracles, Expressions of Salvific Love

We noted earlier that in answer to John the Baptist's question, Jesus makes his identity known by miracles which are all expressions of salvific love. The God who acts in Jesus is not an avenger, but a benevolent, liberating God.

Nowhere in accounts of Jesus' actions do we find one comparable to the one related in Acts 13:11, when Paul struck the magician Elymas Magos with temporary blindness. Far from blinding anyone at all, Christ gives sight to the blind. He never uses his power to fell his enemies. And when he does silence them, it is not by some miracle but by the compelling truth of an argument. He reprimands James and John who want to call down fire from heaven on a Samaritan village that refused to receive him (cf. Lk 9:54-55). Jesus never performed any miracle *against* anyone.

---

[79] "The powerful cry by which Jesus summons Lazarus out of the tomb is only the external echo of the cry by which he, God's envoy, calls all men who believe in him to the life of God" (Schnackenburg, *Johannes II,* 414).

157

This principle of Jesus' behavior poses the problem of the historical accuracy of two Gospel accounts which record miracles of punishment or destruction. The withering of the fig tree, punished for not bearing fruit out of season, is a strange case. According to Matthew, the fig tree lost all its leaves instantaneously (cf. Mt 21:18 ff.). According to Mark, however, the withering was noticed only the next morning (cf. Mk 11:20 ff.). But the most authentic version is perhaps Luke's (13:6-9), which does not relate one of Jesus' miracles but tells a parable. The parable of the fig tree rebuked by its master for not bearing fruit may have been told after passing a fig tree on the road. The rebuke is addressed to Israel, and the fig tree suffers no damage.

Even more suspect is the account of the driving of the demons into a herd of two thousand pigs (cf. Mk 5:12-13; Mt 8:28-33; Lk 8:32-33). This account follows the one about the deliverance of the possessed man of Gerasa which seems authentic. Now, the combining of the two involves an inconsistency. For after Jesus has expelled the impure spirit he reportedly speaks to him as if he were still present, to ask his name. There is obviously an amplification here. It can be accounted for by the Jewish revulsion against pigs, but it contradicts Jesus' unswerving attitude of never having recourse to miracles to destroy the property of others.

This is not to say that salvific love excludes all combat. Jesus fights against the spirit of evil, and those miracles described as involving the deliverance of possessed individuals emphasize his victory.[80] We cannot eliminate *a priori* the possibility that these included persons truly possessed by demons.[81] However, in detailed accounts of healing like the one about the young epileptic, the boy afflicted by "a spirit of dumbness" that threw him to the ground (cf. Mk 9:18) was simply a sick boy suffering seizures, and the expulsion of the spirit signifies his bodily healing (cf. Mk 9:25). By taking this approach, adapted to the mentality of those around

---

[80] Cf. on this subject, L. Sabourin, "The Miracles of Jesus, Jesus and the Evil Powers," *BTB* 4 (1974), 156-157.

[81] "No compelling objection, to our mind, has been proposed against the traditional affirmation that Jesus, at least in certain cases, expelled demons from persons who were really possessed" (Sabourin, *ibid.*, 167).

him, Jesus wanted to symbolize the spiritual liberation he was bringing to mankind. The miracles of Jesus attest to much more than a victory over sickness. They are a triumph over the spirit of evil. What Jesus has come to destroy is the kingdom of Satan. And from this point of view his miraculous actions witness to his divine power.

In response to his embarrassed adversaries who try to attribute his casting out of devils to Beelzebul, prince of devils, Jesus says that if that were the case the kingdom of Satan would be divided against itself. "But if it is through the finger of God that I cast out devils, then know that the king-dom of God has overtaken you" (Lk 11:20). So the finger of Jesus is "the finger of God." It is an admirable way of point-ing to the power of God over devils present in the healing finger of Jesus. As was true of God's walking on the sea and of his extended hand, what has been said metaphorically in the Old Testament [82] can be said in strict reality in the Gospel. Now there is a human finger that is in very truth the finger of God. Besides, Jesus identifies his coming with the coming of the kingdom of God. He does not merely say that in de-sroying the rule of Satan he is establishing the kingdom of God. He affirms that this kingdom "has overtaken" us, that it is present, that is to say, present in him.

Any aspect of destruction in Jesus' miracles is only the reverse side of the salvation or of deliverance granted to man-kind. We can find no derogation of the principle that Jesus' miracles are always expressions of divine compassion. In this Jesus has wanted to reveal the authentic face of God.

In this connection, we should also mention the many mir-acles Jesus performed on the sabbath. Since the sabbath is God's day, the miracles worked on that day were meant to manifest the beneficent action of God in a more special way. We know that Jesus justified these miracles by the Father's

---

[82] The image had been used with respect to the plagues sent down on Egypt: "This is the finger of God" (Ex 8:19); to the Law "inscribed by the finger of God" (Ex 31:18; Dt 9:10); to the Creation, the work "made by [Yahweh's] fingers" (Ps 8:3). In the parallel text, Matthew says "through the Spirit of God" (Mt 12:28) instead of "by the finger of God." But the earlier expression is probably Luke's. The words "through the Spirit of God" seem to be an adaptation of the more customary language, giving pref-erence to the idea over the image.

activity to which he wanted to conform his own behavior: "My Father goes on working, and so do I" (Jn 5:17).

This justification in John's Gospel complements what is said concerning violations of the sabbath in Mark's Gospel. In the latter, things are approached from man's point of view. How can a man presume to claim power to permit violations of the sabbath, such as the disciples' gleaning grain from the harvest? Jesus answers that since the sabbath is made for man and not the reverse, the Son of Man is the master of the sabbath (cf. Mk 2:27). Here, since there is question of a miracle performed on the sabbath, the objection is made from God's point of view. The argument given is that the miraclous cure of the cripple could not be the work of God who decreed the sabbath and chose to rest on the seventh day of Creation. Jesus rectifies this way of conceiving God's activity by saying that the Father never stops working, even on the sabbath. [83] Therefore the miracle performed on this day is altogether in harmony with God's true way of acting. In thus changing the habitual behavior of the Jews on the sabbath, Jesus wants to change the doctrinal interpretation of the origin of the sabbath in God.

Jesus' enemies condemn his words as a claim to equality with God: "But that made the Jews even more intent on killing him, because, not content with breaking the sabbath, he spoke of God as his own Father, and so made himself God's equal" (Jn 5:18). Jesus claims to act like God, with divine authority, [84] and he claims to offer a new image of God, one that is truer than the one presented in the Old Testament. The miracles on the sabbath reveal God's unceasingly active love for men.

Now, the incarnational emphasis of Jesus' declaration that the Son of Man is the master of the sabbath in no way contradicts what he says about the decisive value of the Father's

---

[83] Schnackenburg (*Johannes II*, 127) thinks that Jesus' words are based on a rabbinical argument which commented Gn 2:2 ff. by affirming that on the seventh day God had stopped the work of building the world but not his work for the benefit of men. Be this as it may, the text shows a determination to restore the true image of God.

[84] "The assumption of a uniform activity common to Jesus and to God could only mean that Jesus was equal to God" (Barrett, *John*, 214).

160

action. For it is through the man Jesus who performs miracles on the sabbath that the Father wills to reveal the great love that motivates his action. God's action in the world takes on its definitive form in Jesus' actions.

3. *The Incarnation of God's Presence*

a - The Temple and the House of God

We have several Gospel testimonies that concur in showing that Jesus defined himself, by comparison with the Temple of Jerusalem, as the real temple: "Now here, I tell you, is something greater than the Temple" (Mt 12:6). He affirmed a superiority comparable to his superiority over Solomon and Jonah. As the essential value of the Temple lay in the divine presence within it, only this presence could be superior to the Temple. Thus, Jesus implied that in his person the authentic presence of God lay hidden. [85] Indeed, Jesus' enemies, quickly grasping that he was implying he was superior to the Temple, branded this a blasphematory claim, as is clear from the trial before the Sanhedrin. Jesus was accused of appropriating a privilege that belongs exclusively to God.

Another image used by Jesus suggests the same idea: "I tell you most solemnly, you will see heaven laid open and, above the Son of Man, the angels of God ascending and descending" (Jn 1:51). In the Genesis account, the angels of God ascended and descended on the ladder in Jacob's dream. Here the Son of Man represents either the ladder that rises up to heaven, or the place that Jacob called "a house of God," because "Yahweh is in this place" (Gn 28:17-17). The Son of Man is therefore the earthly place where God is present. He is concretely God's presence on earth. [86]

---

[85] Lagrange remarks: "It seems as though Matthew deliberately avoided using the masculine, which would have placed greater emphasis on the person of the Messiah" (*Matthieu*, 233). The divine presence assured by Christ is the foundation of a new spiritual building, superior to the Temple. The neuter is also used to express superiority over Jonah and Solomon (Mt 12: 41-42) so as to designate the new economy of Revelation along with the person of Jesus.

[86] According to Brown, whatever the interpretation of the image, "the vision means that Jesus as Son of Man has become the locus of divine glory, the point of contact between heaven and earth. The disciples are promised

b - *Ego eimi*

(1) - The meaning of the affirmation

John records a declaration that forcefully stresses the incarnation of God's presence in Jesus: "I tell you most solemnly, before Abraham came into being, I Am" (Jn 8:58). The words "I am" (*ego eimi*) refer to the scene of Exodus (Ex 3:14) where Yahweh revealed his name to Moses: "I am: 'I Am.'"[87] Yahweh was not using this name to appropriate an abstract existence, one that could suggest the translation: "I am the one who is." He was defining himself in terms of a concrete presence. He is always present, with a presence that cannot be destroyed and that remains immutably faithful. The "I am" guarantees the promise made to Moses for the success of his mission: "I shall be with you" (Ex 3:12).

This divine presence now resides in Jesus. The affirmation stresses the opposition between the "becoming" of Abraham[88] that belongs to creatures (cf. Jn 1:3), and the "to be" of the "I Am" anterior to all becoming.[89] The context shows that the "I Am" affirmed by Jesus is that of the Son (cf. Jn 8:54). It is distinct from the Father's, and therefore introduces a hitherto unknown distinction in the "I Am."

In John's Gospel, this attribution of the "I am" occurs more than once. Jesus tends to call for a faith that addresses itself to his "I am": "If you do not believe that I am He, you will die in your sins" (Jn 8:24). "When you have lifted up the Son of Man, then you will know that I am He" (Jn 8:28). "I tell you this now, before it happens, so that when it does happen you may believe that I am He" (Jn 13:19). The Greek expression *ego eimi* can be translated either "I am"

---

figuratively that they will come to see this; and indeed, at Cana they do see his glory" (*John*, I, 91).

[87] The shade of meaning of the *ego eimi* of Jn 8:58 is different from the other absolute *ego eimi*'s (8:24-28) because of the accent placed on the eternal being of Jesus, according to R. Schnackenburg (*Das Johannesevangelium*, II, Freiburg-Basel-Wien 1971, 300). This brings out more clearly the allusion to Ex 3:14.

[88] It could be translated "before Abraham was born," for the Greek verb can have this meaning (Barrett, *John*, 292). But it is more probable that the contrast indicated is between "to be" and "to become."

[89] Barrett translates: "Before Abraham came into being, I eternally was, as now I am and ever continue to be" (*John*, 292).

or "it is I." The allusion to the declarations of Second Isaiah [90] suggests the translation "it is I." We must indeed compare Jn 13:19 with Is 43:10: "I tell you this now, before it happens, so that when it does happen you may believe that I am He." [91] In Second Isaiah the formula "it is I" (*ānī - hū*) refers to the I of Yahweh. It is less explicit than the affirmation "I am Yahweh." [92] By using it, Jesus refers to his divine identity, while refraining from pronouncing the name of God. He adopts an expression that, by reason of its indetermination, can be used in human dialogue without necessarily shocking one's listeners and yet reveals its mystery only to those who want to enter into it.

We should note that the formula allows Jesus a perfect incarnation of his affirmation of divine identity. It permits him to say "It is I" (or "I am he") just as other men do when they want to be recognized by their friends or associates.

That is why we find the expression "It is I" or "I am he" in other Gospel contexts — for example, at the time of Jesus' conversation with the Samaritan woman (Jn 4:26), at the time of his arrest (Jn 18:5-9) — in which the words have first of all the ordinary meaning implied by the dialogue but also a mysterious sense suggested by the context.

Indeed, Jesus offers the Samaritan woman living water that wells up to eternal life (Jn 4:10-14). Thus, when he declares he is the Messiah by saying "I who am speaking to you, I am he" (Jn 4:26), he sets this messianism on a divine level by claiming the power to communicate divine life. The intimation of a divine mystery is likewise attested to when Jesus says "I am he" to those who have come to arrest him, making some of them fall to the ground as if forced to acknowledge his sovereignty in spite of themselves. [93]

Of particular interest is the concordance of the Fourth Gospel with Matthew and Mark in the episode when Jesus walks on the waters of the lake. All three include the for-

---

[90] Is 41:4; 43:10-25; 46:4; 48:12; 51:12; 52:6; cf. Dt 32:39.

[91] Cf. Feuillet, "Les *ego eimi* christologiques du quatrième évangile," *RSR* 1965, 5-22.

[92] The texts of Isaiah perhaps contain an allusion to Ex 3:14-16 (cf. Barrett, *John*, 283).

[93] Bultmann comments: "… the way one bows before an apparition of God" (*Das Evangelium des Johannes*, Göttingen 1952, 495).

mula: "It is I! Do not be afraid" (Mt 14:27; Mk 6:50; Jn 6:20). [94] This is the "It is I" of a man calling out to his friends, but also the cry of one who is revealing his divine power by his mastery over nature. [95] Behind these words we again find Second Isaiah: "Do not be afraid, for I have redeemed you ... For I am Yahweh, your God, the Holy One of Israel, your saviour" (Is 43:1-3). It even seems as though Jesus has walked out on the lake to justify this comparison, for the oracle also said: "Should you pass through the sea, I will be with you; or through rivers, they will not swallow you up" (Is 43:2). The entire incident unfolds as though Jesus were the "incarnation" of this prophetic announcement by visibly passing over the waters of the lake to be with his disciples. His "It is I!" resounds like Yahweh's in the Old Testament, and even in a certain sense in a more poignant way, through a palpable human presence. According to Matthew's testimony, the disciples recognized the presence of a divine mystery in Jesus, since they bowed down before him and said "Truly, you are the Son of God" (Mt 14:33). [96]

The agreement of John's Gospel with the Synoptics [97] confirms that the formula *ego eimi* is soundly rooted in tradition and is not John's theological invention. The context has the great advantage of showing that Jesus could use this locution in the most natural way, while enriching it with a secret

---

[94] While denying that in this case the *ego eimi* is a stereotyped formula of revelation which would identify Jesus purely and simply with God, Th. Snoy remarks: "By identifying himself as the one who walks on the waters, Jesus reveals himself to his disciples in the exercise of an extraordinary cosmic power, thus implying the truly superhuman quality of his personality, and hence, in a certain way, his divinity, although the text tells us nothing specific about the relationship of Jesus to God" ("La rédaction marcienne de Mc, VI, 45-52," *ETL* 44, 1968, 433, note 162). The context shows that the formula is not stereotyped, but also that it retains its value as revelation.

[95] The imperative "Do not be afraid!" corresponds to the style of theophanies, according to Snoy (*ibid.*, 434).

[96] The words "Truly, you are the Son of God" indicate that the declaration *ego eimi* must be understood strictly as a formula of divine Revelation," according to J. D. Kingsbury ("The Title 'Son of God' in Matthew's Gospel," *BTB* 5, 1975, 19).

[97] This is the only point of contact between John's Gospel and the Synoptics for this formula, and it is therefore more significant, according to Schnackenburg (*Johannes* II, 69).

meaning by virtue of the circumstances and by evoking prophetic texts.

The Synoptics (at least Mk 14:62 and Lk 22:70) present
the formula on still another occasion. This is the most solemn
and decisive declaration Jesus ever made of his identity. Jesus'
ego eimi in answer to Caiaphas cannot be interpreted as meaning simply: "Yes, that is right," in other words, "Yes, I am
the Son of God." Jesus certainly means to affirm that he is
the Son of God, but he does so in his own language, using
"it is I" or "I am" the way Yahweh did in the Old Testament.
He knows that by giving this answer he is blaspheming in the
view of his enemies and bringing on his own death sentence.
But his use of this formula implies a persistence in being that
can overcome death. The *ego eimi* has the value of a presence
that can never again be snatched from this world.

Finally, after the Resurrection, it is by this formula that
Jesus gets his disciples to recognize him: "Look at my hands
and feet; yes, it is I indeed" (Lk 24:39). In this last instance
we must conclude that even in his new risen state his divine
presence remains incarnate.

Jesus promises this presence in perpetuity to his disciples:
"And know that I am with you always; yes, to the end of
time" (Mt 28:20). The formula of the Old Testament covenant "I shall be with you" (Ex 3:12) now takes on its definitive
form with an essential innovation, namely, that henceforth the
divine presence will continue to be a human presence as well.
The fully incarnate "I am" or "It is I" is now even more inseparable from the "with you."

There is confirmation here of the value of the ontological.
In the great moment when Jesus sends his disciples out on
mission, he promises them his help and the communication of
his power: "All authority in heaven and on earth has been
given to me. Go, therefore, make disciples of all the nations"
(Mt 28:18-19). But he does more. He promises to be present
to them. He wants their mission to be rooted in this accompanying presence.

The presence Jesus promises his disciples is essentially
dynamic. The words "to the end of time" are more than a
chronological reference. They suggest that all of history, along
with the development of the Church, will bear the mark of

the incarnational dynamism that will progressively permeate humankind until the requisite degree of incarnation for the fullness of time is attained.

(2) - The theology of the *ego eimi*

The expression *ego eimi* has first of all an anthropological sense that corresponds to the human situations in which Jesus says: "It is I." Starting from these situations, it goes on to evoke a mystery and imply a theology. The words "It is I" are best suited to make others recognize a familiar presence. It is in this context that Christ chooses to reveal his identity. Let us note carefully that the primary purpose of the formula is to affirm not a remoteness, but a proximity.

The most meaningful example is Jesus' walking on the lake, because when he says: "It is I! Do not be afraid" (Mk 6:50; Mt 14:27; Jn 6:20), he wants to be recognized as a a friend who is not to be feared. At the same time, Jesus insinuates his divine identity by the miraculous mode of his approach and the allusion to a prophetic oracle in which Yahweh's "Do not be afraid . . . for I am Yahweh" (Is 43:1-3) is meant to banish fear. Consequently, to translate the intent of "It is I!" one would have to paraphrase: "I do not want anyone to be afraid, for though my 'I' is divine, I want you to recognize me as your very close friend."

Contrary to what the translation "I am" might suggest, the accent is on the presence rather than on existence as such. Already in the Old Testament, the name that Yahweh used in identifying himself to Moses, "I Am: 'I Am'" (Ex 3:14), was meant to give a pledge of perpetual presence, in fidelity to the covenant: "I shall be with you" (Ex 3:12). Each time Jesus uses *ego eimi* he wants to affirm his presence, that is to say, an existence that is not turned inward on itself but oriented toward men and in contact with them. Presence is "existence for others."

When Jesus says "I am he" to the Samaritan woman who awaits the coming of the Messiah in some indefinite future, his words express the gift of a presence here and now. Even when Jesus' attention bears on the eternity of his existence, he is referring to his presence: " . . . before Abraham came into being, I Am" (Jn 8:58). According to the dialogue, Jesus

166

wants to affirm that he was already present to Abraham, and that this presence will continue for those who claim to be of Abraham's lineage. When he calls for faith in the *ego eimi*: "so that . . . you may believe that I am He" (Jn 13:19; cf. 8:24-28), he is speaking of faith in his presence as well as of faith in his identity.

At the time of his arrest, Jesus says "I am he" with the intention of dominating his enemies with his presence. In answer to Caiaphas he says "*ego eimi*" to affirm a presence that can never be snatched away, thus guaranteeing the coming of the Son of Man on the clouds of heaven. After the Resurrection, the triumph of this presence rings out in the words "it is I indeed" (Lk 24:39). The promise of a perpetual presence is solemnly addressed to the disciples.

This last promise shows that Jesus' presence is oriented toward the future. Henceforth the "I am with you" presence will be the developmental principle of the history of humankind, the force that will lead the way to the last days (cf. Mt 28:20). Creation will be brought to completion not only by the Absolute Being who immerses himself in its becoming, but also by the presence of an "I" who wants to gather all men around himself.

The presence implicit in Jesus' "I am he" is essentially benevolent. Far from condemning the Samaritan woman, it draws her to conversion and faith. The "It is I" of the one who walks on the waters brings succor to the disciples threatened by a violent storm and offers to communicate to Peter his own power over the waves. During his Passion, Christ's "I am he" reveals his accessibility and courtesy to his enemies, and his refusal to enter into a hostile encounter with them. The "I am with you" of the risen Lord, which literally translates as "I with you am," expresses in the Biblical Greek the unbreakable bond that joins the "I am" to the "with you." The covenant is in some way incorporated into the "I am" of Christ. Even what is most personal to Jesus, his "It is I," is henceforth shared with his disciples.

The formula *ego eimi* therefore contains an affirmation of love. Admittedly, it lifts the veil on Jesus' divine transcendence, for through these words he expresses his dominion over the flow of time, past and future, a serenity that places him

167

above the tumult of events, above the roar of seas and winds, and finally points to his triumph over death. Yet he highlights the power of the *ego eimi* only in view of communicating it to his disciples for their benefit. He reveals his eternal being for the purpose of achieving communion.

Lastly, it is important to stress that the "I" of the formula is not a self-centered "ego." It is the "I" of the Son who lives by his relationship to the Father. This is clearly shown by the context of the three *ego eimi's* in the 8th Chapter of John. This is also the meaning of the supreme declaration before the Sanhedrin meant to guarantee the identity of the Son of God, as recorded in the Synoptics. Jesus' final promise, "I am with you," comes after he has affirmed that all power has been given to him (cf. Mt 28:18). It is as the Son of the Father that Jesus remains present among his own.

c - The presence, a source of life

Presence takes on still another aspect in the metaphor of the vine: "I am the vine, you are the branches" (Jn 15:5). Here Christ's presence involves a permanent communication of life. It is no longer merely a "remaining with" but a "dwelling in." Jesus now gives his disciples this command: "Make your home in me, as I make mine in you" (Jn 15:4).

The divine presence incarnate in Jesus thus tends to extend its power of incarnation to the disciples. The divinity of this presence is emphasized by the image of the vine from which the life-giving sap emanates. Only God can be the wellspring of life. If we ask ourselves what is most authentic in John's depiction of presence as source of life, we must attribute the image of the vine to Jesus. [98] Presence as a "dwelling in" therefore goes back to Jesus' own thinking, at least in the measure that it explains the image. Now, this image signifies a constant vital influx into the branches joined to the vine. [99]

---

[98] The literary style is that of the *mashal,* as in the text of the good shepherd. Brown notes that in John the element of allegory is stronger than the element of parable (*John,* 668). The Evangelist tends to emphasize the ontological aspect of Jesus.

[99] The image is clearly related to the Eucharist; however the application is more general and concerns the whole of the life communicated by Jesus. We do not agree with R. Brown when he says that "the relation is primarily

There is question of a dynamic presence. The accent is no longer on person-to-person relations, as in the "to be with" or the image of the good shepherd. The presence now involves the vital welling up of life, the transformation of human nature.

This image is closely related to the Eucharist, and Jesus uses it in his commentary on the Last Supper. It shows that the wine given as the blood of the covenant is not merely a transitory or intermittent gift. It is the expression of a deeper gift of ongoing presence.

It is therefore in the context of this presence that the institution of the Eucharist attains its full meaning. The words "This is my body" ("my flesh") and "this is my blood" are, as it were, a special incarnation of the "it is I." Flesh and blood certainly have their concrete material signification, but they designate the human reality by implying the presence of the person. They cannot be detached from the *ego eimi,* or from the "And know that I am with you always; yes, to the end of time" (Mt 28:20). In the promise of the Eucharist, as recorded by John, the affirmation "I am the bread of life" (Jn 6:35-48), [100] "I am the living bread which has come down from heaven" (Jn 6:51; cf. 6:41) recurs with the explanation: "the bread that I shall give is my flesh, for the life of the world" (Jn 6:51).

Jesus affirms that he actualizes what the manna of earlier times had figuratively announced. He actualizes it in an "I am" or "it is I" that evokes the supremely living being that is God himself. And so he not only gives life, but is himself life (cf. Jn 11:25; 14:6).

The Eucharist has too often been conceived as an isolated reality. There has been a failure to adequately discern the sacramental presence of Jesus as a special manifestation of the more extensive presence he promised to his disciples. The Eucharist has too often been thought of as a self-contained whole. There has also been a tendency to consider it solely

---

one of love [and faith] and only secondarily eucharistic" (*John,* 674). We prefer to say that the relationship involves an infusion of life whose most typical expression is the Eucharist.

[100] In itself, the affirmation of Jn 6:35 does not allude directly to the Eucharist. It has a broader significance, but the Eucharistic finality is present (cf. Schnackenburg, *Johannes* II, 59).

in its immediate functional aspect: the aspect of food and drink, that makes it resemble other meals. This functional aspect is essential, but it cannot overshadow the ontological aspect, which is still more fundamental. Jesus does not affirm: "this is your food," "this is your drink." He says: "This is my body," "this is my blood." It is an affirmation of his personal presence in his own body, flesh and blood, in their glorious state and filled with the spirit (cf. Jn 6:63), but which remain flesh and blood and insure the incarnation of the divine presence.

While we must safeguard the Gospel context of the institution of the Eucharist, the fulfillment of this Eucharist in memory of Christ must take place in the perspective of his "it is I." Indeed, the "memory" is simply the actualization of the presence. The meal is the penetration of this same presence into the innermost life of each of the disciples.

CHAPTER VI

KENOSIS AND GLORY

The words through which Jesus revealed his identity do not have the fulgurant brightness we might have hoped for or anticipated from someone who wanted others to recognize him as the Son of God. They continue to be subject to debate because of the obscurity that surrounds them. Jesus never swerved from his discretion of manner. He could so easily have affirmed openly that he was God, yet he never did so. He proceeded by way of allusions, intimations, or veiled proofs that left untouched the aura of mystery that surrounded him.

There is no cause for surprise, therefore, that exegetes can be at odds as to the true significance of Jesus' testimony about himself. First of all, there are the inevitable deficiencies in the transmission of his words in the Gospel texts, and the special coloration each Evangelist brought to his account. Then, too, there is the difficulty caused by the language that Jesus deliberately chose to use, and whose meaning is not immediately evident. It is a way of speaking that poses problems, provides many converging clues as to the answers, but still does not have the luminous and irrefutable content that would eliminate all uncertainty as to the truth affirmed.

A. THE OBSCURITY OF THE REVELATION

1. *The Difference between the Language Jesus Used and the Language of the Community*

Jesus never spoke about himself in the terms the primitive Christian community used to designate him. Even though the Gospel texts sometimes insert into his recorded words titles

171

such as Son or Son of God, they allow us to discover his own way of speaking about his identity, in which no title in the strict sense of the word appears.

We cannot say that "Son of Man" is a title, at least in the sense of a quality that directly reveals Jesus' mission or transcendent personality. It is an expression which in itself signifies no more than "man." That is why it was not absorbed into the language of faith of the community. Actually, Jesus used it in a sense that indicated his mission and his transcendent personality, but this meaning escaped his hearers.

The difference between the language of Christian faith and the language Jesus spoke is a guarantee of the authenticity of his testimony. [1] The primitive community could not have invented language different from the one it used, and it could only record Jesus as saying what it said about him. For those who vigorously professed that Jesus was the Lord and the Son of God, it would have been almost inconceivable to present this same Jesus speaking in an obscure manner about his identity.

We are therefore brought into contact with Jesus in his own mysterious way of presenting his divine identity, of saying "Abba" and "it is I," of calling himself the Son of Man, identifying himself with the covenant, claiming and exercising divine powers, explaining that he is God's Word and God's presence, acting as the master and center of the kingdom. He had a unique way of speaking about himself, and it has remained unique. In explicating its faith, the Christian community could not remain at this stage. What the community attributed to Jesus was always based on what Jesus had said and done, but had not himself formulated in the same way.

The difference between what the Christian community said about Jesus and what he himself said retains its relevance. It enables us to grasp the fundamental meaning of Jesus' revelation of himself, a revelation that goes far beyond all subsequent formulations.

This difference makes us understand the inadequacy of any approach that would claim to find in the primitive community,

---

[1] The value of the criterion of discontinuity is unanimously admitted by exegetes. Cf. Latourelle, "Critères d'authenticité historique des Evangiles," Gr 1974, 622.

rather than in the historical Jesus, the origin of the Christian faith. The dynamism of Christology stems from Jesus himself, and more precisely from the awareness that Jesus had of his identity. We find this awareness expressing itself in the Gospels in a way that takes precedence over all formulations. It inspired the formulas of faith, without however ever being totally encompassed by them. That is why it will always remain the primary testimony to which faith must turn as its point of reference.

2. Jesus' Abstention from the Use of Titles

Why did not Jesus present himself by titles that would have been much more clear-cut, such as Messiah, Son of God, Lord, God?

If he had used these titles, he would have run the risk or incomprehension. He could have led his hearers into error.

If Jesus had identified himself as the *Messiah,* his entourage would have expected to find in him the answer to their hopes of an earthly and political messianism. We know that the Jewish populace was looking for a national liberator, and that, on the occasion of the multiplication of the loaves and the fishes they thought they had found in Jesus their long-awaited king. The disciples likewise hoped for the restoration of the kingdom of Israel. Indeed, as is shown by their question at the time of the Ascension, they expected this restoration until the very last moment.

We can understand why Jesus avoided calling himself "Christ" or "Son of David." If he had, he would have been giving a false idea of himself, granted the prevailing attitudes of his contemporaries. When Peter made his profession of faith saying, "You are the Christ" (Mt 16:16), he went on immediately to show that he had not understood the meaning of a messianism destined to be realized through death and resurrection. In actual fact, it was only after Jesus' definitive departure from this world that he could be called the Christ or the Messiah according to the true significance of the titles, and without danger of ambiguity. [2]

---

[2] The messianic secret therefore comes to an end with the glorification of Jesus, because this spiritual glorification definitively removes all doubt as

Why did not Jesus choose to identify himself as the "*Son of God*," the title that would be used to identify him in the pronouncements of faith? Even when he answered the solemn questioning on his identity during his trial, he avoided repeating the expression used by the high priest, despite the affirmative nature of his response.

The appellation "Son of God" could not have expressed the uniqueness of Jesus, at least in the light of the various attributions it had been given in the Old Testament. It had been used to denote the angels (Ps 29:1; Jb 1:6; 2:1; 38:7); the people of Israel (Ex 4:22; Ho 11:1; Jr 31:9,20; Ws 18:13); the Israelites in general (Ho 2:1; Dt 14:1; Is 1:2); certain individuals who enjoyed eminent social dignity, princes and judges (Ps 82:6), and above all kings (2 S 7:14; 1 Ch 17:13; 22:10; 28:6); individuals endowed with exceptional moral perfection, the just (Ws 2:18; 5:5; 12:19), and the charitable (Si 4:10); the messianic king (Ps 2:7; cf. Ps. 89:27).

In the face of such an array of applications, Jesus could not use the title "Son of God" to identify himself in a unique way. He retained the broad meaning of the expression when he called peacemakers "sons of God" (Mt 5:9), and those who love their enemies sons of the Father (Mt 5:45; Lk 6:35). He likewise bestowed the title "children of the resurrection" (Lk 20:36) on those who have risen from the dead and whose life is henceforth like that of the angels.

In any event the expression "son of God" applied better to others than to himself. In itself, it is not the most exact term to describe the person of Jesus. By distinguishing the son from God, it suggests that this son is simply a man. Now, as Son of God, Jesus is God. In strict interpretation, "Son of God" would signify that he is the Son of the trinitarian

---

to the nature of the messianic power of the Savior of mankind. This explains why, after the Transfiguration, Jesus could order his disciples to keep silence "until the Son of Man has risen from the dead" (Mt 17:9; Mk 9:9). Now, G. Minette de Tillesse (*Le secret messianique dans l'évangile de Marc*, Paris, 1968, 506) has tried to attribute the messianic secret of Mark to a "Paschal rereading of the life of Jesus." Such a view seems to misunderstand the true origin of this secret, which belonged to the earthly life of Jesus and had no need to be maintained after Easter. It was the mortal Jesus who needed to avoid any danger of having his contemporaries misunderstand his messianic quality and who had to be extremely prudent in making it known.

God, and hence his own Son and the Son of the Holy Spirit. In the correct use of the term, Jesus is the Son of the Father, he is God the Son in relation to God the Father. The Christian community gave expression "Son of God" the meaning that corrected any imperfect interpretation, i.e., the sense of "God the Son." Jesus was being meticulously exact when he abstained from applying this title to himself. [3]

Could not Jesus have forestalled debates as to his divine identity by bluntly affirming that he was *God*? Even such an affirmation would not have sufficed to obviate all doubts and controversies, for there were bound to be attempts to elude its meaning.

Certain recent interpretations of the expression "true God," used by the Council of Chalcedon, have sought to reduce it to the meaning of "true manifestation of God." This shows that even the most clear-cut affirmations can be subjected to distorted exegeses. [4]

And yet in this case too, there would have been a serious risk of error. If Jesus had declared he was God, he would have seemed to be identifying himself with the Yahweh of the Old Testament, whom Israel had learned to look to as a Father. Now, Jesus could not let anyone think he was the Father. He could claim to be God only by making it clear that he was the Son, personally distinct from the Father. As it was not easy for his hearers to grasp this distinction between divine persons he avoided making an affirmation that would most certainly have created misunderstandings.

If Jesus had simply presented himself to this contemporaries as God, he would have brought them only a misleading insight and roused even more hostile reactions. His claim would have seemed still less acceptable for being misconstrued.

---

[3] P. Benoit has remarked that Jesus could not come out and clearly say: "I am the Son of God" at a time "when such an assertion could not be understood in its true meaning" ("La divinité de Jesus dans les évangiles synoptiques," *LV* 9, 1953, 59). But it is important to add that besides the difficulty of making the meaning of such a title clear, the title in itself did not have the desirable exactness.

[4] Thus, Hans Küng explains "true God" by affirming that Jesus is a representative of God, and that in him God reveals himself to us (*Christ sein*, Munich-Zurich 1974, 439-440), but he expressly refrains from acknowledging that Jesus is really God.

Finally, let us ask ourselves why Jesus did not assume the title that the first Christian community later gave him by preference, the title of "Lord." The answer is reliably suggested by several of Christ's words recorded in the Gospels. The title of "Lord" would have had the advantage of implying a certain distinction between the Son and the Father. This is the terminology Paul adopts when he proclaims faith in "one God, the Father, ... and one Lord, Jesus Christ" (1 Co 8:6).[5] But if Jesus had assumed this title, it would have had the disadvantage of sounding like a claim to domination. Now, if there is any attitude that is fundamental to Jesus, it is the desire to serve. The term "Lord" would have been inappropriate to express this attitude.

According to John's account, Jesus brought out the contrast between the appellation "Lord" and the humility that consisted in washing his disciples' feet: "You call me Master and Lord ..." (Jn 13:13).[6] This most striking contrast presupposes that the title of Lord did not square with the disposition to humble service. If Jesus had called himself "Lord" he would have given a false image of his innermost intentions and attitudes.

3. A Revelation Addressed to the Poor

Why did not Jesus use a more precise terminology to define his identity? While avoiding titles that might lead to confusion, he could have offered a certain number of clarifications that would have made the task of future interpreters and theologians easier. Indeed, this might have spared the Church the violent Christological controversies of the early centuries.

---

[5] Moreover Paul was only adopting a terminology that had preceded him, as we see for instance in Rm 10:9: "If your lips confess that Jesus is Lord and if you believe in your heart that God raised him from the dead, then you will be saved." Langevin stresses that a study of this text shows how deeply the confession of the Lord Jesus "is imbedded at the heart of Pauline faith" (*Jésus Seigneur et l'eschatologie,* 314).

[6] According to St. John, Jesus adds: "and rightly; so I am" (Jn 13:13). This clarification seems to explicate the inner meaning of Jesus' words. The point of the lesson could be paraphrased: "Since you call me Lord and you have seen me wash your feet, you are under the greater obligation to wash one another's feet." The Evangelist did not want to give the impression that Jesus was refusing the title of Lord.

It is a fact that Jesus did not speak on a level of philosophical speculation or even of conceptual pronouncements. He abstained from using learned terminology of any kind. When he said he had been sent "to bring the good news to the poor" (Lk 4:18), he pinpointed the essential reason for this abstention. He wanted to speak a language understandable to all, and especially to those who had not had the advantages of advanced academic training. Even so, we must rightly understand his intention. He did not mean to impoverish his self-revelation by refusing to disclose certain aspects of his identity and of his message to those with insufficient education.

Jesus' art consists in expressing himself in simple terms, which he fills with a very dense and rich meaning. The result is that he reveals to his hearers the essence of his identity and mission, together with the plan of salvation, in language that they can understand. The proof of this lies in the way his disciples, who were not particularly well educated, accepted and grasped the revelation offered to them: "The mystery of the kingdom of God is given to you" (Mk 4:11). The "mystery" refers in this context to God's secret plan. [7]

Let us take an example. Jesus never explicitly affirms that he is the Son begotten of the Father from all eternity. But he presents himself as actually possessing a unique sonship

---

[7] If Jesus' language is so accessible, how does it happen that many do not comprehend it? The answer is: "to those who are outside, everything comes in parables" (Mk 4:11). These words apply especially to the crowds who hear the parables without grasping their meaning. However, several exegetes, and Taylor in particular (cf. *Mark*, 256), remark that verses 11-12 constitute an insertion. and that we do not know their primitive context. According to Taylor, the translation should be: "everything comes to be a riddle." This is the sense proposed by J. Jeremias (*Les paraboles de Jésus*, Le Puy 1966, 19 ff.). G. Minette de Tillesse would expand the meaning of the word "parables," extending it — following E. Lohmeyer — to Jesus' symbolic actions. According to Mark, the crowd remains at the level of a general instruction without grasping the mystery of the kingdom, which is an absolute Innovation (*Le secret messianique*, 215 ff.). If the phrase is not limited to the specific context where Mark inserted it, "those who are outside" would denote, strictly speaking, not the crowd but those who do not accept the message of the good news. The mystery or secret of salvation escapes these latter, for the most they can do is retain the images, the outer wrapping of Jesus' words and actions. What is involved here is not Jesus' language but the receptiveness of those exposed to his words.

with respect to the Father. It is the plenitude of this sonship that matters at the moment he reveals it. The antecedents that it implies will later become the object of theological investigation. They are of no immediate interest to Jesus' hearers who simply need to know that he is the Son in the most complete sense of sonship.

4. The Various Ways Transcendence is Expressed

If we seek the reason why Jesus abstained from making precise formulations as to his identity, we can discern in particular his determination to prevent the truth he was bringing from being reduced to formulas. He wanted to provide testimony concerning himself that would overflow the limits of any formulation whatsoever.

At a still deeper level, we perceive the fact that Jesus realized the impossibility of finding adequate terms in which to tell what God is. The revelation of Jesus' identity poses the problem of the revelation of God, and of the defectiveness of all human language to present this revelation.

This explains the various *modes of expression* used by Jesus.

a - The use of questions

On the one hand, Jesus invites questions, either by his way of speaking about himself: "Who are you?" (Jn 8:25); [8] "Who is this Son of Man?" (Jn 12:34); "Are you a greater man than our father Jacob ...?" (Jn 4:12); or by his way of acting: "Who can this be? Even the wind and the sea obey him" (Mk 4:41 par.).

On the other hand, Jesus himself asks questions of his own: "David himself calls him Lord, in what way then can he be his son?" (Mk 12:37, par.); "But ... who do you say I am?" (Mk 8:29).

---

[8] Barrett sees in this question an example of the misunderstanding typical of the Johannine style. The Jews understand Jesus' *ego eimi* as an unfinished sentence (*John*, 283). However, the questioning arises spontaneously because of Jesus' way of affirming himself, and he seems to deliberately invite this interrogation, at least on the part of those who do not immediately agree with the views he expresses.

This method of interrogation is rooted in the principle that God is the one who poses the most fundamental question to man, a question that in a certain respect is beyond all possible answers. Every revelation of God is first of all a question.

b - Transcending the past

Jesus declares he transcends even the most sublime manifestations or messengers of God in Judaism: "Now here, I tell you, is something greater than the Temple" (Mt 12:6); "... and there is something greater than Jonah here" (Mt 12:41); "... and there is something greater than Solomon here" (Mt 12:42); "I tell you most solemnly, before Abraham came into being, I Am" (Jn 8:58).

The neuter is used for the "greater than" of Jonah and of Solomon, suggesting that the transcendence involves more than the superiority of one person over another. There is a still greater reality, one that is above human realities. [9]

c - The double meaning

Jesus makes use of expressions which, underneath their obvious meaning in human relations, take on a transcendent significance by virtue of the context or the circumstances. A characteristic example is Jesus' use of "it is I" (*ego eimi*). Within the "it is I" of a man who identifies himself before those around him, surfaces the "I Am" or "it is I" of God himself.

The name "Son of Man" likewise has a limited, literal signification that identifies someone as a man, but Jesus uses it in such a way as to bring out his divine origin, attributes, and sonship.

Those who want to elude the mystery are free to stop at the first meaning. But those who are fully open to the search for God discover the deeper, more hidden meaning.

---

[9] Grundmann comments: "neuter, and therefore mysterious," preferring this rendition to the use of the masculine, adopted by a few manuscripts (*Matthäus,* 321).

d - The human appropriation of God's ways of speaking and acting

Jesus speaks with the authority of God himself: "Amen," "I tell you most solemnly," "but I say to you." He acts with the powers of God: he performs miracles, forgives sins, considers himself above the sabbath, and in general behaves as the master of the economy of salvation.

Within his human language and action, the divine is hidden, and at the same time revealed. The simplicity of Jesus' way of acting and speaking seems disproportionate to the transcendence he affirms through these words and actions. Here again, those who refuse to accept his transcendence can point to their inherent simplicity.

e - Intimacy with the Father

The close contacts Jesus maintained with the Father placed him on a footing of equality with God. "Abba" attests to the absence of any remoteness between Father and Son.

Exegetes often refer to Christ's relations with God. It would be more accurate, and more in keeping with Jesus' mode of consciousness, to speak of his relations with his Father. The innovation consists in the fact that a man addresses God as Father habitually, thereby attesting that this man's true condition is not simply that of a creature before God, but of a son who shares the Father's own life.

Jesus' human language expresses his divine transcendence only indirectly. "Abba" points to his closeness to the Father rather than to the distance that separates God from man. But precisely because of this, the word "Abba" indicates that the distance has been spanned and that in consequence he can remedy the ineptness of human notions concerning intimacy with God.

f - Convergence

Since human terms are always inadequate to express the divine identity they seek to reveal, Jesus strengthens their evocative power by using them to confirm one another. In instances where a term might seem to lack clarity and provoke doubts, its convergence with other terms strengthens the intimation of divine identity. For instance, when the affirmation "there is something greater than Jonah here" (Mt 12:41) is isolated, it can easily give rise to disagreements. But when it is used in relation to others like "greater than Solomon," "greater than the Temple," its aptness to denote divine identity is enhanced.

Convergences such as these enable us to discern Jesus' inference of his divine identity in many of his sayings. They help us to realize that the Gospel texts are filled with hints of Christ's divinity; but only those who are disposed to discover his divinity acknowledge these convergences. The variety of the affirmations brings to light the many-faceted aspects of the human presence of God that are fused in the person of Jesus.

5. The Permanence of the Mystery

The common denominator of the diverse kinds of expression is that they all bring out the inadequacy of the revelation as compared with what is being revealed. The identity of Jesus remains a mystery.[10] Jesus could certainly have made doctrinal declarations regarding his identity. But if he had done so, he would have led his hearers to think that the innermost reality of his personality could be grasped through some intellectual pronouncement. A divine identity can be revealed as it really is only by manifestly exceeding all our human concepts. Jesus continually inspired those around him with a sense of the intense mystery of his person.

From this we cannot conclude that he could not or would not express his divine person in a human way, or that everything he said amounted to a stammering that left us at the thereshold of the underlying reality. Jesus has truly introduced us into the mystery of his person, while allowing the mystery to retain its unique quality. By taking a thoroughly existential approach to humanity he expressed what God is in a human life in the most comprehensible way. The ob-

---

[10] The term "mystery" is more appropriate than "secret." A mystery denotes a reality that in itself objectively exceeds any effort to know it, whereas a "secret" can relate to a subjective attitude of reserve and silence. In Jesus, we find more than an attitude of discretion. There is a transcendent reality that cannot be adequately expressed in human terms.

scurity of the revelation cannot allow us to ignore the divine light he has brought us. Jesus has shown God in such a way that whoever has seen him has truly seen the Father. There could not have been a more complete and accurate way of presenting the invisible God than the way Jesus chose. The incarnation of the revelation has been perfect to the extent of human capacities for expressing it.

B. A Call to Faith and a Kenosis

Judging from the way Jesus revealed his divine identity, it is evident that his discretion was more than a kind of prudence resulting from circumstances. Admittedly, prudence was necessary so as not to subject his hearers to a shock that might have shattered them. The monotheistic faith of Israel could not but resist the revelation of someone who presented himself as the Son of God. Yet the need to adapt to the mentality of the people among whom he lived — an act of adaptation that was one of the aspects of the Incarnation itself — was not the only reason for Jesus veiled affirmations concerning his identity. At a deeper level, there was a need to adapt the revelation of God to human realities as such.

This adaptation of a more universal sort was part of the economy of salvation destined to inaugurate the order of faith in Christ, and that presented him in the "emptied" state of kenosis.

1. *The Call to Faith*

Jesus' revelation addresses itself to faith. That is why it eschews prodigies that would situate his earthly coming in the order of vision rather than of faith. Above all, it demands an active faith that involves an effort at discovery. If Jesus had revealed himself in a way that explicitly said or made known everything about him with the greatest possible clarity, faith would have been forced upon its recipients for their passive acceptance. To the contrary, the mark of Jesus' self-revelation is to demand collaboration. Thus, it is the duty of those who receive it to penetrate into the mystery of his person, and it is the task of the Christian community to formulate its own commitment of faith.

Jesus is not content simply to lead his disciples onto the path of faith in God. Essentially, the faith demanded in the Gospels is a new faith, faith in Jesus himself. This faith must take on a firm consistency, find expression among his loyal followers. Jesus does not formulate their faith for them. He presents the reality to be believed, and above all his own divine person. But he does so in such a way that this presentation, by reason of its mystery, will stimulate the effort of believers to know and express what they believe.

2. Incarnation and Kenosis

Finally, we discover the reason for the obscurity in which faith in Jesus, God Incarnate, developed. This obscurity is explained by the plan of the Redemption and by an Incarnation that is fundamentally sacrificial. We are now on the threshold of the mystery of kenosis.

Let us call to mind the passage of the Christological hymn used by the primitive Christian community and adopted by Paul to exhort the Philippians to imitate the sentiments of Christ Jesus:

"Who, being in the form of God,
   did not consider equality with God
      something to be grasped,
   but emptied himself,
      taking the very nature of a servant,
      being made in human likeness.
And being found in appearance as a man,
   he humbled himself
      and became obedient to death —
         even death on a cross!" (Ph 2:6-8)

It is remarkable that this very ancient hymn should conceive of the Incarnation as a "making into nothing," an "emptying." Even though certain exegetes would prefer to interpret this annihilation as applying only to the redemptive sacrifice, it is difficult to deny that Paul is referring to the very act of the Incarnation, inasmuch as the one who was "in the form of

God" "emptied himself, ... being made in human likeness" and "taking the form of a servant"? From this point of view the hymn brings out very clearly a sacrificial aspect that is only discreetly suggested in the hymn of John's Prologue: "The Word became flesh" (Jn 1:14). John insist on the aspect of "glory" that the Incarnation manifests, whereas Paul lays greater stress on its orientation toward redemptive sacrifice. The boldness of thought expressed in Paul's hymn consists in discerning a sacrifice in the very fact of the Incarnation, in the passage from a divine state to the condition of a servant, and in seeing the sacrifice of Calvary as the consummation of this primordial sacrifice.

Of its nature, the Incarnation could have been of a glorious sort. The flesh could have manifested the splendor of the divine state from the start. But kenosis implies the choice of a different kind of Incarnation, one that contrasts with Adam's sinful act. For the first man had heeded the voice that told him: "you will be like gods" (Gn 3:5). In other words, he had wanted, in his human condition, to grasp at equality with God. Christ, on the other hand, although by nature divine, refused to grasp this equality. He preferred to assume "the very nature of a servant."

Let us consider the meaning of the affirmation: "Who ... did not consider equality with God something to be grasped" (Ph 2:6). We have already indicated the difficulty it raises. Many commentators have interpreted this equality as being identical with the "form of God." As a result, they have not given the proper sense to the act of grasping. For when one already possesses equality, he does not have to "cling" fearfully to it. These exegetes have translated Paul's words to mean: "cling jealously to." But this does not preserve the full force of the term. This is made quite clear by the reference to Adam. Equality with God is not the simple fact of "being in the form of God." Rather, it is to live man's life as Adam would have wanted to, [11] after the manner of God and

---

[11] We cannot minimize this reference to Adam by asking: "Where is the temptation of the second Adam?" (J. Ernst, *Die Briefe an die Philipper, an Philemon, an die Kolosser, an die Epheser*, Regensburg, 1974, 67). We might answer first of all that Jesus was indeed tempted to follow the path of miraculous interventions. But more fundamentally still, here the opposi-

enjoying his sovereign prerogatives. It designates the glorious state that Christ did not want to usurp during his earthly life and that he received subsequent to the sacrifice of the Cross.

So we see that the Incarnation was effectuated in a renouncement so total that it is defined by the words "he emptied himself." How did Christ who was "in form of God" empty himself? Certainly he was not divested of his divine nature, for he "was existing" in the form of God. [12] The intimation seems to be that since Christ, before his Incarnation, was living in the glorious state of God himself, he had a certain right to appear on earth in his divine glory, that is, to assume the state of "equality with God" or of glorified humanity. He renounced this right, and, in this sense, by entering the human condition "he emptied himself."

The kenotic character of the Incarnation shows more forcefully how even the type of revelation Jesus adopted was part of a sacrificial choice. If he had wanted a revelation of the glorious kind that would show his divinity in its splendor, he would have wanted to grasp, as man, "the equality with God." Jesus' enemies, or more generally those who could not make themselves believe in him demanded prodigies that would provide this glorious evidence. By rejecting such requests, Jesus restated his adherence to the divine plan of an Incarnation along the lines of an emptying and of a sacrifice.

3. Jesus' Affirmation of the Kenosis

What is the source of this idea of kenosis expressed in the Christological hymn? It presupposes reflection on the very act of the Incarnation, but it is essentially based on what Jesus said about himself. We can establish a parallel between the hymn and Jesus' declaration about the ransom: "For the Son of Man himself did not come to be served but to serve, and to give his life as a ransom for many" (Mk 10:45; Mt 20:28). [13]

---

tion between Christ and Adam is not based on the idea of temptation but on their contrary modes of behavior. The evocation of Adam need not encompass all aspects of the account of the Fall.

[12] The Greek use of the participle indicates an enduring state, as is the case of the present participles used by Paul with an aorist.

[13] The corresponding text of Luke 22:27 is different. According to

Here we find outlined in a very simple way the two stages of the emptying, first the stage of the Incarnation strictly speaking, then the stage of the redemptive sacrifice. Christ Jesus whose "state was divine" and who "became as men are" is paralleled by the "Son of Man" who has come: This Son of Man whose state in Daniel's oracle was divine, is seen here in a coming that implies a preexistence. Now, he has come not to be served, that is to say, not to grasp the condition of equality with God, but to serve, to assume the condition of a slave.

To give one's life "as a ransom for many" indicates the ultimate meaning of the emptying in the redemptive sacrifice. This sense is evoked in the hymn by the humiliation and death of the cross. The difference lies in the point of view. The hymn tends to stress the moral value of the abasement, and Paul sees in its an example for Christians to imitate. Jesus for his part, deliberately indicates his intention to obtain the salvation of mankind. [14] He affirms more explicitly his concern for others and the salvific efficacy for many, whereas the hymn focuses on the person of Jesus, on his abasement and on the glorious elevation that results from it.

Despite a notable difference in vocabulary, the doctrinal concordance is remarkable. We can conclude that Jesus expressed the kenosis in equivalent terms when he rejected any claim to be served by others and presented the coming of the Son of Man as a service and a sacrifice.

Moreover, Jesus' own words indicate most effectively the altruistic meaning of kenosis. The Christological hymn closes with a picture of the triumph of Jesus, before whom the whole of creation "should bend the knee" (Ph 2:10), so that he who has assumed the condition of a slave finally attains a glorious state where he is served. This approach makes us rediscover the perspective of the Son of Man described in Daniel's oracle,

---

Jeremias (*Théologie du N.T.*, 366), it consists in the literarily independent composition of one and the same group of logia.

[14] Paul stresses elsewhere the redemptive value of Christ's actions. The failure to mention the salvation of mankind helps to show that the hymn did not originate in Paul's thinking. The vocabulary and other aspects of the hymn likewise lead to this conclusion: there is a substitution of the dialectic of preexistence-emptying-elevation for the schema death-resurrection (cf. Ernst, *Philipper*, 65 ff.).

a personage served by all nations. Now, Jesus specifically set his conception of the coming of the Son of Man in opposition to Daniel's. The Son of Man did not come to be served. He meant to fulfill the prophecy in an altogether different way, the way of the suffering servant. It would be hard to claim that when Jesus declared he did not want to be served but to serve, he nevertheless was oriented toward a destiny that would allow him to be served after a short period of service on his part. Jesus' orientation toward service did not change when he passed from kenosis to glory.

When thus understood, Jesus' words make us understand kenosis in its truest sense. Since kenosis is the act of the Son of Man who has come to serve, it expresses the profoundly humble love known as service. If the Incarnation had been accomplished in a glorious manner, it might have seemed to result from a certain divine pride that was extending its dominion and making its splendor shine forth in a human nature. Certain images of the Old Testament might well have suggested that God took pride in his omnipotence and in his claims over the world. The emptying of the one who comes to serve shows an entirely different motive, the motive of humility in self-giving.

Jesus' altruistic intention persists in his glorious state. While it is true that Christ is destined to be recognized by all as Lord and that he thus fulfills Daniel's oracle, it is no less true that it is for the salvation of mankind that he became and remains Lord. As Paul writes elsewhere, Christ "was raised to life" for the living (2 Co 5:15), "to justify us" (Rm 4:25). This thought rounds out the perspective of Paul's hymn in Philippians.

Kenosis was only a temporary state that came to an end with Christ's entry into his glorious state. Yet its quality of love and of service to others is destined to remain even in the state of glory. So kenosis does not completely disappear, for the altruistic attitude by which it merited Jesus' elevation to the glorious state had to be permanent.

This quality of love, so essential to kenosis, is the ultimate reason for the obscure manner in which Jesus revealed himself. We have already mentioned his determination not to force human acceptance of himself by dazzling men with his divine splendor. In this he showed respect for the human person, which is one of the marks of love. Likewise inspired by love is the economy of faith which demands of every human person an active collaboration with the God who reveals. This is an actuation of the covenant in which God does not want to act alone. But all these aspects of love depend in the last analysis on the love that impelled the Son to come in the condition of a servant. The humility of service and of sacrifice called for an unassuming revelation. The very act of revealing had to be a service and a sacrifice. Better still, it had to be a kenosis, an emptying, so as to witness to the love that commanded it. The discretion with which Jesus made himself known in his personal reality bespeaks the intensity of his love for men.

A problem still remains. On the one hand we have noted that the mysterious mode of Christ's self-revelation stems from his divine transcendence that cannot be adequately expressed in human terms. In this sense the mode seems to belong to the respective natures of God and of man. On the other hand, we have attributed the discretion of Christ's self-revelation to the economy of salvation and especially to its aspect of kenosis or emptying. From this point of view, the determining factor is no longer the divine nature of Christ but a free divine choice on his part.

Actually, the two points of view are in agreement, for in his plan of salvation God freely decided to reveal himself in his infinite transcendence. More specifically, he chose to make known a love that gives itself in total sacrifice. It is precisely this love which, in Christ, is the supreme revelation of the depths of God.

C. The Revelation of the Glorious Christ

1. *The Obscure Manifestation of the Glorious State*

Even the Resurrection remains shrouded in the obscurity that characterized Jesus' earlier self-revelation. The glorious state attained by the Savior after his sacrifice appears to us as a snatching away from the conditions of earthly life. It is not a triumphal reentry into this world in an aura of divine glory.

In this state we must recognize the consummation of the Incarnation. Jesus' human nature is henceforth permeated, filled to overflowing with divine life, by virtue of a total transformation. But just so, this transformation confers upon Christ the man a heavenly state that accentuates his mystery and his remoteness from the ordinary human condition.

Let us note the diverse aspects in which this remoteness or snatching away is manifested.

(1) The first glorification of Christ relates to his soul, his "spirit," which he committed into the Father's hands as he was dying (cf. Lk 23:46). This glorification remained invisible, and we have no witness to it. The Evangelist Matthew strives to describe its repercussions on earth in terms of an earthquake, the opening of tombs and the rising of the dead. Yet this description can be scarcely more than an effort of the imagination to picture the impact of Jesus' death upon the universe. Peter's First Letter says of Jesus: "In the body he was put to death, in the spirit he was raised to life" (1 P 3:18), and he went to bring the good news to the dead. This is not an eyewitness report but the result of reflection on what presumably happened to the Savior immediately after his death. [15] Nothing is said of the glorious state to which Christ acceded after he breathed his last.

(2) The first sign of the Resurrection is the empty tomb. Of itself, this fact would not suffice to prove the Resurrection. [16] It could be subjected to a variety of interpretations, and from the beginning its significance was apparently challenged (cf. Mt 28:13). For the major event of the work of salvation, the first indication is presented with great discretion and leaves a major role to the intuition of faith. John's state-

---

[15] Concerning the theological meaning and implications of this · text, cf. *Jesus, Our Liberator, op. cit.,* Rome, 1982, Franciscan Herald Press, 1989, p.329-357. Cf. also J. J. Strynkowski, *The Descent of Christ among the Dead,* Rome, 1972.

[16] This is one of the reasons for admitting the historicity of the discovery of the empty tomb. It could not even have been presented as a proof of the Resurrection. Other indices of historicity can be mentioned, in particular the fact that the primitive Christian community would not have invented the story of a discovery of the tomb by women (cf. J. Kremer, "Zur Diskussion über 'das leere Grab'," E. Dhanis, *Resurrexit,* 137-168).

ment about the beloved disciple: "he saw and he believed" (Jn 20:8) suggests a considerable distance between what is evident, namely the absence of a body in the tomb, and what is to become an object of faith, the Resurrection.

(3) The appearances of the risen Christ to the women and to the disciples have greater demonstrative power. Even so, they are merely the indirect attestation of an event which nobody has personally witnessed. No one saw Jesus come forth from the tomb.

Besides, these appearances retain the element of great discretion. They are granted neither to the crowds nor to enemies. In other words, they are not addressed to those who would seem to be in greatest need of irrefutable proof.

Jesus appears only to those who are at least disposed to believe. The appearances of the risen Christ occur over a period of time with no evident continuity, and in circumstances where they remain a privilege for those who witness them.

Jesus' presence makes itself known in a mysterious way, outside the laws of ordinary human encounters. Those who have known him well have trouble recognizing him, even when he comes very near. Doubts arise concerning his true identity, which seems to indicate that his facial features are not so easy to see, and that the encounters are above all a call to faith.

(4) The event of the Ascension, which puts an end to Jesus' appearances, is also enigmatic. It is a departure, a disappearance behind the clouds that leaves the disciples with their eyes raised to the heavens, as though waiting for something that does not happen. In a certain way, this is the last time they look for a prodigy. But the angels who jolt the men of Galilee from their reverie (cf. Ac 1:10-11) make them understand they must stop waiting and turn their eyes toward the earth on which the one who has been taken from them will come.

The Ascension is the ultimate stage in the glorification of Jesus, a glorious elevation that has been interpreted as taking his place "at the right hand of God" (Mk 16:19), and entering into full possession of his filial messianic power. It is the mystery of the establishment of Christ's divine kingship. In itself it is not seen by any human eye, and the appearances of the event as perceived by earthly witnesses remain quite humble, far below the grandeur of the reality signified. All that is seen is a man who rises into the heavens and is permanently withdrawn from sight by a cloud.

Up to its very climax, the revelation of Jesus remains shrouded by a veil of humble discretion, of deliberate reticence, that contrasts with the greatness of the person revealing.

2. *The Demonstration Announced by Jesus*

The Resurrection has been considered the decisive proof of the truth of Jesus' revelation, implying its manifest divine approbation as well as the Father's acceptance of the redemptive sacrifice.

However, Jesus did not announce his Resurrection simply by way of a proof. When he foretold the Passion and death of the Son of Man to his disciples, he added that he would "be raised up on the third day," as we read in the three successive announcements recorded in the Synoptics (Mt 16:21; 17:23; 20:19; and par.). The purpose of announcing the Resurrection was evidently to complement the foretelling of his death, and thus to describe the entire drama of the Redemption to its final outcome. Christ's death and Resurrection form an inseparable whole, and the meaning of his death can appear only in his Resurrection.

In spite of its major importance, the Resurrection was not an event unfolding before men's eyes and in itself a sort of proclamation to the world. We have already noted how discreet the risen Jesus was in revealing himself. He showed himself only to a few, in an indirect way, through the discovery of the empty tomb and by apparitions, and under conditions when seeing him, far from making faith unnecessary, demanded a faith strong enough to overcome all doubts.

When Jesus affirmed his identity as Christ and Son of God before the Sanhedrin, he foretold the demonstration of the truth of his words. This was not to consist, strictly speaking, in his Resurrection, but in his coming in a divine mode: "... I tell you that from this time onward you will see the Son of Man seated at the right hand of the Power and coming on the clouds of heaven" (Mt 26:64). [17]

This coming has often been interpreted as the final coming at the end of time. [18] However, Jesus declares he does not know the date of the end of time (cf. Mt 24:36; Mk 13:32), whereas he announces the coming of the Son of man "from this time onward." [19] He also declares to the members of the Sanhedrin that they will witness it with their own eyes, that they will "see" it. He cannot, therefore, be talking of the Parousia.

When Jesus spoke in this instance of being "seated at the right hand of the Power" he was alluding to his Ascension. The power it signified was to be deployed by the coming of the risen Christ into the world. This coming would not be in the flesh, according to a human mode, as was the first coming of the Son of Man, but a coming "on the clouds," that is, according to a divine mode. It would be brought about by the Holy Spirit and be inaugurated on Pentecost. Jesus could say with complete truth that it would occur "from this time onward," and that it would occur before everyone's eyes. Already Pentecost touched persons of every race. In a broader sense, the expansion of the Church, the manifestation of the actual coming of the Son of Man would thrust itself upon the members of the Sanhedrin as well as on the other Jews.

The proof that Jesus is truly the Christ, the Son of God, lies in this expansion of the Church. The development of the Church is the visible testimony of the coming of Christ through the Holy Spirit among men. [20]

---

[17] Concerning the various interpretations of this text, cf. J. Dupont, "'Assis à la droite de Dieu,' L'interprétation du Ps 110.1 dans le Nouveau Testament" (Dhanis, Resurrexit, 347-370).

[18] We have commented on this text in our work La conscience de Jésus, Gembloux-Paris, 1971, 237-241.

[19] J. Dupont (art. cit., 363) declares that "the formula cannot possibly go back to the source." Yet we wonder where this evidence comes from. The fact that it makes Jesus' statement harder to understand is not a reason to hold it suspect. Rather it is a reason for admitting its primitive character. It is an affirmation of the imminence of the eschatological coming, which agrees with other similarly orientated affirmations.

[20] J. Dupont (art. cit., 355) has mentioned a remark by Ph. Vielhauer to the effect that what we remember of the enthronement at the right hand

Let us emphasize various distinctive aspects of this demonstration. We should note first of all that it completes the mystery of the Incarnation by the diffusion of Jesus' spiritual presence among men. The coming of the Son of Man, that occurred once in a single place on earth, with all the limitations of an individual human life, is now multiplied in a great many places, since it is a coming according to a universal, divine mode.

This demonstration does not consist, as does the proof of the Resurrection, in a visible unfolding of the personal reality of Jesus. It is accomplished through the efficacy of the divine power of the risen Christ which transforms mankind. Finally, the proof of the identity of Jesus, the Christ and the Son of God, is to be found in all men, and in a special way in the Christian community.

The demonstration thus follows the trajectory of self-giving love. The divinity of Jesus is manifested by communicating itself to others. Christ infuses his own divine life into men. This coincides with the argument used by the Fathers of the Church: by reason of the fact that Jesus divinizes us, we must admit that he is God.

Proceeding by way of love, such a demonstration reveals more clearly what manner of God Christ is. It is in no sense a proof of a sovereignty that would subjugate human beings through pride or egoism. It manifests the love of a God who shares his divine riches with mankind.

The revelation of Christ's divine identity in the development of the Church also bears the mark of kenosis. The earthly Church must live, in the image of Christ, in the condition of a servant. It cannot claim to rule in glory or earthly triumph. For this reason the reaction against certain triumphalist tendencies in the Church is justified. The Church cannot "grasp at" equality with God any more than Christ did. While it lives by the mystery of the Resurrection, this mystery still remains hidden within the earthly condition where the mys-

---

of God is simply its result in the coming on the clouds. This helps to answer the objection that we have not seen Christ seated at the right hand of God. What we see is the coming on the clouds (that is to say, his coming within the Church), which is the exercise of the power of the One who sits at the right hand of the Father.

tery of the Passion must be lived simultaneously. The visible defeats of the Church are of the same order as the defeat of the Cross. The Church attests, through a life of kenosis, to the penetration of the divine life of Christ within humankind.

To conclude, we would point out that the demonstration of Christ's divine identity has not been completed. Jesus showed us its starting point: "from this time onward" (Mt 26:64). He did not set any terminal date. The demonstration will be complete only when the Church has reached out to embrace all men. It will keep pace with the ongoing incarnation of Christ within the human milieu until history comes to an end.

CHAPTER VII

THE ESSENTIAL CHARACTERISTICS
OF THE BIBLICAL CHRIST

A. IN SEARCH OF A SYNTHESIS

How to define the image of Christ derived from a study of the witness of Scripture?

We might begin by asking a preliminary question: Is there a single image or are there several images of the biblical Christ? As we have already pointed out, certain exegetes and theologians insist on the diversity in the Christologies of the New Testament authors. In the opinion of these scholars there is not one biblical Christology, but several. We have noted the diversity in the points of view adopted by the Evangelists, as well as the difference between the way Jesus speaks about himself and the way he is denoted by the primitive community or by St. Paul.

Nonetheless, the differences do not eliminate the similarities. In fact, they help to bring out more clearly the traits of Christ commonly agreed upon. The determination of these general traits of Christ is necessary to the believer who engages in research on the person of Christ. Faith's commitment cannot address itself to a multiplicity of images. It is not enough that the theologian, as believer, understand the thought of each of the men who transmitted or commented on the Gospel message in the earliest days of the Church. He cannot be content to answer the question: "Who is Jesus?" by saying "This is what Paul says, or Mark, or John ..." He must achieve for himself, as well as for others, the synthesis of the elements provided by the various authors.

Moreover, the inspiration of the Books of the New Testament is orientated toward such a synthesis. In guiding the composition of these writings, the Holy Spirit wanted them to converge toward a larger, all-encompassing whole. He exceeded the inevitably limited horizon of each of the sacred writers and made use of their complementarity to present a single message. To consider divine inspiration only within the context of each individual writing would result in an unduly fragmented conception of what it is. The intention of the whole array of writings is fundamental. While the Holy Spirit apparently abetted the interpretations of each individual author, he did so in order to arrive at a more balanced and richer synthesis. In striving for this synthesis the theologian does not proceed arbitrarily. He seeks to arrive at the unity already present in the scriptural entity by virtue of God's intent.

Besides, the assembled writings embrace the whole Bible, including the Old and the New Testaments. For the Old Testament was inspired with Christ in view. Jesus in turn continually referred to the Scripture that had preceded him to highlight the fulfillment of its announcements and prophetic figures. The Christian community, for its part, also searched the Old Testament for confirmations of the authenticity of Christ's revelation. In St. Paul's words, the mystery kept secret for endless ages, now revealed itself to all the nations "by means of the prophetical Scriptures" (Rm 16:26). That is to say, when Christ appeared, so too did the true meaning of Scripture according to God's plan. The supreme role of the Old Testament is to elucidate the New and provide a better understanding of who Christ is.

B. THE DYNAMISM OF INCARNATION

The first distinguishing mark to discern is the dynamism of incarnation that finds expression in Jesus.

1. *The Movement of Incarnation that Preceded Christ*

Christ made his appearance at a particular moment of history, contiguous with the past of the Jewish religion. When he inaugurated his mission by the baptism of John, he professed his conformity with the tradition that had preceded him and with the messianic expectations it involved. He appeared, therefore, as the culmination of a long historical process. Now this historical process consisted in an incarnation of God among men. We are here using the word "incarnation" in its broadest sense, and not in the unique sense it assumes when applied to the person of the Word made flesh. Incarnation is the entrance of God into the world and into human lives, as it was revealed to the Jewish people.

The covenant that established the general framework of the Jewish religion lay great emphasis on God's will to place himself on a level of equality with men by concluding reciprocal commitments. God made his contacts with mankind incarnate through certain human relational forms. Among the characteristic marks of this relationship are the following:

— a *horizontalism* instituted by a sovereign and transcendent God;
— an *accessibility* by which God enters into dialogue with men to the point of granting them certain rights over himself;
— *collaboration* required of man in developing this relationship;
— *responsibility* left to man for fulfilling his obligations and thereby providing for the preservation of the covenant and the attainment of its goals.

God's determination to involve himself fully in these contacts was manifested by the love expressed in them. The covenant was not merely a pact addressed to action but a pact of love. God instituted it as an expression of his fatherhood. He wanted to be a Father to Israel, and he demanded a filial attitude in return. Even more emphatic in its horizontal orientation is the image of the matrimonial union in which Yahweh appropriates the role and the sentiments of the Bridegroom. The institution of a father-son, husband-wife relationship is an authentic incarnation of God's love.

This was complemented by the incarnation of God's word in "the Law and the prophets," of God's action in the history of the Jewish nation, of God's presence in the midst of the people, a presence localized in the Tent of Meeting and later in the Temple. So God adopted all the ways by which men

197

communicate with one another: he spoke, he acted, he was present.

In this movement of incarnation, we discern God's intention to enter into relations with men by every possible means, and through every kind of interpersonal contact. One might refer to it as a totalism of incarnation that would be the exact opposite of autocratic totalitarianism. The difference consists in this: God, who could assert himself in all his transcendence, preferred to have humankind accept him freely, and this he did by addressing himself to men at their own human level.

2. *The Movement of Incarnation in Jesus: Continuity and Innovation*

The movement of incarnation is condensed in Jesus. Everything contracted to in the Old Covenant is perfectly fulfilled in a new and unique form. The newness consists in the fact that Christ is himself the whole incarnation. He joins in himself everything previously achieved in bringing God and man together. He *is* the covenant, he *is* the Bridegroom, he *is* the Son in whom the Father gives and reveals himself, he *is* the Word made flesh, he *is* the power of God at work in this world, he *is* God's presence destined to remain permanently among men.

This involves a "condensation" in the sense that the interior movement of incarnation attains maximal intensity. The term might lead some to think that Christ is the product of an anterior evolution. In actual fact, far more than a difference in degree is involved in the leap from one stage of incarnation to the other. While it is true that all aspects of the impetus to incarnation are concerntrated in Jesus, this has not been simply the result of past historical development. It has happened by reason of divine intervention which, while remaining in continuity with the past, goes far beyond it. The essential difference consists precisely in that the incarnation of God has now become identified with a person.

Let us pause and reflect on these aspects of continuity and innovation.

First to make its appearance is the element of *historical*

continuity. Jesus did not interrupt the course of human history. He became fully a part of history and constantly identified himself by references to the history of the Jewish people. We can clearly sense his intention to painstakingly gather the fruit of this historical development which involved God's entering the universe of creatures and making a place for himself within the world of men and women.

We have already noted how Jesus recapitulated in his person the great figures of Israel: Abraham, Jacob, Moses, and David. By evoking them he showed that nothing of this history had been lost, that all of the past came alive again in his own earthly existence. Everything God had once accomplished in these men for the progress of his people was present in Jesus, carried to a higher level inasmuch as Jesus by far transcends all the personages who prefigured him. The same holds true of the liturgical feasts whose significance Christ recaptured, at the same time transforming it. The Temple as the epitome of worship was destined to find its definitive meaning in his person. So, too, the lineage of the prophets whose supreme heir Jesus declared himself to be.

Nevertheless, within this historical continuity the incarnation achieved in Jesus can readily be perceived to be a *radical innovation.* Christ's transcendence showed that he was not the product of a human evolution or of an anterior religious development, even one deeply permeated with a divinely inspired dynamism. This newness even insinuates a reversal of causality. Within a linkage of historical succession whose culmination Jesus appeared to be, the divine reality that asserted itself in him was the ontological basis of all that had preceded and of all that was to follow. Jesus is the reality of the covenant, and all the covenants made before him were only its prefigurement. He is the reality of the Temple since he is God's presence in person, whose material sign was the Temple. The doctrine he taught contains the total reality of the message God wanted to transmit to men, and prophetic oracles were simply the provisional and partial expression of this message. He is the Word. He is the reality of the history of salvation because within him the salvific action of God is efficacious for all men, whereas the religious history of the Jews was only its figurative announcement.

It is the conformity between figure and reality that makes us see Jesus as the ontological foundation of the figurative announcements that preceded him. In Jesus there has not been merely the historical fulfillment of what had been announced, a fulfillment carried to its plenitude. If that had been so, Jesus would have been only the highest point, the consummation of an evolution. Jesus contains within himself the total reality of what had been merely figurative before his coming. Now, a figure or symbol derives all its support from the reality prefigured or symbolized. In God's plan the reality of Christ has been the fulcrum, the foundation of the figures of the Old Covenant.

This elucidates the sense in which Christ is the center of the history of the world. He is at the heart of history not simply because he is the midpoint in the saga of human development, setting apart the "old" from the "new." He is the center within which divine eternity is perfectly incarnated in human time, endowing the latter with a transcendental quality. [1] Christ is at once a part of human history and the one who is above all history. By reason of this transcendental quality he is the foundation of a past that has meaning only through him, and he is likewise the foundation of the future.

John the Evangelist has highlighted the transcendence of Christ in relation to the economy of the Jewish religion, emphasizing the difference between the Law given by Moses on the one hand and the grace and truth that have come through Jesus, the only-begotten Son. John recorded the words through which Jesus presented himself as the light, the truth, and the life, and stressed the ontological weight of these words. These affirmations point to a superiority over what was said of Yahweh in the Old Testament. Yahweh declares: "I form the light" (Is 45:7). Jesus not only forms the light, he is

---

[1] O. Cullmann has correctly pointed out that for the New Testament, in contrast to Judaism, the center of time is no longer situated in the future, but in the past (*Christ et le temps,* Neuchâtel, 1957, 58). But he has not adequately recognized the transcendent quality of this center, in which the superiority of divine eternity over human time finds expression. Incarnation does not abolish transcendence, but introduces it into the world of time. Cf. also the present author's work, *The Mystery of Christian Hope* (New York: Alba House 1977).

the light: "I am the light of the world" (Jn 8:12). We find
the same crescendo in a number of other passages:

- "It is I who deal death and life" (Dt 32:39) — "I
  am the resurrection" (Jn 11:25).
- "I will go before you" (Is 45:2) — "I am the Way"
  (Jn 14:6).
- "I, yes I myself, have spoken" (Is 48:15) — "I am
  the Truth" (Jn 14:6).
- "I, I am your consoler" (Is 51:12) — "I am the
  bread of life" (Jn 6:35).

Whence this superiority which, at first sight, might seem
paradoxical? Is it not absurd to think that Christ is superior
to God? Actually, the superiority lies in the new mode of
God's intenvention in the world. The incarnation realized
in Christ is far superior to all anterior divine action among
men. It is in his flesh, that is, through the Incarnation, that
Jesus is the bread of life. It is by his human speech, expressing God's Word, that he is truth. It is by the resurrection of his body that he communicates eternal life to men.

The Incarnation consummated in Jesus is the apex of
God's intervention among men, an apex that goes incomparably beyond all of his preceding interventions.

3. *From the People to the Individual and from the Individual
   to the People*

When we compare the incarnation of God in the Jewish
religion with the Incarnation accomplished in Jesus, we note
certain differences from the point of view of the relationship
of the people to the individual.

In the Jewish religion God's incarnation related essentially
to the people as a whole. It was with them that he made a
covenant. It was Israel that God the Father looked upon
as a son, or God the Bridegroom accepted as his bride. It was
in the history of the Jewish nation that God's action unfolded.
It was to the people that God's word and presence were
granted. Human mediators played only a secondary role, and
the intervention of a supreme mediator of unique stature,
who was to be the Messiah, was expected in some future time.

In the new economy, God's incarnation was accomplished in a single individual. The reason this Incarnation completed and went beyond the incarnation effected under the Old Law was that this individual now represented the people, and even more than the people. A corporate personality must be attributed to him, but the meaning of this term calls for explanation. It is in the Gospel texts that we see how Jesus himself suggested the corporate or representative quality of his person.

We have the first indication of this in Jesus' use of the name "Son of Man." In Daniel's oracle the name had a corporate value, since the power attributed to the Son of Man signified a power attributed to the people of the saints of the Most High. In the parables of Enoch the name "Son of Man" tended to apply more particularly to an individual, with an emphasis on the transcendence of the personage in question. In Jesus' use of the term this transcendence is highlighted, but while it is a strictly personal designation, it implies a certain quality of universal representation.

In contrast to "Son of David," which Jesus avoided applying to himself, "Son of Man" tends to make Christ appear not as the man of a particular people, but as the man of all mankind. The Son of Man is the man who belongs to the whole family of man, who has bonds of solidarity with all humans, the man whose universality will not brook the divisions of nationalism and of the various particularisms. The very name implies the intention to reconcile all men in the unity of the human condition and of a single destiny.

The universal representative sense of the term "Son of Man" does not result simply from his human reality. It stems from his divine person. In the picture of the last judgment, it is the Son of Man, possessing divine power as judge, who declares he is present in every man, whoever he may be, receiving as done to himself his charitable acts as well as his refusals to help his brothers. In this case the universal representation involves a certain mode of presence. Thanks to his incarnate being, Jesus is really present in every human person. His solidarity with all men takes on an ontological dimension because of his incarnate presence.

This solidarity is so far-reaching that in Jesus' sacrifice

it assumes the aspect of a substitution. The Son of Man has come "to give his life as a ransom for many" (Mk 14:45; Mt 20:28). Here the Son of Man is claiming to represent not each individual but the whole of mankind. He represents humanity by offering his life in its place. His capability to represent mankind is justified by the divine stature of the "Son of Man." A mere man would not have a life to offer whose value would equal that of all men. But a divine person who is of infinite value can make a human offering not only equal but superior to the value of all human lives taken together.

The image of the vine is particularly illuminative of the meaning of the corporate personality. Israel had on several occasions been compared to a vine. Jesus adopts the image, applying it to his own person: "I am the true vine, ... I am the vine, you are the branches. Whoever remains in me, with me in him, bears fruit in plenty; for cut off from me you can do nothing" (Jn 15:1,5).

The comparison was destined to determine the relationship between Jesus and his disciples in the future. It announced the Church and its development. Whereas the image of the ransom referred strictly to the Savior's sacrifice and to a unique event in history, the image of the vine tends to reveal the permanent state of the community assembled around Christ. He was not to be merely an agent of reunion, a rallying point for the Christian community, but its source of life. From him would flow the life-giving pith to nourish the branches. Jesus is therefore a corporate personality in the sense that the life he communicates to his disciples is present in him in its totality. Everything that the disciples can become in the unfolding of their own Christian lives is first of all contained in Christ. If the new people of God is a vine, it is in the sense that this people is born completely from Jesus himself, and receives all its growth from him.

We can therefore discern the various modes in which Christ, through his Incarnation, is a corporate personality. He represents everything that is universal in man, he is present in each man, he represents mankind before the Father in his sacrifice, and by his total presence in the community he fills it with his own life.

It is under this last-mentioned aspect that the dynamism of incarnation manifests its true dimensions. It is concentrated in Jesus in order to be more completely transmitted to all mankind. The Son of God is the vine through which divine life is communicated to all the branches, so that the entire vine may live by the life force of God. The Incarnation is eminently personal, so as to become universal.

C. THE RICHNESS OF DIVERSITY IN UNITY

1. *The Face of Christ Seen from Four Angles*

We have already said that the Christological approaches of the four Evangelists must not be viewed solely in terms of their differences. Rather, they need to be unified into a single, inclusive portrait of Christ. They are complementary, and express points of view that are essential to any research on the person of Jesus.

As Mark describes him, Christ will always be the one who, though bearing the features of a man just like ourselves, remains a mystery. In his human sentiments and acts there is something more than the purely human, something that suggests his divine transcendence. However clear the pronouncements of faith, the person of Jesus inevitably retains this aura of mystery. The only way we can touch the reality of God within him is to perceive his mystery as mystery. Besides, far from diminishing his humanity in any way, his mystery is manifested through his humanity. For his whole human nature bears his divine reality.

In Matthew's perspective, Christ is the master of the kingdom, the one who determines its essential structure and establishes its laws with divine sovereignty. In this capacity he is everything that the Messiah was expected to be, but at a transcendent level. This conception of Christ's divine power needs to be complemented by the one Luke offers us. According to Luke, Jesus is Lord, the master of the kingdom in a more hidden way, and his action is exercised in depth, through the power of the Spirit.

Now, Jesus' title of Lord, involving the action of the Holy Spirit, is the one specifically given him by the primitive

Christian community. After Pentecost more than in his earthly life, Christ asserted himself in the development of the Church as "Lord and Christ," that is, as an absolute master who exercises the divine power of sending the Holy Spirit. He appeared in the Church as the master not only of the present but also of the entire future. The invocations "Maranatha" (1 Co 16:22) and "Amen, come, Lord Jesus" (Rv 22:20) imply his total sovereignty over history.

Christ's mystery clarifies his relationship of sovereignty to mankind. But a still more fundamental relationship remains to be defined, involving his position within God. John's Gospel has preserved and stressed whatever in Christ's words and actions pointed to his identity as Son and to his intimacy with the Father. Because John highlights this divine Sonship, he can unhesitatingly call Jesus "God" without fear of confusing him with the Father. This Jesus of whom John speaks is "God the only Son" (Jn 1:18).

It is the quality of Son that ultimately determines the personality of Jesus and allows us to penetrate to the depths of his mystery. However, what might seem the last stage of Christological inquiry corresponds to the earliest indication Jesus gave of his identity. The term "Abba" is the intimate expression of the transcendent divine Sonship. Besides, we must not forget that the revelation of this divine Sonship was forceful enough to provoke the interrogation of the high priest and to elicit Jesus' decisive answer.

None of the four aspects mentioned can be omitted in any effort to determine Christ's identity: his mystery, his power over the kingdom in its external organization, his power of interior and spiritual action within this same kingdom, and his personality as Son. The four Evangelists, later symbolically identified with the four figures in Ezekiel's vision that accompanied the manifestation of God (Ex 1:3-28), are all indispensable to an understanding of the revelation of God in Jesus. Each of the Evangelists, while having his own distinct orientation, also presents the traits of Christ' physiognomy that are given greater prominence by the others. The difference in the Christology of the four sacred writers lies in the emphasis each one places on one of Christ's distinctive qualities, rather than in any essential divergences in their views.

The fact that the Church has spoken of "the Gospel" according to Matthew, Mark, Luke, and John, rather than of "the Gospels" in the plural, confirms the underlying unity of the four Gospel accounts of Jesus and points to their complementarity.

Pedagogically, we might even propose the four Christological approaches as four stages in the discovery of Jesus. First of all, the mystery of Jesus comes into view with the questions that the Jesus of the Gospels inevitably poses. For here is a man who speaks and acts as no one ever has before him, who works miracles and makes others sense the nearness of the divine. Then comes the sovereignty with which Jesus founds his religion, establishes his Church by formulating his commandments and a law superior to the Old Law. Thereafter Christ's power is more clearly perceived in the inward influence he wants to exercise over men through the action of the Holy Spirit, in bringing to maturity a kingdom whose deepest reality is spiritual and interior. Thus, the title "Our Lord" more directly implies a vital ascendancy. Finally, the divine lordship of Christ is most profoundly defined in terms of his divine sonship. Jesus is the Son of the Father, he is God with the attributes of a Son. This is what defines his person.

2. *The Three Expressions of Jesus' Personal Identity*

What is most precious in the testimony of the Evangelists is not their own individual and unique way of looking at and understanding Jesus. Rather it is what they transmit to us of Jesus' own testimony as to his person through his words and actions. That is why the effort to ascertain the words actually spoken by Jesus is of greatest importance. Descriptions of Jesus given by others, even those whose authenticity is guaranteed by the authority of divine inspiration, are not equivalent to the information contained in Jesus own language and demeanor.

Fortunately we have excellent indications as to the authenticity of certain of Jesus' sayings which definitively illuminate his personal identity. The first of these is his use of the word "Abba," a radical innovation when applied to God.

206

By using this name Jesus showed he had a totally new understanding of sonship, one that was irreducible to any understanding the Jewish people might have had of God as their Father. In its simplicity the word "Abba" implies that Jesus enjoyed an intimate relationship with the heavenly Father analogous to that of a child with his human father. Therefore Jesus' use of "Abba" intimates his natural divine sonship.

Jesus dealt with God not as would a creature with the Creator but as a son living on the same level of being as the Father, in an intimacy that excluded any distance between them. While he never spoke of himself as the Son of God, he constantly showed by his use of the invocation "Abba" that he was acting as God's Son, with a full sense of his right to do so and without reticence. This was the existential revelation of a unique and transcendent sonship, a divine sonship so thoroughly incarnated that it expressed itself by the word most spontaneously used by a child in addressing his father.

The affirmation "It is I" is likewise a locution commonly used in human relations. And yet in the context in which it is used by Jesus it evokes Yahweh's affirmations in the Book of Isaiah, or even the name claimed by Yahweh in the Book of Exodus: "I Am: 'I Am'" (Ex 3:14). When Jesus says "It is I," he may do so as a friend to identify himself to his friends, but also to evoke the personal presence of God. Like the expression "Abba," the words "It is I" witness to the depth of the Incarnation, this time, no longer in Jesus' relationship to God but in his relations with other men. To declare that he is God Jesus simply needs to say "It is I." For even though he is God, he is perfectly at ease in the midst of men. His self-revelation is existential, because the formula he uses is the fruit of an experience of presence in a human milieu.

In addition to the expressions "Abba" and "It is I" through which Jesus presents himself as Son and as God, his use of the designation "Son of Man" focusses attention on his quality as a man. The Son of Man is the man who, while he is a son of man, is also the Son of God. That is the meaning suggested by the name "Son of Man" when Jesus uses it to refer to the personage evoked by Daniel's oracle and subsequent Jewish tradition. There is no incompatibility between the Son of Man and the Son of God, because man, created in the likeness of God, is the being best qualified to represent and to reveal God. When Jesus calls himself "the Son of Man" he is stressing both his quality as a man like all others and his divine power.

The two movements of incarnation, the descending and the ascending, are linked still more closely to the expression "Son of Man." First, there is the descending movement that Jesus begins to unveil when he declares that "the Son of Man has come," and then the ascending movement that he announces by saying that the Son of Man will "rise again" (Mk 8:31) three days after his death, or that he will "ascend to where he was before" (Jn 6:62). The descent by which the Son of Man embraces a life offered in ransom for many culminates in a glorious elevation. In the Johannine vocabulary, the end of the first movement and the beginning of the second are considered in a single vista. The elevation on the cross is the sign of the elevation in glory: "The Son of Man must be lifted up" (Jn 3:14). Thanks to this lifting up, the Son of Man will be able to come on the clouds of heaven to gather up the elect and exercise his sovereignty as judge.

This "coming on the clouds of heaven" (Mt 24:30) reveals more clearly the destination of the ascending movement. The Son of Man is raised to a divine level even in his humanity, and the Incarnation thereby assumes a glorious form, contrary to the earthly kenosis. But the purpose of this glory is to enable him to carry out his mission as Savior by being a man capable of fully deploying divine power for the gathering up of the Church. The second coming of the Son of Man is indeed a coming upon earth, but one effectuated by the divine power of the Spirit for the purpose of divinizing human lives, of "raising" them up to the stature of the Son of Man himself.

3. Word, Action, and Presence

As we have already said, we cannot disregard any of the Christological viewpoints developed by the four Evangelists. Neither can we neglect any of the aspects of the dynamism of incarnation previously manifested in the Old Covenant. Thus, we cannot think of Jesus solely as God's incarnate Word or Utterance, neglecting his incarnation of God's action and presence.

Certainly, we must recognize the full weight of the identification of Christ with the Word, as presented to us in John's Gospel. This identification explains at least partially why it was the Son, and not one of the other divine persons, who became incarnate. Indeed, it justifies Jesus' revelatory mission. The profound intuition of the Prologue to John's Gospel consists in this: the reason Jesus manifested the invisible Father to us through the whole of his human life is that he already was in his reality as a divine person the Word or Utterance, that is, the Father's expression of himself to himself in God. Being the divine, eternal image of the Father, Jesus is therefore eminently qualified to become his human image, to express in human terms God's message and God as he is in himself.

John's intuition is based on certain intimations and suggestions of Jesus concerning his own identity as the divine Word, Wisdom, absolute Truth, and Light. Jesus' self-revelation is thereby endowed with maximal power, inasmuch as in him the Word revealing is identical with his person. This also make clear why the Christian message cannot be detached from the divine person of Jesus. For this message is contained in the first place in the very person of Christ, and the Incarnation of God's Word is the Incarnation of the person of the Son. The Christian religion is the religion of a person.

It follows from this that the Incarnation of the Word cannot be limited to the communication of a message. The Gospel accounts give adequate witness that this would be much too narrow a viewpoint. Jesus did not merely speak, he acted. In him God's action has been manifested in its plenitude through his inauguration of the kingdom. In him God's action multiplied the signs of its transcendence as well as of its primordial intention to save mankind through the working of miracles. Jesus appears in the Gospels as a great benefactor of mankind, someone who is not content to speak kind words but brings effectual help to human misfortunes. Through the miracles he strews along his path, Jesus reveals the power of divine love and God's immense compassion for all the trials and tribulations of men. And by deliberately choosing to work miracles on the sabbath, he makes men understand he has come to complete the work of creation and demonstrates that God is even more active on the seventh day.

What Jesus achieves through his action is a more completely incarnate divine action, one that is closer to mankind, better suited to transform the destiny of mankind. His action offers not only salvation, liberation from the ills that afflict human existence, but blessings in abundance. His many-faceted miracles witness to his intention to lavish the gifts of divine life upon men.

Jesus' words and actions might be seen as two functional realities. However, this would be too restricted an interpretation. For the great innovation of the Incarnation accomplished in Jesus lies in the coming of the divine person of the Son. It is this divine person who speaks and acts, who gives divine value to Jesus' words and actions. But above and beyond that, we see the importance Jesus himself attributed to the incarnation of God's presence. In addition to expressing the divine presence in the words "it is I," he made allusions to the real temple which would henceforth be his own person and invited men to receive his presence in the Eucharist.

When Jesus sent his disciples out on mission, he was not content to transmit his own divine power to them. He also assured them of his perpetual presence: "And know that I am with you always; yes, to the end of time" (Mt 28:20). In John's commentary on the Last Supper, Jesus asks his disciples to remain in him, as he will remain in them (cf. Jn 15:5-9). He offers them his own permanent presence as the wellspring of their life and action.

Jesus' offer of his presence also highlights the essentially personal quality of the Incarnation. Jesus does not limit himself to transmitting God's words and actions. He hands over his whole person through his presence. In so doing he is telling us that the Incarnation of his divine person as Son is a permanent gift to be perpetuated in all human lives. He gives the dynamism of incarnation a new dimension, a dimension as vast as mankind and the universe.

PART THREE

**THE FUNDAMENTAL AFFIRMATIONS
OF THE FAITH OF THE CHURCH**

CHAPTER VIII

THE FORMATION OF CHRISTOLOGICAL DOCTRINE
IN THE FIRST CENTURIES OF THE CHURCH

The dynamism of faith in Christ was manifested during the first centuries of Christianity in efforts to elaborate Christological doctrine. The goal of Christian thought was to determine who and what Jesus was, and this search made headway only at the price of passionate controversy. It is not our intention to describe this process or even to sum it up briefly, for the history of early Christological thinking is long and complex. We prefer to refer our readers to individual studies and works of synthesis on the subject.[1] We shall simply point out a few distinctive aspects of this history and of its culmination in the formulations of the great ecumenical councils. Our purpose will be to set forth more clearly the concepts that illuminate theological reflection and to offer answers to the fundamental questions posed by the mystery of Jesus.

A. THE ORIENTATION OF DOCTRINAL DEVELOPMENT

We begin by noting the essentially ontological emphasis of early Christological thinking. The efforts of the first Christian centuries focussed on elucidating the ontology of Christ.

We need only point to the problems raised in the early controversies to see that this is so: Is Jesus truly man, en-

---

[1] An outstanding work of synthesis is: Aloys Grillmeier, S.J., *Christ in Christian Tradition, From the Apostolic Age to Chalcedon (451)*, translated by John Bowden, 2nd rev. ed., Atlanta, John Knox Press, 1975. The French translation is entitled *Le Christ dans la tradition chrétienne*, Paris, 1973. Cf. also J. Liebaert, *L'Incarnation, I, Des origines au concile de Chalcédoine*, Paris, 1966; A. Grillmeier - H. Bacht, *Das Konzil von Chalkedon*, 3 vol., Würzburg, 1951-1954.

dowed with a real body? Is he truly God, and in what way? Is he of the same substance as God the Father in his divinity? In his humanity, does he possess a soul, or must we say to the contrary that the Word is immediately united to the body? How is the unity of Christ assured in view of his duality as God and man? Should we speak of one or two persons in Christ, of one or two natures? All these questions, answered by various Councils, concern what Jesus is in himself.

This is not to say his soteriological aspect was ignored. His work of salvation was never disregarded, and indeed the salvific purpose of the Incarnation was explicitly stressed But soteriological considerations tended to be illuminative of Christ's ontology. This is evident in a principle that was often invoked: "What has not been assumed has not been healed." [2] The salvific finality was fundamental, but it served to demonstrate what Christ was, what the Word had personally assumed.

This ontological concern is revealing. It confirms the primordial orientation of the dynamism of Christian faith, which cannot limit itself to an inquiry into the function or mission of Jesus and strives first of all to solve the problems posed by his personal identity.

This is the orientation Jesus himself chose and encouraged, since he asked his disciples the question: "But you, who do you say I am?" (Mt 16:15 and par.). He even laid himself open to a sentence of death by his answer to the high priest's question: "Are you the Christ, the Son of the Blessed One?" (Mk 14:61 and par.). Clearly, for Christ the ontological problem was of decisive importance. The Gospel message demanded that doctrinal elaboration focus first of all on the definition of Christ's identity. There was a continuity between the origins and subsequent tradition.

The priority of the ontological problem can be explained by the very nature of the Christian faith which is a commitment to a person, not merely the acceptance of God's word and trust that the work of salvation will be accomplished. The intellectual effort inspired by faith necessarily focusses on the person of Christ. This explains the passions aroused by

---

[2] This principle was formally stated by Gregory of Nazianzus (*Epist. 101 ad Cledonium*, PG 37, 181 C), but it had already been implied in Irenaeus' argumentation.

controversies about matters that might have seemed far removed from the mundane concerns of men. The reason was that faith was deeply involved in these controversies. True, to some the formulation of who and what Jesus was might seem a secondary problem linked to the meaning of abstract concepts. Yet such a formulation was demanded by a faith seeking to know itself and to define its tenets. The achievement of doctrinal clarity deserved the most persevering effort, even if it involved bitter arguments. It was not in vain that so much energy was expended to achieve a more precise determination of the ontology of Christ.

We would point also to the altruistic character of this ontological inquiry. Those who disregard ontology do so in the view that what matters in the last analysis is what has been accomplished in us through God's action, i.e., the new conditions of our destiny. They feel that what we are should be of greater interest to us than what Christ is in himself. But in addition to the fact that Jesus' achievement can be understood only in the light of what he is personally, there is something more to consider. We cannot lose sight of the fact that faith is inspired by a love addressed to Christ for his own sake. An inquiry which, like that of the first Christian centuries, strives to know Christ in preference to everything else is a manifestation of this love. Moreover it results in a deeper understanding of man by reason of the fact that Jesus is the perfect man. But above all it witnesses to an intellectual effort which, far from turning man's attention inward upon himself, is guided by the fundamental altruism of love to seek to discover the person of the Savior.

B. THE THREE INITIAL PERILS

From its very origins, Christology encountered perils. These dangers correspond to three permanent temptations which faith in Jesus must resist.

1. The Negation of Christ's Divinity

The sentencing of Jesus to death demonstrated how extremely difficult it was for the Jews, imbued with monotheism,

215

to accept that a man could really be the Son of God. This difficulty surfaced in *Ebionism,* a doctrine prevalent among certain Judaeo-Christian communities of the 2nd century A.D. but not generally understood. The Ebionites recognized in Christ a man who had been filled with the Spirit at his baptism, but denied he was the Son begotten of the Father.

Adoptionism followed the same line of thought; its protagonist during the last quarter of the 2nd century was Theodotus the Elder. To the mind of Theodotus, Christ was "simply a man," although he had indeed been chosen or adopted by God as the bearer of an exceptional divine grace. Jesus was a man in whom the Spirit acted as a divine power.

When a unipersonal God is posed as the principle of monotheism it is impossible to attribute the divine personality of a Son to Jesus. He can only be thought of as a man in whom the activity of the one God was deployed in a unique manner. In this view Jesus is considered to be a man who, although filled with divine gifts, is essentially a man and no more. When he is called a son of God, it can only be in the sense of an adopted son, privileged among all other men. [3]

It should be noted that Adoptionism proposes an image of Christ that is the reverse of the Incarnation process. Instead of a God who becomes man, it acknowledges a man who is raised to a certain divine level. But such an ascending Christology is basically incomplete, for the man Jesus does not really become God. Here we find the perspective we noted earlier in the Jewish preparation for the Incarnation, which attributes to man certain divine properties or a divine sonship granted for the sake of a mission. This view remains far removed from Christian Revelation.

However Adoptionism, in eschewing faith in the Incarnation of the Son of God and limiting itself to demanding faith in a special action by God in the man Jesus, was to remain one of the more facile temptations to which Christology would be exposed. We find it in another form during the 3rd century in Paul of Samosata who demanded the elimination of hymns in honor of Christ. He could not accept the

---

[3] Referring to the *Shepherd of Hermas,* Sim. V, Grillmeier remarks that "an absolutely closed Judaistic monotheism necessarily brings adoptionism in its train" (*Christ in Christian Tradition,* 78).

worship of Christ, since in his view Christ was a son of God strictly as a man. Adoptionism reappeared especially during the era of the Protestant Reformation among such anti-Trinitarians as Michel Servet and his disciples who saw Christ merely as a man, a son of God by reason of the action of the Holy Spirit who had conceived, anointed, and glorified him. [4] Adoptionism was resurrected by later theologians who refused to see in Jesus anything more than a human being, while recognizing in him a man privileged by divine grace and in this sense a son of God.

2. *The Negation of the Human Reality of Jesus*

It is surprising but significant that from the start the humanity of Christ was challenged quite as much as his divinity. Docetism, which reduces Jesus' body to the level of an apparition, developed quite early, since John the Evangelist alludes to it in one of his Letters: "There are many deceivers about in the world, refusing to admit that Jesus Christ has come in the flesh" (2 Jn 7; cf. 1 Jn 4:2). [5] Ignatius of Antioch fought against the same error, affirming the truth of the birth and crucifixion of Jesus. [6] Those who reacted vigorously by affirming Christ's humanity were equally concerned with stressing his divinity. John is the only Evangelist who explicitly calls Jesus God, and Ignatius makes still more frequent use of this name. In the face of the opinions that were circulating, they had to combat on two fronts. Against those who saw Jesus as simply a man, they insisted that he was God; against those who recognized him as God under the appearances of a man, they answered that he was in very truth a man.

---

[4] Concerning these theories against which Bellarmine fought, cf. the thesis presented to the Gregorian University by I. Zirdum, *Die Gottheit Christi als geoffenbarte Wahrheit nach der Lehre Bellarmins,* Rome, 1974.

[5] Grillmeier does not consider these "deceivers" to be Docetists in the strict sense, for he concludes that it cannot be proved they were already denying the reality of Christ's body (*Christ in Christian Tradition,* 79). However this reality was being challenged and John forcefully affirmed it. The fact remains that the existence of a clearly defined Docetist theory cannot be proved.

[6] *Smyrn.,* 1-4; *Trall.,* 9; *Magn.* 9,11.

Docetism may have been influenced by the dualism that set spirit in opposition to matter, to the point of considering flesh itself to be evil. But it was apparently dominated above all by a fanatic idea of divine transcendence. For the Docetists the one who is God is so far superior to the material world that he could not have lived in a real body. For them, only a corporeal appearance is compatible with divinity.

The birth of Christ and his Passion are among the events related in the Gospels that were most often interpreted by the Docetists as merely appearances. For Marcion, the Son of God could not have been born as men are. He appeared on earth in the semblance of a body, as an adult. For the Gnostic Valentinus, Christ's body was heavenly and spiritual. It merely passed through Mary but was not born of her. For another Gnostic, Basilides, Christ's Passion was only apparent, for Christ did not really die. He foiled his enemies by putting Simon of Cyrene in his place.

Admittedly, it is not easy to reconcile the suffering of the Cross with divine transcendence. When in later times Hilary of Poitiers declared in his work on the Trinity that Jesus could not have suffered in his Passion because he could not have had the infirmities of the corporeal nature, [7] he was influenced by Docetism. He later retracted, declaring that only Christ's divine nature was exempt from suffering, whereas his human nature was subject to it. [8]

Docetism has remained an ongoing temptation. For faith in the divinity of Jesus, in its efforts to affirm itself vigorously, runs the risk of diminishing the reality of his human nature.

3. Reducing Christ to the Level of a Myth

In the 2nd century, a great number of apocryphal writings led the popular imagination to picture Christ under legendary

---

[7] *De Trinitate*, 10,23, PL 10,363 A: "Habens ad patiendum quidem corpus, et passus est; sed naturam non habens ad dolendum"; 10,35, PL 10, 371 B: "demonstrari non ambiguum est, in natura ejus corporis infirmitatem naturae corporeae non fuisse ..." This doctrine had already been expressed in the *Commentary on saint Matthew*, 31,7, PL 9,1069 A.

[8] Cf. *De Synodis*, 49, PL 10,516 B - 517 A; *In Ps.* 54,6, CSEL 22,151,4; 138,3; CSEL 22,746-7. On this evolution of thought cf. R. Favre, "La communication des idiomes dans les oeuvres de Saint Hilaire de Poitiers," *Gr* 17 (1936) 481-514.

aspects.[9] In these accounts, the life of Jesus became a series of extraordinary happenings. It no longer belonged to the world of history, but to the realm of myths.

The tendency to reduce Christ to a myth appeared at a more intellectual level in Christian Gnosticism. This approach sought to include Christ in a cosmogonic system, as an element of this system, one "eon" among others. The mythical eon was related to the earthly Jesus in various ways, revealing a kind of personal dualism. Thus, according to Valentinian Gnosticism, Christ descended upon Jesus at the time of his baptism. The fact that the Gnostic teachings had considerable influence demonstrates their appeal for many intellectuals.

These mythologizing tendencies should cause no surprise. The historical event of the Incarnation occurred quite outside mankind's universe of religious myths. It was predictable that this universe should seek to assimilate the Christ who was beyond its grasp. Human imagination and intellect had no opportunity to play a creative role in the Revelation of the Son of God to the world and had to accept the evidence of historical fact and of testimony to it. As a reaction against this, they spontaneously took their revenge by "recreating" a Savior of their own choosing.

Christology will always face the temptation to create a Christ to its own specifications, rather than accept the Christ who has actually been given and placed by God within human history.

Through the centuries and up to the present day this temptation has assumed two forms. On the one hand, imagination is inclined to fill in the silences of the historical witness. On the other hand, there are those who want to integrate Christ into an intellectual system developed beforehand. They interpret the testimony of the Gospels and translate it into a new language. As a result Christ is reduced to a segment of this system. The efforts to transform Christianity into a kind of Gnosticism may take on very diverse forms, depending on circumstances. But they commonly attribute to the human intellect control over the revealed deposit.

---

[9] We must not forget that the apocrypha were expressions of a rudimentary faith and theology; they are not without value or interest. On this popular theology, cf. Grillmeier, *Christ in Christian Tradition*, 64-76.

Such intellectual hermeneutics ultimately relegates the Christ of the Gospel to the realm of myths. It retains of Christ only what coincides with certain philosophical views, while considering the rest simply material wrapping whose historical value is debatable.

C. The First Outlines of the Theology of the Incarnation

Among those who reacted against the earliest errors, we shall single out Irenaeus of Lyons and Tertullian, both remarkable for doctrinal views and formulations which anticipated the future development of the theology of the Incarnation.

1. *Irenaeus*

Irenaeus fought against Ebionism, Docetism, and above all against Gnosticism. He was careful to remain faithful to Scripture and relied on the traditional Creed that he knew in its Eastern forms. In the face of what one might call the deluge of Gnostic notions, he understood he should not simply set forth his own ideas, but must hold fast to the unshakable foundation of Scriptural doctrine and of the Church's expressed faith.

He affirmed that Christ was "true man and true God," [10] and vindicated this affirmation by a soteriological argument: Christ is true God, because only God can efficaciously obtain salvation and restore union with men. [11] Christ is also true man because it is man's duty to make reparation for his misdeeds. [12] To reconcile God and man, a mediator was needed who was akin to both.

---

[10] *Her.* 4,6,7 SC 100,452: "ab omnibus accipiens testimonium quoniam vere homo et quoniam vere Deus."

[11] *Her.* 4,33,4, SC 100,811: "How could men be saved if God were not the one who wrought their salvation on earth? Or how can man go to God, if God has not come to man?"

[12] *Her.* 3,18,7, SC 34,325 ff. (SC 211,365-367): "If a man had not conquered the enemy of man, the defeat of this enemy would not have been just; if on the other hand a God had not given us salvation we would not be sure of having it; finally, if man had not been constituted in closest unity with God he could not have had a share in incorruptibility. It was there-

The soteriological argument took on its full meaning in the fight against Gnosticism which claimed to be a doctrine of salvation. Irenaeus showed that salvation lies not in Gnosticism but in Christ. However, this thought was not inspired solely by polemics. It stemmed directly from Christian Revelation. Soteriology demands a clear understanding of the ontology of Christ.

In the man Jesus, Irenaeus emphasized the reality of the *flesh*. He stressed the genuineness of the virginal birth. Christ did not merely pass through Mary's body, he was born of her, he received his flesh from her. [13] Christ was born of a virgin so as to "recapitulate" — that is to say, reassume and renew from its origins — the formation of Adam. [14] But Christ was really incorporated into the generations of man.

While insisting on the true divinity and the true humanity of Jesus, Irenaeus forcefully affirmed the *unity* of this being. Against the Gnostics who distinguished between Christ, the being of heavenly origin, and Jesus, the earthly being, he declared that "Jesus Christ is one and the same" (heis kai ho autos). [15] This expression was adopted in the Chalcedonian profession of faith. It already signified the unity of Christ's person.

Irenaeus conceived unity according to the orientation of John's Prologue: "The Word became flesh." He often spoke of "union" rather than "unity." [16] In most of these instances, he was referring less to the internal structure of Christ than to the communion restored between mankind and God. Sometimes he also spoke of "the man of Christ," [17] that is, of the

fore necessary that the Mediator between God and men, by his kinship with each of the parties, restore friendship and harmony between them and thereby obtain that on the one hand God should assume responsibility for man, and that on the other man should surrender himself to God."

[13] *Her.* 3,22,1 SC 34,373 (SC 211,431): "Those who claim that Christ 'received nothing from the Virgin' are in error."

[14] *Her.* 3,21,10. The value of the virginal birth is also stressed against the Ebionites. Cf. A. Orbe, *Antropología de San Ireneo,* Madrid 1969, 438.

[15] *Her.* 3,16,2.3.8; 3,17,4; cf. A. Benoit, *Saint Irénée. Introduction a l'étude de sa théologie,* Paris, 1960, 212-214.

[16] *Her.* 4,33,11; 4,20,4, etc.

[17] *Her.* 5,14,18, SC 153,183: "the humanity of this one"; cf. SC 152, 264-265, for the justification of this translation as being "clear and faithful to the thought of Irenaeus." Cf. *Her.* 5,14,4; 5,21,2-3.

man assumed by the Word, without thereby insinuating the existence of a human person or a dualism. He used the concrete term "man" for lack of a more abstract vocabulary such as "humanity" or "human nature," but with the same meaning. Here we perceive the need for further progress in terminology to express the ontology of Christ with greater exactitude. Progress in thinking would also be necessary to clarify the presence of a human soul in Christ. Irenaeus admitted Christ had a human soul, [18] but he paid little attention to it when speaking of the Word and of the flesh.

The most remarkable doctrinal element of Irenaeus' Christology is his notion of "recapitulation." [19] This recapitulation situates the Incarnation at the center of the economy of salvation, as the truth that explains everything.

The verb "recapitulate" has three closely related meanings: to reproduce the past in a new way, to sum up the destiny of mankind in one's person, to command the unfolding of history in the role of a leader.

Christ recapitulates creation because the Incarnation reproduces the formation of Adam in a new way. This is a consummation of the work of creation. The Word "through whom everything has been made, who has always been present to mankind, united himself in the last days, at the moment decreed by the Father, to the work he had fashioned and became a passible man." [20]

By virtue of this creative power, the Word Incarnate recapitulates the history of mankind. He sums it up, he concentrates it in himself, achieving the economy of salvation in his flesh and refashioning the destiny of man.

Just as the Eternal Word holds primacy in the invisible world, the Word Incarnate assumes primacy in the visible and corporeal world, drawing all things to himself as head of the Church. This is how Christ "recapitulates all things in himself." [21]

In this way the Incarnation takes on a cosmic significance,

---

[18] Cf. *Her.* 3,22,1.
[19] Cf. A. Houssiau, *La christologie de Saint Irénée,* Louvain, Gembloux 1955, 216-224.
[20] *Her.* 3,18,1, SC 34,310 (SC 211,343).
[21] *Her.* 3,16,6, SC 34,292 (SC 211,313).

without for that matter totally dissolving the historical and personal aspect of the Word made flesh.

2. *Tertullian*

Tertullian adopted positions and discovered formulas that anticipated the answers later provided in the Eastern Church to three great Christological errors: Apollinarianism, Nestorianism, and Monophysitism.

Against Docetism and Gnosticism, he clearly affirmed that Jesus had a human soul, a truth Irenaeus had passed over in silence. "In Christ, we find soul and flesh, according to a simple and clear expression, that is to say, a soul that is a soul and flesh that is flesh." [22] Man is truly composed of body and soul. [23] Against the Gnostic doctrine that Jesus had a "psychic body" Tertullian invoked the soteriological argument to prove the existence of Jesus' soul. In order to liberate our souls, Christ was obliged to take on a soul like our own, and not the "psychic body" or the "fleshly soul" imagined by Gnosticism. This argument was invoked more than a century later against Apollinarianism.

Tertullian's vigorous affirmation of Christ's human soul enabled him to avoid the difficulty Athanasius later experienced in explaining Jesus' emotions and passions, which are not easily situated in an ontology of the Word-flesh variety. Tertullian did not ask himself whether he should impute these sentiments to the flesh or to the Word. He attributed them to the soul.

Tertullian won an important victory against the Monarchianism of Praxeas. In Praxeas' view of the "divine monarchy," Christ was only the manifestation of the Father, and therefore it was the Father, the one and only God, who became incarnate and suffered on the cross. The crux of the error lay in thinking that since God is One, he must be impersonal. Tertullian refuted this doctrine by declaring that the Word is distinct from the Father as a person, while being

---

[22] "In Christo vero invenimus animam et carnem, simplicibus et nudis vocabulis editas, id est animam animam et carnem carnem ..." (*De Carne Christi*, 13,4, CCL 2,898).
[23] "Quid a Patre Christus acceperat, nisi quod et induerat? hominem sine dubio, carnis animaeque texturam." (*De Resurrectione Carnis*, 34,10, CCL 2,965-966, 44-46).

one with him in the unity of their substance. Having introduced the distinction between substance and person in Trinitarian theology, Tertullian expressed it likewise in Christology. This was a significant contribution. By contrast, it would be a long time before the Eastern Church succeeded in extending the use of the term "hypostasis" designating person from Trinitarian doctrine to Christology.

Tertullian's formulation is especially apt: "We see a twofold state, not confused but united in a single person, Jesus, God and man." In this twofold state, "the uniqueness of each of the two substances is safeguarded," together with the distinction of the operations. [24]

Elsewhere Tertullian speaks of the two natures as the equivalent of two substances, stressing the great difference in their properties. [25]

In Tertullian's affirmation of a "twofold state" we discern the emphasis that the Council of Chalcedon would place on the permanence in the distinction between the two natures. He speaks of a "state" to show the stability of the properties of each substance. [26] He specifies that there is no confusion between them. He wants to avoid any notion of a mingling of the divinity with the humanity. He firmly opposes any affirmation of a substance that might derive from the fusion of the two others, as Monophysitism would later seek to do.

In expressly referring to the distinction between the operations, Tertullian rejects what would later be called monenergism. This doctrine that claims there is only one principle of operation in Jesus was condemned by the Third Council of Constantinople.

---

[24] "Videmus duplicem statum, non confusum sed coniunctum in una persona, Deum et hominem Jesum — de Christo autem differo — et ideo salva est utriusque proprietas substantiae, ut et Spiritus res suas egerit in illo, id est virtutes et opera et signa, et caro passiones suas functa sit, esuriens sub diabolo, sitiens sub Samaritide, flens Lazarum, anxia usque ad mortem, denique et mortua (est)" (*Adv. Praxean* 27,11, CCL 2, 1199 ff.).

[25] "Quae proprietas conditionum, divinae et humanae, aequa utique naturae utriusque veritate dispuncta est ..." (*De Carne Christi* 5,7, CCL 881-2). On the importance of the expression, cf. R. Cantalamessa, *La cristologia di Tertulliano,* Friburgo 1962, 97 ff.).

[26] Cf. R. Braun, *"Deus Christianorum." Recherche sur le vocabulaire doctrinal de Tertullien,* Paris 1962, 207:

224

The most impressive of Tertullian's formulas concerns oneness of person. He clearly perceives the distinction between substance and person. Where substance is concerned he sees a permanent duality in Christ; but this duality exists "in a single person." This person is the Word, distinct from the person of the Father. Hence Christ's unity can stem only from his person inasmuch as the substances remain two, united but not commingled. [27] Tertullian thus succeeds in expressing the fundamental ontology of Christ, using the formulas "one person," "two natures," which were later adopted by the Council of Chalcedon.

In carefully distinguishing person from substance and in giving the latter the meaning of nature, Tertullian used a terminology that could have prevented the errors in the Latin translation of the Greek term "hypostasis," which was often rendered as "substance" whereas it means "person."

Thanks to the polemical context in which it is inserted, the affirmation "in a single person" avoids another danger. In contrast to Monarchianism, it refers to the person of the Son, considered on the Trinitarian level as distinct from the person of the Father. [28] The one person in Christ is therefore

---

[27] Grillmeier notes that Tertullian had not yet posed the question whether the man in Jesus had his own *prosôpon* (*Christ in Christian Tradition,* 129). Obviously, Tertullian does not approach the problem the way the Nestorians did. When he speaks of "one person" he clearly excludes a second person attributable to the human nature of Jesus.

[28] Cantalamessa rightly remarks that "una persona" signifies one person of the Trinity, but he adds that the expression is used not in strictly Christological sense but in a Trinitarian sense. For Tertullian opposes his formula to Monarchianism which, by atributing the humanity to Jesus and the divinity to the Father, identifies the Father and the Son as one and the same person. Even more than the term "*in una persona*," the expression "*Deum et hominem Jesum*" would more adequately affirm the unity of Christ. It would therefore be incorrect to point to Tertullian's formula as the one that would later be defined by Chalcedon (*Cristologia,* 171-176). However, the Trinitarian value of "in una persona" cannot conceal its Christological significance. It is true that Tertullian wanted to combat the opinion that the Father and the Son are distinct within "a single person." He declared that in Christ there is a twofold state "in a single person," inasmuch as Jesus is God and man. However, while positing the distinction between the person of the Son and the person of the Father, he focused his attention on the duality and the unity that exist in Christ. "A single person" therefore takes on a strictly Christological meaning. Tertullian wanted to say that Christ's unity stems

this divine person, and not the result of the conjunction of two substances, as Nestorianism would later tend to conceive of him. There is not a "composite" person, but a single divine person who possesses a twofold state or a twofold substance.[29]

It is true the affirmation of "one person" in Christ was not very widely accepted by subsequent Latin tradition. It did not have the repercussions it deserved. Yet it demonstrates that more than two centuries before the profession of faith of Chalcedon the Christological formulation of that Council had already been proposed, thus indicating the admirable continuity of Tradition.

D. THE DIVINITY OF THE WORD: THE ARIAN CONTROVERSY

In Arianism we discern a Trinitarian error and a strictly Christological error. The Trinitarian error, which is by far the more serious, consists in assimilating the Word with a creature. The Christological error consists in the negation of Christ's human soul. Inasmuch as the Trinitarian error likewise dominates the entire Christological doctrine of Arianism, we must consider it at least briefly, as well as its condemnation by the Council of Nicea.

1. Arius: The Word, a Creature

The *profession of faith* that Arius presented to his bishop, Alexander of Alexandria, might indeed have seemed faultlessly orthodox. It affirmed "one God, alone unbegotten, alone

---

from his person, whereas his duality relates to substance. The truth of the matter is that Tertullian was not considering in this context the active role played by the divine person in the Incarnation. He limited himself to considering the fact of Jesus God and man. But his affirmation of a single person already had the meaning it would be given at Chalcedon.

[29] Even though we must admit a certain superficiality in the formula for its lack of metaphysical speculation on the value of the concept of person (cf. J. Moingt, *Théologie trinitaire de Tertullien, II, Substantialité et individualité,* Paris, 1966, 639-643), the fact remains that the affirmation of the two substances united without confusion in a single person is in very truth an anticipation of the definition of Chalcedon.

eternal, alone without beginning, alone true, alone possessing immortality ... who begot his only Son before eternal time." [30] However, what Arius attributed to the one God, he refused to attribute to the Son, whom he relegated to the level of a creature. [31]

In the view of Arius, the Son is not eternal: "God has not always been the Father, but there was a time when God was alone and was not yet the Father. Afterwards he became the Father. The Son has not always existed ... There was a time when he was not. And he did not exist before he was born, but he, too, had a beginning, namely, the beginning of creation." [32] Then Arius makes the following claims:

The Son was created out of nothing, and he is therefore not consubstantial with the Father: "He who is without principle established the Son to be the principle of all creatures, and after having produced him, he adopted him as his son. The son possesses nothing through his own individual substance that is strictly attributable to God. For he is neither equal, nor even consubstantial with him ... The Father is foreign to the Son according to essence, since he is without principle." [33] Since the Son is only a creature, he is imperfect, subject to change, whereas the Father is perfect and immutable.

Arius continues: The Father created the Son in order to make use of him in producing the world, according to a doctrine that calls to mind the Platonic doctrine of the demiurge. God "created a certain being whom he called Logos, Wisdom, and Son, so as to produce us through him." [34]

In the Incarnation, the Word assumed a body that was to be his instrument, a body without a soul, or at least without a rational soul. The reason Arius denies the Word-made-flesh possesses such a soul is "in order to declare more clearly that he is foreign to the essence of the Father." [35] He relates the

---

[30] Athanasius, *De Synodis,* 16, PG 26,708 C to 709 A.
[31] Cf. E. Boularand, *L'hérésie d'Arius et la "foi" de Nicée,* I, Paris 1972, 68.
[32] Cf. *ibid.* 72; Athanasius, *Oartio I contra Arianos,* 5, PG 26,21 A.
[33] Athanasius, *De Synodis,* 15, PG 26,705 A - 708 A.
[34] Athanasius, *Oratio I contra Arianos,* 5, PG 26,21 A.
[35] Boularand, *op. cit.,* 79. The argument was used by the Arians, but is this the primary source of their negation of the soul? Liebaert expresses reservations on this point in *L'Incarnation,* 115.

states of hunger, thirst, fatigue, sleep, suffering, death, and resurrection directly to the Word, who uses the body the way a charioteer drives his chariot. Arius thereby makes it clear that he thinks the Word cannot be the impassible God and that he is merely a creature.

2. Nicea: The Son, Consubstantial with the Father

In condemning Arius' error, the Council of Nicea (325 A.D.) was obliged to use a more precise vocabulary than that provided in the formulas of Scripture, since these had been adopted by Arius who gave them a new, heterodox meaning. "We believe ... in one Lord, Jesus Christ, the Son of God, begotten from the Father as only Son, that is to say, from the substance of the Father, God from God, Light from Light, true God from true God, begotten, not made, consubstantial with the Father, through whom all things were made both in heaven and on earth. For us men and for our salvation he came down from heaven: ... he was born ... and became man. ..." [36]

Therefore the Son was not created from nothing. He was begotten from the substance of the Father, and that is why he is true God from true God.

The term that most characteristically describes the Son is "consubstantial (homoousios) with the Father." "This term, had first been used by the Gnostics and then been condemned by the Council of Antioch because of the use Paul of Samosata had made of it. However the Fathers of Nicea saw in it the term that most clearly indicated the Son's perfect likeness to his Father in his divinity, while avoiding the subtleties of the Arian interpretations. [37]

Exactly what does this consubstantiality mean? It is equivalent to asserting "that the nature of the Son is as divine as the Father's and equal to it in every way." [38] It does not designate what would later be called the numerical identity

---

[36] DS 125; cf. Boularand, op. cit. II, 259. See the commentary, 289-358.

[37] The transmission of the term by way of various theories tends to show that the doctrine of faith is not defined solely by the application of a philosophical concept, and that the vocabulary used derives its meaning from the theological context.

[38] I. Ortiz de Urbina, Nicée et Constantinople, Paris, 1962, 85.

of substance, namely that the two persons of the Father and of the Son are one and the same substance. [39] Yet, in expressing the equality of the substance, "consubstantial" implies numerical identity between them, for in God there is only one substance. The Nicene Creed begins with the affirmation of this divine unity: "We believe in one God ..." If the substance of the Son resembles the substance of the Father in every respect, then the Father and the Son are identically one and the same substance.

The Council did not concern itself with this problem. Its intention was to affirm that the Son was perfectly God, like the Father. While the term "consubstantial" does not occur in Scripture, it simply clarifies what was stated in the Prologue to the Fourth Gospel: "In the beginning was the Word ... and the Word was God" (Jn 1:1). The Council rejected any inferiority on the part of the Son with respect to the divine substance.

This essential affirmation is complemented by an anathema: "As for those who say: 'There was a time when he did not exist', and 'before being begotten he did not exist', and that he was drawn out of nothingness or from another substance or essence, who declare that the Son of God is subject to change or variation, they are anathematized by the Catholic and Apostolic Church." These words specifically exclude some of the limitations placed on the Word by Arianism. The Son of God always existed, he was not called into being out of nothingness, he possesses divine immutability.

E. THE HUMAN SOUL OF CHRIST: THE APOLLINARIAN CONTROVERSY

1. Inadvertence to the Problem: Athanasius

It took the Apollinarian negation to evoke a clearer and more explicit affirmation that Christ had a human soul. While Tertullian and Origen had already insisted on the existence of Christ's soul, the great enemies of Arianism were little con-

---

[39] On this problem, cf. G.C. Stead, "'Homoousios' dans la pensée de saint Athanase," in C. Kannengiesser, *Politique et théologie chez Athanase d'Alexandrie,* Paris, 1974, 231-253.

cerned with challenging Arius' negation on this point. They focused all their attention on the problem of the divinity of the Word.

Athanasius' position is characteristic. In his refutation of Arianism, he made no mention of the soul of Jesus. [40] He adopted a Christology of the Word-flesh (*Logos-sarx*) sort. In his view, the Word became man by assuming a body. He attributed the spiritual qualities of Christ to the Word, whereas his passions belonged to the flesh. To have argued that Jesus had a soul would have made it easier for him to refute the Arian objections. For Arianism based its denial of the divinity of the Word on certain spiritual deficiences, on the fact that Jesus was ignorant of certain things, that he prayed and experienced emotional distress. Athanasius needed only to attribute these to Jesus' human soul, but this explanation did not come to his mind. He preferred to deny any real ignorance in Jesus, and to interpret the agony of Gethsemane as a movement of the flesh or as a "sham fear."

Athanasius was unable to discern an authentic human psychology in Christ. "The idea that the Savior could be a man like other men, inasmuch as he was endowed with a complete human nature, and yet was not like other men because he was God as well as man, did not come to him." [41]

Certainly, he never denied the existence of Jesus' soul, and he firmly held to the traditional affirmation that the Word became man. On one occasion, at the Synod of Alexandria in 362 A.D., he even admitted that Christ had a soul. But he did not incorporate this element into his Christology or recognize its importance. [42]

2. *The Apollinarian Doctrine*

Apollinarius the Younger, Bishop of Laodicea (362-390 A.D.), came under the influence of Alexandrian theology

---

[40] Cf. M. Richard, "Saint Athanase et la psychologie du Christ selon les Ariens," *MSR* 4 (1947) 5-54.

[41] *Ibid.*, 46.

[42] According to Grillmeier's expression, for Athanasius Christ's soul is a physical factor, but not a "theological factor" (*Christ in Christian Tradition,* 286).

through his father, Apollinarius the Elder, a native of Alexandria.

a. Negation of the human soul of Christ

In the Apollinarian view, Christ could not have a human soul because this soul would be a principle set in opposition to the Word: "It is impossible for two spiritual and will-endowed beings to coexist as one." For each would be in opposition to the other through his will and energy. Consequently, the Word has not assumed a human soul." [43] Therefore Christ's humanity could not have been perfect: "If a man had been united to God, perfect man with perfect God, they would have been two." [44]

Even more explicitly, Apollinarius thought that if the Word had assumed a complete man, he would have introduced into his being a principle of sin. A human spirit united to flesh turns away from God and inevitably exists in a sinful condition. "According to Scripture, the 'complete' man is not pure of sin in the present life, because of his inability to make his own energies coincide with the divine energies, and that is why he is not free from death. Therefore, God, having united himself to human flesh, retains the purity of his own energy, since he is a spirit (*nous*) not subject to psychical and carnal affections and governs the flesh in its carnal inclinations in a divine and impeccable way." [45]

However Apollinarius thinks that "the Word did become a son of man," [46] that he is "totally God, totally man." [47] Indeed, in his view, "to become a man" is not to be confused with "assuming a man." [48] For the Incarnation, it did not suffice that God should dwell in a man. He became man through the union of the divine pneuma with the earthly

---

[43] Fragm. 2 (ed. H. Lietzmann, *Apollinaris von Laodicea und seine Schule*, Tübingen, 1904, 204); cf. Liebaert, *L'Incarnation*, 145.
[44] Fragm. 81, Lietzmann 224.
[45] *Kata meros pistis*, Lietzmann, 178-179. Cf. H. de Riedmatten, *La christologie d'Apollinaire*, Studia Patristica, II, Berlin 1957, 213.
[46] *Ibid.*, 177.
[47] *De fide et incarnatione*, 6, Lietzmann 199.
[48] Ps.-Felix, fragm. 186, Lietzmann 318. Cf. Grillmeier, *Christ*, 332.

flesh. It is this union that formed Christ the man, a being composed of body and spirit.[49]

Nevertheless, Apollinarius was forced to admit that in his view Christ is "not a man, but like a man, because he is not consubstantial to man according to the most exact terminology."[50] Even so, Apollinarius never retracted any part of the position he had adopted and according to which it is the Word who, in Christ's humanity, takes the place of soul (*psuchè*) and spirit (*nous*).

b. Unity of the Word with the flesh

To express the relationship of the Word to the flesh, Apollinarius used the notions of prime mover and instrument. The Word moves the body. "The instrument and the prime mover naturally constitute a single energy. Now, just as energy is one, so also is substance. Therefore there is a single substance of the Word and of the instrument."[51]

Such a unity is conceived on the model of the unity of every human nature: there is a unity of the Word with the flesh, just as in other men there is a unity of the soul with the body.

Based on this premise, Apollinarius affirms "a single nature" (*mia phusis*) in Christ. The unity is so complete that it is impossible to distinguish the properties of each by relating some of them to the flesh and the others to the Word. An Apollinarian condemns "those who call Christ a man who was crucified and do not confess that he was crucified in his entire divine hypostasis."[52]

According to this view, the biological unity of the Word with the flesh was assured by the virginal conception. In the ordinary process of generation, the man's role assures the infusion of the soul — Apollinarius was a traducianist —, whereas in the conception of Christ the flesh was quickened by a spiritual and divine Power.[53]

---

[49] Cf. E. Mühlenberg, *Apollinaris von Laodicea,* Göttingen 1969, 165-171, 215-230.

[50] Fragm. 45, Lietzmann, 214.

[51] Fragm. 117, Lietzmann 235 ff.

[52] Fragm. 186, Lietzmann 319.

[53] *De unione,* 13, Lietzmann 191; cf. de Riedmatten, *op. cit.* 216.

Apollinarius likewise spoke of a single person (*prosôpon*) and of a single hypostasis.[54] He appears to have been the first to use the term hypostasis in Christology. Since flesh cannot be considered to be a hypostasis, there can be in Christ only the hypostasis of the Word.

But this unity of the person was reduced to the unity of nature and operation. "In any case, the starting-point from which Apollinarius seeks to understand the unity in Christ is almost always the idea of a vital dynamism," according to Grillmeier.[55]

This *vital dynamism* which permeates all of Apollinarius' doctrine is not only a physical constitutive principle, but also a theological principle of *salvation*. Apollinarius relies on the mystery of salvation to vindicate Christ's unity of nature: "Break the unity of the 'whole' that Christ is, and that is the end of his redemptive death, of baptism in this death, the end of the role of Christ's flesh as well as of the worship we render to him."[56] Indeed, only God could save us by suffering and dying for us: the Son of God "by the blood of his hypostasis has delivered the whole of creation."[57]

3. The Reaction: Affirmation of Christ's Soul

At the Synod of Alexandria of 362 A.D. the soteriological argument was invoked against the Apollinarians. It was declared that the Word became man to save not only bodies but also souls. Hence he must have assumed a soul and a body. The Synod adopted a declaration that "the Savior did not have a body devoid of a soul, devoid of feeling or reason" (*apsuchon, anaisthèton, anoèton*). The Apollinarians signed the formula but interpreted it in accordance with their doctrine, translating *apsuchon* by "without life" and attributing the role of reason (*nous*) to the Word, inasmuch as the formula did not explicitly speak of a human intellect.

Later on when the quarrel was revived, Vitalis, a priest of Antioch opposed to his bishop Paulinus, went to Rome to

---

[54] *De fide*, 6, Lietzmann 198-9.
[55] *Christ in Christian Tradition*, 338.
[56] De Riedmatten, *op. cit.*, 218-219.
[57] *De fide*, 8, Lietzmann 201.

plead the cause of Apollinarianism (375 A.D.). However the pope sent a letter to Paulinus saying: "This heresy, which has been rapidly spreading in the East, must be completely wiped out; that is to say, it must be acknowledged that the Son of God, Wisdom and Word, assumed body, soul, and mind (*sensum*), that is to say, the whole Adam and, to speak more accurately, the whole of our old man except for sin. ... If anyone affirms that the Word replaced the human mind (*sensum*) in the incarnate Lord, the Catholic Church anathematizes him." [58]

In another letter, Damasus went back to the soteriological argument: "If imperfect man was assumed, the gift of God is imperfect, our salvation is imperfect, for the whole man has not been saved." [59]

In 377 A.D., a Council convened at Rome in the presence of Peter of Alexandria and of messengers from Basil of Caesarea, and solemnly condemned Apollinarius, Vitalis and Timothy, the Apollinarian bishop of Berytus.

The decision was confirmed at the Council of Alexandria (378 A.D.), at the Council of Antioch (379 A.D.), at the Ecumenical Council of Constantinople (381 A.D.), and at another Council of Rome (382 A.D.).

After Apollinarius' death, Apollinarianism divided into two schools. The Synusiasts were intransigent, professing belief in the consubstantiality of the flesh with the divinity. The other school was more moderate and came closer to the orthodox Church in stressing the unity of person in Christ. Apollinarian writings were disseminated during the 5th century, falsely claiming to be the work of Gregory the Wonderworker, Popes Felix and Julius, Athanasius, etc.. They had an impact on the development of Christological thinking.

---

[58] *Per Filium*, PL 13, 356 B.
[59] Fragm. *Illud Sane*, PL 13, 352 B.

F. THE ONE PERSON OF CHRIST: THE NESTORIAN CONTROVERSY

1. *Dualism in the Antiochian School*

In the face of the Alexandrian School which affirmed the unity of Christ and tended to highlight his divinity, the Antiochian School clung to his duality and concerned itself with acknowledging the integrity of Jesus' humanity.

An opponent of Apollinarius, *Diodorus of Tarsus* († 394 A.D.), was accused after his death by Cyril of Alexandria of being the founder of Nestorianism. This accusation is excessive, but it does point to a dangerous emphasis by Diodorus on duality. Diodorus still professed a Christology of the Word-flesh sort, and he deepened the separation between the Word and the flesh. In his view, it cannot be said that the Son of God is the son of David in the strict sense, or that he was born of Mary. The man born of Mary, said he, is the son of God through grace, whereas the Word is the son of God by reason of his nature. However, Diodorus refused to speak of two sons of a single Father: "Let us grant this: the two are a single son, and let us leave what is impossible in the form of words." [60] This sentence reveals Diodorus' dilemma, the difficulty he experienced in conceiving a unity of person in Christ.

Theodore, Bishop *of Mopsuestia* (392-428 A.D.), was considered during his lifetime to be a defender of orthodoxy against the Arians and the Apollinarians. After his death, however, he was accused of Nestorianism by Cyril of Alexandria, and solemnly condemned by the Fifth Ecumenical Council (the Second Council of Constantinople, 530 A.D.).

To this day, he remains a controversial figure. Msgr R. Devreesse has pointed to the falsification of texts produced to induce his condemnation, [61] whereas F. A. Sullivan has concluded that the condemned texts were indeed written by Theodore. [62] The current trend is to highlight Theodore's positive

---

[60] Fragm. 30, in M. Brière, "Fragments syriaques de Diodore," *Revue de l'Orient chrétien* 30 (1946) 231-283.

[61] *Essai sur Théodore de Mopsueste*, The Vatican 1948.

[62] *The Christology of Theodore of Mopsuestia*, Rome 1956. On this

contribution to Christology, while acknowledging certain imperfections of language and thought stemming from the epoch in which he wrote.

(1) Contrary to Diodorus of Tarsus, to whose views he was greatly indebted, Theodore adopted a *Word-man* Christology.

He affirmed that the Word became incarnate by assuming a man, by dwelling in a man, by clothing himself with the man Jesus. Thus, this is not a theology of the Word becoming man. Theodore used the traditional expression: "The Word became man." But if he had adopted it as a theological principle it would have had the disadvantage of suggesting a change in the Word, as the Arians claimed there was. Theodore therefore sought another theological explanation of the Incarnation: the assumption of the man by the Word.

He wrote: "The only-begotten Son of God, God the Word, deigned, he alone for the salvation of all, to assume one among us, so as to raise him from the dead. He made him rise up to heaven, joining him to himself and placing him at the right hand of God." [63] Because of this formulation Theodore was suspected of Adoptionism. Actually, he had in mind the assumption not of a human person but of a human nature: "He assumed our very nature ..." [64]

(2) Theodore stressed that he was speaking of a *complete human nature*. In Christ, he said, the natures remain distinct, without confusion, in their indissoluble conjunction. He highlighted the role of the soul as a theological principle.

How did Theodore of Mopsuestia conceive of the problem of the Incarnation? He saw it in the context of a soteriological problem. The Redemption must be the work of God himself, but it must also be the redemption of the human will in the exercise of its freedom. Now, Christ is he "in whom God the Word accomplishes the Redemption of mankind through the free activity of a perfectly obedient man." [65] The

---

point the demonstration is considered convincing by J. Daniélou (*RSR* 1956, 604).

[63] *Hom. cat.*, X, 1,2; ed. R. Tonneau, The Vatican 1949, 537.
[64] *Hom. cat.* II, 1, Tonneau, 161.
[65] R. A. Norris, *Manhood and Christ, A Study of the Christology of Theodore of Mopsuestia*, London, 1963, 237.

236

dualism of Theodore of Mopsuestia can therefore be explained by his concern to emphasize the role of man in the work of salvation.

This concern led him to show the development of the man assumed, his interior struggles, the help of grace that he received. Theodore made a very laudable effort to discover Christ's psychological and spiritual life.

(3) *The union of the two natures* is conceived by Theodore as stemming from "the indwelling" of the Word in man "through his good pleasure." Yet this union is not strictly a moral one, or a union of grace. For Theodore affirms the unity of the person. "The natures are distinct, but the *prosôpon* is completed as a single entity through the union. This means that when we set about distinguishing the nature, we are to say that the *prosôpon* of the man is perfect, and perfect also is [the *prosôpon*] of the divinity. Yet when we focus our gaze upon the union, we affirm that the two natures are a single *prosôpon,* inasmuch as the humanity receives through the divinity an honor that exceeds its capacities, and inasmuch as the divinity accomplishes all justice in the humanity." [66]

A doctrine such as this is not perfect, because it seems to presuppose that the personal unity results from the union of the natures, and it manifests a certain ambiguity in the notion of *prosôpon* which is applied to each of the two natures. Nevertheless, the final affirmation is that there is a unity of *prosôpon,* conceived in such a way that the work of the man in Christ is attributed to a divine subject, the Word. Theodore of Mopsuestia still fell short of the idea that the Word is the one and only person in Christ.

Theodore's formulas were deficient, they considerably antedated the Council of Chalcedon. Even so, it cannot be said that Theodore ever deviated from orthodoxy or that he was a Nestorian ahead of his time.

The only incident in connection with the propagation of Theodore's ideas came from the opposition he expressed to calling Mary the "*Theotokos.*" But he later corrected these unfortunate statements and explicitly accepted the name "Mother

---

[66] H. B. Swete, *Theodori Episcopi Mopsuesteni in Epistolas B. Pauli Commentarii,* II, Cambridge 1882, 300.

of God." [67] John of Antioch cited this example when he wrote to Nestorius in 430 A.D., inviting him to accept the term *"Theotokos"* and redress his doctrine to make it agree with that of Pope Celestine. [68]

2. *Nestorius*

When Nestorius became Bishop of Constantinople in 428 A.D., he found himself confronting a controversy that was already raging. There were those who rejected the term *Theotokos*, "Mother of God," and would accept for Mary only the title of "mother of the man" (*anthrôpotokos*), thereby arousing the indignation of the others. Nestorius took a position in favor of the name "mother of Christ" (*Christotokos*).

Nestorius has been accused of asserting there are two persons in Christ, and a third who is the fruit of their union. That is not what he really taught. Recent historians have posed the question: Was Nestorius a Nestorian? Several of them have sought to reinstate him.

Actually, two deficiencies in Nestorius' doctrine must be pointed out:

(1) On the one hand, he was unwilling to accept certain elements of Tradition. In Grillmeier's words: "We must ... fault Nestorius for not having taken the tradition of the *communicatio idiomatum* seriously enough and not having thought it through sufficiently. ... This tradition should have spurred him to reconsider his speculative presuppositions. But he was more inclined to measure the tradition by his own speculative framework than vice versa." [69]

According to the fundamental principle of the *"communication of idioms"* (i.e., the communion of attributes), the one Christ possesses both divine attributes and human attributes. Thus, the Word possesses the distinctive hallmarks of human life with its infirmities and sufferings, whereas the man Jesus is endowed with the attributes of divinity. This principle had already been incorporated into traditional Christo-

---

[67] *De Incarn.*, 15, PG 66,991 B.

[68] *Epist. 1 ad Nestorium*, 3, PG 77,1453 B C.

[69] *Christ in Christian Tradition*, 518. However, in an ecumenical spirit, Grillmeier seeks to understand Nestorius' position and to defend whatever validity it had.

logy, and its abuse by the Arians and Apollinarians had not robbed it of its intrinsic value.

It was this principle that found expression in the term *Theotokos,* and in the affirmation that the Word was born, suffered, and died. But Nestorius rejected the title *Theotokos* in the strict sense, a title that had been used since the Council of Nicea by Alexander of Alexandria as well as by the majority of the theologians of the 4th century including Eusebius of Caesarea, Athanasius, Cyril of Jerusalem, Epiphanius, Didymus, Gregory of Nazianzus, and Gregory of Nyssa.

In consequence, Nestorius denied it was proper to say the Word was born of Mary, that he suffered and died. He rejected the formula *Deus passus.* In so doing he set himself in opposition to the Creed of Nicea which attributed to the Son of God both eternal generation and the Passion and Resurrection. Nicea declared that one and the same subject, "true God" begotten by the Father, suffered and rose again.

(2) Philosophically, Nestorius failed to develop the concept of person as distinct from nature.

Nestorius conceived the *prosôpon* to be the appearance of the essence, the aggregate of attributes that concretely determine a nature (*ousia*) and make of this nature a "substance" (*hupostasis*). The hypostasis designates the complete nature. For Nestorius, there are in Christ two natural *prosôpa,* for in this union the two natures are complete. (On this point, the Council of Chalcedon was to approve the Nestorian position.) However, each of the natures in Christ has its own hypostasis (and for Nestorius hypostasis did not signify person). But the union of the two natures forms a concrete whole; hence there is a *prosôpon* of union which he called the "common *prosôpon* of our Lord Jesus Christ."

Now, for Nestorius the unity of this *prosôpon* is realized by the compensation of the *prosôpa,* that is to say, by an exchange of appearances, inasmuch as the Son uses a human *prosôpon* to represent him and the human *prosôpon* receives a glorious divine form. This unity is also realized by a mutual compenetration (perichoresis) of the *prosôpa.* The compenetration occurs through the indwelling of the Word in the man as in a temple. Nestorius even spoke of a mingling of the two natures without confusion, namely, God-made-man and man made into God. [70]

However, the compensation and compenetration of the two natures, the divine and the human, do not suffice to verify the true unity of Christ. Nestorius sought an ontological principle of the unity of the two natures and did not succeed in finding one. He would have needed a concept of person that was more than the expression of the concrete individuality of the nature. And this concept never came to him.

If Nestorius had accepted the Christological data of Tradition he might have remedied these deficiencies and orientated his thinking toward the correct solution. For these data posited the Word as subject of all of Christ's human activity and opened the way to finding in the Word the ontological principle of the unity of his natures.

3. *The Reaction against Nestorianism: the Authentic Expression of Faith in the Unity of Christ*

The reaction against Nestorius

Cyril of Alexandria reacted violently against Nestorius' teaching. He defended the use of the term *Theotokos*. He formulated the principle that the qualities of Christ must be attributed to the Word, and that the Word united himself "*according to the hypostasis*" to the flesh he assumed. Here appeared for the first time an expression that would be accepted by Tradition in the notion of the "hypostatic union."

However in the anathematisms he hurled against Nestorius, Cyril also spoke of a "union of nature" (*enôsis phusikè*), for he did not yet grasp the distinction between hypostasis and nature. In his treatise against Nestorius he affirmed "a single incarnate nature of the God Word," a formula that had come to him from an Apollinarian writing which falsely claimed Athanasius as its author.

Nestorius refused to yield to Cyril, and asked Pope Celestine for his support. But the Pope convoked a Council at Rome which condemned the Nestorian thesis. The Emperor Theodosius II, for his part, convoked a Council at Ephesus.

---

[70] Cf. Grillmeier, *Christ in Christian Tradition*, 516.

The Council of Ephesus

Cyril of Alexandria opened the Council in 431 A.D., without waiting for the arrival of the Fathers from Antioch. Cyril's second letter to Nestorius was read, and the Fathers were asked if it conformed to the Creed of Nicea. After the approbation of Cyril's letter, Nestorius, letter was read. The Fathers held that Nestorius' views were not in conformity with the Creed of Nicea and deposed him. The verdict was confirmed by the Pope's delegates who arrived a few days later.

What the Council of Ephesus defined was not the doctrine of Cyril's anathematisms, but the essential content of his second letter to Nestorius. This content can be summarized as follows: *The eternal Son of the Father is he who, according to carnal generation, was born of the Virgin Mary; for this reason Mary is legitimately called Theotokos, Mother of God.* The expression "union according to the hypostasis" is not defined as such. It simply refers to a union that is more than moral or accidental. In Christ there is a unity of the subject of attribution: the divinity and the humanity form "one single Lord, Christ and Son."

The Formulary of Reunion

While the Eastern Fathers grouped around John of Antioch rejected the position taken by Nestorius, they did not accept the decision of the Council of Ephesus. They condemned Cyril's anathematisms and excommunicated him and his followers. To restore peace, John of Antioch proposed a formulary written by Theodoret of Cyrus. In 433 A.D., this profession of faith was accepted with a few slight changes by Cyril, and so became the "Formulary of Reunion." It might well be called "the Creed of Ephesus." [71]

This profession of faith avoids the unacceptable terms used by Cyril, such as "one nature," "union of nature," and on the contrary affirms *two natures* in union (*duo physeôn enôsis*).

On the one hand, the Formulary affirms the *identity of person* of the Son of God before the Incarnation with Jesus Christ: "We therefore confess that Our Lord Jesus Christ, the only-begotten Son of God, perfect God and perfect man

---

[71] Cf. Grillmeier, *Christ in Christian Tradition*, 498-500.

in his rational soul and in his body, born of the Father before the ages according to his divinity, is the same who, consubstantial with the Father according to his divinity is also consubstantial with us according to his humanity. The union of the two natures has indeed been effected. That is why we confess one Christ, one Son, one Lord." [72] To express the union, care was taken to avoid the word *"sunapheia,"* used by Nestorius, meaning conjunction, and the stronger term *"enôsis"* was used instead.

The Creed of Ephesus also sanctions the use of the name *"Theotokos."* "According to this notion of a union without confusion, we confess the Holy Virgin to be the Mother of God (*Theotokon*), because God the Word became flesh and man, and through the very conception united himself to the temple taken from her." The image of the temple, so eagerly proposed by the School of Antioch, is used here in the explanation of the term *Theotokos.*

Cyril added to the Formulary a declaration on the *apportionment of the operations* of Christ, to forestall incorrect interpretations of his Fourth Anathematism: "As to the words of the Gospels and of the Apostles concerning the Lord, we know that theologians apply those words that unify to a single person (*prosôpon*), and those that divide to the two natures, attributing those that befit God to the divinity of Christ, and the humbler ones to his humanity." [73]

G. THE TWO NATURES: THE MONOPHYSITE CONTROVERSY AND THE COUNCIL OF CHALCEDON

1. *Eutyches, the Spokesman for Monophysitism*

Proclus, Patriarch of Constantinople (434-446 A.D.), had offered a formula for reconciling the theologies of Antioch and of Alexandria: "two natures in one hypostasis." However Eutyches, an archimandrite of Constantinople, insisted on retaining the formulas of Cyril of Alexandria on unity of nature. He spread a Monophysitic doctrine, and was accused of heresy. Patriarch Flavian invited him to appear before the Synod of

---

[72] DS 272.
[73] DS 273.

Constantinople in 448 A.D., where the following Christological formula was proposed to him: "We confess that since his Incarnation Christ is of two natures in one hypostasis and in one person."

Eutyches rejected this formula, and expressed his essential position in this way: "I confess that Our Lord has been of *two natures before the union,* but *since the union* I confess *one single nature.*" Inasmuch as he refused to admit in Christ a nature consubstantial with that of men, he was declared a heretic and excommunicated. He appealed to Pope Leo, who wrote a letter to Flavian (*Tome to Flavian*), confirming the condemnation of Eutyches. [74]

Meanwhile Emperor Theodosius, who supported Eutyches, convoked a Council at Ephesus in 449 A.D. Presided over by Dioscorus of Alexandria, this Council refused to read the "*Tome to Flavian*" and rehabilitated Eutyches. The Pope condemned the Council, which he called "the Robber Synod" and held to be null and void.

After the death of Theodosius, his successor Marcian convoked another Council at Nicea, but the Council was actually held at Chalcedon in 451 A.D. This Council deposed Dioscorus and pronounced a definition of faith which excluded Monophysitism.

2. The Definition of Faith of Chalcedon

"Following the holy Fathers, therefore, we all with one accord teach the profession of faith in the one identical Son, our Lord Jesus Christ.

"We declare that he is perfect both in his divinity and in his humanity, truly God and truly man composed of body and rational soul; that he is consubstantial with the Father in his divinity, consubstantial with us in his humanity, like us in every respect except for sin.

"We declare that in his divinity he was begotten of the Father before time, and in his humanity he was begotten in this last age of Mary the Virgin, the Mother of God, for us and for our salvation.

"We declare that the one selfsame Christ, only-begotten

---

[74] Cf. DS 290-295.

Son and Lord, must be acknowledged in two natures without any commingling or change or division or separation; that the distinction between the natures is in no way removed by their union but rather that the specific character of each nature is preserved and they are united in one person and one hypostasis.

"We declare that he is not split or divided into two persons, but that there is one selfsame only-begotten Son, God the Word, the Lord Jesus Christ. ..." [75]

The elements of this definition stem from four earlier documents: Cyril's second letter to Nestorius, the Formulary of Reunion of 433 A.D., Flavian's formula, and Leo's Tome.

(1) The Council adopted *the earlier elaboration of Christological doctrine* in its entirety:

— The Son is "one selfsame," according to the formula used by Irenaeus.

— This Son is truly God and truly man, a truth opposed to the teaching of the Gnostics and the Docetists.

— As man, he is composed of a rational soul and a body, in refutation of the Christological error of the Arians and the Apollinarians.

— He is consubstantial with the Father, a reminder of the *homoousios* of Nicea.

— He is consubstantial with us, an affirmation opposed to the views of Apollinarius and Eutyches.

— He was born of the Virgin Mary Theotokos, a reminder of the Council of Ephesus. Indeed, everything said concerning the unity of Christ (in great part borrowed from the Formulary of Reunion) harks back to Ephesus.

(2) The Council of Chalcedon affirmed the *duality of the natures* in Christ, a duality that has been maintained ever since. The formula proposed by Anatolius, Patriarch of Constantinople, and inspired by Flavian's formula, used the expression "from (*ek*) two natures." The Chalcedonian definition reads: "in (*en*) two natures." The Pope's legates, with the support of the Antiochene bishops, had demanded this change. Dioscorus declared he was willing to admit that Christ is "from two natures," but refused to admit that there are "two na-

---

[75] *The Church Teaches, Documents of the Church in English Translation* (Rockford, Ill., Tan Books and Publishers 1973) 172. Cf. also DS 301-302.

tures" in him. The Council's formula eliminated all ambiguity, and flatly condemned Monophysitism.

Chalcedon insisted on a permanent duality in Christ. His two natures are "without any commingling or change." According to the terms of Cyril's second letter, the distinction between the natures was not removed by the union. The Council gave greater force to Cyril's terms by adding "in no way." According to a statement in Leo's *Tome to Flavian,* the specific character of each nature has been preserved. Leo had explicated the principle with greater precision by declaring that the operations of each of the natures are uniquely its own, "the Word performing what belongs to the Word and the flesh performing what belongs to the flesh." [76] However the Council did not enunciate this distinction between the operations, which follows from the distinction of the natures. If it had done so, it would have been more successful in forestalling the dangers of monenergism and monothelitism.

(3) The Council affirmed, on the other hand, that the natures are "without division or separation," in accordance with the views of Alexandrian theology. Above all, it declared that in Christ there is " *one selfsame person and one selfsame hypostasis.*" This was probably taken from Flavian's formula. It is an important addition because "hypostasis" has a more metaphysical significance than "*prosôpon*" and indicates more clearly that the unity of the person is ontological.

The meaning of the term hypostasis was not defined, but the expression "one selfsame hypostasis" gives full ontological value to another expression that is easy to understand: "one and the same," a very concrete formula whose meaning is very clear.

---

[76] "Agit enim utraque forma (scil. Dei et servi) cum alterius communione quod proprium est, Verbo scilicet operante quod Verbi est, et carne exsequente quod carnis est. Unum horum coruscat miraculis, aliud succumbit injuriis" (*Act. Conc. Const.* II, 2, 1, p. 28). The formulation of the distinction between the operations was still very imperfect, for it reflected the schema Word-flesh. Besides, instead of clearly pointing to the divine nature as the principle opposed to "the flesh," it referred to the Word, thereby designating the person.

H. THE TWO WILLS: THE MONOTHELITE CONTROVERSY

1. *The Development of Monothelitism*

Monothelitism was born of efforts to reconcile the Mono-physites with orthodoxy by way of intermediary formulas that might satisfy both parties.

Sergius, Patriarch of Constantinople, began by proposing monenergism, according to which, after the union of the two natures, there was a single "energy" or operation in Christ, the theandric (divine-human) operation.

This doctrine was attacked by Sophronius who soon after-ward became Patriarch of Jerusalem (630 A.D.). [77] Sergius thereupon abandoned this solution on the grounds that it was not possible to speak of either one or two operations in Christ. In his answer to Sergius, Pope Honorius wrote: "We confess one single will in our Lord Jesus Christ." What he meant by this was that Christ's human will is one through its conformity with the divine will which it has never contradicted. When separated from its context, the Pope's affirmation could be interpreted in a Monothelitic sense. Sergius published an "explanation" (*ekthesis*), in which he proposed Monothelitism in the strict sense by affirming that Christ has only one will.

The Popes were to react against this view, and Emperor Constantius II published a decree that prohibited any affirmation of monothelitism or dyothelitism, monenergism or dyenergism, so as to put an end to the debate.

The error of Monothelitism consists in considering only the unity of the person in the matter of operation. The Monothelites interpreted the will as an impulsion proceeding from the person, and in so doing they changed the sense of the word. Besides, they failed to consider the duality of will and operation that results from the duality of natures. [78]

2. *Affirmation of Two Wills in Christ*

Monothelitism was condemned by the *Lateran Council* convoked and presided over by Pope Martin I (649 A.D.). This was not an ecumenical council, but Martin I later made

---

[77] On this author's doctrine, cf. C. Von Schönborn, *Sophrone de Jérusalem, Vie monastique et confession dogmatique*, Paris, 1972, 191-224.

[78] Cf. M. Jugie, "Monothélisme," *DTC* 10, 2307-2323.

vigorous efforts to have its canons accepted as a profession of faith for the entire Church. [79]

The condemnation was renewed and made more explicit by the 6th Ecumenical Council (3rd Council of Constantinople, 680-681 A.D.). This Council adopted the terms of Chalcedon and then affirmed that in Christ there are "*two natural wills and two natural operations* [i.e., energies], without division or change, without separation or commingling." The term "natural" was explicitly used according to the terminology of St. Maximus of Chrysopolis, a great enemy of the Monothelites. The Council refused to use the Monothelitic terminology of "hypostatic" will or operation.

Moreover the Council declared that the two natural wills are not in opposition, for the human will follows submissively and without resistence or opposition the all-powerful divine will. It thereby answered the Monothelitic objection that a duality of wills was incompatible with the unity of Christ because it necessarily implied an opposition.

Finally, the Council affirmed that the divinity of Christ, far from eliminating his human will, safeguards it.

I. Conclusion of the Patristic Period

The Council of Chalcedon enunciated in a profession of faith the results of the Christological advances of the first centuries. We have seen how it incorporated everything that had previously been affirmed against the various errors. In a well-balanced position, it joined together whatever was valid in the opposing Alexandrian and Antiochene Christologies. It accepted both the unity and the duality of Christ, and explained how both points of view were to be held simultaneously and harmoniously, i.e., unity of person and duality of natures.

This was a definitive step forward. True, the temptation has persisted through the centuries to challenge the pronouncements of Chalcedon, as did Harnack when he called the Council of Chalcedon a synod of robbers and traitors. [80] Following the

---

[79] DS 510-511.

[80] According to Harnack, the Eastern Church was "robbed of its faith" (*Dogmengeschichte*, 2, Tübingen 1931, 395-396).

thinking of liberal Protestantism, Harnack would have liked to restore a certain Adoptionism or Nestorianism, and he saw Chalcedon as a triumph for Apollinarianism or Monophysitism. Grillmeier, on the contrary, in his study of the formation of Christological doctrine during the first centuries, concludes that the dogma of Chalcedon, far from being a deviation in either direction, expresses the authentic Tradition of the Church: In his words: "Few councils have been so rooted in Tradition as the Council of Chalcedon." [81]

No valid Christology can be developed, therefore, outside the path blazed by Chalcedon. The starting point of Christology remains unity of person and duality of natures. A theology of Christ should not reach back beyond Chalcedon to search for another solution than the one this Council so laboriously achieved to the problems posed by the unity and duality of Jesus. It follows that it is useless to seek any unity of Christ other than the unity of person. Neither the unity of an indwelling of God in man nor a simple unity of consciousness or of the subconscious can explain the revealed deposit on Christ and provide a foundation for his unity.

The terms of the definition of Chalcedon may appear abstract. However we should note that in the thinking of the Fathers who composed the formula, the two natures and the one person or hypostasis were considered concretely: the one person is the person of the "one selfsame" Jesus Christ; the two natures are on the one hand his divinity and on the other the humanity by which he is in all things like us. Chalcedon did not canonize any particular philosophical concepts or system of thought. Its decisions were governed rather by concern to discover the best way of expressing what concretely exists in Christ. It set out to translate the Gospel sources, for the Fathers of the Council always referred back to this fundamental revealed deposit.

While Chalcedon is the authentic expression of Patristic Christology, it does not in any sense put an end to doctrinal research. On the contrary, it remains the point of departure for new research. It is a stage in the doctrinal progress of the Church, a stage that can never again be brought into question but which must open the way to further advances.

---

[81] *Christ in Christian Tradition*, 550.

For instance, the Chalcedonian formula of faith does not go into explanations of what nature is or what person or hypostasis is. It does not even concern itself with defining the act of the Incarnation, but limits itself to declaring what exists in Christ. It does not specify the relationship between Christ's ontological constitution and his redemptive mission, but limits itself to a general affirmation: "For us and for our salvation." In no sense is its goal to show the value and the significance of the unity of Christ and the duality of his natures for the human community he came to transform.

It has been and remains the task of subsequent theological inquiry to build on the solid foundation of Chalcedon and to elaborate a more complete metaphysics of the Incarnation. In so doing, theology continues to depend on the basic revealed deposit that guided the first Councils and that still guides the doctrinal labors of the Church: Holy Scripture, and in Christology, the Gospel witness in particular.

PART FOUR

THE ONTOLOGY OF THE INCARNATION

How can theological reflection on the deposit of Revelation define the ontology of the Incarnation? Such reflection is enriched by the contribution of Tradition over the centuries in its efforts to clarify the identity of Christ. But theology also sets out to attain a deeper understanding of certain aspects of Christology which were not adequately adverted to in the controversies of the first centuries.

We are speaking not simply of the ontology of Christ but of the ontology of the Incarnation *per se*. Revelation shows us a beginning of incarnation in the Old Covenant and then draws our minds to the process by which the Word became incarnate.

Let us make ourselves very clear: our thinking is not based exclusively on a conciliar definition, but rests on the testimony of Scripture. We rely on the declarations of the great Councils, Chalcedon in particular, in order to rightly interpret the meaning of this testimony, but our horizon is much broader. Our inquiry into the area of ontology rests on the totality of Revelation concerning Christ and the Incarnation, and not solely on the individual affirmations that settled certain specific controversies once and for all.

CHAPTER IX

THE ACT OF THE INCARNATION

The Council of Chalcedon did not specifically consider the dynamism of the Incarnation, even though it determined the ontological structure that clarifies its meaning. However, in affirming there is one single person in Christ, it has shown us that the Incarnation consists in a personal involvement on the part of God. The Incarnation is the action of a divine person.

A. INCARNATION IN THE OLD TESTAMENT

Already in the Old Covenant there was an authentic incarnation which involved God in the life of mankind, or more precisely in the life of a chosen people. We have noted how God established relations with men in the form of human covenants. He involved his thought by expressing it through human words. He involved his action by deploying it in the history of Israel. He involved his presence by localizing it in the Tent of Meeting, then in the Temple, in order to be more humanly accessible.

We can say that this involvement was total in the sense that it encompassed the whole of God's being: his thought, his will, and his activity. The offer of his permanent presence is especially indicative of his intention to give himself totally to men.

However this divine involvement differed essentially from what it would become in the New Covenant because it was not yet as personal as it would be in the Son of God become man.

It is certainly true that God appeared in the Old Covenant

as a personal being. But he did not yet reveal himself in his Trinity. He simply manifested his unity. The personal qualities attributed to him, such as those of father and bridegroom of Israel, were applied to him in a general way, without any distinction of persons. Fatherhood characterized God as God, not strictly the divine person of the Father. The same holds true of the quality of bridegroom, claimed by the Son in the Gospel, which had been hitherto attributed indistinctly to Yahweh.

We can conclude that reconciling certain of these attributions could pose a problem. The quality of fatherhood is not easily identified with the hallmark of a bridegroom, if they are to be interpreted as something more than imagery. The problem finds an answer in the distinction among the persons which is emphasized in the New Covenant, where the Father appears as distinct from the Bridegroom. In Jewish Revelation, however, God kept hidden the deepest aspect of his reality: the mystery of the three divine persons. The distinction among the divine persons was not revealed until one of these persons began to live an authentically human life [1].

It is not by chance that the distinction between the Father, the Son and the Holy Spirit makes its appearance in the Gospel account of the Annunciation. Nor for that matter that in the Prologue of John's Gospel the eternal preexistence of the Son and of the Father is clearly affirmed to introduce the affirmation: "The Word became flesh" (1:14). It is through the Incarnation of the Word that God's innermost life was revealed. This revelation is not a simple manifestation of truth, but the distinct gift of each of the divine persons.

The incarnation of God in the Old Testament, which did not attain to the level of this personal involvement, enables us to more surely measure, by contrast, the significance of the

---

[1] If indeed the Trinity reveals itself in the Incarnation, we cannot affirm with Küng (*Christ sein,* 468) that this Trinity signifies only the manifestation of God in the man Jesus through the power of the Spirit; nor can we agree with Schoonenberg that the distinction of the Father from the Son and from the Spirit became interpersonal through the Incarnation ("Trinity — The consummated covenant: Theses on the doctrine of the trinitarian God," *Studies in Religion — Sciences Religieuses* 5, 1975/6, 114-115). In Christ the Trinity is revealed as a trinity of divine persons, and as a preexistent Trinity.

Incarnation in the New Covenant. Even though the God of the Jews expressed the will to give himself to his people and to establish a horizontal relationship of love with them, there was profound reserve in his self-giving. His remoteness was stressed as well as his closeness. Indeed, in the Old Testament God intervened only through the mediation of human persons, i.e., the leaders of the people or the prophets. He entered the universe of men yet remained a stranger to it, and he affirmed his transcendence in his contacts with men.

God manifested his intention to give himself totally only through signs and mediations which announced and prepared the way for what was to follow. His self-giving was finally consummated in the action of the Son who became personally present to men as one of them and thereby bridged the gap that separated God from man.

B. The Son's Act of Incarnation

1. *The Son's Involvement*

a. An act of self emptying

In the Christian community the value of the act of the Incarnation was highlighted very early, as witnessed by the Christological hymn of the Epistle to the Philippians (2:6-8). Christians did not limit themselves to affirming that Jesus is the Son of God. They wanted to celebrate the action which, starting from the invisible God, explains this truth. The description of a descending Christology appears to have been one of the first expressions of the Christian faith and liturgy.

God's personal involvement is stressed in the act which, for the one who "being in the form of God," consisted in "emptying himself" and "taking the form of a servant," that is to say, becoming a man like other men. The importance of the decision emerges from several elements of the text.

First of all, there is the contrast between permanent subsistence in the divine nature and passage to the condition of a servant which occurred at a specific moment.[2] It is the con-

---

[2] The self-stripping does not consist in abandoning the "form of God" in order to take on another form, that of a "servant." It consists in taking

trast between a preexistence that involves life at the level of eternity and entrance into the time of mankind, into the "becoming" of men.

Besides, the contrast between the condition of God and the condition of a servant shows the vast distance spanned. It is the distance between the divine "to be" and the human "to be," [3] but with the emphasis on the humble condition of man's ordinary life, far removed from God's splendor.

The passage from one condition to the other is described as a deliberate refusal to assume a glorious condition: "he did not deem equality with God something to be grasped" (Ph 2:6). [4] Christ's attitude, described in contrast with Adam's sin, manifests a strong decision regarding the kind of incarnation he adopted.

The most characteristic expression "he emptied himself" attests not only to a personal decision on his part, but to a mode of action that profoundly affected his person. Paul proposes this mode of action as the model of humble love.

The deep interior disposition of humility that Paul re-

---

on the form of a servant while subsisting "in the form of God." P. Grelot comments: "Now Christ is *in* this inexpressible form of God. He exists and subsists *in it* ... He manifests in a certain way, in his very being and through the mediation of his humanity, the invisible 'features' of the living God. In fact, he is and remains 'in the form of God', 'with the features of God', even when he empties himself by taking on the form (= the features) of a servant." "While there is no direct speculation on his preexistence, still the fact of his being 'in the form of God', 'with the features of God', *presupposes* his full and total participation in the divinity of the Father, at the very moment he intentionally conceals it" ("Deux expressions difficiles," *Bi* 1972, 506-7).

[3] The term "form," as we have already noted, relates to the essence in its expression or manifestation. Cf. J. Behm, *TWNT* 4, 750-760; R. P. Martin, *Carmen Christi (Philippians II, 5,11) in Recent Interpretation and in the Setting of Early Christian Worship,* Cambridge 1967, 99-133; Grelot, *art. cit.,* 503-507, which relies in particular on the text of Flavius Josephus (*Contra Apion.* II, 22, 1901), in which God is said to be "inexpressible for us with respect to his form and to his greatness."

[4] We should remember that equality with God must be understood, according to the context of the hymn, as referring to the glorious state that was not "grasped," but received through obedience. *Harpagmos* does not mean something to be jealously preserved but something to be grasped at. Paul is saying very simply: Christ refused to grasp at the glorious state of equality with God. (Cf. P. Grelot, "La valeur de *ouk ... alla,*" *Bi* 1973, 25-42.)

commends to Christians was first exemplified in Christ Jesus. This gave the act of the Incarnation a moral quality.

Very probably the hymn Paul chose to use was primarily intended to present Jesus as a model to be imitated. It set out above all to proclaim the generosity that had motivated the Incarnation, to make known the vast love implicit in Christ's human life, and thereby to provide a better understanding of the entire work of salvation. Yet even totally apart from any thought of an ascetic example, it emphasizes the interior dispositions that governed the act of the Incarnation. Paul's use of the hymn simply draws attention to the exemplary value of these dispositions.

The act of the Incarnation, therefore, is not a comfortable and superficial extension by God of his glory. The Son's making himself "nothing" indicates the depth of his self-giving and the innermost reality of his involvement.

b. The start of a life of becoming

The affirmation "The Word became flesh" (Jn 1:14) in John's Prologue does not seek to indicate the interior disposition that inspired the mode of the Incarnation. Rather it describes the act itself in an objective way.

First of all, we should note that the affirmation is inserted as a prelude to the Gospel account: everything that can be related about Jesus begins with this first act and is illumined by it. The true origin of Jesus is not to be sought in the world. It is hidden in eternity.

Here again we discern the need for a descending Christology in order to understand the mystery of the Incarnation. The Evangelist realized that without such a prologue an essential dimension would be lacking to the testimonies concerning the history of Jesus. This history requires a primordial relationship to what preceded it.

The act of the Incarnation proceeds from eternity to time. The contrast between being and becoming is stronger here than in Philippians. The hymn established the contrast between "being in the form of God" and "being made in human likeness" (Ph 2:6-7). In the Prologue we find the eternal existence of the Word stated more explicitly: "In the beginning was the Word" (Jn 1:1). The condition of the one who "was" is clarified through his personal relationship to the Father and through his nature as God. The strong sense of the verb "to be" — repeated three times from the very beginning — is confirmed by the statement that "the Word was God." It is made more cogent by contrast with the becoming of creatures: "Through him all things were made (became)" (Jn 1:3).

He who in his eternal being is the cause of the becoming of creatures now embarked on a life of becoming of his own.[5] He assumed a mode of existence radically inferior to the one that was intrinsically his from all eternity.

For the Word Incarnate, becoming was an involvement. In contrast to creatures, he existed before he became, and the reason he became was because he wanted to involve himself in the life of creatures.

St. John does not write that the Word "emptied himself," but by saying that he "became flesh" he seems to evoke a life destined for sacrifice. In so doing he makes it clear that the Word was personally affected by his human existence. To "become flesh" is a stronger term than "to take on the flesh of a man." The verb "to become" implies an involvement of the person who wants to be something other than he was before. The term "flesh" designates man in his weak and mortal aspect, and shows the depth of the abasement.[6] When the Word embarked on a life of becoming he accepted all that was destructible about this becoming.

---

[5] The force of the Johannine expression is highlighted by the objections it has provoked. Thus, Barrett thinks that John could not have meant to say "he became," since the Word continues to be the subject of other declarations. It is the Word who "lived among us," etc. "The Word was to continue being the Word" (St. John, 138). The fact that he continued to be the Word did not stop him from becoming flesh. That is the mystery John is affirming. Moreover, we should note, as does R. E. Brown (*John, I,13*), that John does not say the Word became *a* man (which might presuppose a substitution of persons), but that he became flesh, that is to say, man.

[6] The word "flesh" is meant to indicate "the great condescension of God. The Logos came down from his heavenly homeland and consented to become a member of our poor human race in order to reveal to us the secrets of the divine world and to lead us back to God" (A. Feuillet, *Le prologue du quatrième évangile*, Paris, 1968, 98-99).

260

c. A coming

From the very start Christian liturgy pondered and proclaimed the act of the Incarnation because its truth had been intimated by Jesus' own words. The formulation of the substance of this act is not a simple conclusion from the fact that Jesus, being the Son of God, made a transition from his divine condition to the human condition. It results more directly from the dynamic perspective that Jesus opened up on his human condition when he said: "The Son of Man has come."

The hymn of Philippians simply comments on Jesus' own words. The evocation of the one who, "being in the form of God, did not consider equality with God something to be grasped, but emptied himself, taking the form of a servant" (Ph 2:6-7), seems to stem from the declaration: "For the Son of Man himself did not come to be served, but to serve ..." (Mk 10:45; Mt 20:28).

Jesus was therefore the first to express the dynamism of the Incarnation. By saying of himself "the Son of Man has come," he showed that he considered his earthly life a dynamism coming from above. It was the coming of a preexisting divine personage.

In this coming, God's personal involvement for the salvation of mankind was realized. The Son of Man came "to seek out and save what was lost "(Lk 19:10), because God's love for sinners refused to remain remote from men in a divine sphere. The Son involved himself in a human life in order to express in human terms the love of a God searching out those he wants to save.

Likewise, Jesus' refusal to be served makes clear his choice as to the mode of his Incarnation. It is part and parcel of the involvement of the Son of God among men, revealing God's intention to serve mankind.

It is true that Jesus did not use the verb "to become" to indicate his passage from the condition of Son of God to the human condition. But by using the title "Son of Man" he implied this becoming. He thereby suggested that he was indeed the Son of God who had become man.

The reason Jesus preferred to speak of a coming rather than of a becoming was probably because he wanted to take an approach based on his personal relationship to mankind.

Jesus defined the involvement of the Incarnation in terms of his intention to come close to men more than by the fact of his becoming man. He was more concerned with persons than with natures. His way of proceeding consisted in a coming. We should also remember that John's Prologue does not limit itself to saying "The Word became flesh" but adds: "he lived among us" (Jn 1:14). This second and more interpersonal aspect corresponds directly to what Jesus wanted to emphasize in the dynamism of the Incarnation. It is expressed in a way that stresses the dynamism of the Incarnation process as well as the fragility of the dwelling: "he lived under the tent among us." [7]

2. *The Father's Involvement*

Jesus constantly pointed to the Father's primordial involvement in his earthly life. He said he had been sent by the Father, and he acted the part of an envoy.

In John's Gospel the expression "the one who sent me" is often spoken by Jesus to designate the Father. [8] In the Synoptic Gospels this sending likewise appears as the determinant of Jesus' entire life. [9]

Here, then, is the wellspring of the dynamism of the In-

---

[7] The commentators mention the allusion to the *Shekinah*, the dwelling of God in the midst of Israel. They likewise note that the Word realizes what had been said about divine Wisdom, come to pitch her tent among men (cf. Si 24:8). Barrett concludes nonetheless that "John probably did not mean to say anything more than that the Word took up a temporary residence among men" (*St. John*, 138). It would be difficult to disregard the reference to the *Shekinah*, but in any event the use of the verb "to live under the tent" retains its value as indicating the transitory nature of the dwelling, a meaning that agrees with the affirmation that the Word became "flesh," that is to say, man, embracing the perishable nature of human life. Besides, the tent, being mobile, aptly evokes the dynamism of the coming.

[8] Jn 4:34; 5:23,24,27,30,37; 6:38,44, etc. This expression taken by itself would suffice to show that in Johannine terminology "Father" must be understood to designate the divine person of the Father. It is not acceptable to say that this term "does not designate the first person of our Trinitarian Creed, but the personal God of the faith of Israel and of Jesus" (S. Gonzalez de Carrea, *Cristo, Revelador del Padre en San Juan, La Trinidad en la Biblia, Cristo, Revelador del Padre y Emisor el Espíritu en el Nuevo Testamento*, Salamanca 1973, 156).

[9] Mt 10:40; 15:24; 21:37; Mk 9:37; 12:6; Lk 4:43; 9:48; 10:16.

carnation. When Jesus said the Son of Man had come, he never meant to suggest that he had come solely on his own initiative. For Jesus, to come and to be sent were one and the same thing, as can be seen for instance by comparing the two affirmations: "For the Son of Man has come to seek out and save what was lost" (Lk 19:10) and "I was sent only to the lost sheep of the House of Israel" (Mt 15:24). Jesus' most characteristic attitude, his benevolence toward sinners, can be explained by the mission he had received. The dynamism of salvific love manifested in all of his activity stemmed from the Father.

A similar equivalence can be seen as between Mark's logion: "that is why I came" (Mk 1:38) and Luke's version: "that is what I was sent to do" (Lk 4:43). Jesus' goal, proclaiming the good news of the kingdom of God, was assigned to him by the Father when he sent him.

In itself, a sending does not necessarily involve the one who sends. It can even, in certain cases, tend to mean a disengagement on the part of the sender. Someone may send another so as not be become personally involved in a delicate situation, to avoid the difficulties experienced by the one who is directly confronting certain problems.

In Jesus' case, however, his being sent implies the Father's total involvement. This is indicated in several ways.

First, the sending is the supreme demonstration of the Father's love for mankind. That is how Jesus depicts the Father in the parable of the homicidal vinedressers. He relates the story of the master of the vineyard who first sent his servants to the vinedressers; but this master "had still someone left: his beloved son. He sent him to them last of all ..." (Mk 12:6). Obviously, the sending of the beloved son represents the Father's supreme involvement in the vineyard. It implies a greater love than the sending of servants. This is precisely the difference between God's involvement in the Old Covenant and the involvement of the Incarnation of the Son in the New. The Father gives his Son instead of merely sending servants. He could not have given a greater gift.

Besides, God's involvement is shown by the fact that his paternal presence accompanies his Son. Jesus reveals it: "Anyone who welcomes one of these little children in my name, welcomes me; and anyone who welcomes me welcomes not me but the one who sent me" (Mk 9:37). That is a way of saying that the Father's presence is involved in the presence of the Son among men.

Finally, the Father's involvement is indicated above all by his will to deliver his Son to sacrifice. Actually, the sending implicit in the Incarnation cannot be separated from its culmination. Sacrifice was the end to which the Incarnation process was directed, as Jesus himself has said: "But it was for this very reason that I have come, for the sake of this hour" (Jn 12:27). [10]

In announcing his coming Passion and death, Jesus attributed them to an imperative stemming from the divine plan. And at Gethsemane he saw his imminent crucifixion as being willed by the Father: "But let it be as you, not I, would have it" (Mk 14:36).

Paul and John discerned in this paternal will an involvement of the Father in the Son's sacrifice. God loved us "when he sent his Son to be the sacrifice that takes our sins away" (1 Jn 4:10). "Since God did not spare his own Son, but gave him up to benefit us all, we may be certain, after such a gift, that he will not refuse anything he can give" (Rm 8:32). The allusion to Abraham's sacrifice highlights the immensity of the Father's gift. [11] In sending his Son into the world, the Father destined him to the immolation of the Cross; thus the totality of his Father's love was involved in this sending forth.

We can readily see how, in Paul's eyes, the Father's giving his Son up to sacrifice involved all other gifts as well, and was to perpetuate his involvement in the life of mankind. Since the Father did not refuse to give his own Son, he could

---

[10] As in other passages of John's Gospel, "for this reason" refers to what follows, namely, "this hour." "I have come" has the sense of "place" rather than of time. "For the sake of this hour" expresses a finality, not merely a termination in time. That is why the translation "But it was for this very reason that I have come, for the sake of this hour" is preferable to: "But it was for this very reason that I have come to this hour" (The Jerusalem Bible).

[11] Cf. Gn 22:12,16. In the Targumic tradition, this account had been commented upon with an "emphasis on Abraham's love for his son, the beloved, the only-begotten," especially in the writings of Philo and Josephus (R. Le Déaut, La nuit pascale, Rome, 1963, 198).

not refuse men anything else. The Father's involvement is therefore at the origin of the life of grace of every Christian, as well as of the growth of the whole Church. From this point of view, the dynamism of the redemptive Incarnation extends to the entire future of human history. The Father who gave himself to men in his Son can never stop giving himself to mankind.

3. The Involvement of the Holy Spirit

The role of the Holy Spirit in the Incarnation is expressly mentioned in the account of the Annunciation: "The Holy Spirit will come upon you and the power of the Most High will cover you with its shadow" (Lk 1:35). It is worth noting that the conception of the child was not attributed solely to the power of the Most High, but to the more personal action of the Holy Spirit. In Matthew's Gospel, the announcement made to Joseph contains a similar inference: "she [Mary] has conceived what is in her by the Holy Spirit" (Mt 1:20). Whereas we might have expected the angel simply to affirm a work of God without any other details, the designation of the person of the Holy Spirit takes on its true importance. It is part of the plan of the New Covenant in which the personal involvement of the Son in the Incarnation is accompanied by the involvement of the two other divine persons, and the revelation of the action of the Word involves the revelation of the Trinity. [12]

According to Luke's account, the action of the Holy Spirit was not purely physiological in its effect, namely, the formation of the child's body. It resulted in conferring a divine sonship on the child. "And so the child will be holy and will be called Son of God" (Lk 1:35). Admittedly, the expression "Son of God" apparently does not refer to the eternal divine sonship. It refers rather to the divine sonship assured to the human being who has been conceived. The child is considered to be the Son of God in his human life, and not in an anterior divine life. The preexistence of Christ is not yet under con-

---

[12] Obviously, there is no question yet of a formal expression of the Trinity as such in the account of the Annunciation. But in this account the distinction between the persons begins to appear.

sideration. But the essential affirmation remains that Jesus is indebted to the Holy Spirit for the fact that he is the Son of God in his human reality.

The dynamism of the intervention of the Holy Spirit found expression in his "coming." The Spirit did not limit himself to an act he could have effectuated "from afar." When he came upon Mary he performed an action that attested to his personal involvement. Spiritually, this coming preceded and preformed the coming of the Son of Man.

Why this intervention by the Holy Spirit, when we might have been tempted to attribute the conception of the child to the Father, since this child was to be the Son of God? Obviously, we cannot deny the action of the Father. But the Father acted through the Holy Spirit, who alone is named as the person who produced the miracle in an immediate way.

The role of the Spirit can be explained in the light of Jewish tradition. The Spirit had been thought of as the life-giving power through which God renewed and sanctified human existence, making it capable of actions until then impossible. [13] In particular he was going to rest upon the Messiah (cf. Is 42:1; 61:1).

The Holy Spirit appears in the account of the Annunciation endowed with these marks of a superior life-giving power. To "come upon" signifies passing from the supreme divine heights to the level of earthly things, and the immensity of the distance makes it easier for us to surmise the power deployed in this coming. It is this power that justifies the closing words of assurance: "nothing is impossible to God" (Lk 1:37).

In comparison to the action of the Spirit as presented in the Old Testament, a great innovation is evident here. *The Spirit did not come directly upon the Messiah, but on the mother in order to produce the generation itself.* [14] In con-

---

[13] "The Spirit is a vital force which, like the wind and the air, permeates man's flesh, transforms his life, and empowers him to accomplish concrete actions of which he at first felt incapable" (H. Cazelles, "L'Esprit Saint et l'Incarnation d'après le développement de la révélation biblique," in *Le Saint-Esprit et Marie*, II, Bible et Spiritualités, *Etudes Mariales* 26, 1969, 13). Cf. also H. M. Manteau-Bonamy, "Et la Vierge Conçut du Saint-Esprit," in *La Vierge Marie et le Saint-Esprit*, Paris, 1971, 12-25.

[14] Cf. Cazelles, *art. cit.*, 17, which, after pointing out that "the texts

sequence, he wanted not only to inspire the Savior's actions, but to constitute his human reality. The ontological must precede the functional. The effect of the action of the Spirit was to be the child's identity as the Son of God, which was to be his hallmark.

The meaning of the intervention of the Holy Spirit becomes clearer in the light of the Johannine affirmations: "God loved the world so much that he gave his only Son ..." (Jn 3:16). "This is the love I mean: not our love for God, but God's love for us when he sent his Son to be the sacrifice that takes our sins away" (1 Jn 4:10). The love of the Father who sent his Son assumed a personal consistency, so to speak, in the Holy Spirit. It is through the Spirit that the Father is united to mankind. When the Holy Spirit came upon Mary, all of the love of the Father who wanted to give his Son to men was gathered up in the Spirit.

The involvement of the Holy Spirit was thus the involvement of divine love in the innovation of the sending of the Son by the Father.

Like the Father's involvement, the involvement of the Holy Spirit was prolonged in Jesus' earthly life and then in the life of the Church.

The account of the intervention of the Holy Spirit at the time of Jesus' baptism is similar to the account of his coming at the Incarnation. The Spirit came upon Jesus in the same manner as he came upon Mary (cf. Mt 3:16 and par.). The imagery of the account shows God bridging the distance that separates him from men: The heavens open to allow the Spirit to descend, and the voice coming from heaven indicates that the Spirit accompanies the Father as he gives his beloved Son to men. The symbol of the dove indicates the intention of love and peace that inspires the coming of the Spirit. [15]

of the Old Testament admitted this action of the Spirit even before birth when the Savior had only been conceived," adds: "Luke goes further and shows the Spirit resting not on the Savior in his mother's womb, but on the mother herself. I have found no trace of this theology in the Old Testament "

[15] On this symbol, cf. A. Feuillet, "Le symbolisme de la colombe dans les récits évangeliques du baptême, *RSR* 46 (1958), 524-544; J. De Cock, "Het symbolisme van de duif bij het doopsel van Christus," *Bijdragen* 21 (1960), 363-376.

This intention was confirmed by Jesus when, in the synagogue of Nazareth, he applied Isaiah's oracle to himself: "The Spirit of the Lord is on me" (Lk 4:18), and explained the meaning of his mission. It was a mission born of God's benevolence toward men, a mission of good news, light, and liberation (cf. Lk 14:18-19). Jesus' claim to be fulfilling the oracle thus focussed attention on the action of the Holy Spirit who continued to inspire and orientate all of his activities. The involvement of the Holy Spirit that made the Incarnation a work of love persisted throughout Jesus' public life and assured it the same finality.

It is no less significant that Jesus, at the time of his Ascension, announced to his disciples that they, too, would be granted the baptism of the Holy Spirit and would receive his strength in a special degree: "You will receive power when the Holy Spirit comes on you, and then you will be my witnesses ..." (Ac 1:8). The action of the Spirit is defined by the words "come on." The event of Pentecost manifested the power of the coming in a visible way.

The effect of this coming, as Jesus enounced it, deserves our close attention. It is the Holy Spirit who was to make the disciples witnesses to Christ. Thus, the involvement of the Holy Spirit in the Incarnation was prolonged through his involvement in the individual lives of the disciples. [16] And it has been prolonged in such a way as to assure that Christ would be the center of the life of the Church. The Spirit deploys his power to produce witnesses, not to the Spirit himself but to Christ. Pentecost extended the sway of the Incarnation.

C. A New Physiognomy of God

1. *A More Dynamic Physiognomy: the Problem of Mutability*

The revelation of the divine involvement in the Incarnation brings to light a new, more dynamic physiognomy of God.

---

[16] As A. Feuillet remarks: "When Luke related the scene of the Annunciation, he already saw the outlines of the scene of Pentecost" (" L'Esprit Saint et la mère du Christ," in *Le Saint-Esprit et Marie,* I, *L'Evangile et les Pères, Etudes Mariales 25,* 1968, 53.)

It does not permit us to affirm that the immutability of God is such as to exclude any change whatever and to render any "innovation" in divine dispositions and activity impossible. It obliges us to reflect more deeply on God's transcendence and on its conciliation with a certain mutability.

First of all, it is necessary to stress that, theologically speaking, immutability must be attributed to God exactly as it is presented in Revelation. It follows that we cannot determine *a priori* a concept of God's immutability that might afterward be applied to the doctrine of the mystery of the Incarnation and maintain this mystery within certain limits. The Incarnation itself, together with the divine involvement it implies, teaches us what kind of immutability and mutability we must acknowledge in God.

Two approaches have been attempted to justify the mutability inherent in the Incarnation. The first seeks to situate this mutability in the creature. According to a classical explanation, whatever was new about the Son of God after he became man lay in his humanity, whereas the Son of God remained immutable. All change was in the human nature assumed by the Word. In this way, it is claimed, the principle of the absolute immutability of God is preserved.

The formula proposed by Karl Rahner is along these lines, but with an important correction: "God can become something, the immutable in itself can be mutable in another." [17] The formula affirms that the immutable can become mutable. However, if it remains immutable in itself and becomes mutable only in another, mutability is ultimately limited to the creature, that is to say, to the man in Christ. There remains an ambiguity, to say the least, as to the meaning of becoming and as to the area of the mutability.

The other approach consists in affirming that in God there is only an immutability of the moral order. It identifies this immutability with divine fidelity. The Bible presents God as absolutely faithful to the covenant and to the promises related to it. Within this fidelity, God's attitudes may vary in relation to human actions, but these attitudes are all governed by the one selfsame love that established the covenant. There-

---

[17] "Considérations générales sur la christologie," in H. Bouëssé - J. J. Latour, *Problèmes actuels de christologie*, Bruges, 1965, 25.

fore this love is immutable in its fundamental intent, even though there is an implicit mutability in its manifestations. Such an interpretation seeks to avoid the drawbacks of a metaphysical immutability attributed to the being or to the nature of God, and is a reaction in particular against the immobility of Aristotle's God.[18]

Neither of these two approaches seems satisfactory. The former relegates all mutability to the created domain. Now, to explain the mutability of the Incarnation we cannot limit ourselves to admitting a change on the part of the humanity assumed by the Word. There is in fact an authentic involvement of the Son of God who, in becoming man, "empties himself." This means that the act of the Incarnation springs from a decision made by a divine person. And so the newness lies first of all in the realm of the divine, before affecting the human nature of Jesus.[19] Likewise, the involvement of the Father, who sends his Son, stems from a free and gratuitous act in which is affirmed all of God's sovereignty as well as his merciful love for mankind. The involvement of the Holy Spirit is the expression of this love that comes from above to effectuate the conception of the child. This involvement cannot be limited in its effect. The divine dynamism of the Incarnation thus demands the affirmation of an authentic innovation in God himself, and thus obliges us to accept shades of difference in divine immutability.

Moreover, we cannot reduce this immutability strictly to the moral order, and exclude it from the metaphysical domain. It is true that the Biblical message reveals God's absolute fidelity to the covenant, a fidelity that itself involves a varied series of attitudes and reactions toward human behavior. But

---

[18] Cf. H. Mühlen, *Die Veränderlichkeit Gottes als Horizont einer zukünftigen Christologie. Auf dem Wege zu einer Kreuzestheologie in Auseinandersetzung mit der altkirchlichen Christologie*, Münster 1969; H. Küng, *L'Incarnation de Dieu*, Paris 1973, Excursus IV. Immutabilité de Dieu?, 655-663.

[19] Therefore we cannot be content with an "Additions-Christologie," to use the term proposed by W. Maas (*Unveränderlichkeit Gottes*, Munich-Paderborn-Vienna 1974, 176). Here is how he explains this "Christology of addition": "Becoming, suffering, and change affect only the human nature that has been "assumed," "added." God the Word as such remains immune to change. Far from being a simple addition, Christology implies the active involvement of the Word.

it also presents God as a sovereign being, immutable in his deepest reality.

In God's dialogue with Moses, the divine promise of fidelity to the covenant — "I shall be with you" — is rooted in God's name, that is to say, in his innermost reality: "I Am who I Am" (Ex 3:12-14). There is no question here of an abstract, philosophical notion of being, as is suggested by the Septuagint translation ("I am the one who is"). Rather there is a concrete, existential affirmation which poses the immutability of the "I Am" as the guarantee of the immutability of the covenant. Thus, there is a metaphysical immutability that assures the moral fidelity.

In John's Gospel, the great affirmation of the "becoming" of the Word who was made flesh is preceded by the affirmation of his immutability in the order of eternity. He who becomes remains the one who "was" in the beginning. Embarking into a life of becoming destroys nothing of his eternal being. On the contrary, this immutable being gives the Incarnation process all its value.

The problem consists, therefore, in reconciling metaphysical immutability with a real becoming. This becoming can take nothing away from the transcendence of the divine being. And yet the innovation of the act of the Incarnation must be acknowledged not as outside of God and in a created effect, but in the inward act of divine involvement.

To clarify how the two aspects, which at first sight seem incompatible, are reconciled, we must remember that God's immutable being cannot be conceived of as necessarily closed in on itself, incapable of any action directed outside itself. God's immutability signifies permanence and perseverance in perfection, but does not signify immobility. The Bible presents God to us as the supremely Living Being. God is revealed to be full of vitality, an overflowing vitality that is deployed in creation and in his relations with men. Philosophical speculation has arrived at this notion of God by identifying the divine being as "pure act." Pure act is perfect in itself, but it cannot be thought powerless to act outside itself. On the contrary, the interior vitality of God implies an excess of vital capacity directed to creatures. It is in this sense that God's immutability is a capacity for mutability.

Any immobilistic conception of God would deprive God of a fundamental perfection, the power to deploy his action outside himself with sovereign freedom. It would imprison the being of God by making of its infinite perfection an insurmountable barrier.

While mutability results from God's vitality, it assumes in God characteristics that are different from those of human mutability. The difference moreover corresponds to the intention of the Council of Nicea which, when it declared the Son of God to be immutable, [20] meant to exclude from him the mutability proper to creatures.

In creatures mutability is an inevitable condition of existence. Created being cannot evade it. In God, to the contrary, mutability is the expression of his total sovereignty. He enters freely into the life of becoming, and he does so to the extent that he himself chooses.

In addition to this difference, there is another closely related to it. Mutability makes creatures perfectible, whereas God can neither attain greater perfection nor cause himself harm through freely performed actions directed outside himself. If God embarks on a life of becoming, it is through his superabundant vitality that cannot make him either richer or poorer in his innermost being.

God's involvement in the Incarnation, therefore, does not pose a challenge to his divine perfection. This involvement is governed solely by his totally gratuitous love for mankind.

2. *The Son's Human Experience*

There is nothing to fear in admitting the completely real involvement of the Son in the becoming of a human life. Far from being hampered by his divine perfection, the Son is far better able, by virtue of this perfection, to live the human experience integrally. For, as we have already stressed, God's vitality has the power to extend freely beyond the sphere of the divine.

---

[20] DS 126. The definition is against Arianism which attributed to the Word the mutability proper to created being. Cf. Boularand, *L'hérésie d'Arius*, 77-79; *La "foi" de Nicée*, 433-435; Mühlen, *Die Veränderlichkeit Gottes*, 15; Maas, *Unveränderlichkeit*, 143.

It follows from this that the Son incurred no handicap by reason of his own divine personality in the development of his human life. He was unreservedly human. This explains the fact that he was like us in every way except sin. We can even assert that no man ever lived his human life as deeply and fully as he.

We should also guard against the idea that the human experience was of no use to the Son because of his eternal perfection. Since the Word already knew everything there was in man through his divine knowledge, we might be inclined to think his human life could teach him nothing. The truth is that his human life could not add any perfection to his perfect being as God. Even so, while it did not give him any opportunity for greater perfection, his human existence provided him with an irreplaceable experience. Divine knowledge of human realities cannot be identified with man's personal experience of them. It was precisely this experience that enabled the Son of God to know the human universe in a different way than before. This was a real discovery on his part. The Creator rediscovered his creatures through the eyes of a creature.

This was the experience not only of the man Jesus, but of the Son of God. The subject of the experience was the divine person of the Son. We remember the importance of the principle of the "communication of idioms" in the Christological controversies, and above all in the refutation of Nestorianism. By virtue of this principle, the human activities and states of Jesus are attributed to the divine subject. That is why we must affirm that the Son of God was born of the Virgin Mary, that he suffered and died. Such an attribution could not be made exclusively on the basis of semantics or of the requirements of grammatical logic. It means that the Son of God really went through birth, suffering, and death. He himself integrally experienced the life of man, under the same conditions as all other humans.

The depth of Christ's human experience has been evoked for us in the hymn of the Epistle to the Philippians. We have noted that the act of "emptying himself" is identified with the act of becoming like other men. The Incarnation is considered, therefore, as the trying experience of the human condition.

It is not an experience that could have remained "outside" the person of the Son. In dealing with the divine involvement, we have tried to express to what degree the divine person of the Son willed to involve himself in this experience.

In what sense can Christ's human experience be called *an adventure?* It was not an adventure if we interpret the term in the sense of a course of action left to the whims of chance, or a superficial experience that touches only the outward aspects of events. But it was an adventure in the sense that the Son embraced a life in which the unknown element of experience was opened to him and in which he accepted in advance all the consequences of this experience including those of a tragic nature.

The value of this human experience for the fulfillment of Jesus' earthly mission needs no demonstration. Yet we should realize that it continued in the heavenly mission of the glorious Christ. For example, we can point out how Jesus, according to John's Gospel, justified his attribution as judge: "For the Father, ... because he is the Son of Man, has appointed him supreme judge" (Jn 5:26-27). According to the divine plan, the judge of mankind must be one who has personally experienced human life and been subjected to its hardships and temptations.

3. *Newness and Freedom of the Involvement of the Triune God*

The act of the Incarnation is the act of the Son becoming man, thereby revealing the Trinity, as we have already pointed out. In acting in a manner inherently his own, the Son distinguished himself from the two other divine persons. He alone became incarnate.

Nevertheless, the involvement of the Father and the Holy Spirit is inseparable from the Son's. The Fourth Lateran Council declared that the only-begotten Son of God, Jesus Christ, was "incarnated in common by the entire Trinity." [21] "To act in common" does not mean that the roles of the divine

----

[21] DS 801. Cf. DS 535: According to the Council of Toledo, "we must believe that the entire Trinity also brought about the Incarnation of this Son of God, inasmuch as the works of the Trinity are inseparable."

persons are identical. In the Incarnation each of them acted in his own unique way, but in an operation which likewise revealed their unity.

The involvement of the Father enlightens us on the primordial origin of the Incarnation process. Even better than the involvement of the Son, it shows us how the Incarnation proceeds from an act that is an innovation in the life of God. The aspect of sacrifice, which according to the Epistle to the Philippians marks the action of the Son who "emptied himself" (Ph 2:7), can be seen also in the case of the Father. For the greatness of the Father's love is measured by his sending his Son as a victim of propitiation or by his refusal to spare him, as in the case of Abraham. This sacrifical quality reveals the disposition that governs the process. The "newness" of the Incarnation springs from the depths of God. It confirms that the aspect of mutuality cannot be limited to the external effects of the divine act.

The involvement of the Holy Spirit in the Incarnation also attests to the newness that comes from the innermost depths of God. In the Spirit is personalized the inspiration of love by virtue of which the Incarnation was accomplished.

However, does not the affirmation of the newness, of the involvement of the divine persons, bring into question the immutability of the divine being? If the newness comes from the depths of God, does it not imply a modification of the divine nature?

Here we must stress a primordial distinction between the divine being and the free action through which God effectuates the salvation of mankind. We cannot claim that every act of God is identified with the pure act in which his being consists. Nor can it be said that all divine love is identically the love that characterizes the innermost depths of God's being. The acts of God directed outside himself are supremely free. Thus, the creation of the world stems from no interior divine necessity and cannot be confused with pure eternal act. The work of salvation is freer still, and unfolds with absolute liberty on God's part. The love at work in salvation conforms to the love proper to the eternal divine being, but remains distinct from it. Its fundamental characteristic is precisely that it is freely given and cannot be reduced to the necessary being of God.

The newness of the involvement of God's love in the world consists in its being freely given. It leaves the necessary being of God entirely intact, and therefore does not derogate from the immutability of the divine nature. In the work of salvation God remains essentially what he is. He loses none of his intrinsic transcendence. Nevertheless, he involves himself deeply in this work in the sovereign freedom of his love.

Consequently the distinction between necessary being and free act safeguards the double affirmation of God's immutability and of the involvement of his divine love in the work of salvation. The two affirmations are essential elements of Revelation, and are moreover intimately linked. For immutability belongs to divine transcendence, and this transcendence in turn manifests itself through God's liberty of action in the world. From the fact that God is the absolutely perfect being, he has no need of men. When he involves himself in salvific action, he does so with absolute liberty.

4. *The Relational Involvement*

The involvement of the Incarnation is relational, because through it the divine persons enter into relations with human persons.

The two aspects of the Incarnation of the Word, one relating to the natures and the other relating to the persons, were tersely joined in the Johannine affirmation: "The Word became flesh and lived ... among us" (Jn 1:14). To become flesh is to appropriate a human nature. To live among us is to establish permanent relationships with human persons.

It goes without saying that these relationships must be acknowledged in their total reality. The restrictions placed by a certain school of Scholastic philosophy on the relations of God with the world are difficult to defend. To safeguard God's transcendence and immutability, this philosophy has denied that God can have real relations with created beings. According to this approach, while creatures have real relations with God, God can only have "relations of reason" with them. The latter are relations that we posit by virtue of our mode

276

of thinking but which do not really exist as such. To these philosophers, recourse to "relations of reason" seemed the only way to preserve the notion of the sovereign independence of God.

However, while the God of Biblical Revelation presents himself as absolutely transcendent, he addresses himself to men and wants to maintain contact with them. He takes the initiative in establishing real relations with human persons. Hence, it cannot be said that on his part these relations are not real, whereas they are real on the part of the human beings who turn to him. It is God who confers reality on his covenant with men and who by his actions, his involvement, cements very profound relationships of love with mankind.

Far more, we note that in these relationships God does not eschew a certain dependence with respect to men, since he is affected by their behavior. Thus, he is offended by men's sins and he rejoices over their conversion and good deeds. This dependence does not jeopardize his sovereignty, since he himself has freely decided upon it and accepted in advance all of its consequences when he chose to establish loving relations with his creatures.

The mystery of the Incarnation of the Son pushes to the extreme limit the forging of real relations between God and mankind. In an even more explicit way, the reality of these relations does not come from creatures. The purpose of the coming of the Son of God into the human milieu is to establish an enduring relationship between the divine persons and human persons. The divine "I" of the Son seeks to establish the closest possible relations with all the "I's" of the human race.

The first interpersonal relationship implicit in the Incarnation was with the Virgin Mary. The Son of God became the son of a woman. The importance of this relationship has been acknowledged in Tradition by the title "Mother of God." Can we join with St. Thomas Aquinas in denying that Christ's sonship with respect to his Mother is a real relationship, while on the other hand admitting a real relationship of motherhood on Mary's part with respect to the Word? [22]

---

[22] "Therefore the filiation by which Christ is related to His Mother cannot be a real relation, but only a relation of reason" (St. Thomas, *Summa*,

This application of the principle that excludes real relations with creatures on the part of God would be contrary to the purpose of the Incarnation. For when the Son became incarnate he involved himself in a real relationship of sonship vis-a-vis Mary, whose counterpart is Mary's real relationship of motherhood with respect to the Son of God.

In the case of the sonship, the personal relationship entered into by the Word includes a dependence vis-a-vis Mary. But the acceptance of this dependence manifests the love that commanded the Incarnation. God cannot be denied the freedom to love in this manner, that is to say, to love with very humble love, involving the obedient attitude which Luke mentioned as the essential, distinctive mark of Jesus' childhood: "He ... lived under their authority" (Lk 2:51).

This dependence was not assumed only by the Word. It was implicit first of all in the Father's initiative: "... when the appointed time came, God sent his Son, born of a woman, born a subject to the Law" (Ga 4:4). By these words Paul wants to stress the abasement effectuated in the Incarnation, an abasement for which the Father was responsible in the first place. The Father was therefore the first to want a certain dependence with respect to Mary, as a sign of dependence upon mankind. [23]

The Father's involvement in personal relationships with mankind is even more striking in his desire to establish a paternal relationship with all human beings. In the view of the Epistle to the Ephesians, it is the Father who, even before the creation of the world, predestined us to "become his adopted sons, through Jesus Christ" (Ep 1:5). The involvement of the Incarnation thus creates a whole new web of relationships between the divine persons and human persons through the universal extension of the Father's paternity and of adopted sonship in Christ.

III, a. 35, inc.). This position was somewhat palliated by H. M. Diepen, who interprets it in this way: "Christ is really the Son of the Virgin Mary, but without a real sonship" ("La critique du baslisme selon saint Thomas d'Aquin," *Revue Thomiste* 50 (1950) 82).

[23] D. Guthrie, *Galatians*, London, 1969, 119: "That the Son should have been born of a woman is the supreme example of his humiliation."

CHAPTER X

MEANING AND IMPORTANCE
OF THE UNITY OF PERSON

A. The Current Importance of the Notion of Person

1. *Is There Need for a New Terminology?*

Does the notion of person, as it was used by the Council of Chalcedon, still have the value today it did then? Or should it be translated into modern language by a different concept?

Karl Barth, in his explanation of the dogma of the Trinity, expressed the view that the concept of person changed meaning during the 19th century, when it began to be defined in terms of consciousness of self.[1] He proposed replacing the affirmation of three persons in God by the affirmation of three modes of being. However, he acknowledged he was unable to confer on these modes of being any distinctive marks that differed from those that had been attributed to the ancient concept of person.[2]

Karl Rahner in his turn has gone ahead with the modification of vocabulary. He substitutes the expression "three distinct modes of subsistence" for the expression "three persons."[3] In Christology, this author thinks that the modern concept of person is confirmed in the humanity of Jesus, inasmuch as it contains a finite center of consciousness and of created freedom. While refraining from speaking of a human

[1] *Dogmatique* I, 1,2, Geneva 1953, 61.
[2] *Ibid.*, 69.
[3] *Dieu Trinité, fondement transcendant de l'histoire du salut, Mysterium Salutis*, 6, Paris 1971, 121-123.

person, he nonetheless stresses the autonomy of the subjective human center, a center that places Jesus vis-a-vis God. [4] Rahner criticizes monosubjectivism, in which he sees a modern form of Monophysitism. And since he cannot admit a single subjectivity in Christ, he warns against the dangers implicit in the affirmation: "Jesus is God." [5]

Are these propositions of a new terminology justified? First of all, we might point out that the expressions "mode of being" and "distinct mode of subsistence" do not seem any better adapted to the contemporary mentality than the concept of person. On the contrary, they have an abstract and scholastic aspect, and would scarcely fit into a theology that claims to be kerygmatic. Can we really speak of a distinct mode of subsistence that became incarnate? In preaching as well as in doctrine, the notion of person is more accessible, more comprehensible.

The use of the term "mode" has serious drawbacks from the point of view of doctrine, then it seems to involve modalism. In addition we must recognize the value of the concept of person for our time, and the coincidence of the Chalcedonian notion of person with the modern notion.

2. Concrete and Universal Value of the Chalcedonian Concept of Person

The Council of Chalcedon's use of the two terms *prosôpon* and *hypostasis* demonstrates how forcefully it affirmed the unity of Christ's person. Whatever our vantage point in dealing with reality, whether at the more superficial level of the personal physiognomy or at the deeper level of the innermost personal reality, we must agree there is only one person in Christ.

But the Council's affirmation of the ontological unity of Christ's person was not accompanied by a definition or description of "hypostasis." The Fathers of the Council did not want to embark on abstract philosophical considerations. They limited themselves to the concrete notion of person as it emerges

---

[4] K. Rahner - W. Thüsing, *Christologie-systematisch und exegetisch*, Freiburg-Basel-Vienna 1972, 58.

[5] *Ibid.*, 55-57; K. Rahner - A. Darlap, *Sacramentum mundi*, Freiburg 1967-1969, II, 927-929.

from the most commonplace human experience. Man experiences his own person in his social relationships and in his own psychological demeanor. Thanks to this experience we know what a person is, even if we are unable to define person in abstract terms.

On the basis of the common experience of human existence, we must say that in Christ, true God and true man, there are not two persons, but only one. The Council thus refers not to a theory of the person but to an experience inseparably linked to the life of every human being and which, in its innermost reality, remains the same for everyone in every historical era and in every culture. The terms *prosôpon* and *hypostasis* belong to a particular language and to a particular culture, but the experience on which they are based and which they express is constant and universal.

One specific aspect of the notion of person, which necessarily emerges from the Conciliar affirmation, is its distinction from nature. Chalcedon did not define "nature" either. The word has a concrete signification, just as does the term person. The two natures designate Christ as true God and as true man. The word "nature" is also used with reference to human experience, and answers the question: "What is it?" whereas "person" answers the question: "Who is it?" To answer the question: "What is Jesus Christ?" we must refer to his two natures, the one divine and the other human, since he is true God and true man. To answer the question: "Who is Jesus Christ?" we must say he is a single person, the one person of the Son of God who became man.

The concrete value of the affirmation of the "one person" in Christ is confirmed by the Council's intention to express in more explicit terms what had already been said: Jesus Christ is "one identical." This expression appears at the very beginning of the profession of faith of Chalcedon, [6] as if to make it clear that this is the primordial assertion. It reappears later to introduce the second part of the profession, before the affirmation of the two natures.

Even if we were to limit ourselves to this as the founda-

---

[6] DS 301. These are the Council's words: "Following the Holy Fathers, therefore, we all with one accord teach the profession of faith in the one identical Son, our Lord Jesus Christ ..."

tion of the affirmation of the "one person," it is clear that the Council of Chalcedon did not reject monosubjectivism. Nor can it be said that such monosubjectivism is the modern translation of Monophysitism. To the contrary, the Council wanted to affirm that in Christ there is a single subject. It declared that while Jesus is truly God and man, he is "one identical" person, that is to say, a single subject.[7] The Council rejected Monophysitism and affirmed monosubjectivism.

This was the crux of the difficulty. How to succeed in clearly distinguishing one from the other by bringing out the difference between the terms "one nature" and "one hypostasis" which for Cyril of Alexandria were more or less equivalent? The Council definitively repudiated the affirmation of a single nature, and on the other hand affirmed a single hypostasis. Far from being identical, Monophysitism and monosubjectivism are in direct opposition.

Moreover, if we follow the profession of faith of the Council of Chalcedon, we must say that Jesus is God. He is indeed "the one identical Son, our Lord Jesus Christ ... perfect both in his divinity and in his humanity, truly God and truly man ..." While distinguishing the two natures, which cannot be identified with one another, we must affirm that Jesus the man is God. Far from giving a diluted meaning to this affirmation, the Council of Chalcedon stresses that Jesus is "truly God," and that he is one and the same in his divinity and in his humanity. There is a real identity, but an identity stemming from the unity of the subject or person. Rather than hesitate

---

[7] To quote Grillmeier: "Chalcedon leaves no doubt that the one Logos is the subject of both the human and the divine predicates. We can trace quite clearly in the Chalcedonian Definition the wish of the Fathers to take the Nicene framework as their starting point: *ante saecula quidem de Patre genitum secundum deitatem, ... propter nos et propter salutem nostram ex Maria Virgine Dei genitrice secundum humanitatem. ..* In the view of Chalcedon, Christ is not just a *'homo deifer'* or a human subject, *habens deitatem,* but the God-Logos, *habens humanitatem,* or rather, *habens et deitatem et humanitatem. ...* The Chalcedonian unity of person in the distinction of the nature provides the dogmatic basis for the preservation of the divine transcendence. ... But it also shows the possibility of a complete immanence of God in our history, an immanence on which the biblical doctrine of the economy of salvation rests" (*Christ in Christian Tradition,* 552-553).

at the words: "Jesus is God," we must hold them to be an authentic expression of faith. He is "truly God," and he who is God is not a distinct person from the one who is man. He is "one selfsame Son." We must emphasize the identifying power of the verb "is," which comes to it from the one identical subject or person. [8]

3. The Notion of Person as Subject of Consciousness and Freedom

The current accent on consciousness and freedom as attributes of the person does not change the concept of person adopted by the Council of Chalcedon. It throws greater light on certain of its aspects, and enriches it with the fruit of a deeper psychological exploration.

Implicitly, when the Council affirmed there is "one identical" person in Christ, it acknowledged in him a single subject of consciousness and freedom. True, it did not explicitly refer to consciousness or freedom. Yet when it declared that the man Jesus is "composed of body and rational soul," it included in the rational soul the entire activity of knowing and willing. It considered this rational soul as part of Christ's human nature, and therefore situated consciousness and freedom in the

---

[8] Certain scholars have proposed curious interpretations of the formula "Jesus is God," taking great pains to avoid its normal meaning which is a statement of identity. For instance, O. González de Cardedal speaks of a "limit-affirmation" which expresses Jesus' unity with God to the point that Jesus means for us what God is and that God is unthinkable without him, a unity in which Jesus in his total being lives in a relationship of total personal reciprocity with God (*Jesús de Nazaret, Aproximación a la Cristología*, Madrid, 1975, 507). The same author wonders whether it would suffice to define Christ as the one who is not without God and without whom God is not. The same view is expressed by H. Gollwitzer (*Krummes Holz-Aufrechter Gang, Zur Frage nach dem Sinn des Lebens*, Munich, 1971, 253). None of these paraphrases take the affirmation of Chalcedon into account, which is not a limit-affirmation but an expression of the personal identity of Christ: Jesus, in his person, is God. We must carefully exclude any identity between the divine and the human natures. But this distinction does not derogate from authentic unity of person. The verb "is" indicates an identity, and not merely "a relational unity based on origin, ordering, and reciprocity," according to the formula of O. González (*Jesús*, 506, footnote 446).

nature. It saw in the person of Christ the subject of this nature, the subject of all his human attributes and activities.

The Chalcedonian affirmation that Christ has a rational soul was a response to the Apollinarian controversy. It is worth remembering that the problem of identifying consciousness and freedom with the person had already been posed in that controversy. For Apollinarius of Laodicea, spirit, characterized by intellectual activity and even more by the power of self-determination, was identical with the person, with the "hypostasis." [9] As he had to admit there could be only one person in Christ, i.e., the person of the Word, he had to exclude the presence of a human soul. The single vital principle had to be the divine spirit of the Word.

When the Council of Chalcedon affirmed that Christ has a rational soul, endowed with consciousness and freedom, and that he is "one identical" person, it made it clear that the soul and the person of Christ are not identical. The "one identical" person is the person of the Son of God, a divine person. The rational soul, for its part, belongs to his human nature.

Even in our own day, any attempt to identify soul and person would resurrect the difficulty that Apollinarius was powerless to resolve. Person is defined as the *subject of consciousness and freedom,* but a distinction must be made between the subject who thinks and his intellect, the subject who wills and his will. And so it is that in Christ there are two wills, one divine and the other human, that cannot be identified with the one person. The two wills are distinct "without commingling," as is true of the two natures.

This approach need not prevent us from entering into the perspectives of modern psychology which stress consciousness and freedom as attributes of the person. Even in the Chalcedonian conception the person is the subject of rational activity. Therefore the divine person is the subject of the human activities of consciousness and will. These activities in no sense imply that Jesus is a human person. All the results of psychological research concerning the person can be applied

---

9 Cf. M. Richard, " L'introduction du mot 'hypostase' dans la théologie de l'Incarnation," *MSR* 2 (1945) 6-17.

to the person of Christ with respect to his human psychology, to help clarify its role.

To say that the person is the subject of consciousness and freedom is to admit that person is the principle of intellectual and voluntary activity. However, we must not forget that nature is also in its own way the principle of the activity of knowledge and will. How can we pinpoint the distinction between person and nature, which in this instance is the distinction between person and soul? According to the Chalcedonian view, hypostasis designates *the one who* acts, whereas nature refers to *what it is* that acts. The person is the first or dominant principle that produces the unity of the two natures. But this first principle respects whatever belongs strictly to the human nature. *The one who* acts does so through *what it is* that acts. Scholastic philosophy has expressed this by distinguishing the person, "the principle which" (*principium quod*), from the nature (*principium quo*). This is a distinction that we can adopt today, while noting that the nature is not simply a means or an instrument of the person.

4. *Importance of the Unity of the Person*

Unity of person in Jesus implies that in his human nature there is an "anhypostasis" or absence of human personhood. But this anhypostasis does not mean that Christ the man is deprived of personhood. The divine person of the Son has become man and exercises on his human nature the complete ascendancy that stems from the human person in other men. Because of the power of the divine person of the Son, we must even say that this ascendancy is more total and that no human nature was ever so profoundly personified as the human nature of Jesus.

We have noted that person is the principle of the activities of consciousness and will. The divine person must not, therefore, be considered as an external reality that is merely superimposed on Jesus' human nature. The notion of the two natures in the one person would then be static, as if they were simply placed side by side. However, the human nature of Christ is totally permeated by the personal being of the Word. The divine hypostasis is present in his human nature after the manner of a dynamism that vivifies from within the whole human reality of Jesus.

From the point of view of vocabulary, it would be preferable to speak of the hypostatic unity rather than of the hypostatic union, precisely in order to make the unity of person more compelling. This unity is not the result of the joining of the two natures, but is indeed the principle of their union. It is a person, the person of the Son, who assumes a human nature and makes it his very own, thereby uniting it to the Godhead. The expression "hypostatic union" addresses itself first of all to the two natures. However, if we want to approach the Incarnation process from the ontological point of view, we must first of all consider the unity of person and speak of "hypostatic unity."

B. SEARCHING FOR THE DISTINGUISHING MARK OF THE PERSON

While Chalcedon's affirmation that there is one person in Christ retains its validity, there is need for further research into the meaning of person. We need to discover and more clearly discern wherein lies the reality of the person. [10]

In describing the person as the subject of consciousness and freedom, we have already indicated the dynamism inherent in the subject. In short, person is the principle of activity. There still remains for us to delve more methodically into the dynamic ontology of the person.

1. *The Problem of the Distinction between Person and Nature*

How does the distinction between person and nature present itself to us? He have already alluded to the universal experience on which the distinction is based, the experience that makes us spontaneously ask: "Who is it?" and "What is it?" The first question, "Who is it?", reflects our experience of our own "I" and of our encounters with others.

---

[10] The author has dealt with the problem in his book *The Person of Christ, A Theological Insight*, Rome, 1981, Chicago, Franciscan Herald Press, 1983.

It draws attention to the person. The second question, "What is it?", concerns the discernment of the nature.

Do these two questions relate solely to two aspects of one and the same reality, or do they address two distinct realities? The problem of the real distinction between person and nature cannot be settled solely at the level of psychological manifestations. We experience psychologically the influence of the person, the inward impact of our "I" on our behavior, our decisions, our freedom, and our personal responsibility. But this is the influence of our person within our nature. In our experience, person and nature are so intimately linked that we perceive them together and we do not dichotomize their respective roles. Phenomenology does not suffice to enable us to establish a real distinction between person and nature.

Philosophical reflection is necessary if we are to pinpoint the nature of this distinction. Starting from the data of experience such reflection must go back to constituent elements, to the first principles. It must seek to determine what person is and what nature is, as well as their respective positions in being and their mutual relationships. Even though the distinction between person and nature is based on a fundamental human experience, it is of the ontological order. It lies at the level of the fundamental constitution of being itself.

That is why search for the distinctive marks of person and nature is a difficult venture. To seek to determine what formally constitutes personhood is to seek to explore the innermost depths of being. We need not be surprised if it is a slow, groping process and gives rise to divergent theories. Nonetheless, philosophical reflection is needed in order to elucidate as much as possible the distinction between person and nature.

In addition, the formulation of definitions of person and nature is even more arduous. Obstacles arise not only at the level of thought but also at the level of language. A first principle cannot be described in terms of sensible qualities and attributes, inasmuch as it underpins visible reality. Besides, since such a principle is simple it cannot be defined in terms of its component elements. As a result, there is danger of designating it by complex concepts which make it more confusing instead of elucidating it.

The most important comment to make about this inquiry concerns the role of theology in the problematic of the person-nature distinction. Even though this distinction is intrinsic to thought on human ontology, it has actually taken shape only in response to the problems posed by the mystery of the Trinity and by the ontological constitution of Christ. Theological reflection on the affirmations of faith has been a decisive factor in this area.[11] This means that the human intellect has actually succeeded in discerning the ontological constitution of man only by reflecting, in the light of Revelation, on the ontological constitution of God and of Christ.

At the level of vocabulary, we have pointed out that the terms hypostasis and nature did not come to be distinguished clearly in Christology until shortly before the definition of the Council of Chacedon. Greek philosophy had not provided theology with concepts suitable for expressing the distinction. In the history of human thought, this distinction was developed by theology in its efforts to give valid expression to the message of Revelation.

It follows that an analysis of the distinction between person and nature cannot abstract from the light that theology has brought to it. Certainly, philosophical reflection on the data of human experience and psychology must be pursued in accordance with its own method. But in such an arduous realm of knowledge philosophy is fortunate to have the beacons of revealed truth to guide it in its search.

---

[11] In the development of the notion of person, it is the doctrine of the Trinity that evoked the definition in terms of relational being. It is surprising to note, by contrast, how far removed Greek metaphysics had remained from this concept. While Plato had presented, on the existential level, the relational import of the person of Socrates, he left little room in his metaphysics for this dimension of the person. Aristotle had been more open-minded in that he thought of men more as subjects and defined love as concern for the well-being of the one loved. However he never developed the idea that what constitutes the person is precisely relation (cf. C. Lefèvre, " La personne comme être en relation chez Platon et Aristote," *MSR* 30, 1973, 161-184).

2. *The Divergent Trinitarian and Christological Approaches*

There have been various approaches in Trinitarian doctrine and Christology seeking to determine what formally constitutes the person.

To explain the doctrine of the Trinity, there has been a consensus among theologians that relation is what formally constitutes the person. Already in the early Church the Greek and Latin Fathers had defined the divine persons in terms of their relationships. We need only recall the words of Gregory of Nazianzus: "Father is not the name of an essence or of an operation, but of the relationship the Father has with respect to the Son, or that the Son has with respect to the Father." [12]

Augustine enounced the principle still more clearly. He said that the names of Father, Son, and Holy Spirit "signify that by which they are mutually related to one another, and not the substance by virtue of which they are one." [13]

The further development of the doctrine of relations by medieval Scholasticism was canonized by the Council of Florence in its *Decree for the Jacobites*. This Decree adopted a formula of St. Anselm: In God "everything is one, wherever the opposition of relation does not pose an obstacle." [14] There is a plurality, therefore, only where there are relations of opposition. It is these relations that distinguish the persons from one another. Theology has concluded from this that the divine persons are constituted by a relation or *esse ad,* and defined them as subsistent relations. In this way the identity of absolute perfection of the three persons was safeguarded. Each divine person possesses the totality of the divine substance or *esse in,* and none is inferior to the others.

We shall not delve further at this time into the subsequent interpretations of this fundamental principle. These interpretations followed two divergent paths. First, there have been the theologians who held the view that the relations derive their reality from the divine substance itself. They thereby tried to reduce the *esse ad* to the *esse in,* attributing to the nature a complete priority over the persons. They

---

[12] *Or.* 29, 16, *PG* 36, 96 A.
[13] *Epist.* 238, c. 2, 14, *PG* 33, 1043.
[14] DS 1330.

held that in the subsistent relation, the subsistence stems from the nature. In their view, relation subsists inasmuch as it is substance and not as relation. This explanation corresponds to the tendency of Latin theology to accentuate the nature at the expense of the persons, and to insist more on the unity than on the trinity. However, this view was not held unanimously by all Scholastic theologians.

A second interpretation conforms more closely to the principle that person involves an opposition of relations. It acknowledges the value of the *esse ad,* which possesses in itself a relative reality or perfection. [15] It is only by admitting this value that we can speak of an authentic relational being and accept the primordial originality of the person. To refuse to admit that relation has a reality of its own is to reduce the person to a secondary aspect of the nature. A subsistent relation is one that subsists as a relation. It is a relation whose reality consists not in being a substance but in being a subsistence or hypostasis, and thereby differs radically from all other relations.

The Trinitarian doctrine is not an attempt to reconcile the Three and the One through the subtlety of logical distinctions. Its purpose is to recognize the plenary reality of the three persons and the plenary reality of the divine essence by showing how they harmonize, without making them result from one another and without reducing them to one another. The definition of person as subsistent relation makes it possible to attribute plenary reality to the Father, the Son, and the Holy Spirit, without thereby diminishing the plenitude of the divine nature.

In Christology, the theories as to what formally constitutes the person follow various paths, none of which coincides with the Trinitarian explanation. They may seek this constitutive principle in the attribute of independence (the Scotist opinion), or of wholeness (Tiphanius), in a substantial mode (Cajetan and Suarez), or in existence, i.e., *esse* (Capreolus-Billot). [16]

---

[15] Cf. A. Michel, "Relations divines," *DTC* 13, 2135-2156.

[16] On this subject, in addition to the article "Hypostate" (A. Michel) in the *DTC* 7, 411-429, the reader can turn to Ph. Kaiser, *Die Gottmenschliche Einigung in Christus als Problem der spekulativen Theologie seit*

The first of these theories, in that it characterizes personal subsistence by independence or wholeness, has the merit of stressing the aspect of self-awareness and self-determination which distinguishes the behavior of the person. Yet it has the disadvantage of considering person as simply a component of nature. Now, the person is intrinsically original and differs from nature in its innermost reality. It is a principle of being really distinct from nature and cannot be reduced to a quality or an aspect of the latter. In the case of Christ, the theory would lead to two consequences. On the one hand, the human nature of Jesus would not be complete since it would be deprived of an important attribute. On the other hand, the divine person would have to be considered an attribute of this human nature.

The theory of the substantial mode separates the person more completely from the nature, for the mode is conceived as being really distinct. This mode is not considered to be a simple adjacent reality, an "accident" that perfects the substance. Indeed, it is called "substantial." Of the human experience of personality, the theory retains the incontestable fact that being a person involves a certain kind, a certain "mode" of existing. However, the term "mode," which it is difficult to define more precisely, remains rather vague, and still too weak to render the ontological value of the person. It remains too closely related to the idea of a particular quality of the nature. In Christ, this theory leads to the statement that the Word assumes a role as a substantial mode, which would be more appropriate to a Trinity constituted by three modes, rather than by three persons.

The theory that identifies subsistence with existence seeks to emphasize the experiential fact that to be a person is to exist independently. However the element of independence does not appear in the explanation, since in this view the person is constituted by the sole fact of existence. Even if it were necessary to affirm a real distinction between essence and existence, it would be difficult to admit that this distinction is identical with the distinction between nature and person.

der Scholastik, Munich 1968. The present author has made a critical commentary of these theories in his book The Person of Christ, A Theological Insight, Rome, 1981, Chicago, Franciscan Herald Press, 1983, pp. 13-23.

Why would a nature become a person by reason of the fact that it exists, that essence is actuated by existence? This does not seem to be the way to arrive at the authentic entity of the person.

In Christology, the theory gives rise to some difficulties. It would oblige us to say that the human nature of Christ has no human existence, but only a divine existence. This affirmation of "the ecstasy of being," that is, of Christ's deprivation of a human "to be," is scarcely compatible with the definition of Chalcedon. The two distinct natures, "without any commingling," of which the Council of Chalcedon speaks, are two concrete, existing natures. They are not abstract essences. Christ's human nature possesses the totality of the human "to be," the totality of human existence. It would therefore be a "commingling" of the two natures, a partial Monophysitism, to attribute a divine *esse* to the human nature so that the latter might have its own existence.

In addition to the difficulty of maintaining the integrity of the human nature, the theory would tend to call into question the notion of the hypostatic union. In its thinking, this union is accomplished within the divine being, that is to say, within the divine nature and not strictly in the divine person; consequently it would no longer be a hypostatic but a substantial union. While in its Trinitarian theology the theory goes to great pains to distinguish the persons from the being of their substance, in its Christology it would consider the *esse ad* and the *esse in* of Christ to be identical.

3. *Evaluation of the Divergences*

What is the root of the divergence in the theories that explicate the meaning of person in Christology and in Trinitarian theology? It sems to lie primarily in the fact that in Trinitarian theology attention is focussed on the divine person as such, whereas in Christology theologians have striven to define person in terms of the human person. It is certainly true that in the Incarnation the "one identical" person in whom the two natures are united is a divine person. It is therefore not impossible to abstract from the notion of person as it has been elaborated in the doctrine of the Trinity. But

292

inasmuch as in the case of Christ the specific problem consists in justifying why the absence of a human person does not imply the diminution of the human nature, theological speculation has concentrated on the human person.

How does it happen that in explaining the human person, the search for the formal constituent of the person has been sought in an absolute element rather than in a relative element? Specifically, it is because the designation of the human person encompasses the entire reality of the human being. When we speak of a person, in common parlance, we do not distinguish between person and nature, but consider the whole being, the person together with the nature he possesses. Thus, for instance, the person appears to us as an intelligent and free being. The definition given by Boethius: "an individual substance of a rational nature" [17] stresses this rationality. By using the term "substance," an ambiguous translation of the Greek "hypostasis," it moreover nurtures the confusion of person with nature.

To the extent that we consider the totality of the human being, we are inclined to attribute an absolute substantiality to the person. We are likewise inclined to define the person in terms of consciousness and freedom, because we do not take care to distinguish what belongs strictly to the nature and what belongs to the person as such.

When the problem of the distinction between nature and person is posed more explicitly, person can no longer be described as the totality of the human being but must be characterized by what in this whole belongs specifically to the person. Person is then understood in a more restricted sense that no longer coincides with the total psychological experience of the person, which involves experience of person within nature. A far-reaching and well-coordinated intellectual effort is needed, as we have already pointed out, to disentangle the two entities, the first two principles, which are so profoundly united and interrelated.

It is therefore necessary to pinpoint what formally constitutes person as distinct from nature in the concrete whole that is the human person. In such a determination, the orien-

---

[17] "*Persona est naturae rationalis individua substantia*" (*De persona et duabus naturis,* III, *PL* 64, 1343 D).

tation of Christology cannot be fundamentally divergent from that of Trinitarian doctrine. If, in God, person is defined by the *esse ad,* it cannot be defined in man in a diametrically opposed way, in terms of absolute being or of an absolute attribute of being. Ontological research on the human person must be addressed to relational being.

Similarly, the solution of the Trinitarian and the Christological problems cannot be sought in two contrary directions. At first glance, these two problems probably seem to reflect inverse situations, inasmuch as in one case the problem is to explain the presence of three persons in a single nature, and in the other case the presence of two natures in a single person. Despite this difference, they present a fundamental analogy. The difficulty consists in showing, in both cases, that the person does not contribute perfection in the order of nature.

Indeed, where the Trinity is concerned, there is need to explain why the Father is not more perfect than the Son or the Spirit, and how each of the persons, though he is not one of the others, lacks no perfection. In Christology, the problem is to show why Christ is perfectly man without being a human person. In both cases, the solution can be found only through recourse to a relative element, i.e., relational being.

If we attribute to the person as such an absolute quality or property of being, we must admit that insofar as it constitutes a reality, a principle of being, it contributes a perfection of the absolute order. We should then conclude that the divine persons do not possess an identical perfection and that in Christ the absence of a human person implies a deprivation of perfection for his nature as man. In Trinitarian doctrine, the need to resort to relational being has been seen more clearly. In Christology, efforts to identify the person with an attribute of nature, with a mode, or with existence, cannot provide a solution. The only way to explain how the absence of a human person in Christ does not make him less perfectly a man is by situating the formal constituent of the human person in relational being.

C. The Underlying Reality of the Person

1. *The psychological experience of the person*

If we seek to determine what person is through our psychological experience, we discover that the person is discovered essentially in our relations with others. Consciousness of our own "I" is illuminated by the relationships it establishes with "you's."

This fact deserves to be given the highest priority. For in striving to grasp the reality of person in the act of consciousness, we might be led to characterize person in terms of an "I" that clings to itself and turns inward on itself. Indeed, consciousness is the "I's" apprehension of itself, a knowledge that focusses on the "I." It might easily lead to an egocentric notion of the person.

Two considerations must be introduced here. First, while it is true that consciousness perceives the "I," it is part of an activity of knowing which, for its part, is essentially directed outward. It is by knowing an object extrinsic to me that I become aware of myself. Consciousness is never the simple perception of one's "I." It always accompanies the perception of something outside the self, and this something else is the primary object of knowledge. Only a reflexive effort can distinguish within the act of knowing what belongs strictly to the act of consciousness of self. This is to say that the act of consciousness of self cannot be separated from orientation toward other beings, since it is this orientation that elicits the act in the first place.

However, this relationship with external reality is at first concerned only with things, with the immediate objects of knowledge. Another specific relationship is established in encounters with persons. By virtue of the encounter with a "you," the knowing subject is revealed to himself as an "I." In order to discover myself as an "I," I need to be confronted with another person. At the same moment the "other" is seen by me as a "you," I perceive myself as an "I."

This experience is constantly being confirmed in every person's life. Interpersonal relations, encounters with others, are necessary if a person is to take cognizance of himself. This is true of the development of consciousness from its earliest stages. A child experiences himself as an "I" in his developing relationships between himself and his parents or other persons. If he were not situated in a personal milieu, his personality could not assert itself or develop to maturity. His personality is nourished by contacts with the persons that surround him.

There is no better way to express this essential psychological experience than by using the words used to describe the mystery of the Trinity. Persons are manifested in the "opposition of relation." Truly, there is an opposition here, not in the sense of hostility or contrariety, but of a relational confrontation in which one person finds himself facing another and experiences the impact that the mutual encounter produces on each.

An encounter presupposes that the eyes of the two participants meet. It would not suffice for their eyes to be turned in the same direction in a communion of orientation. For an "I" to develop consciousness of itself, there has to be a genuine face-to-face contact, an encounter with a "you."

From the "opposition of relation" results the perception of the "incommunicable" character that has been traditionally considered the distinctive mark of the person. When the "I" faces a "you," it becomes aware of what it is in itself, of what it can neither cease being nor renounce being. It will always be the same "I" that nobody can ever snatch away, that another "I" can never assimilate. For every other "I" will always face it as a "you." The "opposition of relation" is a constant factor in the universe of persons. Each "I" is situated vis-a-vis all the others, and retains this position indefinitely. Even when two "I's" face in the same direction, thereby forming a "we," they cannot eliminate their face-to-face stance which remains their primary relationship.

Perhaps it is better not to speak of "incommunicability," for this might suggest the impossibility of communication and the imprisonment of the person within an absolute individualism. Rather, let us speak of the fundamental inalienable originality of the person. The "I" possesses an originality that makes it unique in its kind, different from all other "I's." It can never be deprived of this originality or divest itself of it. This originality is so radical that it cannot be defined. The concrete reality of each "I" cannot be described conceptually. It cannot be reduced to something else. Each "I" postulates the possession of an inimitable individuality within itself.

The reason the self-awareness of the "I" is not *per se* an act of egoism or egocentricity is that it occurs within a relationship with another or others. The "I" does not become aware of itself as an absolute. It can think and say "I", "me", only in the measure that its contacts with other persons develop. The experience of the "opposition of relation" enables the "I" to discover its irreducible originality, but in an inherently outgoing attitude toward other "you's."

The altruistic orientation of the "I" is seen still more clearly in the act of love. Love and consciousness are characteristic activities of the person, corresponding to the two spiritual faculties of will and intellect. Now, only love can fulfill the person's destiny. Consciousness is in a certain sense merely a point of departure. When the "I" becomes conscious of itself and perceives itself as an "I", it is so that it may give itself to a "you," and enter into communion with that "you." In the world of persons, self-giving is self-fulfillment. The underlying reality of the "I" is completed, therefore, only when the altruistic intention is fulfilled.

To sum up, in the psychological activity of the person orientation toward others is of capital importance. For even in the act of consciousness in which attention is focussed on the "I," contact with a "you" is essential; and in the act of love the person tends to give himself to a "you," in communion with whom the "I" seeks its completion.

2. *The Ontology of the Person*

From this fundamental psychological experience an ontology of the person emerges. While the person's psychology is not identical with his total reality, it manifests its hidden depths.

If psychology attests to a dynamism of the person orientated toward others, to the point that contact with others elicits the awakening of consciousness and that the destiny of the person is consummated in union with another or others, then ontology must acknowledge that the reality of the person is of the relational order.

Every person also possesses a reality not of the relational order, what might be called a substantial perfection. Such, for instance, is perfection of soul, endowment with intellect and will. Indeed, every person possesses an individual human nature. But when we try to distinguish in this concrete personal entity what belongs strictly to the nature and what to the person, we come to the conclusion that we should define person in the strict sense as a relational being. Nature embraces the rich reality of body and soul, including the faculties of thought and action. The person is the relational entity that energizes the nature by directing its activity toward others in knowledge and love.

We speak of person as "relational being" and not "relative being," because the designation "relative" is better suited to nature. Things are relative to others, that is, dependent on others. Thus, to express the dependence of human nature upon God, we speak of its relativity. The term "relational" is better suited to designate person-to-person relationships. When we affirm that the person is a relational being, we are referring to relationship with other persons, to the dynamism of the person orientated toward others.

This means that the person exists as a reality relating to other persons. That is the translation in ontological terms of basic psychological experience. The "I" exists only in relation to other "I's" because its innermost reality consists in this relationship.

We are dealing here with an altogether unique relationship, considerably different from others. Logical or philosophical considerations on the notion of relation can be applied in this instance only with careful discernment. In order to determine the aspects of a person's relationality one must take into account what is observable in the person's psychological experience.

To define person as relational being is not to define one person by another. In fact, the definition does not mean that the reality of the person is "ecstatic," i.e., that it is situated in others. The reality of the person finds psychological expression in his "I." And this "I" is not identical with the "you." For relation involves a certain opposition, a vis-a-vis, as we have already indicated. The "I" is defined with reference to the "you," but never becomes the "you." When we speak of a "relational being," we must include within it this inherent opposition. Relationships can never make the "I" lose its own originality and reality.

To claim that the person, as a relational being, is adequately defined by others is to imply it is not a real relation. To interpret person as a simple relation of the logical order is to misconstrue the meaning of person. A person is a relation that possesses a reality of its own. This relation does not derive its reality from nature, as we have already pointed out in differentiating what constitutes person as distinct from nature. Man consists on the one hand of nature, with its absolute determinations; and on the other hand he is endowed with personhood, whose reality, far from deriving from these absolute determinations, is relational . The two principles of being are intimately united in a single whole that can be called a concrete person, each with its own unique reality.

Moreover, the " relation" that constitutes the person cannot be included in the category of " accidents." We are speaking here of a relation that exists independently and not of a relation that adds a secondary perfection to a being already in existence. It deserves the name of subsistent relation, or hypostatic relation.

However, the relational being of the person appears in concrete relationships with others, that, according to Aristotelian terminology, can be called accidental relations in the sense that they do not enter into the constitution of the individual but merely contribute to his perfection. The principle of being that is called relational being unfolds within these relationships, even though it cannot be identified with any one of them in particular.

Besides, the term "accidental relations" can be used only through a transposition . For here accident cannot be opposed to substance according to the normal distinction, which is situated in the order of nature. A person is not a "substantial relation." This expression would imply that the person is a substance or nature, that it draws its reality from substance. That is why we speak of person as subsisting relation, or better still, as hypostatic relation. This avoids ambiguity and distinguishes hypostasis from substance, person from nature.

Still another question can be raised. In spite of the distinction, is it not possible to affirm an "identity" between hypostatic relation and nature? Do we not say of a person that he is a man, and do we not thereby imply a certain identity between person and nature? Actually, since there is a profound distinction between these two principles of being, there is no identity between them inasmuch as the reality of the person is not the reality of the nature. Yet there is a dynamic identity between them in this sense: the person possesses the nature and quickens it with his relational being. The person is the subject of all the activities of the nature. The nature, for its part, is dominated, governed by the person, and belongs to the person. All the determinations, qualities and attributes of the nature are appropriated by the person. Inasmuch as he is the subject, the person is what he possesses. We can therefore speak of identity, but with certain reservations, noting that the unity of person and nature is comparable to no other and does not enter into preexisting categories.

The notion of identity, therefore, can be applied to the unity of person and nature only with reservations and in a very carefully defined sense. The relational being, in recognizing itself as an "I" and acting as an "I," appropriates everything that exists in the nature. Consequently, while the human person is not, rigorously speaking, his human nature, person personalizes nature to the point of totally possessing it. In this sense, the nature is identified with the person.

3. *The Illumination Given by the Trinitarian Doctrine*

We have already mentioned the necessity of a convergence between Trinitarian doctrine and the Christological doctrine of the person. This convergence is based on the analogy between the divine persons and human persons. If each divine person is a subsistent relation, then the human person must likewise be a subsistent relation, their essential resemblance not being eliminated by the ontological distance that separates God from man. In man as in God, the person is a relational being.

There are those who have difficulty accepting this analogy. The theory of relations appears to them a subtlety resorted to by Trinitarian theology in order to justify the unique and ex-

300

ceptional case in which there are three persons in one and the same nature . In their view, the Trinity is an exceptional case that is absolutely unique with God. It could not have any analogy in any other being. The notion of the divine person as subsistent relation would thus remain exceptional, without parallel in the human person.

Still more simply, the difficulty might be stated this way: in God person must be explained in terms of relation because there are three persons in a single nature. In man, in whom there is no need to make this harmonization, person must be explained in a different way and can be defined in terms of an absolute entity.

Yet this would presuppose that person is defined as relation for lack of a better definition. It would imply that the ideal would be to define person as an absolute reality, but that the Trinity presents an obstacle to such a definition. Then the ideal of the person would be realized in man, whereas in God person would possess only a diminished, less subsistent reality.

Now, the opposite is true. The ideal of the person is realized in God. It is the human person who is a copy and reflection of the divine persons. Even though the community of the three divine persons in one nature is a unique reality that can never be repeated as such in mankind, it remains the exemplary model from which all human exemplars derive, because of the resemblance of creatures with their Creator. The divine community of persons forms the model of all communities and persons.

First, the divine community of persons in the Trinity is the model of all communities. The Trinity forms the most perfect communion of persons. It is the primordial reason why human beings were created in community. God did not create one solitary human individual as the generative principle of all other humans. Rather, he created a couple consisting of a man and a woman, a community destined to grow in size. Therefore human persons are essentially communitarian. Man and woman were created to be complementary to one another, intrinsically relational to one another, and their community reflects the divine community.

Secondly, the Trinity is also the model of every person.

Inasmuch as they are subsistent relations, the Father, the Son, and the Holy Spirit realize the plenitude of perfection of the person. We must therefore admit that in every person, whoever he or she may be, reality and perfection consist not in an absolute entity but in a relation. This relation is not something flimsy or tenuous. It is endowed with the solidity and power of being turned toward others. It is a dynamism whose reality seeks to deploy itself, to communicate its riches.

The infallible affirmations of Trinitarian doctrine confirm the result of our fundamental psychological experience. They clarify the ontology hidden within this experience, and lend support to the bold inquiry that concludes to the relational being of the human person. Moreover, in the development of human thought, it is the theology of the Trinity that first identified person and relation. Our understanding of God thus indirectly enlightens us on the innermost reality of man. It helps us to distinguish person and nature within ourselves, and to define our own person in terms of relationality. We cannot disregard the fact that the distinction between person and nature has been the accomplishment of theology rather than of philosophy.

As we have already said, Christology depends just as much as Trinitarian doctrine on the definition of person as relational being to explain one of its intrinsic problems. The fact that in Christ there is no human person does not entail any deprivation of the absolute perfection that lies in man. The reason is, of course, that person is constituted by relation and not by an absolute human element, attribute, or quality. The lack of personhood in Christ, therefore, does not make him any less a man.

In addition, Christology needs to stress the fundamental analogy between the divine persons and human persons. How, indeed, could the Word perform the normal role of a person in Christ's human nature if this analogy did not exist? If the person of the Word were totally different from human persons, he could not vivify and personalize a man's nature. This means the divine person of the Word could not form, in the humanity of Jesus, the personality that performs within it all the functions that in other men are assumed by the human person. Since the divine person of the Son is a relational being, he can play an authentic role as person in Christ the man only if human persons are likewise relational beings.

4. The Limitations of the Human Person

In comparison with the divine person, the human person is seen to have the limitations inherent to creatures. In the analogy, there is a fundamental likeness, but also some differences. We shall focus our attention on these differences. An initial limitation lies in the originality of the human person. The divine persons are constituted by relations of origin: the Father is truly himself by virtue of his paternal relationship, the Son by virtue of his filial relationship, and the Spirit by virtue of his procession of love from the Father and from the Son. None of these origins is the replica of the others. The three differ among themselves, and each origin has its characteristic mark that makes it unique. That is why each of the three divine persons is totally original. By contrast, human persons do not differ from one another in the same way by reason of their origin. Obviously, each human person is brought into existence by the Creator in a unique manner, but in this regard the origin of each human person is like that of all the others. His relational being is not determined by his origin, and in consequence his originality is much less radical.

However, the originality of each human person is a universal fact. For the origin of every man is a creative act which calls him forth individually and causes him to spring into being in an "opposition of relation" with respect to all other persons. This creative act confers an originality that nothing can wipe out. It is a definitive work of God and the authentic reflection of the irreducible originality of the divine persons. Once again, let us stress that this limitation of the human person does not destroy the likeness.

This analogy justifies concern on the part of human persons to preserve and develop their originality. The eradication of all differences among persons could never be held up as an ideal. These differences need to be preserved, just as they are preserved in the Trinity. Far from being an impediment to union, originality constitutes the riches that the "I" contributes to the community.

303

The second limitation of the human person concerns the union that exists among human persons. The three divine persons possess the same totally identical nature and share in this nature without reservation or limitation. All three possess the same richness of being, the same knowledge and the same love. Each human person, on the contrary, possesses his own individual human nature, and this limits his potential for communion. Each human person must promote what is best for his nature, and from this point of view safeguard his own best interests. The fact that a human person possesses his own distinct nature may tend to make him consider himself as an absolute, and to set himself up as the center of everything around him. The danger of individualism is obvious, and it has provoked an egocentric or even a monadic conception of the person. Indeed, the person has been defined as a being who not only lives through his own dynamism but lives for himself, who lives like an "I" that behaves as the sovereign master of its existence and of the surrounding world.

In actual fact, human nature is intended to contribute to the communion of persons. While the individuation of nature in each human person does not permit the identical perfection, knowledge and love that are uniquely possessed by the divine persons of the Trinity, it is no obstacle to the development of a community of thought and love. This community is even a compelling need of human nature, inasmuch as human intellects are called to arrive at the one truth, and human wills are destined to come together in mutual self-giving. Even though fundamentally limited by individual natures, the communion of human persons should reflect the communion of the divine persons in God.

A third limitation of the human person concerns the development of personality. In God, the persons are established in the perfection of their personal reality from their origin, and cannot become more perfect. Human persons are governed by a law of growth and progress. The person is destined to develop his virtualities, to exercise his dynamism, and thereby to better actualize what he is meant to be. The human person is perfected through his own activity.

Each of the divine persons is a relational being completely determined by his origin. Thus, the Father is perfectly a Father in relation to the Son and cannot attain additional perfection in the paternal relations he inaugurates with men. Conversely, each human person is a relational being that does not possess its full perfection from the beginning and must perfect himself through concrete relationships with others. His relational being is destined to pass from potency to act, to become more completely realized through human contacts. Human persons not only have personality, they are also subject to growth in personality. A human person gradually becomes more of a person and the reality of his person develops. This maturation is provided by the activation of his relational dynamism. In relating to others, the person becomes more profoundly himself.

While created being is inherently limited we must say that, like the other limitations of the person, this one is not solely negative. To need to develop is to experience one's own limitations, but it is also to overcome them and to become more actively a person. The unfolding of relationships with others amplifies the relational being, and gives the person greater solidity. From this point of view, human persons reflect the plenitude of the divine persons. The persons of the Trinity have possessed this plenitude from all eternity; man, on the other hand, continues his unending quest for personal fulfillment. Personalization is the tendency to come as close as possible to the perfection of personality realized in God.

D. THE RELATIONAL BEING OF CHRIST

1. *The Son, Perfect Man*

The notion of person as relational being helps us to understand how Christ can be perfectly man without being a human person. In the theology of the Trinity the equality in the perfection of the divine persons is explained by the distinction between the absolute perfection of the single undivided nature possessed by the Three and the relational reality of each of the persons. All three divine persons possess the same absolute perfection. One differs from the others only in his unique entity as person; and since this entity is relational, it does not contribute any absolute perfection. In Christology, the solution to the problem is similar. The incarnate Son possesses all the absolute perfection that pertains to human nature, and it is because of this that he is perfectly man.

In Christ there is no human relational being. The relational being of the Son of God vivifies and possesses the human nature. Now, Christ's human nature is complete, endowed with all its attributes and qualities, above all, wholeness and autonomy. It lacks nothing that is present in other men. The Son of God is a man like all others, with the sole exception of sin; and this does not denote a difference in nature but in behavior.

Jesus' human nature is fully endowed with human reality and human existence. It does not exist by virtue of a divine existence, and is not deprived of its human "to be" through an "ecstasy of being." Christ is "truly man," "consubstantial with us," to use the words of Chalcedon. In particular, he has a human soul with a human consciousness and a human will, a soul that acts according to the laws of human psychology and remains distinct from his divine spirit, "without any commingling."

Without losing any of its own qualities, this human nature is personalized by the relational being of the Word. Jesus' human activity is not governed by a human "I," but by the "I" of the Son of God which inspires and guides it. That is why the man Jesus possesses a completely filial personality, capable of enhancing in the most complete way all that is human about him.

2. The Coming of the Relational Being of the Son Among Men

The notion of relational being clarifies the meaning of the dynamism of the Incarnation. Relational being cannot be defined as a static reality that might emerge from abstract theories concerning relations. It is a dynamic entity inasmuch as it defines person as a reality reaching out to other persons.

The relational being of the Son has established concrete relationships with men at their own level. A divine dynamism permeates the interpersonal relations of Christ's humanity.

This explains the importance of the unity of Christ's person. If there were not one divine person in two natures, the marvel that is the Incarnation would not exist, i.e., that a divine person has made contact with men not only from his own divine level but by freely coming down to the level of men. In becoming man, the relational being of the Son inaugurated horizontal relationships with men. His contacts were no longer directed solely downward from above. They were henceforth to be made on a level of equality with human nature. Through this human nature, a divine relational being entered into human interpersonal relations.

The Prologue of St. John's Gospel gives us an insight into the depth of this downward movement into humanity. First, it presents the Word to us in his eternity. This Word was "toward God" (1:1), that is to say, from all eternity he has been turned toward the Father. [18] His eternal existence as Son was relational to the Father. He now directed his inward dynamism toward humanity: "The Word became flesh, he dwelled among us" (1:14). The Incarnation consists not only in becoming flesh by taking on a human nature, but also in entering into personal contact, at the human level, with human persons. To dwell among us is to establish stable relationships of proximity with us within the human community.

We find the same movement expressed in the words: "No one has ever seen God; it is God the only Son, who is toward the Father's heart, who has made him known" (1:18). The One who was reaching out with his whole filial being toward the Father in the most complete intimacy now turned toward us to reveal to us the innermost reality of God.

Thus, all the dynamism of the Son's relationality to the Father was directed toward mankind. This explains the power of Christ's approach to men, and likewise the complete solidarity with which he shared their existence. Jesus expressed the horizontality of his personal relations by calling his disciples friends (cf. Jn 15:14) and by looking upon all men as his brothers, without allowing the least of them to be thought of as remaining at an inferior level (cf. Mt 25:40).

Just as in eternity there have always been horizontal

---

[18] The literal sense "toward" has often been weakened in translations, but deserves to be maintained even if the expression "to be toward" seems strange. "To be toward" indicates a dynamic ontology. Cf. I. de la Potterie, "L'emploi de *eis* dans S. Jean et ses incidences théologiques," *Bi* 43 (1962) 379-387; "'Je suis la voie, la vérité et la vie' (Jn 14:6)," *NRT* 88 (1966) 934.

relations between the Word and the Father, so, too, since the Incarnation, the Word has had truly horizontal relations with mankind. One and the same relational being is the subject of these relationships.

By entering the world of human relationships through his divine relational being, the Son transformed the universe of human persons. This transformation has consisted in an elevation of men correlative to his descent. By the very fact of descending to the human level, he raised human persons to the level of the three divine persons of the Trinity. Through the horizontality he established with human beings, the Son opened to them the path of horizontality with the Father. From the moment of the Incarnation, there has been a divine "I" in the midst of the "I's" of men. As a result, all human "I's" have been given access to the "You" of the Son of God. The infinite distance between God and man has been spanned by the relational being of the Word. While the two natures of Christ, the divine and the human, retain their identity, man and God have been drawn together by the person, the relational being of the Word.

3. Christ, the Covenant

When person is defined as relational being, we can understand why Jesus found it possible to identify himself as the covenant (cf. Mk 14:24; Mt 26:28). The person of the incarnate Son, the "one, identical" relational being in two natures, constitutes the definitive and permanent bond between the community of the three divine persons in God and the community of all human persons. It unites the two communities, by placing the divine persons at the level of human persons, and human persons at the level of the divine persons.

Here we see the intimate bond between the functional and the ontological. Christ's mission was to inaugurate between God and mankind the covenant figuratively announced in the Old Testament and that was to be given a new and eternal form in the fullness of time. Now, he established this covenant in his own person. Granted, he did not consummate it until the end of his earthly life through his redemptive sacrifice. Yet this sacrifice simply carried to its utmost limits the relational dynamism within him. In other words, the sacrifice of Calvary expressed in all its concrete implications the ontological reality of Christ. This sacrifice was the supreme moment of Christ's filial relationship of love with his Father, as well as of his loving relationship with men, bringing the incarnation of the relational being of the Word to its fulfillment.

It is important to understand the meaning of this covenant. It is more than the union of two natures, the divine and the human, in one person. It unites the entire world of human persons with the three divine persons of the Trinity.

The relational being of the Son profoundly transformed human intersubjectivity by entering into it through the Incarnation. He conferred a new value upon human persons by offering them the opportunity to dialogue with himself, and with the Father and the Holy Spirit. In so doing he amplified the personalities with which he entered into contact, making them participate in the greatness of his own divine personality by means of horizontal relations.

In a more specific way, Christ appears in the Gospels as the one who leads men to the Father by sharing his filial relationship with them. The words recorded by John as spoken by Jesus at the Last Supper give us the itinerary of Jesus' whole life: "I came from the Father and have come into the world and now I leave the world to go to the Father" (Jn 16:28). Now, Christ wanted to lead his disciples toward the Father to whom he was going. When, after the Resurrection, he spoke of "my Father and your Father" (Jn 20:17), he meant he had communicated his filial relationship to his disciples.

And so the Christian's filial attitude does not consist merely in a certain moral behavior that responds to the Father's love. It is rooted in the ontology of Christ's filial relationship, on the relational being of the Son who makes all men share in his own innermost reality. It is likewise based on the ontology of the Father's paternal relationship which, addressing itself to the Son, includes all men within its embrace.

Earlier we mentioned that in the Old Testament the covenant found expression in a paternal relationship that God wanted to establish with his people. This relationship could have consisted simply in an efficacious love, in a paternal affection expressed by benevolence. Now, by virtue of the presence of the Son's relational being among men, the Father based his fatherhood on his own relational being as Father. He extended the scope of this fatherhood by turning, through his Son and beyond him, toward those who would henceforth be united in the divine sonship of Christ. Fatherhood, like sonship, thus has an ontological value that underlies its functional value.

This ontological value helps us to perceive more clearly the basic reason for the universality of Christ's mediation in the relations between men and the Father. Whether they are Christians, Jews, Moslems, or pagans, all genuine contact between men and God really passes through the relational being of the Son. Christ gives Christians an explicit awareness of this filiation that stems from his own Sonship and that gives them the most intimate access to the Father. He invites them to utter the name "Abba" when they pray, as he himself has done. As for pagans, he inspires them, through their myths and ritual acts, to an attitude of relationship to God which, although denying its ultimate foundation, follows the secret course impressed on mankind by Christ's relational being. Every prayer finds its way to the Father through the Son, even if it cannot name either the Father or the Son and lies totally outside the perspectives of the Gospel.

4. The Reason for the Son's Incarnation

The role of the Son's relational being enables us to grasp the reason why the Son, and not the Father or the Holy Spirit, became incarnate. Strictly speaking, it cannot be claimed that the incarnation of one of the other divine persons would have been impossible. [19] We are not forbidden to opine that the Father or the Spirit might have become incarnate. We cannot restrict the options open to God in his plan of salvation, eliminating options different from the course he actually chose.

---

[19] Rahner has held an opposing view (*Myst. sal.* 6, 35-40) above all in protest against the idea that, according to Trinitarian theology, any one of the three divine persons might have become incarnate. On the contrary, theology owes it to itself to determine why the Word, rather than one of the other divine persons, became incarnate.

Yet we must strive to discover, in God's actual plan of salvation, why it was fitting that the Son should become incarnate.

Inasmuch as the Word is the image or perfect expression of the Father, it devolves upon him to make the Father known, to express the Father in a human nature. The mission of revelation, therefore, is appropriate to the Word made flesh.

In addition, since his relational being is that of a Son, he is qualified to represent and lead mankind in a filial return to the Father through the homage of prayer and sacrifice.

As a matter of fact, the Redemption achieved by Christ was the activation of his filial relationship carried to its extreme limit. In offering up his sufferings and death, Jesus revealed he was completely a Son, indeed to the point that his relational being was turned toward the Father in a disposition of total filial surrender. Jesus' whole life was dominated by the purpose to return to the Ftaher because this movement was implicit in his very person of a Son.

This clearly manifests the dynamic aspect of the unity of Christ's person. The one "identical" relational being of the Word is not simply a static link, a bridge between two natures. Rather, it takes possession of the human nature in order to bring to all men a divine presence that is very close to them, and to lead them to the Father. The covenant personified by Christ's relational being achieves the reconciliation of mankind with the Father, as well, for that matter, as the reconciliation of all men among themselves. As subsistent relation, the Son draws together and unifies all men.

5. *The Transformation of Relations Among Human Persons*

The coming of the Son's relational being into the human community put human persons in contact with the three divine persons. It also transformed the horizontal relationships of humans among themselves. This transformation can be defined from three points of view, because of the fact that the person of the Son takes on the aspect of an "I," a "you," and becomes the foundation of the "we."

As an "I," the Son incarnate established a new relationship of love between humans and their human brothers and sisters. Charity is the essence of the new commandment. the one that is uniquely Jesus' own: "my commandment" (Jn 15:12). This is not simply the precept he decreed. It is the impulsion of love that his "I" came to create within all men: "Love one another; just as I have loved you, you also must love one another" (Jn 13:34; 15:12). The innovation does not consist, strictly speaking, in love for neighbor, which had been formulated as a law in the Old Testament (cf. Lv 19:18). It lies in the words "as I have loved you ..." The relational being of the Son reached out to men with the same dynamic love he addressed to his Father. He wanted to communicate the vital power of divine love to Christians. Christ's "I" thus remains the permanent wellspring of a superior love of charity, capable of exceeding all human limitations.

The incarnate Son inaugurated the same superior relationship of charity, but from the opposite point of view, in his quality as a "You." While the "I" of Jesus is the source of our love for our brothers and sisters, his "You" remains nonetheless the term of this love. We find this principle enunciated in the picture Jesus gave of the final judgment: "I tell you solemnly, in so far as you did this to one of the least of these brothers of mine, you did it to me" (Mt 25:40). Wthin each human "you," therefore, the "You" of Christ lies hidden, feeling personally every act of love or rejection. It is this "You" of Christ that stores up for the day of judgment everything that has been given in the love of charity.

It is important to understand that this presence of Christ's "You" applies to every man, woman, and child, whoever they may be. It is not to be confused with his presence of good pleasure and friendship in his disciples. It is an ontological, universal presence that stems from the Incarnation. Henceforth the relational being of the Son, in the quality of a "You," maintains a personal relationship with each and every human being, and he does so through all the "you's" of mankind.

Finally, this relational being of the Word incarnate is the foundation of the "we." "For where two or three meet in my name, I shall be there with them" (Mt 18:20). In this affirmation, no less than in the preceding ones, Christ is speaking of far more than a moral presence. It is an ontological presence, the presence of the relational being who brings his disciples into contact with one another and forges a bond of divine union among them.

In consequence, all aspects of the interpersonal relations of mankind, in the "I," the "you," and the "we," have been raised to a divine level through the coming of the person of the Son into the human milieu.

PART FIVE

THE PSYCHOLOGY OF CHRIST

The great Christological controversies of the first centuries concerned the ontology of Christ. While they certainly dealt with his psychology at least peripherally, their essential purpose was one of ontological clarification. The Fathers wanted to determine what Christ is in his innermost reality. They did not linger over psychological investigations.

It is characteristic that Athanasius, the great opponent of Arius, had given no thought to the soul of Jesus prior to the Apollinarian controversy, and thus omitted consideration of his human psychology. No less significant is the delay that occurred in defining the two types of activity in Christ after the definition of his two natures. Two hundred years and more elapsed between the Council of Chalcedon (451 A.D.) and the 1st Lateran Council (649 A.D.) and the 3rd Council of Constantinople (680 A.D.).

It has only been in recent times, since the development of psychological research, that theologians have sought to analize the psychology of Christ in a more systematic way. They attempted to understand the data of the Gospel in the light of the psychological experience of the human person. Even if the Evangelists did not adopt the viewpoint of psychological description, they provide many clues concerning the psychology of Jesus. Obviously, theology must take into account the uniqueness of Chrit's ontological constitution. Yet, inasmuch as Jesus was truly man, he had a true human psychology.

Chapter XI

THE CONSCIOUSNESS OF JESUS

A. The Human Consciousness of a Divine "I"

1. *The Human Consciousness*

The first fact to emphasize is the reality of Jesus' human consciousness. In the Gospel texts we discern manifestations of this human consciousness that allow us to affirm that Jesus was a man like other men.

We are speaking of psychological consciousness, that is to say, of the interior knowledge a person has of himself and of his inner reactions. We are not dealing here with the moral awareness known as conscience, which relates to the responsibility a person assumes for his way of acting and which we shall consider when we study the freedom of Christ.

As is the rule for all of Christ's activities and kinds of knowledge, we must maintain the distinction between his divine consciousness and his human consciousness. We cannot describe Jesus' psychology as stemming from a commingling of his divine consciousness with his human consciousness. The principle of the duality of Christ's "operations," without commingling, was declared by the Third Council of Constantinople, [1] and is based on the Gospel witness itself. In the Gospels, only Jesus' human consciousness is discernible. There is not a single Gospel episode in which the divine consciousness of Christ is manifested directly. The reason we are obliged to admit the existence of this divine consciousness is that Jesus presented himself as the Son of God, and that, being a divine person, he necessarily possesses a divine con-

---

[1] DS 557.

sciousness. The reason is not that any Gospel text provides immediate testimony to support it.

We shall not concern ourselves with the problems that the divine consciousness, common to the Father, the Son, and the Holy Spirit, might pose. For these belong to the domain of Trinitarian theology. We shall limit ourselves to a consideration of Jesus' human consciousness, as it was revealed to us during his earthly life.

Let us forestall a possible ambiguity. Certain authors speak of Jesus' divine consciousness, meaning thereby the awareness of his divine identity. Thus, V. Taylor would have us discard the expression "messianic consciousness," and adopt instead the term "divine consciousness." The latter he defines as the consciousness Jesus had of "being more than a man, of sharing during his earthly existence in the life of Deity itself." [2] The expression has a descriptive value, but in a more specific sense which distinguishes Christ's human nature from his divine nature, there is need of making it clear that Christ's awareness of possessing a divine nature sprang strictly from his human consciousness. The "consciousness" of which Taylor speaks is a perception of the human order. To avoid all ambiguity, we shall limit ourselves to the term "human consciousness."

2. The "I" of Jesus

Does Jesus possess a human "I"? There can be no doubt that Jesus possesses an "I" perceived in a human way by his human consciousness. But must this "I" necessarily be a human "I"? Are we obliged to admit that there are two "I's" in Christ, one divine and the other human, or must we say, on the contrary, that there is in him only the one identical "I" of the Son of God?

If we turn for guidance to the witness of the Gospel accounts, we discover that Jesus often says "I" or "me" in a way that implies an allusion to his divine personality.

The most obvious statement of this sort is the *ego eimi*. Jesus says: "I am" or "it is I," evoking passages of the Old Testament in which Yahweh revealed his name to Moses (cf.

---

[2] *The Person of Christ in New Testament Teaching*, London, 158, 156.

Ex 3:14), or assured the people of his sovereign presence. The "I" belongs to a person who is insinuating his divine identity. The reference, therefore, is clearly to a divine "I." The most explicit statement in John's Gospel leaves no room for doubt: "I tell you most solemnly, before Abraham came into being, I Am" (Jn 8:58). It demonstrates that the "I" of Christ is different from the "I" of any other man: it does not owe its origin to a human birth, it does not belong to the becoming of creatures, but is situated in the "to be" of God.

We have already pointed out that what is affirmed more explicitly in certain Johannine declarations can be discerned implicitly in the "it is I" of other contexts of John's Gospel or the Synoptics. Jesus says "It is I!" in the spontaneous and ordinary way a man announces his presence to his friends. But each time the context indicates an insinuation of his divine personality. Thus, for example, when Jesus walks on the water, he wants his disciples to recognize him as a familiar, friendly presence, and so he says: "It is I! Do not be afraid" (Mt 14:27; Mk 6:50; Jn 6:20). And yet at the same time this "I" dominates the forces of nature and manifests his divine grandeur. It is as though he were secretly inviting them to discover the divine quality of his "I."

Jesus' self-description: "I am the good shepherd" (Jn 10:11) needs to be understood in the light of Ezekiel's oracle: "For the Lord Yahweh says this: I am going to look after my flock myself and keep all of it in view. . . . I myself will pasture my sheep ..." (Ez 34:11,15). Jesus describes himself in other ways that likewise evoke the "I" of Yahweh: "I am the light of the world" (Jn 8:12); "I am the resurrection and the life" (Jn 11:25); "I am the Way, the Truth and the Life" (Jn 14:6).

When Jesus exercises the divine power to send out prophets and to change divine law on his own authority, he perceives his own "I" as being on the same level as God's: "You have learnt how it was said. . . . But I say this to you" (Mt 5:21-44).

These words and similar statements attest that Jesus was conscious of having a divine "I," not in an exceptional, sporadic way, but habitually. Obviously, we are not speaking of a divine "I" that manifests itself as such in its pure state, but of a divine "I" in a human context, of an "I" that asserts itself within a human consciousness and in human language. It is the divine "I" of a man who is living a genuinely human life.

However, another clue is essential. From the texts cited we might get the impression that the "I" of Jesus is identified purely and simply with the "I" of Yahweh. Actually, these texts occur within the context of Jesus' relations with the Father. To interpret them correctly we must take into account the invocation "Abba" which expresses the depth of these relations. This invocation, which accompanies and characterizes Jesus' prayer reveals his awareness that he is and acts as a Son with respect to the Father, and enjoys an intimacy with him that implies their complete equality.

Consequently, Jesus realizes he has a divine "I," but that it is the "I" of a Son. This does not keep him from claiming the "I" of Yahweh as his own. But he appropriates for himself the "I" of the Son within the Yahweh who, in the Old Testament, was still indistinct with respect to persons.

At the same time, it is not permissible to discern in Christ the presence of a second "I," a human "I" within and different from the divine "I." Thus, when the crucified Jesus says: "I am thirsty" (Jn 19:28), the one who thirsts is none other than the one who has said "I am" or "It is I!" There is no dichotomy of the "I" of Jesus, any more than there is any dichotomy of his person. All that we can point to by way of difference is that in certain cases the accent is placed on the divine quality of the "I," whereas in others the human condition tends to be the focus of attention. Even so, this human condition can conceal an allusion to Christ's divine identity. Thus, even the words "I am thirsty" can imply the spiritual thirst of the Son of God, the Savior of mankind. This symbolic sense pierces through in Jesus' request of the Samaritan woman: "Give me a drink" (Jn 4:7). In any case, the "I" to which Jesus refers is always identical to himself. It is a divine "I" engaged in a human existence.

The question: "My God, my God, why have you deserted me?" (Mt 27:46; Mk 15:34) might pose a difficulty. These words might seem to imply that the "I" of Jesus was in a confrontation with God, since God had abandoned him. This "I" would then be purely human, excluding the abandonment of the divine person of the Son by the Father.

However, here again the existence of a human "I" is not necessarily posited. The unusual form "*Eli,*" "My God," is explained by the fact that Jesus is citing Psalm 22 and addressing his Father. The "I" that has been deserted is the "I" of the Son, but within his human nature and within the human situation in which he is involved. There is no dichotomy of the "I" here, any more than in any other instance. It is the divine "I" of the Son of God, whose human agony Jesus is expressing at this particular moment.

B. THEORIES CONCERNING A HUMAN "I" IN CHRIST

Several theories have been proposed to justify the existence of a human "I" in Christ.

1. The "I" of Christ the Man vis-a-vis the Triune God

According to Déodat de Basly, [3] Christ must have a human "I" because the man Jesus is an autonomous individual, endowed with his own intellect and will. It is this individual who is "an Acting Being, a Loving Being" ("*un Agisseur, un Aymeur*"). Now, the subject of action and love is an "I."

This human "I" stands vis-a-vis the Trinity, for the Triune God is an Absolute Being who, for his part, is likewise an autonomous individual, "a unique and indivisible spiritual power of intellect and will." [4]

Between the two individuals, the Triune God and Christ the Man, or the *Assumptus Homo,* there occurs a tournament of love. The Triune God, by an unsurpassable act, creates

---

[3] *La Christiade Française,* Paris, 1927; *En Christiade Française,* I, "L'Assumptus homo. L'emmêlement de trois conflits, Pélage, Nestorius, Apollinaire," *Fr F* 11 (1928) 265-313; *En Christiade Française,* II, "Le Moi de Jésus-Christ, Le déplacement des autonomies," *Fr F* 12 (1929) 125-160, 325-352; "Inopérantes offensives contre l'Assumptus homo," *Fr F* 17 (1934) 419-474; 18 (1935) 33-104; *Structure philosophique de Jésus, l'Homme-Dieu,* I, "Ma ligne de cheminement," *Fr F* 20 (1937) 5-40; this article continued in 1937 p. 315, and in 1938, p. 5, remained unfinished at the time of Déodat de Basly's death in 1937.

[4] "Structure philosophique de Jésus," *Fr F* 1937, 33.

the man Jesus so as to be loved by a being extrinsic to himself, and this man vows to the Triune God a love whose
heroism is likewise unsurpassable.

What, then, is the bond between the "I" of Christ the
Man and the Word who belongs to the Triune God? It is
an external bond, and hence the conjunction between the two
produces only a heterogeneous entity. To say that Christ the
Man is God means that he forms a single entity with God.
It is not the Word who accomplishes the human actions of
the Jesus of the Gospel.

What remains of the unity of person in Christ? Déodat
de Basly indicts the concept of person as a source of confusion and would substitute for it the notion of the intelligent
individual. The two intelligent individuals confronting each
other are the Triune God and Christ the Man.[5] Similarly,
he would prefer that there be no further mention of the Word
Incarnate, or of the Incarnation for that matter, but rather
of a "deifying assumption" ("*susception déitante*").

Following the logic of this theory, one of Déodat de Basly's
disciples, L. Seiller, has attributed human personhood to Christ the
Man.[6] And he endows this "Man" with all the attributes and
characteristics proper to the person.

2. *A Human "I" Required for the Psychological Autonomy of Christ's Human Nature*

Father P. Galtier stresses the distinction between person
and consciousness,[7] but he likewise wants to distinguish the
"I" from the person. By reason of the fact that we must
admit Christ has a human consciousness and that consciousness
is nothing else than "nature becoming aware of itself in its
own acts,"[8] we must admit a human "I" that is really identical with the human nature. This human "I" is more than
an empirical, phenomenological "I"; it is an underlying, sub-

---

[6] L. Seiller, "La psychologie humaine du Christ et l'unité de personne,"
Franziskanische Studien 31 (1949) 49-76, 246-274. The article was placed
in the Index of Forbidden Books. Cf. *AAS* 43 (1951) 4-12, and *NRT* 83
(1951) 1095.

[7] P. Galtier, *L'unité du Christ, Être ... Personne ... Conscience*, Paris, 1939.

[8] *Ibid.*, 335.

stantial "I", an "I" that is "the principle or immediate support of the psychogenic acts." [9]

In Galtier's view, this human "I" of Christ is manifested in the Gospel. When Jesus speaks, the "I" of a man gives voice to affirmations. When he prays, a human "I" addresses itself to God, to the three divine persons.

For Galtier, this human "I" of Christ does not differ from the "I's" of other men. Nothing sets it apart from the "I" of a human person. Its psychological autonomy is complete, and nothing of the divine person can be discerned in the human consciousness. However, the human "I" is not a person because the human nature of Christ is not a person.

Despite its autonomy, Jesus' human psychology is totally dependent ontologically on the Word. This dependence stems from the fact that the Word appropriates the entire human activity of Jesus, without intervening in it psychologically. The hypostatic union "is in no sense operational." [10] The divine person does not act in the strict sense in Christ's human psychology. It is the human nature that acts, and its actions are attributed to the concrete entity that is the person of the Word Incarnate. So reasons Galtier.

Moreover, in the realm of activity, Christ's human nature depends more on the Trinity than on the Word. The Word alone possesses the human nature, but the divine impulsions of this nature stem from the divine nature and hence from the three divine persons. The Father and the Holy Spirit exercise just as much influence over the human actions of Jesus as does the person of the Word.

While Galtier's doctrine contains many more subtle distinctions than that of Déodat de Basly, it has the same essential structure. There is a principle of human activity that is the human "I," identified with the human nature, related to a principle of divine activity that influences the former and is identified with the divine nature.

Nevertheless, in a controversy with Msgr. Parente, Galtier modified his views, and denied the existence of a human ontological "I." [11] Instead, by stressing the distinction between

---

[9] *Ibid.*, 343.
[10] *Ibid.*, 262.
[11] " La conscience humaine du Christ," *Gr* 32 (1951) 535.

the "I" and the "self" he situated the "I" in the divine person [12] and posited several human psychological "selves" in Christ, as would be true of any other man, depending on the tenor of his affirmations such as, for example: "I control myself" and "I distrust myself."

3. The Distinction between the Divine "I" and the Human "Self"

Several authors explain the psychology of Christ by distinguishing in him a divine "I" and two "selves" — a divine "self" and a human "self." It is readily apparent that this distinction is modeled on the one the Council of Chalcedon established between the one "identical" person and the two natures.

This is the theory proposed by Msgr. Gaudel, who sought to make the notion of two "selves" for a single "I" more acceptable. He based this view on the common experience of every man who, while having a single "I", has a diversity of "selves" according to his various psychological states. On the one hand, the "I" of the Word necessarily and eternally appropriates the divine "self" common to the three divine persons. On the other hand, by his own free choice and in the temporal context, he takes possession of the human "self" that he assumes. He prevents this "self" or "vital human center" from saying "I" and becoming a closed entity. [13]

According to Philippe de la Trinité, the distinction between one divine "I" and two "selves" corresponds to the meaning of the "I", which expresses the metaphysical personality, and to the meaning of the "self" which "expresses the content of the psychical states in the context of nature." Inasmuch as there are two natures, there are two "selves." [14]

Nevertheless, according to this view, the problem of the human consciousness of the Word Incarnate would really be spurious. In actual fact, so the theory goes, the human consciousness is the consciousness of the humanity and not of the

---

[12] "La conscience humaine du Christ," *Gr* 35 (1954) 228.

[13] A. Gaudel, *Le mystère de l'Homme Dieu*, II, Paris, 138-140.

[14] Philippe de la Trinité, "A propos de la conscience du Christ: un faux problème théologique," *Ephemerides Carmeliticae* 11 (1960) 22.

divine personality. The Word Incarnate knows that he is God "by divine consciousness and knowledge, even within his human nature which has been assumed." [15]

Charles V. Héris protests vigorously against any identification of the "I" and the "self." He applies this distinction which exists in every being to the Gospel testimony. "When Jesus says: 'I', without any doubt he is referring to the divine 'I', to the second person of the Trinity, to the Word himself. When he says 'me' [referring to his "self"], he is speaking either of his human nature or of his divine nature." Inasmuch as, in the Word, "the divine nature is identical with the Father and the Spirit," the impulsion of the divine "self" on the human nature is "the impulsion of God himself in his essential unity, rather than of the Word in person." [16]

In this approach, the distinction between the "I" and the "self" is of primordial importance. Héris pinpoints it even further by discerning in the "I" the subject to which everything is attributed, whereas the "selves" are constituted by various interior phenomena. "There is the corporeal 'self', the affective 'self', the intellectual 'self', and the volitional 'self': I suffer, I see, I want, I think. The fact that these various 'selves' can be in opposition certainly demonstrates that they are not identical with the 'I', even though they are united to it while sometimes in conflict with one another." [17] St. Paul witnesses to this plurality of "selves" when he confesses that he does not do the good he wants to do, but instead does "the sinful things" he doesn't want" (cf. Rm 7: 19). So does Jesus at Gethsemane, where the stark contrast is revealed between the sensible "self" that is repelled by suffering and death and the volitional "I."

Certain affirmations of St. Thomas Aquinas have also been invoked to justify the existence of a human "self" in Christ. While St. Thomas most probably never used the expression "human self," yet in the opinion of A. Patfoort certain of St. Thomas' statements are along those lines. This is true for instance of the argument proposed to legitimize the In-

---

15 *Ibid.*, 37.
16 C. V. Héris, "Problèmes de christologie. La conscience de Jésus," *Esprit et vie* 81 (1971) 676.
17 *Ibid.*, 674.

carnation in a human nature. "Now this fitness in human
nature may be taken ... according ... to its dignity, because
human nature, as being rational and intellectual, was made for
attaining to the Word to some extent by its operation, viz.
by knowing and loving Him." [18]
    From this text of St. Thomas and others, it can be con-
cluded that human nature provides the divine incarnate person
a "second center of perception and decision granted to the
world in which he had come to dwell." On the basis of this,
a human "self" without the connotation of ontological autonomy is not only a reality in Christ, but a kind of necessity
and law of the Incarnation. [19]

C. The Psychological Expression of the One Person
and of the Human Nature

1. The Divine Person and the Divine "I" in the Human Consciousness

    The authors who affirm the existence of a human "self"
in Christ are motivated by the desire to emphasize the truth
of the human psychology of the Word Incarnate. They want
at all costs to avoid a monophysitism or a monopsychism which
would take into account only the divine consciousness of the
Word or at least a divine consciousness that would so en-

---

[18] *Summa Theologica*, III, Q. 4, a. 1.
[19] A. Patfoort, "Amorces en S. Thomas de l'idée d'un 'moi humain' dans
le Christ?" *RSPT* 48 (1964) 198-204. Elsewhere, in the review of an earlier
article by Héris ("A propos d'un article sur la psychologie du Christ," *RSPT*
43 (1959) 462-471; cf. J. Galot, "La psychologie du Christ," *NRT* 80 (1958)
337-358), the author had expressed his own personal opinion: "Both from
the point of view of the immediate principle as well as from the point
of view of the direct object of consciousness, human nature constitutes an
'empirical me' distinct and unified in itself, that is at the same time really
but only very partially *the* 'Me' of the Word: the human nature is the human
'me' of the Word, and the organ through which the Word becomes humanly
conscious of what he has become through the Incarnation" (*Bulletin Thomiste*,
Vol. X, 698). He adds: "To avoid any taint of Nestorianism, it suffices to
bear in mind that the human nature endowed with this consciousness recognized and saw itself substantially united to the Word, to the point that
through it and in it the Word could forcefully and easily apply to his "self"
both his divine attributes as the Word and what he experienced within his
human consciousness" (*ibid.*, 699).

lighten Jesus as to make a human consciousness useless. The defense of a genuinely human psychology in Jesus is certainly legitimate. Such a psychology is even a requirement of the Incarnation. But does this imply the existence of a human "I"? We have already alluded to the distinction between consciousness and the "I." Human consciousness does not coincide with the human "I." A distinction exists between consciousness and the "I" analogous to the difference between nature and person. Psychologically, the "I" is to consciousness what person is to nature, ontologically speaking.

The theories of a human "I" in Christ are based on his human nature, considered as the principle of psychological activity, either as an acting and loving individual or at least as the center of perception and decision. Nature is considered to be the subject or the object of the act of consciousness. And as this is a matter of human consciousness, the "I" that finds expression through it is described as a human "I."

Yet at this point a question arises: Is the nature really the subject and the object of the act of consciousness? Can it be identified with the "I"? If we turn to the ordinary experience of human psychology, we discover that we identify our "I" with our person. Galtier acknowledged that the words "me," "myself," or "I" are commonly used to mean "person." [20] He considered this an incorrect use of these words since, according to his theory, the underlying "I" is identical with the nature. Still, this colloquial terminology has its importance. It reflects the ordinary way human persons perceive themselves. And should not universal experience remain the starting point of psychological theories?

When anyone speaks of his "I", he is speaking of his person, of what is most profoundly original about him, most exclusively his own. This "I" is the subject that thinks and acts, that becomes aware of itself in thought and action, and realizes it is transparent to itself. It is indeed the "I" — as well as the "you" or the "he," other ways of designating the person — that answers the question: "Who is it?"

In philosophical language, the term "I" is often used as the equivalent of person. Thus, community may be defined as a plurality of individual "I's" gathered together in unity.

---

[20] *L'unité du Christ,* 337.

To affirm that Christ has a human "I" therefore entails a certain danger of ambiguity, for it might seem to imply that there is a human person in him. Even if it is explicitly stated that in Christ there is ontologically only one person, the divine person of the Word, it is almost inevitably implied that, psychologically speaking, Christ presents all the appearances and manifestations of a human person.

To put it more precisely, the theories of a human "I" in Christ attribute the role of a person to his human nature.

Déodat de Basly, as we have already said, situated the Man Jesus (*Assumptus Homo*) vis-a-vis the Triune God as if they were two "autonomous individuals" exchanging a mutual love. In so doing he erected the two natures of Christ, the human and the divine, into two persons. In fact, he conceived these two natures as subjects of activity and love, facing one another after the manner of an "I" and a "you." In this confrontation, Déodat is actually setting the man Jesus in opposition to the Word, and as a result he can no longer speak of unity of person or of the Word Incarnate. Such a theory does not respect the ontological structure of Christ.

The other theories are less radical, in the sense that they take care not to set the Word and the human nature of Christ in opposition as a "you" and a "me." They distinguish a divine "self," or rather a divine "I," and a human "self." This corresponds to the distinction between the human nature and the divine nature.

Thus, Galtier recognizes a principle of divine activity, common to the Trinity, that is above the human "I" of Christ. Héris speaks of the impulsion upon the human nature of Jesus of a divine "I" that he identifies with God in the unity of his divine nature. In this case, the two natures are considered to be subjects of activity just as persons are. That is the crux of the misunderstanding. For the duality of the natures is transformed into a duality of persons, whereas it should be integrated into one "identical" person.

Attribution of a human "I" to Christ results in conferring upon him a psychological structure that is profoundly different from his ontological structure. Galtier recognized the divorce of the two structures when he affirmed that "the hypostatic union is established in the order of the substances" and not in the order of the operations. [21] According to Galtier, the union realized at the level of being had no impact on Christ's psychological activity. The person of the Word, in his view, did not act upon the human nature. Such a compartmentalization is not acceptable. Action conforms to being. It follows that the deployment of psychological activity must stem from the ontological structure and manifest this structure.

The upshot of all this is this: while we must admit the role of the human nature as a "natural" principle of human activity, we cannot eliminate the role of the divine person of the Son as the "personal" principle of this same activity. Indeed, the person of the Word is the subject of the actions and operations. And inasmuch as it is the subject of Jesus' human psychology, this divine person is posited as the "I" of his human consciousness.

The ontology of Christ demands that there be only one "self" in his psychology, the "I" of the Son of God. We must completely exclude a second "self," a second subject of conscious and free activity. [22] Moreover, the affirmation of a single "I", the "I" of the Son, conforms to the Gospel testimony. When Jesus says "I" or "me", he is referring to his "I" as the Son of God, without any duality of subjects.

Thus, psychology does not develop along different lines than ontology. It is simply an aspect of the dynamism of this ontology. Besides, the ontology of Christ as it has been defined in the Councils has simply expressed what the psychology of Jesus has revealed to us according to the testimony he gave of himself.

The very close relationship between psychology and ontology explains why it is not possible to admit a kind of psychological Nestorianism by positing a human "self", without immediately facing the danger of ontological Nestorianism. The transition is easy from the affirmation of a human "self" to the affirmation of a human person, and the logic of it seems hard to refute.

---

21 *L'unité du Christ*, 262.

22 The Encyclical *Sempiternus rex* declared that "it is not possible to conceive of the human nature of Christ as constituting a subject *sui iuris*" (AAS 43 (1951) 638: D S 3905). The Encyclical explicitly rejects, as contrary to Chalcedon, the theory that in Christ there are two individuals, the "*homo assumptus*" and the Word.

The "self" is the person inasmuch as it is the subject and the object of consciousness. In Christ, a divine person is the subject and the object of human consciousness. The "self" of Jesus is divine, even though it takes on a human psychological coloration.

2. *The Unity of the "Self"*

As we have already pointed out, various scholars have invoked a plurality of "selves" or psychical states to justify the presence of a human "self" in Christ. They have also pointed to the distinction between the "I" and the "self" to the same end.

No one will deny there are contrasts and struggles within man's psychology. But must we infer from this a plurality of "selves", different "selves" none of which would be identical with the "I"? When we speak of the affective "me", the intellectual "me", or the volitional "me", are we not indeed speaking of the same "me"? Is it not the same "self" given different coloration by the interior phenomena of affectivity, thought, and volition, but nonetheless identical to itself within all these phenomena?

Indeed, it is this very identity within the contrast that makes the conflict all the more acute. The inner struggle is more violent because the same "self" is torn between affective tendencies and the force of the will. St. Paul's cry of anguish over his sinful condition (cf. Rm 7:19) finds an explanation in the conflict of a personality that yearns to achieve self-mastery but does not succeed in dominating its actions. The poignancy of Paul's cry comes from the identity of a "self" aware of itself as dramatically torn apart and as powerless to make its actual actions coincide with what it wills.

Similarly at Gethsemane, the "I" that suffers and wants to push away the chalice is identical to the "I" that wants to submit to the Father's will. That is why the conflict is so deep. On Calvary, if the "self" that feels abandoned were not the "self" of the Son, the drama would be much more superficial. This is the same "self" that commits itself into the Father's hands, gaining mastery over its ordeal by this very act of trust. Truly, the "self" that has been abandoned is the "self" that abandons itself to the Father.

The phenomenological descriptions of the affective "self", the volitional "self", or other "selves" cannot make us forget a basic fact of experience: these "selves" refer to one and the same person. The one who speaks about his various "selves" actually thinks of himself as fundamentally one as he passes through diverse psychological states.

The distinction between the "I" and the "self" cannot for that matter be conceived apart from an underlying identity between them. The difference results quite simply from the diverse aspects of man's psychological makeup. The "I" expresses the person as the subject of activity. The "self" tends rather to express the person in the act of taking cognizance of himself as the object of activity. Indeed, the difference between the two is not absolute. It varies with the semantic customs of different languages. In any case, the identity of the "I" and of the "self" underlies all human language, because it defines the fundamental experience of every person, namely: there is one subject of all his psychological states and activities. Indeed, each of us relates the words "I", "me," and "myself" identically to himself.

Therefore the data of psychology do not allow us to assert a difference between the "I" and the "self" that would result in the "I" referring to the person while the self would refer to the nature. That would mean that in Christ there is a divine "I" and a human "self."

Moreover, Gospel terminology would not favor such a distinction. We have noted that the Greek expression *ego eimi* can be translated "I am" or "It is I." The affirmation made bv Jesus can include both nuances, depending on whether the emphasis is placed on the verb "to be" (*eimi*) or on the personal pronoun "I" (*ego*).

How, then, can we interpret the *ego* spoken by Christ if we want to relate the subject "I" to the person and the predicate nominative "I" to the nature? And how can we show that this profound difference in meaning emerges from the text itself? In fact, the *ego*, "I", whether subject or predicate nominative, asserts itself as divine and refers to the divine person in a human psychology: the "I" or "self" is the "I" or "self" of a man, for Jesus thinks and speaks truly as a man. The *ego* therefore really designates a divine person in a human nature.

Just as the "self" cannot be identified with the human nature, so too, the "I" of Christ cannot be referred solely to the divine nature. It cannot be claimed that this "I" is the "I" of God in the unity of his nature, and that the Father and the Holy Spirit are encompassed within it. The Gospels would certainly not suggest that Jesus' words about his divine "I" should be extended to include the three divine persons. His "I" remains exclusively his own and belongs to him personally. He behaves vis-a-vis the Father as an "I" confronting a "You."

3. *The Autonomy of Jesus' Human Psychology*

The principle we stressed earlier that ontology is expressed in psychology shows us how we are to understand the autonomy of Jesus' human psychology. This autonomy signifies that Jesus' psychological activity is deployed according to the laws pertaining to all human psychology. Since Christ is truly a man, he has a real human consciousness. His divine person does not substitute his divine consciousness for this strictly human process. Nor does his divine consciousness interfere in any way with the normal human mode of his conscious activity. Jesus does not have a single divine-human consciousness, since the two activities, like his two natures, are distinct, "without any commingling," as Chalcedon says.

The autonomy of Jesus' human psychology likewise accounts for the fact that his divine "I" manifests itself only in an integrally human consciousness. We have already noted that this "I" did not reveal itself in its pure state. It always appeared within a human consciousness, and its expression was entirely human. The reason certain scholars have tended to speak of a human "I" in Christ may stem from their desire to emphasize this fact. However, while the "I" of Christ asserted itself within a profoundly human psychology, it remained the divine "I" of the Son.

The autonomy of Christ's human psychology, which is required for the distinction between his two natures, does not entail independence vis-a-vis the person. We cannot picture the psychology of Christ as not subject to the influence of his divine person. The Word does not limit himself to appropriating the phenomena of consciousness and of the psychological states that really come into being without him. Nor can we consider Jesus' human nature as the center of perception or of separation, facing the Word after the manner of an autonomous "I."

Actually the divine person of the Son exercises in the psychology of Jesus the role that ordinarily devolves upon the human person. It is the "*principium quod,*" to use Scholastic terminology, the "principle which" acts, the subject of all psychological operations and consciousness. The divine person never acts independently of the nature, the latter being the "*principium quo,*" the "principle through which" the person acts. The divine person of the Word, in operating through the nature, does not modify the laws of this nature's behavior. The Word respects the human nature and conforms to all of its limitations. And so it is that while preserving the autonomy of the human psychology the person of the Word commands its development.

Here we discern the psychological aspect of the dynamism of the Incarnation. When the Son became man, he entered into a human psychology in order to express himself through it in a human way. He impressed a filial attitude on this psychology. That is why the thoughts, sentiments, and activities of Jesus are imbued to their core with a deep, intimate filial relationship with the Father. Far from being absent psychologically, the influence of the person of the Son makes itself felt in the totality of Christ's behavior, as recorded in the Gospel texts.

Jesus declared he was transmitting the teaching of the Father, that he was working miracles in the name of the Father, that he had come from the Father and was going back to him. He thought and acted in true human fashion, but as a Son. His psychology is thus seen to be totally governed and dominated by a filial "I." This fact demonstrates the primordial role of the divine person of the Son within his human psychology.

D. The Consciousness of His Sonship

1. *The Problem*

How did Jesus become aware of his divine sonship? We must begin by clarifying the elements of the problem. We cannot pose the question simply in this way: How can a man become aware that he is God or the Son of God? When thus formulated the question would imply a radical disproportion between the subject of the act of cognizance, namely, a man, and the object of this act, namely, the God of whom he becomes aware. This disproportion assumes major importance for those who admit that in Christ there is a human "I" at the center of his knowledge and consciousness. How can this human "I" know that it is the "I" of the divine Word?

Yet, as we have already pointed out, we cannot posit a human "I," i.e., an autonomous center of consciousness that would assert itself both within the Word and vis-a-vis the Word. Nor can we accept the theory, proposed for instance by Galtier, that in becoming conscious of his human "I," Jesus would spontaneously have thought he was a human person had he not been saved from this error by the beatific vision. To quote Galtier: "If Christ's human nature had known itself solely by way of direct consciousness it could and would have appeared to itself as being a person." [23] The psychology of Jesus would have been distorted if, simply by virtue of his becoming conscious of himself, he had thought he was a human person. Such an act of consciousness would have been lacking in truth. An extrinsic element such as the beatific vision could have contributed only a superficial remedy to a fundamental error in the functioning of his psychology. It was necessary for Jesus to perceive his "I" for what it really was through his own human consciousness.

Now, we have seen the profound disproportion between the man who becomes aware and the God of whom he becomes aware. The problem changes however if we remember that it is not merely a man who becomes aware, but the Son of God. The problem is not how a man becomes conscious that

---

[23] *L'unité du Christ*, 350. Analogous views are expressed in Charles V. Héris' article, "A propos d'un article sur la psychologie du Christ," *RSPT* 43 (1959) 468.

he is the Son of God, but *how the Son of God becomes humanly conscious of himself.*

A normal consequence of the Incarnation is that the Son of God became the subject of human psychological activity. In becoming man and assuming a human nature, he exercised the activity proper to this nature. That is the way the divine "I" of Jesus became humanly aware of itself.

But how does this ontologically divine "I" appear in the human psychology of Jesus as the "I" of the Son of God? An "I" does not present itself to the consciousness with a label detailing its identity or its qualities. In order to describe our "I," our " self," we need to reflect on our intimate experience of it, on the relationships we establish with others, on the totality of our environing world that helps us to situate our personality.

How did Jesus become conscious that he was the Son of God? Through what experience and what mode of thought was he able to recognize this identity?

2. *The Truth of the Psychology of Jesus*

The ancient explanation that the consciousness of the divine sonship resulted from the beatific vision (i.e., the beatific knowledge) of Christ has quite often been supplanted by another that invokes an external, rather than an internal illumination on his part. Some theologians have thought they discerned the sign of this revelation in the episode of Jesus' baptism. If we adopt Mark's version (1:11) and Lukes's (3:22), we find that the divine words were indeed addressed to Jesus himself: "You are my Son, the Beloved." According to this view, that was the precise moment when Christ discovered God looked upon him as his only-begotten Son. Others set the beginning of this awareness at a later time, even as late as the Resurrection.

However these explanations do not take the facts into account. It is not possible to situate the beginning of Jesus' awareness of his divine sonship after his death. The Gospel texts clearly witness to this consciousness during his earthly life. His great debate with his adversaries focussed on his claim to be the Son of God, and this was the reason why he was condemned to death.

Besides it is not possible, on the basis of the baptism account, to situate the first revelation of Jesus' transcendent sonship at the start of his public life. We have already observed that the theophanic declaration could have had its origin in the Transfiguration event.

Then, too, does it not seem improbable that Jesus received a revelation of his true identity only when he was thirty years old? That would have been a very belated moment for him to become aware of his true "I." He would not have had time to assimilate this truth so as to express it clearly to others. The revelation of his divine sonship would have come to him as a shock as he was about to enter upon his mission, just as it was to shock those to whom he declared it, provoking the intransigent opposition of his enemies. It is unrealistic to think he might, at the age of thirty, suddenly and completely reverse his earlier understanding of who he was. For there is a vast distance between the condition of a mere man and that of the Son of God. Such a psychological about-face on his part would be difficult to accept.

We must not undervalue the basic law of Jesus' psychology, namely, its conformity with the truth. We have already pointed out how important it is not to divorce Christ's ontology from his psychology. Jesus unquestionably had to live in the psychological truth of what he really was. He could not have been ignorant of his true identity or been mistaken about it during the years of his childhood and youth. If by virtue of the Incarnation the Son of God became humanly conscious of himself, this consciousness could have no other object than his innermost personhood. His psychological development could not have consisted in a transition from awareness of his human identity to the discovery of his divine identity. It had to be a gradual increase and deepening of his human consciousness that he was indeed the Son of God.

In addition to the fact that the divine process of the Incarnation, by its very nature, had to conform with the truth, there is an implicit demand for truth in Christ's mission of revelation. How could he who was destined to bring God's definitive Revelation to mankind have thought of himself, during many long years, as a mere man, when he was in fact the Son of God? Or how could he have been ignorant of the central truth around which his whole message was to take shape? To acquit himself of his mission, which involved personal witness to his divine identity, Jesus had to have become conscious of this identity in accordance with the truth he was entrusted to communicate and to have grasped it in such a way that it permeated his whole psychology.

From the beginning of his earthly life, therefore, Jesus' psychology must have developed around the unfolding consciousness that he was the Son of God. We have a confirmation of this in the Gospel texts. The only episode that has come down to us about Jesus' boyhood concerns his stay in the Temple when he was twelve years old. [24] Now, according to Luke, we have Jesus' affirmation of his divine sonship: "Did you not know that I had to be in my Father's house?" (Lk 2:49). These words were mystifying to Mary and Joseph, who did not understand them. Mary spoke of "your father" and Jesus' answered "my Father," alluding to someone else. As we have already pointed out, Mary probably used the word "Abba," and Jesus repeated the word, giving it a divine sense unknown to Judaism. The episode attests that Jesus' understanding of his sonship had not come to him from the Jewish religion and certainly went far beyond anything his mother knew of his origin. For Jesus, the heavenly Father held the place a human father holds for any other child. God is Jesus' Father in the strict sense of the word. And so Jesus' words revealed his true origin to Mary and the nature of his divine sonship, thereby showing that even as a child he had already become aware of his exceptional filial relationship with the Father.

3. The Mystical Filial Contact

Jesus' use of the name *Abba* clarifies our understanding of Jesus' psychology. It is, in fact, the most spontaneous expression of his filial identity, an expression that belongs uniquely to him and is independent of Jewish religious terminology. By contrast with the locution "the Son of Man" and the affirmation " *ego eimi,*" Jesus did not borrow the word *Abba*

---

[24] On the historical value of the account, cf. R. Laurentin, *Jésus au Temple. Mystère pascal et foi de Marie en Luc 2,48-50*, Paris, 158-161.

from the Old Testament. Its use affirmed all that was unique and unprecedented in the "I" of Christ.

The name *Abba* reveals an intimacy with the Father, profoundly rooted in Jesus' psychology. This closeness had developed in his innermost consciousness, making him realize he was the Son of this Father in a plenary sense, in no way inferior to the relationship *between a human child and his human father.*

To explain the development of this intimacy we must attribute to Jesus an experience of the mystical order. The mystics give witness to their intimate contacts with God. They experience the feeling of God's presence, they receive the impression of being fused with divine life, of being immersed in it. This involves a kind of perception of the union between God and man that is achieved through the life of grace. The perception occurs less on the intellectual than on the affective level. The whole personality senses its involvement in the contact.

The "great mystics" are not alone to have this experience. It occurs in the hidden, interior life of many Christians, who experience at first hand, deep within themselves, peaceful union with God.

And so we have some idea of what must have taken place psychologically in Jesus. His mystical contacts with the Father enabled him to discern his own filial identity, and to grasp the truth of his divine "I" through his human consciousness.

These contacts must have begun quite early, as his child's consciousness began to develop. In fact, this consciousness had an imperative need to grow in truth. Just as other children become aware of their own personalities through their relations with other persons, and first of all their parents, so, too, Jesus became aware of his divine personality through his intimate relations with the Father. And this consciousness became increasingly clear in the light of his mystical contacts of a filial nature. By positioning himself before the Father and contemplating him with the inner contact of his soul, he discovered his own condition as a Son.

All mystical experience comes from God, and in the case of Jesus the initiative in these contacts came from the Father, linked to the initiative of the Incarnation. It may help us to better understand it by comparing it with the generation of the child Jesus. The virginal conception was the work of the Father, who wanted to be the only Father of the child, and who produced the generation through the Holy Spirit. Yet the Father wanted to be the father of Jesus not only ontologically, but also psychologically. Through the Holy Spirit, he acted within the psychological makeup of Jesus in such a way as to make himself known as Father. He provided a psychological development in continuity and harmony with Jesus' physical generation.

In Jesus, mystical experience took on the specific form of an essentially filial contact with the Father. Whereas the mystics often speak of their fusion with God, Jesus always speaks of his intimate relations with the Father: "just as the Father know me, and I know the Father" (Jn 10:15); "the Father is with me" (Jn 16:32; cf. 8:29); "the Father is in me and I am in the Father" (Jn 10:38; cf. 14:11; 17:21). Clearly, therefore, Jesus' mystical experience is filial. Its outstanding hallmark is that it is the relationship of a Son.

In addition, this mystical contact of Jesus with the Father bears the mark of reciprocity. Let us quote again from the Gospels: "... and no one recognizes the Son except the Father, just as no one recognizes the Father except the Son...." (Mt 11:27). "... all I have is yours and all you have is mine" (Jn 17:10). Whereas the mystics often feel submerged by God's majesty, Jesus expresses mutual relations that reveal profound equality, even though the Father always comes first and is considered to be the origin of everything.

There is a boldness in this mystical relationship of Jesus with his Father that cannot be discerned in any mystic. While certain mystics interpret their states as indicating an identification with God, they always remain aware of the abysmal inferiority of their respective persons vis-a-vis the transcendence of God. Jesus, on the contrary, enters into this transcendence by affirming he is the Son on a level of equality with the Father. Only an extraordinary mystical experience could give him such assurance.

We might add that this mystical experience of Jesus during his earthly life was not limited to a few moments of particularly intense religious emotion. Jesus experienced such moments to be sure, as we see in his hymn of jubilation (cf. Lk 10:21; Mt 11:25). But his demeanor was habitually that of the Son, and the invocation *Abba* which he ordinarily used in his prayer indicates his ongoing intimate contact with the Father. The sense of the Father's presence and of his filial rapport with him was the normal accompaniment of his various states of consciousness.

Specifically, the Father made Jesus sense and understand through an interior experience that he was truly his Father. And so he called into being a human filial consciousness in the One whose "I" was the "I" of the Son, but who needed to be enlightened in his human psychology as to the underlying value and reality of this "I."

From this point of view likewise, we can discern the harmonious interrelationship of Jesus' psychology and ontology. Person is defined as a subsistent or hypostatic relation: we have emphasized the relational nature of the person. The Son, a divine person, is defined by his filial relationship. Now, he became humanly conscious of himself through his filial relations with his Father. *It was by becoming aware that he was the Son that Jesus became aware that he was God.* The Father revealed himself to him in very deep mystical contacts that made him grasp his identity as the Son of God.

This gradual growth in consciousness developed according to the laws of human psychology. Jesus possessed at the start the consciousness of a child, then the consciousness of an adolescent, and finally the consciousness of an adult. His filial consciousness was enriched by what he learned from the Jewish religion, and especially from the Bible. But the "key" to this consciousness lay in the filial relationship he developed with the One who gave himself to him in the intimate light of mystical contacts as his real Father.

Let us add that Jesus' filial psychology continued to develop throughout his public life. It was not by chance that the name *Abba,* so often used by Jesus, has been recorded for us only once in the Gospel texts, i.e., during his prayer at Gethsemane (Mk 14:36). At a moment of deep soul-searching conflict, Jesus cried out "*Abba!*" to his Father with a poignancy that would never be forgotten by those who heard it. Following this, his death on the Cross, by which he entrusted

342

his spirit into his Father's hands, became the pinnacle of his filial experience.

To conclude, Christ's filial consciousness was nurtured by all aspects of his human existence. He lived this experience in a profound mystical rapport with his Father that enabled him to situate and to grasp the reality of his divine "I."

CHAPTER XII

THE KNOWLEDGE OF JESUS

A. THE THEOLOGY OF THE THREEFOLD KNOWLEDGE

1. *The Medieval Theory*

Medieval Scholasticism developed a doctrine of Christ's threefold knowledge.[1] The Conciliar definitions, and that of the 3rd Council of Constantinople in particular, simply established the distinction between the divine knowledge and the human knowledge of the Word Incarnate. The theological thinking of the Middle Ages focussed on Christ's human knowledge, and it is within this knowledge that a threefold division was proposed.

According to this doctrine,[2] Jesus possesses in the first place the knowledge enjoyed by the blessed in heaven, a knowledge that consists in the vision of God and is accompanied by beatitude or happiness. For, it argues, we cannot deny to Christ the perfection of knowledge and happiness toward which he is leading mankind, a perfection that postulates the glorious state of his soul from the moment of his conception. Through this knowledge, the soul of Christ sees the divine essence and likewise knows in the Word the sum total of reality. The only thing he lacks is knowledge of everything God can do, for his knowledge of the possible is limited to what creatures can do.

---

[1] For the elaboration of this doctrine, starting with the Augustinian theory of "morning knowledge" that clearly sees everything in the "Word," and "evening knowledge" that knows things in themselves in a more obscure way, cf. J. T. Ernst, *Die Lehre der hochmittelalterlichen Theologen von der vollkommenen Erkenntnis Christi*, Freiburg, 1971.

[2] Cf. Thomas Aquinas, *Summa Theologiae*, III, Q. 9 through 13.

This doctrine also holds that Christ enjoys the privilege of infused knowledge, for it would be inconceivable that he should be lacking in a mode of knowledge enjoyed by the angels and granted to certain humans such as Adam and some of the saints. It is a supernatural knowledge that makes possible the knowledge of things in themselves, in contrast to the beatific knowledge that perceives them in the divine essence. Concerning the extent of Jesus' infused knowledge, opinions have varied. St. Thomas himself changed his mind about it. However, in the *Summa* he expresses the view that all realities, both natural and supernatural, outside of the divine essence, constitute the object of Christ's infused knowledge.[3] There are those who specify that the soul of Christ was endowed with infused knowledge from the first instant of his earthly existence.[4] Thus, in addition to "the beatific knowledge by which the soul of Christ knows the Word and things in the Word," there is his "infused knowledge by which his soul knows things in their proper nature."[5]

It might have seemed that these two kinds of knowledge, in view of their superabundance, would make any other type of knowledge superfluous. Yet medieval scholasticism adds a third, namely, acquired knowledge. For the soul of Christ had to exercise its intellect actively. Infused knowledge from above would not have sufficed. It was only after considerable hesitation that medieval theologians admitted this acquired or experimental knowledge in Christ.

At first, St. Thomas rejected it as irreconcilable with infused knowledge,[6] but he gradually came to accept it quite explicitly.[7] He extended its object to everything the intellect can know through its own activity. Yet he denied that Christ could have learned anything whatever from other human beings. For, in his view, this would not have befitted his dignity as head of the Church, come to bring the doctrine of truth to all men.[8] Thomas therefore concluded that Jesus acquired

[3] *Summa*, III, Q. 11, Art. 1.
[4] Cf. H. Bouëssé, *Le Sauveur du monde*, 2, "Le Mystère de l'Incarnation," Chambéry-Leysse and Paris, 1953, 408.
[5] *Summa*, III, Q. 9, Art. 3.
[6] *Sent*. 3, d. 14, a. 3, q. 5, ad 3; d. 18, a. 3 ad 5.
[7] *Summa*, III, Q. 9, Art. 4.
[8] *Summa*, III, Q. 12, Art. 3

knowledge by personal experience, through his contact not with men but with the works of God in the world.[9]

This theology of Christ's threefold human knowledge draws its inspiration from a principle of perfection: Christ must have possessed all knowledge in all its perfection. In this view, "Jesus therefore lived our very own intellectual life, just as he lived the intellectual life of the angels, the intellectual life of the saints, and the intellectual life of God." And C. V. Héris adds: "Let anyone who might be tempted to wonder at this multiple knowledge remember that all these forms of knowledge harmonize with one another because they are all rays of divine light illuminating the created intellect."[10]

2. Critical Observations

In our own day, the doctrinal construction of Christ's triple knowledge seems very artificial.[11] In itself, this doctrine lacks coherence and can be maintained only by compartmentalizing the human intellect of Christ. How could Christ know the same things twice over, once through his beatific knowledge and again through his infused knowledge? And how could he learn through acquired knowledge what he already knew in two other ways?[12] This would divide Christ's knowledge into three compartments. But is such a division compatible with Christ's authentic human nature?

The principle of perfection, as it has been manipulated in the theory, leads to obviously extravagant conclusions. Nor could the ideal solution be that Christ's human knowledge be equivalent to divine knowledge and to angelic knowledge. The correct view is that Christ knew the way a man knows. This could not have involved Christ's acquiring factual and experi-

---

[9] This is also the position taken by A. Michel in his article "Science de Jésus-Christ," DTC 14, 1658.

[10] Ch. V. Héris, Le mystère du Christ, Paris, 1928, 98-99.

[11] A critical analysis of this scholastic doctrine has been made by J. Rivière, "Le problème de la science humaine du Christ, position classique et nouvelles tendances," BLE 7 (1915-1916), 241-261, 289-314, 337-361.

[12] Cf. the presentation of Christ's acquired knowledge by A. Michel, art. cit., DTC 14, 1651: "Like ourselves, Christ was obliged to acquire knowledge. This is not to say that he thereby learned something he did not know before, but that he acquired through his 'acquired knowledge' a knowledge he already possessed through another kind of knowledge."

mental knowledge of all that is humanly knowable. And yet this is what the Carmelites of Salamanca sought to demonstrate. In applying St. Thomas' principle of perfection to the universality of Christ's acquired knowledge, they did not hesitate to attribute to Christ every kind of natural knowledge. Thus, in their view, Christ was "not only the best dialectician, philosopher, mathematician, physician, moralist, and statesman, but also the best musician, grammarian, orator, artisan, agronomist, painter, navigator, soldier, and so on." [13] The only limitation they set to these attributes was that they were possessed by Christ as habitual capacities and not necessarily in actual practice. [14] The extravagance of such an affirmation brings out the flimsiness of the argument. Perfection for a human being does not consist in knowing everything. And so Christ had no need to encompass within himself every kind of knowledge, all the arts, as well as all the crafts and professions. Nothing could be further from the Gospel message than to call him the best navigator or the best soldier the world has ever seen. [15]

To better understand the import of the medieval theory, we must remember its historical point of departure. In the early days of scholasticism, certain writers had maintained that by reason of the hypostatic union, Christ's human soul possessed, through grace, everything that God possesses by nature, and in consequence possessed all the wisdom of God. In particular, this was the opinion of Hugo of St. Victor who denied Christ's human knowledge was equal to God's, but solely for the reason that his soul had received from outside itself what God possesses in himself. Allowing for this difference, according to Hugo, the plenitude and the perfection

---

[13] " Universaliter tenendum est quod omnis vera scientia naturalis fuerit in Christo," *Collegii Salamanticensis Carmelitarum Discalceatorum Cursus Theologicus,* Tract. 21 "De Incarnatione," Disp. 22, Dub. 2, 4, No. 29 (Paris-Brussels, Geneva, 1880, Vol. XV, 320).

[14] "Secundum habitum" (*ibid.*).

[15] Quite as whimsical, among the logical consequences of St. Thomas' principle, is the affirmation of A. M. Lépicier. After declaring that Christ possessed knowledge exceeding that of all other men, he draws certain concrete conclusions: "We can infer that Christ, when he saw the grasses, plants, and trees, unhesitatingly discerned on his own the rules and classifications of botany," etc. Then he refers to other fields of knowledge, such as mathematics and political science (*Tractatus de Incarnatione Verbi,* I, Paris, 1905, 461).

of Christ's human wisdom and divine wisdom were identical. [16]

The upshot of this opinion was to admit that Jesus the man possessed divine wisdom "beyond measure." [17] As such, this view is unacceptable, for it does not respect the distinction between Christ's natures and operations, and attributes divine perfection to Christ's human activity. While its supporters claim St. Fulgentius held this view, [18] it is not free of Monophysitism.

This theory was subsequently corrected to indicate a difference between Christ's divine knowledge and his human knowledge. However, in this correction the medieval theologians preserved the underlying principle, attributing to Christ's knowledge the highest possible perfection and most universal extension. [19] From this principle stemmed the affirmation of Christ's beatific knowledge, then the adjunction of the infused knowledge. The type of knowledge that should have been affirmed in Christ in the first place, namely, acquired or experimental knowledge, was considered only after the others, and found more difficult to accept.

A contrary procedure should have been followed. Rather than positing *a priori* perfect models of knowledge which needed to be proven as present in Christ, the point of departure should have been the Gospel witness regarding the kinds of knowledge Jesus actually manifested, taking into account the principle of the Incarnation according to which Christ, during

[16] Hugo of St. Victor, *De sapientia animae Christi, PL* 176, 853 A B; *De Sacramentis,* Lib. 2, P. 1, c. 6; *PL* 176; 383 D-384 A. Cf. Gerhoh of Reichersberg, *De gloria et honore Filii Hominis, PL* 194, 1135 B C D-1136 A (which cites the *De Sacramentis* of Hugo of St. Victor); *Epist.* 21, *PL* 193, 581 C D; the anonymous author of *Summa Sententiarum,* c. 16; *PL* 176, 74 B C.

[17] Hugo, *De Sapientia, PL* 176, 853 B: "Sine mensura gratiam acceperat, quia cum immensa gratia erat possibilis natura."

[18] *Epist.* 14, q. 3, 25-34, *PL* 65, 415-424. Fulgentius attributes to Christ's soul the full knowledge of the divinity, i.e., in his humanity Christ possesses all wisdom, because in this wisdom resides the fullness of divinity. Cf. especially 29-30, *PL* 419-420: "In humanitate sua totam habet divinitatis suae substantiam, ... totam sapientiam, totam omnipotentiam" (420 BC). This opinion does not sufficiently distinguish between the two natures in Christ.

[19] Peter Lombard's position is characteristic. While he denied that Christ's soul could do everything that God does, he affirmed that it knew everything that God knows, but not with the same clarity. Christ's omniscience was clearly posited: "Omnia ergo scivit anima illa" (*Sent.* III, Dist. 14, n. 2; *PL* 192, 783-784).

his earthly human life, was like us in all things except sin. The only valid point of departure for our reflection on Christ's various kinds of knowledge is the concrete man Jesus himself, as he lived among men. The doctrinal elaboration of the threefold knowledge of Christ offers us an example of a "descending Christology," incorrectly understood. Starting out with divine perfection, an effort was made to determine Jesus' human perfection by a long and circuitous route which made it difficult to actually grasp the experience of his human life.

B. EXPERIMENTAL FORMS OF KNOWLEDGE IN JESUS

We are not speaking here of an acquired or experimental knowledge distinct from the other kinds of human knowledge in Christ. In Jesus there is only one human knowledge. In this knowledge, as the Gospel testify, there are experimental kinds of knowledge as well as knowledge of superior origin.

It is important first of all to realize that Jesus acquired knowledge through the normal exercise of his intellect, like all other men. These forms of knowledge were necessarily limited, and they progressed by the ordinary stages of human intellectual development.

There can be no question of omniscience in Christ's human intellect. [20] Not only would it be arbitrary to attribute to Jesus scientific and technical knowledge superior to that of his contemporaries, but the Gospel sources also lead us to a contrary conclusion. Jesus never manifested knowledge of this sort. During his thirty years at Nazareth, he lived what outwardly appeared to be a commonplace existence. He did not make known any scientific discovery, he did not invent anything, and he did not contribute to any notable advance in the technique of his craft. The people of Nazareth never noticed anything outstanding or extraordinary about him. That is why they were so surprised when he entered upon his public life. Even those who had been closest to him, his cousins or

---

[20] Writing in opposition to the positions taken by the Carmelites of Salamanca and Lépicier, Vigué declared: "A Christ who had acquired all scientific knowledge would not seem authentic to us" ("Quelques précisions concernant l'objet de la science acquise du Christ," *RSR* 10 (1920) 27).

"brothers," wanted to drag him home when he began to preach because they had not discerned any remarkable aptitude in him.

To appreciate this essential fact, it is not enough to speak of the knowledge of "Christ's soul," in accordance with Scholastic terminology. It was the Son of God who slowly and progressively acquired various kinds of experimental knowledge, with the limitations necessarily inherent in them.

The "adventure" of the Incarnation involved the Word, the possessor of divine omniscience, in the lowly development of a human intellect. By assuming a human condition identical to our own, the Word accepted the limitations of a knowledge bound up with a particular milieu, a particular historical epoch, and a particular trade.

Are we obliged to attribute ignorance and error to the Son of God? As far as inculpable ignorance is concerned, we must indeed. [21] Humanly speaking, the sum total of the things Jesus knew was far less than the things he did not know, for that is the condition of all experimental human knowledge. Thus, for example, he did not know the scientific truths that have been discovered since his time; a present-day scientist knows much more than he did on the innermost composition of matter.

The fact of this ignorance, which is undeniable, takes on special importance in the light of the Incarnation. Jesus conferred a superior significance upon human ignorance, since it was not found unworthy to be assumed by the Man who is God. He certainly tried to overcome ignorance by acquiring all the kinds of knowledge that were available to him. Yet,

---

[21] We are not referring to the Scholastic notion that ignorance is a "penal state that presupposes the deprivation of a knowledge that the subject ought to have," according to Rivière's formula (*Le problème,* 349). Ignorance of this sort should not be imputed to Christ. It is on the basis of this conception of ignorance ("privatio illius scientiae quae inesse deberet") that Suarez affirms that Christ "was never ignorant, but possessed the plenitude of knowledge": "et ita Christus nihil eorum nescivit seu ignoravit quae opportuit scire, considerata dignitate personae, conditione naturae et ratione status seu officii; et ita, simpliciter loquendo, ignorantiam non habuit, sed plenitudinem scientiae" (*Dissert.* 24, sec. 3, n. 8; t. 17, 663). According to this vocabulary, the conclusion is correct, but we prefer to keep the more common meaning of the word "ignorance": a lack of knowledge. In this sense, Jesus was ignorant, and this ignorance has a special quality of participation in the human condition.

like all other humans, he learned through experience that the more human science develops, the greater the evidence of a still greater ignorance on the part of man. Sometimes Jesus allowed his awareness of ignorance to show through: "The wind blows wherever it pleases; you hear its sound, but you cannot tell where it comes from or where it is going" (Jn 3:8). At the same time he gives an inkling of the value of this ignorance which helps to open man's mind to the mystery of God.

Where error is concerned, however, the problem is different. In fact, in the strict sense error implies a contradiction with the truth. It does not result purely from ignorance, but presupposes that one has tried to affirm more than one knew. By reason of his integrity, Jesus never made any affirmation that exceeded what he knew. For example, he was ignorant of the innermost constitution of matter and of the ordering of the sidereal world, and so limited his statements to the discernment of their outward appearances. He chose to be a teacher only in the domain of religious doctrine. His freedom from error was due in a special way to a humility that accepted the limitations of his knowledge.

It was this same humility that enabled Jesus to seek instruction from others, contrary to what certain theologians following St. Thomas have thought, [22] that Jesus had to learn everything for himself through his own personal experience. In their view, he learned everything through contact with the things or the works of God in the world, but could not have received any knowledge from other men because this would have been contrary to his dignity as Teacher.

This opinion is based on an incorrect notion of perfection applied to Jesus' human nature. There is in fact no impertion involved when a child or an adult learns something from others. To the contrary, a man must know how to learn from others as a member of a society in which there is a mutual teaching-learning relationship. Before assuming his role as Teacher, Christ was a member of the community of men and accepted the conditions of this membership. In childhood he was subject to the authority of his parents. The submission affirmed by Luke (2:51) was not simply a matter of

---

[22] Cf. Michel, "Science de J.C.," *DTC* 14, 1658.

appearances. He truly acquired many kinds of knowledge as he grew to maturity. Mary and Joseph exercised a real influence on his psychological development.

For that matter, the entire human milieu in which Jesus lived left its mark upon him, in particular on his mode of thinking and speaking. The Gospel texts show that he did not withdraw within himself, or remain impervious to the influences to which he was exposed. Even during his public life when he had openly declared himself as a teacher, he continued to acquire knowledge through his contacts with those around him. It would be an exaggeration to say that every time Jesus asked a question or sought information he was simulating ignorance and learning nothing new from the answers given him.

Such a view involves the danger of Docetism. In order to exempt Christ from any possibility of imperfection, it seeks to discern only an appearance of learning on his part, [23] only the adoption of a façade when he asks questions or converses with others who are normally in a position to teach him something new. Contrary to such an approach, the mystery of the Incarnation demands that Jesus be truly instructed by his parents, that he really acquire knowledge and savoir faire in his dealings with others.

Even in the area of religious knowledge and behavior, Christ learned a great deal from others. His mother certainly played a significant role in his religious and moral formation. [24] Then, too, the Jewish cultic milieu put its mark on him, especially by the use it made of the Bible. While Jesus' religious life was bound up with his awareness of his unique filial identity and with his knowledge of his redemptive mission, it was considerably enriched by the familial and social influences of his early life.

Jesus did not experience any reticence in accepting the

---

[23] Thus, A. F. Claverie thought that Jesus had no need of guidance from Joseph and Mary: "Indeed, he had already formulated the right answers in advance in accordance with his will" ("La science du Christ, science acquise," *RT* 18, 1910, 777).

[24] J. Mouroux remarks:: "It was from his Mother that Christ was to learn human behavior and communication with others; it was from her ... that he would 'learn' God himself ...." ("La conscience du Christ et le temps," *RSR* 47, 1959, 333 ff.).

contributions of others to his own fund of knowledge, nor did he consider them merely inevitable necessities. Rather, he delighted in establishing social contacts in order to experience a more completely human life. The importance he gave to these contacts in his public life is significant. In his conversations with his human brothers he wanted to receive as well as to give. The adventure of the Incarnation involved the Word in a search for the most authentic human life possible, one that would be nourished by concrete experience and knowledge within the social relationships in which he was deeply immersed.

C. Jesus' Knowledge of God

1. *The Theory of the Beatific Vision*

In Scholastic doctrine, the beatific knowledge offers a basic solution to the problem of how Jesus knew God.

It also provides a solution to the problem of Christ's awareness of his identity as the Son of God. However, on this point a difficulty at once arises when we consider the essential nature of consciousness. Consciousness cannot be explained merely in terms of vision. According to the language of the Scholastics, the soul of Christ, in seeing God, sees the Word.[25] It is "the vision of the divine nature that enables him to say he is God through his very humanity."[26] The difficulty arises from the fact that a vision is not equivalent to an act of consciousness. To see the divine nature as the object of knowledge is not to become conscious of one's own divine personality. Vision and act of consciousness tend

---

[25] This is the language of St. Thomas that we find, for example, in H. Bouëssé, *Le Sauveur du monde.* Concerning the beatific knowledge, four questions are studied: "Whether the soul of Christ comprehended the Word or the divine essence?", that is to say, did Christ's soul know the Word with an exhaustive knowledge? "Whether the soul of Christ knew all things in the Word?" "Whether the soul fo Christ can know the infinite in the Word?" "Whether the soul of Christ sees the Word or the divine essence more clearly than does any other creature?" (Vol. II, 395). These questions are taken from the *Summa,* III, Q. 10, Art. 1-4).

[26] Galtier, *L'unité du Christ,* 371.

rather to be in opposition. What is seen as an object cannot be considered to be its own subject.

In fact, the entire manner in which the problem is posed calls for some rectifications. When one says that the soul of Christ sees the Word, one seems to forget that the Word himself is the principle and subject of all human knowledge in Jesus. Are we then to say that the Word, through Christ's soul, sees God and the Word himself? In addition, between the vision of the divine nature and the consciousness of a divine person, there is a considerable difference that makes it impossible to explain one by the other.

Even an "immediate vision" that would not be a "beatific vision" [27] could not account for Jesus' consciousness of being the Son of God. For the difficulty stems not only from the beatific quality of the vision, but also from the fact that the vision of an object is not equivalent to the consciousness of a subject. Immediate as this vision may be, it remains a vision, and the object that is seen is not equivalent to a subject who takes cognizance of himself.

We have already examined the problems of this act of consciousness, and sought to solve it apart from any recourse to a vision of God. Even if this element of vision were assured in the case of Jesus, it could only contribute externally to the act of consciousness, complementing and rectifying it so as to prevent Jesus from thinking of himself as a human person. But far from being assured, there is no foundation for it. More importantly, it is in profound disagreement with the Gospel witness and with the entire economy of the Incarnation.

There is no basis for the claim that Jesus enjoyed the beatific vision during his mortal life, for neither Scripture nor the Patristic Tradition attest to it.

Even while affirming Christ enjoyed the beatific vision during his earthly life, Galtier admitted that it cannot be proven on the basis of the Gospel texts. [28] The passages in

---

[27] This is the theory proposed by K. Rahner, who sees the immediate vision as resulting from the consciousness of Christ's soul that it is in the Logos ("Problèmes actuels de christologie," in *Ecrits théologiques*, I, Bruges 1969, 142).

[28] P. Galtier, *De Incarnatione ac Redemptione*, Paris, 1947, 258-259.

which, according to St. John, Jesus affirms he has seen the Father can refer to the divine vision prior to his earthly life, as is suggested by the past tense "has seen" and the context of the Prologue where the eternal intimacy of the Word with the Father is presented as the source of Jesus' mission of revelation. No Gospel text points to a human vision during Jesus' earthly life.

Moreover, in all of Patristic Tradition we can find no unchallengeable, explicit testimony in favor of the assertion that Christ possessed the beatific vision during his earthly life. [29] When Augustine comments on the Johannine texts on the vision of the Father, he does not make it clear whether he is speaking of the eternal divine vision or of a human vision during Christ's earthly life. The other Patristic texts which have been invoked are even less conclusive. [30]

As for the theological argument based on the exigencies either of the hypostatic union, the fullness of grace, or the communication of the beatific vision to the elect, it remains extremely vulnerable.

It is not possible to deduce the necessity of the beatific vision from the hypostatic union. For if a divine person becomes incarnate in order to live an earthly life like all other men, it is not evident why this mortal life should possess a perfection that belongs to human life in its eternal condition. Why should it be thought impossible for the Son of God to

---

[29] *Ibid.*, 256; " L'enseignement des Pères sur la vision béatifique dans le Christ," RSR 15 (1925) 54-68. Galtier nevertheless did consider retaining one of Augustine's texts as the only explicit testimony (*De Div Quaest.* 83, 65; PL 40, 60). However it must be admitted, with T. Van Bavel, (*Recherches sur la christologie de saint Augustin,* Fribourg 1954, 166) that there is nothing explicit in that writing. In his turn, Van Bavel thought he had found a more conclusive and even decisive text (*Contra Maxim.* II, 9,1, PL 42, 763). But this text is no more convincing than the others, for when Augustine comments on Jesus' words: "Not that anybody has seen the Father, except the one who comes from God" (Jn 6:46), he does not seek to affirm a current human vision. Rather, his purpose is to point out the divinity of Christ, and therefore his eternal divine knowledge.

[30] We refer the reader to Galtier's remarks. Regarding the text of St. Fulgentius (*Ep.* 14, q. 3, 25-34, PL 65, 415 ff.), we have noted earlier that it attributes to Christ not a strictly beatific knowledge but a divine wisdom in his humanity, and that this involves a deviation in the direction of Monophysitism.

have lived among us without the beatific vision? [31] How can the "true God" be an obstacle to the "true man"?

As for the fullness of grace, even when possessed in its supreme degree as in the case of Jesus, it requires the beatific vision only as its ultimate consummation after death, not during earthly life. It cannot be held to be identical with the fullness of glory.

Neither does the gift of the beatific vision to the elect provide a valid argument. It is produced by the glorious Christ. In Jesus it implies a kind of summit of vision that is the wellspring of its communication to others, but it implies the glorification that followed Jesus death. In his earthly life, Christ had to merit glorification and the extension of its benefits to mankind. Before his death, therefore, he had not yet entered into possession of the beatific vision.

It would seem that no testimony of Scripture or Tradition nor any theological reasoning calls for the affirmation that Jesus possessed the beatific vision during his earthly life. Moreover, this affirmation is contrary to the truth of Jesus' evangelical presence and of the authentic meaning of the mystery of the redemptive Incarnation.

As described to us in the Gospel accounts, Jesus could not have enjoyed the beatific vision. He lived a life that was like our own, not only in appearances but in very truth. Now, if he had enjoyed the contemplation and the happiness of the elect, this identification would have been only a sham. What sense would there have been to his exhaustion, his human emotions, his sadness, his anguish, if they had served merely to screen a beatitude of heavenly dimensions? The very integrity of the Incarnation would have been put into question. The Word would not have experienced human life and would not have truly shared our mortal condition.

The presence of the beatific vision in Jesus' mortal life would have directly contradicted his kenosis. The "emptying" of the hymn in Philippians 2:6-11 obviously could not have been real in one who, during his mortal life, enjoyed the privilege of the elect. The glorious state would be incom-

---

[31] Bouëssé has admitted that it is impossible to "establish an intrinsic contradiction in the notion that the soul of the Man-God is not endowed with the vision of God" (*Sauveur du monde*, II, 377).

patible with the merit attributed to Christ in the work of salvation, inasmuch as anyone who possesses the glorious vision of God can no longer merit. In a still more general way, this would deprive the redemptive sacrifice of all value. How can we admit that Christ could really have suffered in his human nature the terrible trial of the Passion if he already possessed the beatitude reserved for the elect in heaven? How, too, could we take the agony of Gethsemane and the dereliction of Calvary seriously?

We know that certain Spanish theologians have tried to solve this dilemma by proposing the hypothesis of a suspension of the state of glory during the time of the Passion, or at least a suspension of the spiritual joy produced by the beatific vision.[32] This amounted to admitting both that the beatific vision was incompatible with Christ's redemptive mission, and that this vision was not necessary to human existence.

Since the entire process of the Incarnation is orientated toward the work of the Redemption, the beatific vision must be excluded from Jesus' earthly life. This exclusion restores to us a Christ who is truly man, endowed with a human psychology like our own. Other historical epochs and other mentalities may well have delighted in the contemplation of Jesus' most sublime perfections. In our own day, we tend to be more interested in what the incarnate Son of God has in common with our human way of life.

Christ, "true man," did not live a heavenly life here on earth either in the intellectual or in the affective sphere. He did not have the immediate vision or the beatitude of the vision.

2. The Filial Knowledge

The truth that the theory of the beatific vision sought to guarantee, but which it did not succeed in expressing in its real form, is the fact of Jesus' unique knowledge of God during his mortal life.[33] Christ was aware that he was the

---

[32] M. Cano, De locis theol., 1, 12, c. 13 in fine; G. de Valencia, De Incarnatione, disp. 1, q. 9, punct. 2; A. Salmeron, Commentar. 10, tract. 11; Maldonat, In Matth. 26, 37.

[33] A decree of the Holy Office of June 5, 1918 has declared that we must admit as certain that in Christ's soul, during his sojourn among men,

Son of God and he knew the Father through intimate relations of an exceptional kind, which were in keeping with his identity as the Incarnate Son of God.

The problem of knowing God confronted Jesus in a different way than it does other men. Christ is not a man positioned vis-a-vis God, he is the Son who is God. In his very person he is within the Trinity and his human knowledge of God is determined by this unique personal relationship: he knows the Father and the Spirit, and he is aware that he is the Son.

We have already discussed how this knowledge and awareness developed in Jesus. Through his filial contacts with the Father which unfolded in his child's psychology under the influence of graces analogous to those of mysterical experience, Jesus received what can be called infused illuminations that enabled him to recognize the Father as his true Father in the full meaning of the word. But this illumination from above was integrated into the natural development of his child's con-

---

there existed the knowledge that the blessed in heaven possess (DS 3645). This declaration concerns only the security of the teaching (*tuto doceri*) and abstains from any direct doctrinal affirmation. It can be explained by the necessity of mounting a defense against Modernism (cf. No. 32-35 of the Decree *Lamentabili*, DS 3432-3436), and more specifically by the fact that Christ's beatific knowledge had been denied by those who did not admit that Jesus was aware of his divinity. It is this awareness that must be maintained, according to the fundamental intention of the declaration.

As for the beatific knowledge, it stems from a Scholastic theory that is now outdated. We find the affirmation in the Encyclical *Mystici Corporis* (1943), which attributes to Jesus, from his mother's womb, the beatific vision as well as the knowledge of all the members of the Mystical Body (DS 3812), and in the Encyclical *Haurietis aquas* (1956), according to which in Christ the act of charity is illumined and governed by a twofold knowledge, the beatific knowledge and infused knowledge (DS 3924; AAS 48, 1956, 328). But in both encyclicals, these are affirmations of secondary importance which do not affect the essential points of the doctrine enounced. Regarding the significance of the 1918 Decree of the Holy Office we must call to mind the position adopted, concerning certain decrees of the Biblical Commission, by the Secretary of this Commission in a letter addressed to Cardinal Suhard in 1948 (DS 3862-3863). One cannot attribute an unduly absolute value to these decrees, born of a defensive reaction against certain theories; and it is important to distinguish between the truth of faith that they sought to preserve and that must be maintained, and the private opinions of Scholastic theory that do not possess the same degree of certitude.

sciousness. In the psychology of Jesus there is no compartmentalization between the acquired and the infused.

This means that Jesus was not conscious of his identity from the very first instant, as the theory of the beatific vision would imply. Christ's human life began in unconsciousness, just like every other human life, and his consciousness awakened gradually. This process was not accelerated in Jesus, since the Incarnation did not involve any speeding up of the laws of nature.

However in this awakening of consciousness, special graces of illumination enabled the child to discern his true Father, and to develop psychologically in the truth of his filial identity. Besides, this development was aided by the rich Jewish contribution to the knowledge of God. The features of Yahweh's countenance delineated in the Old Testament helped Jesus to discern his Father's face, to grasp the meaning of his innermost experience and to situate it within the context of his human life.

Thus, the earlier message of Revelation was entirely incorporated into Jesus' personal relationship with his Father. These contacts, illumined from above, determined the essentials of Jesus' knowledge of God. What Jesus, as the Son, revealed of the Father, considerably exceeded the stage of knowledge of God to which Judaism had attained, and rectified certain aspects of the Jewish presentation. This explains why the keyword of Christ's revelation of God was not derived from the language of the Old Testament but stemmed from his own personal experience of intimacy with the Father.

It should be emphasized that this experience, far from being a heavenly experience comparable to that of the elect, was fully integrated into Christ's earthly existence. Jesus knew his Father and recognized himself as the Son in all the circumstances of his human life. That is why the knowledge of the Father to which Christ bore witness possessed a pronounced existential savor, and found expression in concrete situational terms.

In the life of the Word Incarnate there was an authentic human discovery of the Father. Jesus learned to discern the mysterious features of his Father's presence amid the events and realities of the world.

D. The Knowledge Stemming from a Superior Source

1. *The Fact*

In addition to his knowledge of the Father, Jesus had other knowledge that could not have resulted from his experience or from the normal exercise of his intellect, and which can only be explained as stemming from a higher source.

The Gospel texts provide us with several examples of Jesus' *superior knowledge of situations or events.*

In the Synoptic Gospels, the instructions given to the disciples before the entrance into Jerusalem denote an astonishing prevision of detailed circumstances: "Go off to the village facing you, and as soon as you enter it you will find a tethered colt that no one has yet ridden. Untie it and bring it here. If anyone says to you, 'What are you doing?', say, 'The Master needs it and will send it back here directly.'" (Mk 11:2-3; cf. Mt 21:2-3; Lk 19:30-31). The same holds true of the instructions for the preparation of the Passover supper: "Go into the city and you will meet a man carrying a pitcher of water. Follow him, and say to the owner of the house which he enters, 'The Master says: Where is my dining room in which I can eat the passover with my disciples?' He will show you a large upper room, furnished with couches, all prepared. Make the preparations for us there'." (Mk 14:13-15; cf. Lk 22:10-12).

No less remarkable is the *knowledge of men's hearts* that Jesus demonstrated on several occasions.

The Synoptic Gospels tell us that Jesus knew the innermost thoughts of those who accused him of blasphemy when he forgave the paralytic's sins, and Mark specifies that he was "inwardly aware that this was what they were thinking" (Mk 2:6-8; cf. Mt 9:3-4; Lk 5:21-22). Similarly, Jesus responded to the secret thoughts of Simon the Pharisee (cf. Lk 7:39-40). He also knew what was going on in his disciples' hearts (cf. Lk 9:47-48; Mk 9:33-34).

According to John's Gospel, Jesus showed he knew Nathanael's loyalty the very first time he met him (cf. Jn 1:47). He likewise knew the hypocritical duplicity of Judas at the time he called for the profession of faith in the Eucharist: "Yet one of you is a devil" (Jn 6:70-71). He foretold his betrayal when his disciples could not believe it was possible and had no idea as yet what he meant (cf. Jn 13:21).

Far more important still was Jesus' *knowledge of religious doctrine* which could not stem entirely from Judaism since it exceeded, complemented and corrected the doctrine heretofore proposed. The divine origin of this doctrine appears in the authoritative way it was presented (cf. Mt 7:29 and par.) and in the fact that Jesus did not hesitate to present it as superior to the doctrine of the Law (cf. Mt 5:21 ff.).

Jesus' teaching implied a profound knowledge of Scripture which had no apparent human cause, first of all because Jesus was not a learned man as witnessed by the reaction of his fellow Nazarenes (cf. Mt 13:54 and par.); and also because he presented a new interpretation of the Biblical texts that could not have come to him from any earlier tradition.

Jesus' *knowledge of the plan of the Redemption* was made particularly clear in his foretelling of his Passion, death, and Resurrection. In addition to the explicit threefold prediction of the Synoptics (cf. Mk 8:31; 9:31; 10:30-34 and par.), we find other announcements or allusions such as the one about the sign of Jonah (cf. Mt 12:40) or the destruction of the Temple (cf. Jn 2:19), the departure of the bridegroom from his friends (cf. Mk 2:20 and par.), the cup and the baptism (cf. Mk 10:39; Mt 20:22; Lk 12:50), the murder of the vineyard master's only son (cf. Mk 12:1-11 and par.).

These predictions were accompanied by the announcement of significant details. The anointing at Bethany presaged the burial and would be proclaimed along with the good news (cf. Mt 26:6-13; Jn 12:1-8); Judas' betrayal was foretold (cf. Mk 14:17-21 and par.), as were Peter's three denials (cf. Mk 14:26-31 and par.; Jn 13:38).

There is such complete convergence in the testimonies and the predictions are so much a part of Jesus' public life that it is hard to deny the fact that Jesus knew in advance the main events of the drama of the Redemption. Likewise, if we are not to systematically minimize the historical foundation of the Gospel accounts, we must recognize that Jesus manifested eminent knowledge that is inexplicable in natural terms in the area of religious doctrine, and that he possessed information stemming from a superior source concerning persons and events on various occasions during the course of his public ministry.

2. *The Origin*

Jesus' knowledge of things that cannot be explained by his own experience and that points to a superior source does not suffice to attribute infused science to him. For infused science presupposes a superior mode of knowing the real world. Now, Christ's knowledge stemming from a superhuman source was limited to the demands of his mission. It was not universal in character. Thus, under certain circumstances Jesus demonstrated that he knew the innermost thoughts or the particular situation of the individuals he encountered. Yet one cannot conclude from this that he knew the secrets of all hearts or the facts of all human situations. He possessed certain pieces of infused information, but he did not possess infused science *per se*.

We should note that this kind of knowledge was not possessed by Jesus alone. We know of examples of it in other human lives. There are circumstantiated accounts that John Mary Vianney, in the exercise of his priestly ministry, received the gift to know the inner life as well as the previous or current situations of a number of persons who consulted him. [34] The difference is that in Jesus' case his knowledge of men's hearts and of events was interrelated with a much vaster body of religious knowledge of a superior kind. We cannot discover such abundant knowledge in any other human life.

In addition, Christ's knowledge of supernatural origin was accompanied by the working of miracles. Thus, after Jesus affirmed that Lazarus was dead, he returned to Bethany to resurrect him. In a more general way we see that Christ received illuminations and powers of divine origin. In knowledge as well as in action, he was endowed with exceptional gifts that exceeded the unaided capacities of human intelligence and power.

---

[34] Cf. F. Trochu, *Les intuitions du Curé d'Ars,* Lyons, France, 1931-1939, 3 vol.

Nevertheless, the extraordinary breadth and depth of Jesus' knowledge was never exhibited for the sake of making a supernatural display. It was always addressed to the fulfillment of his mission. For example, Jesus surprised Nathanael by revealing to him that he had seen him before, thereby confirming the accuracy of his judgment as to Nathanael's loyalty and bringing him to believe in his message.

Jesus' knowledge of religious doctrine and of the plan of the Redemption was related to his knowledge of the Father through his awareness of his filial identity. Strictly speaking, the knowledge was not a necessary fruit of the awareness, since its extension was measured by Christ's mission and not by the implications of his identity. Yet Jesus himself attributed his knowledge to the Father, recognizing it came to him from his filial contacts with him. "And therefore what the Father has told me is what I speak" (Jn 12:50). Besides, he insisted on this divine origin to validate the authority of his teaching: "For what I have spoken does not come from myself; no, what I was to say, what I had to speak, was commanded by the Father who sent me" (Jn 12:49).

The link between Christ's filial consciousness and his knowledge of the redemptive sacrifice was emphasized in the account of the twelve-year-old boy in the temple. When Jesus said: "Did you not know that I must be in my Father's house?" (Lk 2:49), he used the verb "must" which was to be the hallmark of his predictions of the Passion. He made it clear that it was because he belonged to the Father that a sacrifice was demanded of him. Actually, the boyhood episode appears to be a prefiguration of the Paschal mystery during which Jesus would remain for three days in his Father's house. And so Christ's knowledge of the sacrifice to come was bound up with his awareness of his filial identity.

The development of Jesus' filial consciousness was accompanied by the development of his knowledge of his redemptive mission. This twofold development led Jesus, when he was twelve years old, to reveal his unique and essential quality of a Son and to foretell the awesome denouement to come.

Psychologically speaking, we rediscover here the intimate bond between the ontological and the functional. To become aware that one is the Son of God is to become aware of having been sent by the Father for a mission that demands the complete gift of one's human life, and likewise to become aware of the absolute necessity of belonging to the Father and leaving everything else.

3. Jesus' Knowledge of Eschatological Events

(a) - Jesus Accused of Error

Was Jesus mistaken about the exact moment the world will come to an end? Protestant exegetes have often attributed this error to him. As early as 1835-1836 David Frederick Strauss sought to prove this on the basis of the close link established in Christ's eschatological discourse between the destruction of Jerusalem and the end of the world. [35] As this link was not fulfilled in history Strauss claimed that Jesus deceived his disciples by a fraud, albeit perhaps a "pious" fraud, or else was in error. Thus, he concluded, "one of the pillars of Christianity went crashing to the ground." [36]

Among those who inherited Strauss' view, we might mention Albert Schweitzer, who thought that Jesus, convinced the Parousia would come immediately after his death, could not have envisaged an intermediary period for the duration of the Church. [37] We realize the magnitude of such an error inasmuch as it would have prevented Jesus from acting as the founder of an enduring Church. Oscar Cullmann, while claiming Jesus made this error, sought to reduce its impact by suggesting that Jesus had really envisaged an intermediary era but had estimated its duration at a maximum of a few decades. [38] For Cullmann, this was an error of secondary importance, involving only a miscalculation in timing. But this attempt to minimize the error does not eliminate the difficulty. The fact remains that if Jesus had indeed made such an error he would have been mistaken on a matter that directly con-

---

[35] *Vie de Jésus,* French translation by Littré, Paris, 1864, II, 335 ff.

[36] The expression used by Reimarus to stress the importance of the prophecy on the Parousia, was adopted by Strauss in that declaration, *op. cit.,* 339.

[37] A. Schweitzer, *Geschichte der Leben-Jesu Forschung,* Tübingen, 1951, 407.

[38] Oscar Cullmann, *Christ et le temps,* Neuchâtel, 1947, 106.

cerned his mission as the founder of the Church. Moreover, would not Jesus' error have been confirmed by the error of the first Christians who expected an early end to the world?

(b) - Jesus' Ignorance of the Day and the Hour

The disciples thought that the ultimate consummation of the world was of a piece with the destruction of the Temple. In answer to their question, Jesus made a clear-cut distinction between the two.[39] He made it plain that the eschatological events he had just described in his discourse would occur in the near future, for "before this generation has passed away, all these things will have taken place" (Mk 13:30; Mt 24:34). As for the exact time of the end of the world, he gave no clue. "But as for that day or hour, nobody knows it, neither the angels of heaven, nor the Son; no one but the Father" (Mk 13:32; Mt 24:36).[40]

This explicit declaration of ignorance on Jesus' part is truly astonishing. It does not do credit to the Master, and at first glance might seem hard to reconcile with the knowledge he was required to have of the divine work of salvation. This would seem to indicate the statement is an authentic record of Jesus' own words. The Christians would never have attributed such ignorance to their Master.

We are dealing here with a very real ignorance. We cannot claim that Jesus knew the date, but not with a communicable knowledge. Jesus says that "the Son" does not know it. It is more likely that the words he used were "the Son of Man," which would have emphasized more forcefully that this was an ignorance of the incarnate Son of God. Divine omniscience was not in question here. It was a matter of human ignorance, but an ignorance that was not merely apparent.[41]

---

[39] This distinction has been discerned in the study by J. Winandy, "Le logion de l'ignorance (Mc XIII, 32; Mt XXIV, 36)", *RB* 75 (1968) 63-79.

[40] Winandy explicates: "As for this particular Day and Hour, *on the contrary,* nobody knows anything about it .... ("Le logion ...", 71).

[41] The Decree of the Holy Office of June 5, 1918 is less categorical on the matter of omniscience than of the beatific knowledge. It says that Catholic institutions of learning must accept the opinion favoring the universal knowledge of Christ's soul, in preference to the more recent theory of a limited knowledge (DS 3647). It considers as not secure the teaching according to which "the

In actual fact, Jesus' ignorance is justifiable by the principle on which his supernatural knowledge rested, namely, the requirements of his mission. Jesus had no need to know the date of the end of the world, because it was of no interest for his mission. He was ignorant only of what he had no obligation to know. [42]

This ignorance belongs to the state of emptying or kenosis that was the mark of Jesus' earthly life. The fact that the Word made flesh assumed human ignorance, even in the area of religion, is worth stressing. Christ chose to bear the burden of ignorance out of a sense of solidarity with human life which is so limited in the scope of its knowledge. He experienced personally the obscurity against which the desire to know runs afoul, especially in the exploration of the mystery of God's plans.

Now, Jesus' very clear affirmation of his ignorance excludes the possibility that he might have thought or indicated that the end of the world was near, especially as his statement contrasted with his allusion to the proximity of the eschatological events referred to in his discourse.

The belief that the end of the world was near at hand resulted from the identification of Jesus' two statements. Jesus himself did not make this identification. On the contrary, he made a clear distinction between this end of the world and the eschatology he was announcing.

---

opinion cannot be held as certain which holds that the soul of Christ was ignorant of nothing but knew everything in the Word from the beginning ..." (DS 3646). According to the terms of the Decree, this opinion can be called "certain," but it is not obligatory to do so. (*Potest* is not equivalent to *debet*.) Jesus' own affirmation of his ignorance in the Gospel text cannot lightly be disregarded.

[42] Winandy ("Le logion," 64) cites other examples of ignorance due to the limits of Christ's mission: with regard to the places of honor (Mt 20:23; Mk 10:40), the number of those to be saved (Lk 13:22-30), the fate in store for John (Jn 21:21). This last example is open to question, for here Jesus did not appear to be demonstrating ignorance in the strict sense. The first two, however, are characteristic. As the logion on the date of the end of the world indicates, they concern areas where the sovereignty of the Father operates with the cooperaiton of human freedom.

(c) - Jesus' True Eschatological Perspective

The confusion regarding Jesus' eschatological announcements resulted from an overly concrete interpretation of the apocalyptic images used to represent the events. It is by recognizing the symbolic value of these images and not interpreting them literally that we rediscover the eschatological perspective of Christ.

The first image is the one of the destruction of the Temple. We know how John the Evangelist commented on Jesus' words: "Destroy this sanctuary, and in three days I will raise it up" (Jn 2:19). He understood them as the announcement of Jesus' death and Resurrection (cf. Jn 2:21-22). Jesus' adversaries, on the contrary, understood his words in a material sense involving the destruction and rebuilding of the Temple. And it is in this material sense that Jesus' other allusions to the destruction of the Temple have too often been interpreted. Jesus was talking of a spiritual destruction of the sanctuary, which would be consummated by his condemnation to death, but these words have been interpreted as the announcement of the disaster of the year 70 A.D.[43]

The material destruction also allowed stone to be left on stone (cf. Mk 13:2 and par.). It is part of an historical unfolding of events on which Jesus abstained from making any predictions. When Christ spoke of the "disastrous abomination" (Mk 13:14; Mt 24:15), he had in mind the great profanation that the Jewish people would commit against his sanctuary by condemning him to death. And when he said "Your house will be left to you desolate" (Mt 23:37-39; Lk 13:34-35), he was speaking of a spiritual vacuum in the Temple. The tearing asunder of the Temple veil, reported by the Evangelists in describing Jesus' death (cf. Mk 15:28 and par.), expresses symbolically the spiritual destruction of the building henceforth to be deprived of God's presence. The prophetic announcement of this spiritual destruction, which was close

---

[43] Luke's Gospel offers an example of the interpretation of Jesus' words by this event. Whereas Mark and Matthew speak enigmatically of "the disastrous abomination set up where it ought not to be" (Mk 13:14; Mt 24:15), Luke specifies: "When you see Jerusalem surrounded by armies, you must realize that she will soon be laid desolate ...." (Lk 21:20-23).

at hand, therefore alluded to the drama of the Redemption, and enables us to grasp its full meaning.

The other apocalyptic images Jesus used are those of the coming of the Son of Man on the clouds, to be preceded by calamities that were to afflict the earth and by a cosmic mourning. The coming of the Son of Man was solemnly announced at the moment of the trial, as a demonstration of Jesus' identity as Messiah and Son of God: "... I tell you that from this time onward you will see the Son of Man seated at the right hand of the Power and coming on the clouds of heaven" (Mt 26:64). If these words were interpreted to refer to the final Parousia, we would have to admit that Jesus committed an error inasmuch as he assured his adversaries they would see the coming of the Son of Man on the clouds, and "from this time onward" (Mt 26:64; cf. Lk 22:68).

But this coming which was so close at hand was not the Parousia. It was to accompany the seating of Christ at the right hand of God. Now we know that this seating designates the glorious exaltation of Christ, particularly after the Ascension. It signifies the enthronement of Christ, his entering into possession of the divine power of universal dominion. The coming that was to result from this seating was to take place in a divine manner, "on the clouds of heaven." This refers to the coming of Christ through his Spirit, which differed from his first coming in the flesh and was inaugurated on Pentecost. In short, this was the spiritual coming of Christ in the world, which brought about the gathering together of the Church. It was this coming that Christ's adversaries would be able to "see" as they contemplated the expansion of the first Christian community, proof that Jesus was in truth the Messiah and the Son of God. If we will stop externalizing the coming of the Son of Man on the clouds and picturing a theatrical entrance amid a decor of billowing mists, we can understand that Jesus was announcing his real coming, a coming of the spiritual and divine order, to be realized in the development of the Church.

Christ announced this gathering together of the Church in even more explicit language in his eschatological discourse: "And then they will see the Son of Man coming in the clouds with great power and glory; then too he will send the angels to gather his chosen from the four winds, from the ends of the world to the ends of heaven" (Mk 13:26-27). The great eschatological event which is the high point of the discourse is not the Parousia but the coming of the glorious Christ. For after Pentecost he gathered up all men into the Church throughout the world. Jesus made other statements alluding to this same coming: "I tell you solemnly, there are some of these standing here who will not taste death before they see the Son of Man coming with his kingdom" (Mt 16:28). "I tell you solemnly, you will not have gone the round of the towns of Israel before the Son of Man comes" (Mt 10:23). "But when the Son of Man comes, will he find any faith on earth?" (Lk 18:8).

In the eschatological discourse, this coming is preceded by various calamities: wars, famines, earthquakes, wild flights, the convulsion of the universe. These apocalyptic images should not be taken in their literal and material sense. They are meant to give an insight into the immensity of the tragedy that was to occur on "the day of Yahweh," before the Messianic coming. "For in those days there will be such distress as, until now, has not been equalled since the beginning when God created the world, nor ever will be again" (Mk 13:19). This unique catastrophe in the history of mankind can only be the one that preceded the new creation: the death of Christ. It was in this death that the misery of mankind, the suffering and death of all human beings was, so to speak, gathered up.

The evocation of the cosmic mourning calls for the same interpretation: "But in those days, after that time of distress, the sun will be darkened, the moon will lose its brightness, the stars will come falling from heaven and the powers in the heavens will be shaken" (Mk 13:24 and par.). Already in the Old Testament this darkening of the heavenly bodies had been used to describe the day of Yahweh (cf., for example, Is 13:9-13). The image was particularly apt for stressing the participation of the universe in the death of Christ. Actually, it was in a certain sense adopted by the Evangelists in their account of his death: "... there was darkness over all the earth" (Mt 27:45 and par.). Such universal darkness reaches far beyond the horizons of the witnesses to the crucifixion and can only be a symbolic expression of the mourning of the whole earth. When Jesus, in his eschatological discourse, announced the mourning of the entire cosmos, he was relating it to the event of his death.

Jesus therefore used apocalyptic images of the events of the last days to announce their fulfillment in his Passion and in his glorious coming to follow. That is why he affirmed so insistently that the eschatological events would occur during the lifetime of his own generation, that, indeed, they were imminent.

On the other hand, he foretold "the end of the world" at a later time, at an undetermined date in the future. Whereas his disciples could already see the portent of the end of the world in the destruction of the Temple, Jesus showed them that the desolation he spoke of was not to be identified with the end of the world: "... this is something that must happen, but the end will not be yet. . . . This is the beginning of the birthpangs" (Mk 13:7-8). He clearly dissociated his imminent Passion from the last days of the world.

Jesus even explicitly pointed to an intervening period. His Passion would only begin the painful childbirth, for it was to continue in the persecutions that would befall the Church (cf. Mk 13:9-13). During this period, the Gospel would be preached throughout the earth, and the end would come only after this universal evangelization was completed (cf. Mk 13:10): "And then the end will come" (Mt 24:14). Jesus was therefore expecting the Church to develop over a long period of time. What he did not know was the exact date when this development would reach its highest point and culminate in the end of the world.

While Jesus stressed the proximity of the ordeal and the glorious coming of the Son of Man, he pushed back the end of the world to a much more distant future. The error has come not from what Jesus said but from those who misunderstood or misinterpreted his words.

Instead of condemning Jesus for an alleged error, we should rather admire the grandeur of his vision which adopted Jewish eschatology with its most characteristic images in order to announce its imminent realization in his death and glorious triumph. His eye scanned the whole religious history of Judaism and of mankind.

370

Three characteristics of this approach to eschatology deserve special attention on our part.

The first is that Jesus demythologized eschatology. He stripped the traditional images of Jewish eschatology of their mythical quality. He announced the realization of these images not through outwardly astounding events but through the drama of the Redemption which, by his Passion, would bring about his new coming into the Church. He thus conferred meaning on these images in the unfolding of human history. He gave them a reality that was not merely mythical but historical.

A second distinctive mark consists in the positive view Jesus took of the end of the world. He evoked this denouement with great discretion and presented it as the completion of the work of evangelization. This was to be the consummation of the Church's mission in history — a mission to be accomplished amid persecutions and trials of every kind which were to be the sign of the Son of Man, the sign of his coming. When the disciples asked what sign would serve as a prelude to the catastrophe, Jesus answered by indicating tribulation would be the sign of imminent triumph.

Finally, the third aspect concerns the meaning of history. In Jesus' eyes, the great eschatological event was not his Parousia, but his coming within the Church. This view gives history its full meaning. For history is now seen to consist in this coming, in the work of evangelization which is the reason for the historical process. Indeed, as soon as the work is completed, history will be consummated and come to an end.

E. THE DEVELOPMENT OF THE MESSIANIC AWARENESS

From what we have discovered concerning Jesus' knowledge of the plan of the Redemption we are not encouraged to think that he simply followed clues received from events in developing his Messianic consciousness. There are those who have thought that at the start of his public ministry Jesus hoped to succeed in his mission of evangelizing the Jewish people and did not in fact expect an abrupt interruption of this mission by being sentenced to death, nor for that matter the subsequent extension of his message and of his followers to the ends of the earth. In their view, the opposition of his compatriots led him to accept the prospect of a personal sacrifice as his crowning achievement. It was this opposition that made him hope for a better reception of the Gospel by other nations, having a more universal vision of the Church. The need for an expiatory offering on his part would have been, to their mind, simply his way of reacting to the turn of events. [44]

This interpretation of the development of Jesus' Messianic consciousness would imply not merely a development in Jesus' notion of his mission, but a radical change, a complete reversal of his perspectives. Indeed, the truly essential elements in Christ's mission are on the one hand its fulfillment in his sacrifice and on the other hand his intention to save the whole of mankind. How could Christ, in his Messianic consciousness, have failed to perceive these elements from the very start of his public life, and how could he have integrated them into his goals only belatedly under the pressure of events?

To justify such a radical change in Jesus' plan of action, we would need conclusive evidence from the Gospels. The evidence we do have does not support this hypothesis.

The first testimony is the account of Jesus' sojourn in the Temple as a child of twelve, which presupposes that even then he understood enough of the essential reality of the Paschal mystery to cause Mary and Joseph the great anguish of thinking they had lost him.

Then at the start of his public life Jesus allowed himself to be baptized by John the Baptist. While there may be reservations as to the historical value of the theophany accompanying the baptism, the fact of the baptism is soundly historical and is generally admitted by exegetes of every persuasion. In fact, the account of this baptism was an embarrassment to Christians inasmuch as it ostensibly placed Jesus in a relation of inferiority vis-a-vis John the Baptist. This event was incorporated into the Gospel because it marked the beginning of Christ's public life.

Now, John's baptism was a baptism of penance. In submitting to it Jesus must have accepted it as involving the re-

---

[44] A. Vögtle, "Exegetische Erwägungen über das Wissen und Selbstbewusstsein Jesu," in *Gott in Welt,* I, Freiburg 1964, 624-634.

mission of sin. Yet knowing he was without sin he could do so only for the sake of others, assuming the burden of men's sins in order to purify them of sin. This acceptance of the weight of the people's sins, though he himself was innocent, had been announced in the Book of Isaiah as applied to the suffering "servant of Yahweh" (cf. Is 53:4-12). Jesus therefore realized from the start of his ministry that he was fulfilling the prophecy of the servant. He also knew that according to the oracle the servant was to obtain the salvation of the multitudes by his own personal sacrifice of expiation. In other words, before Jesus even began to preach he already knew the painful destiny in store for him as well as the universal scope of the salvation he would bring to mankind, as described by the prophet.

It is true that at the start of his preaching Jesus did not announce the events of his Passion and Resurrection. He reserved the clearest predictions of these events for the second stage of his public life, thereby showing a gradual evolution in his teaching. This change is expressed in the Gospel text: "And he began to teach them that the Son of Man was destined to suffer grievously ..." (Mk 8:31).

Did this evolution result from a change in Jesus' thinking? On the contrary, it appears to have been part of his method of teaching. For it was only when the disciples had progressed to the point of professing their faith in the Messiah that Jesus taught them exactly what kind of Messiah he was. It was not Christ's thinking that changed, but the thinking of his disciples.

Besides, when Jesus announced his Passion he did not present it as forced on him by the turn of events. He faced his Passion with the affirmation: "I must," indicating it was demanded of him by God's plan. The drama of the Redemption was commanded not by circumstances but by the Father's decree.

In addition, it would be arbitrary to claim all of Jesus' allusions to his coming sacrifice were made toward the end of his public life. We have only to remember his announcement of the day the bridegroom would be taken away from his friends (cf. Mt 9:15 and par.),[45] his references to those who suffer

---

45 Cf. A. Feuillet's commentary on this logion: "Contrary to what certain critics have claimed without foundation, Jesus was not forced to change his

persecution (cf. Mt 5:11-12; Lk 6:22-23), to the sickle to harvest the crop (cf. Mk 4:29), and to the need to lose one's life (cf. Mt 10:39; 16:25, and par.). These allusions all seem to show that Jesus' teaching was imbued with this essential orientation.

Universality of intention likewise inspired the whole of Jesus' thinking. It underlies the name "Son of Man" that Jesus chose in preference to "Son of David." It inspired an attitude that did not accept nationalistic prejudices or discrimination of any sort, and revealed his intention to call the pagans to faith in him.

For all these reasons we cannot accept the view that any profound changes in orientation occurred in Jesus' Messianic consciousness. However, there was a development in this consciousness, as there was in Jesus' whole psychology. Wherein did this development consist? The Gospel texts do not offer us any unchallengeable guidelines in this area. We can however point to three elements that contributed to the development of Jesus' Messianic consciousness.

The first element was experience. While Jesus understood the drama of the Redemption in its essentials, he gradually came to see more clearly, through the hostility that escalated against him, the concrete way this drama would be carried out. Through the force of circumstances he came to realize the course his sacrifice would take.

The second element was Scripture. By meditating on the prophecies and on the history of his people, Jesus came to a deeper understanding of God's plan and of the value of the ordeal to which he was destined.

The third element was the knowledge that came to him from above as events unfolded. Knowledge of this supernatural sort enabled him to foretell Peter's threefold denial.

Messianic program, although it is true his human understanding of this program gradually become clearer. Even though it is hard to pinpoint the date of the controversy over fasting, it was probably anterior chronologically to the great announcements of the Passion. We can therefore conclude that Jesus did not need failures in his Galilean ministry to understand his task as the suffering Servant. We already knew this from the accounts of the baptism. A scrutiny of the logion on the Messianic bridegroom who was violently taken away fully confirms this conclusion" ("La controverse sur le jeûne (Mc 2,18-20; Mt 9,14-15; Lc 5,33-35)," *NRT* 90 (1968) 257).

Jesus' Messianic consciousness continued to develop, in harmony with the growth of his filial consciousness. For it was in understanding fully that he was the Son of the eternal Father that Jesus understood with ever greater clarity the need for his sacrifice to be the oblation of a loving Son.

CHAPTER XIII

THE HOLINESS AND THE FREEDOM OF JESUS

A. THE HOLINESS OF JESUS

1. *The Fundamental Consecration*

It is easy to understand that Jesus, being the Son of God, could not fail to possess the plenitude of human holiness. Yet it is harder to determine precisely in what this plenitude of holiness consists.

Jesus alluded to the fundamental consecration implicit in his Incarnation when he called himself "someone the Father has consecrated and sent into the world" (Jn 10:36). The consecration relates to his human nature. This nature belongs totally to the Father because it is the nature of the Son sent into the world. This consecration encompasses the whole of Jesus' being, prior to any activity on his part, but was destined to be manifested specifically in the accomplishment of his mission.

It should be noted that holiness, as conceived in the Jewish religion, did not signify first of all moral rectitude but a belonging to God. In Jesus this belonging was realized by the assuming of a human nature by the person of the Son. Besides, this human nature was totally at the service of the Father so that he might accomplish his works through it. When Jesus declared he was "consecrated" by the Father he wanted to show his enemies that he was truly accomplishing the Father's works and was in very truth the Son of God (cf. Jn 10:33-38).

In this consecration of Jesus we see the prototype of Christian holiness, which was to consist in a consecration of the human "to be" before involving moral purity of behavior. The belonging of the human "to be" to God, realized at the start of every Christian life, was to be the reflection of the consecration of Jesus' human "to be" accomplished through the mystery of the Incarnation.

If we try to express the holiness of Jesus in the context of this Christian holiness, of which it is the wellspring, we must recognize it as the model of "character" and of "grace." Character is the consecration imprinted in the "to be" in a definitive, indelible way. Grace — and more specifically habitual or sanctifying grace — is the interior life through which this consecration finds expression by the communication of divine holiness. The distinction between character and grace, which was to be discerned later in theological reflection on the sacraments, was already present in a certain way in the mystery of the Incarnation.

In Jesus' own words recorded by John, the distinction is outlined between the initial consecration, the work attributed to the Father, and the consecration realized in Christ's sacrifice. [1] "... for their sake I consecrate myself" (Jn 17:19). Obviously, this is not a second consecration simply added to the first. Rather it is a concrete realization of the initial consecration, but one in which Jesus reveals more clearly his personal responsibility, as well as the freedom with which he gives himself.

2. A Progressing Holiness

The affirmation "I consecrate myself" (or "I sanctify myself") implies a development in holiness, since Jesus had to consummate this holiness himself through his sacrifice.

The problem of Jesus' progress in grace could not be posed if we claimed his grace was infinite. In fact, since grace is a transformation of human nature, it has the limitations of a created reality and therefore cannot, even in Christ's human nature, have the infinite perfection that belongs to the divine nature as such. Since Jesus' grace was finite, it was susceptible to progress. [2]

---

[1] The distinction is stressed by R. E. Brown from the exegetical point of view (*John,* 766). The consecration of Jn 10:36 evokes that of the prophets and priests, whereas the consecration of Jn 17:19, being the work of Jesus himself, tends to evoke the consecration of victims in sacrifice.

[2] The attribution of the beatific vision to Jesus during his earthly life, in Scholastic doctrine, prevented the affirmation of such progress. Thus, in

Luke took care to affirm the fact of Jesus' growth in every area: "And Jesus increased in wisdom, in stature, and in grace with God and men" (Lk 2:52). The grace Luke was referring to cannot be identified with sanctifying grace. According to the text of Proverbs (3:4) from which these words were borrowed, "grace" relates to the favor one finds before God and men. It is therefore an external designation. However, if God's good pleasure in this child kept growing, we must admit it corresponded to an inward reality. Jesus, through his spiritual growth, merited to draw God's favor increasingly upon himself.

This is confirmed by Jesus' growth "in wisdom." Luke had already emphasized this growth in an earlier passage: "Meanwhile the child grew to maturity, and he was filled with wisdom; and God's favour was with him" (Lk 2:40). Wisdom signifies more than a quality of intellect. In fact, in the Biblical sense, it evokes a way of thinking and living which is communicated by God to men. The development of wisdom in Jesus embraces his total religious outlook.

So we can say that Jesus truly grew in grace and holiness. This development was not limited to external manifestations, and could not be limited to his behavior. [3] It was Jesus' interior attitude that developed. Luke's intention was to stress inward as well as outward growth, growth that was moral and spiritual as well as physical.

There is no reason to be surprised by this progress of Jesus in holiness or grace. To claim that because he was perfectly holy, he could not experience such progress would not

---

his article "Jésus-Christ," (DTC, 8, 1284), A. Michel poses the following as a principle: "Christ's habitual grace was not susceptible to growth." He explains this by saying: "From the first instant of his conception, Christ, in his soul, was a perfect 'comprehensor.' Now, a soul that has thus attained its ultimate goal through the intuitive vision is no longer capable of progress and of greater perfection in the grace it possesses and in the operations that stem from it." This so-called "theologically certain" conclusion is alleged to clinch the argument that would have made of Jesus' mortal life a life not of this earth but of heaven.

[3] Michel (ibid., DTC 8, 1284) states that by reason of their doctrinal position the Scholastics were obliged to interpret Luke's affirmation as referring solely to progress in outward manifestations, excluding all real progress in wisdom and grace. However, the clarity of the Gospel affirmation should outweigh speculative considerations.

be true to the conditions of human existence. Human holiness, of its very nature, matures slowly over a period of time. In espousing the normal human way of life Christ also chose to develop in holiness gradually.

Obviously, for Jesus progress in holiness could not consist in amending his ways or passing from a defective stage to one that was less imperfect. Jesus always possessed the maximum holiness befitting each phase of his human development. Luke's words "Jesus grew filled with wisdom" (Lk 2:52) express this nuance exactly. Jesus was filled with a grace that was constantly increasing, without ceasing, at each stage, to be a fullness of grace.

By reason of this, we can say that Jesus advanced in the virtues. The Epistle to the Hebrews described the full power of this increase with respect to his obedience: "Although he was Son, he learnt to obey through suffering" (Heb 5:8). That is to say the experience of his Passion was necessary to confer the fullest depth to Jesus' obedience.

Jesus himself declared that the summit of love consists in giving one's life for others: "A man can have no greater love than to lay down his life for his friends" (Jn 15:13). He looked upon his ultimate sacrifice as the summit of his love for men. He thereby implied that his love for men had continued to grow until it attained its maximum degree in his death. Nothing had been lacking to his love at any earlier stage of Christ's life, but only death could provide him with the opportunity to give himself totally.

3. Jesus and Faith

Did faith play any part in Jesus' religious attitude?

Scholastic theology which attributed the beatific vision to Jesus during his earthly life could not even pose the problem. However, when we no longer claim that Jesus enjoyed the beatific vision and accept his earthly condition as one of authentic kenosis, the question requires examination.[4] Indeed, kenosis involves a certain obscurity in the activity of the intellect under the ordinary conditions of human existence. In itself, this obscurity can be compatible with faith.

---

[4] Cf. H. Urs von Balthasar, *Sponsa Verbi*, Einsiedeln 1961, 45-79; L. Malevez, *Pour une théologie de la foi*, Paris-Bruges 1969, 159-216.

When we compare Jesus' religious attitude with the Christian's disposition of faith, we immediately discern a first difference between them. Christian faith is essentially addressed to Christ as its object and cannot exist in the same way in Jesus himself. The problem has often been raised in terms of faith in God. That is too abstract and too partial a point of departure. Concretely, the essential mark of Christian faith is that it is faith in Christ. It recognizes God in Jesus. From this point of view, Jesus' position is different. The Son of God is aware of his divine "I." While this awareness involves the inherent limitations and obscurity of every human psyche, it stems from an inward certitude that cannot be reduced to an act of faith. Besides, the fact remains that the One who apprehends is the Son of God. It is not only man who becomes aware that he is God and who might be comparable to other men who believe in God. There is question here of a divine person who becomes humanly conscious of his identity as the Son of God.

It is also significant that Jesus never at any time said that he "believed." When he spoke of his relations with the Father, he declared that he knew him and not that he believed in him. When he affirmed the power of faith, he did so to encourage others to believe and not to describe a power he himself possessed. Several scholars have interpreted the words "Everything is possible for anyone who has faith" (Mk 9:23) as referring first of all to Christ's personal experience. [5] However the context shows that Jesus was speaking of the faith of his interlocutor, and that the latter understood his words in this way since he answered: "I do have faith. Help the little faith I have!" (Mk 9:24). [6] Likewise, the image of the mountain that casts itself into the sea was not intended to

---

[5] W. Grundmann, *Das Evangelium nach Markus,* Berlin, 1968, 190; G. Ebeling, *Wort und Glaube,* I, Tübingen, 1960, 240.

[6] The father of the epileptic challenged Jesus' power: "but if you can do anything ..." (Mk 9:22), and Jesus' answer pointed out the real problem by reversing the point of view. The crux was not the power of Christ which was beyond challenge, but the power of the one who was asking for a miraculous cure. And this power was given in proportion to the petitioner's faith.

emphasize the strength of Christ, but that of the disciples who have faith (cf. Mk 11:23-24 and par.).[7]

Jesus demanded not only faith in God, but faith in himself. According to the Synoptics, he did not speak of faith in himself with one exception (cf. Mt 18:6). However, he made it clear that this was the faith he was calling for. When he demanded faith of others in order to work miracles for them, he was obviously referring to faith placed in himself. In John's Gospel, the meaning of this request is explicit. It is a matter of believing in Jesus with the same faith one addresses to God (cf. Jn 14:1). Christ thus presented himself not as the one who believed but as the one in whom others must believe.

Yet the profound difference between Christ and other men in the matter of faith does not eliminate all similarities. We discern two characteristic elements of faith in Jesus' religious attitude: an intellectual element, namely, knowledge, and an affective element, namely, trust.

Jesus was the one who "recognized the Father" in the earthly context of his human life and who revealed him to men (cf. Mt 11:27). And that is why the faith of the disciples was formed through the communication of this knowledge of the Father. Jesus shared with his followers his discernment of the Father in the visible manifestations of his action in the world.

Jesus likewise witnessed in many ways to his trust in the Father. It was from the Father that he awaited the fulfillment of the plan of salvation, and above all, his glorious triumph: "Father, ... glorify your Son ...." (Jn 17:1). The supreme act of his life was an act of abandonment into the Father's hands (cf. Lk 23:46). His preaching and the formation he gave his disciples tended to inspire in others this disposition of trust and surrender.

It can also be pointed out that at Gethsemane and during his Passion Jesus went through an interior trial in many ways

---

[7] Regardless of Ebeling's interpretation which applies these words first of all to Jesus (*ibid.*), they were clearly addressed to the disciples: "I tell you ... everything you ask and pray for, believe that you have it already, and it will be yours" (Mk 11:24). Any link between this advice and the episode of the fig tree would appear to be artificial.

similar to the trials of faith. In the hour of darkness it was not easy for him to recognize the Father in events and to abandon himself into his hands. This involved a deep inner struggle on his part, as is witnessed by his cry: "My God, my God, why have you deserted me?" (Mk 15:34; Mt 27:46).

Consequently, there were in Christ's dispositions certain essential elements of faith and he inwardly experienced ordeals closely resembling the trials of faith. From this point of view Jesus must be considered as the model of our faith. At the same time, he is the source that communicates faith, for it is from him that spring the knowledge and the trust that constitute Christian faith.

Be this as it may, since Jesus is the Son of God and possesses the consciousness proper to this sonship, it is impossible to attribute faith to him in the strict sense of the word. Nor can we forget that the hallmarks of faith, namely, knowledge of God and trust in him, assume a special orientation in us, because this knowledge and trust are addressed essentially to Christ himself. The differences inevitably result from the vast distance that separates a divine person from human persons.

4. *Jesus and Hope*

The mark of Christian hope is certitude amid uncertainty.[8] During his earthly life the Christian cannot possess the absolute certitude that he will be ultimately saved and will enter into the eternal happiness of the possession of God. This uncertainty comes from his freedom, whose final option cannot be determined in advance. His awareness of this uncertainty is heightened by the experience of his weakness in the face of temptations and his awareness of the forces within him that tend toward evil. And yet in the midst of this uncertainty, a certitude develops, the certitude that salvation is really within the reach of every human being. The Christian is certain he can attain the happiness won for him by Christ. By putting his trust in the divine love that has manifested its benevolent power in the coming and in the work of the Savior, he overcomes all uncertainty, for he turns his gaze on

---

[8] J. Alfaro, "Certitude de l'espérance et 'certitude de la grâce'", *NRT* 104 (1972) 3-42.

this love more than on himself and on his sinful state. [9] His hope is founded on Christ alone, it is purely theological and "Christological."

In asking ourselves to what extent Jesus could really hope during his earthly life, we must first of all note that, as in the case of faith, there is a basic difference between the Christian's hope and the hope of Jesus. For the Christian puts all his hope in Christ who died and rose again. His hope results from the event of Christ's coming, from the Redemption he brought to all men.

Notwithstanding, Jesus did hope during his mortal life. The Christ who trod our earth hoped for his glorious triumph. But there was no uncertainty in his mind as to the outcome of his destiny. He was sure of it in advance. He foretold his Resurrection. He knew his human will could not stray into the path of sin.

While Jesus did not share the universal human uncertainty as to the capacity to resist evil, he did share with other men a hope founded on trust. It was above all at the moment of his death that he manifested the trusting abandonment to God which underlay his hope of resurrection.

Above all, we must consider the *communitarian dimension* of hope. Hope cannot be constricted within the horizons of a single individual. Jesus hoped for the ultimate gathering together of all men within his Church in the course of subsequent history, as a prelude to the eternal assembling of the blessed in the heavenly community. We glimpse this hope especially in his eschatological discourse, in which he outlined the future development of the Church amid persecutions through the evangelization of all nations until the final consummation (cf. Mk 13:10; Mt 24:14). Jesus also affirmed this hope in his priestly prayer, where it was addressed above all to the unity and holiness of the Church (cf. Jn 17:9-24).

This communitarian hope possessed a certain all-encompassing certitude with respect to the total Christian community that was being called into being and launched upon a course

---

[9] " A radical lack of self-assurance and a sense of responsibility in the face of God's love bring man face-to-face with the one and only salvific decision, the decision of hope, ... total commitment to the mystery of God-Love" (*ibid.*, 42)

of development. It did not eliminate uncertainties as to the ultimate fate of each individual human being after death, for it could not do away with the indeterminations of individual choice. Even in Jesus, communitarian hope did not exclude these uncertainties. But in his person it was filled with trust in the Father's love, a love resolved to do everything possible to promote the salvation of every human being, and it was rooted in the certitude of the universal efficacy of his sacrifice.

Jesus' communitarian hope is the wellspring and model of Christian hope.

5. The Impeccability of Jesus

The absence of any sin whatsoever in Christ's life has been mentioned in the Church's professions of faith promulgated at the Council of Florence.[10] It touches upon a fundamental aspect of Jesus' holiness.

According to the testimony of the Gospel, Jesus showed he was thoroughly aware of the irreproachable quality of his demeanor: "Can one of you convict me of sin?" (Jn 8:46). There is a bold challenge in this question such as no other man would have dared to lay down. His intention was to attest to the credibility of his teaching, to the absolute purity of the doctrine that he, as the Son, was communicating to men from the Father.

Jesus' humility never expressed itself in the confessing of sin, and the only prayer in which he formulated a petition for forgiveness, the Lord's Prayer, was meant to be recited by others. For it was in answer to the request of one of the disciples that he taught them how to pray (cf. Lk 11:1).

In the Epistles the absolute innocence of Christ is affirmed several times, to stress the contrast between the absence of sin in Jesus and the sacrifice he chose to suffer so as to bear the weight of the sins of mankind. He is called "the sinless one" (2 Co 5:21; 1 P 2:22; 1 Jn 3:5). This also brings out a difference between Christ and other men within the context of their likeness. He is "the one who has been tempted

---

[10] *Decree for the Jacobites*, DS 1347: "sine peccato conceptus, natus et mortuus."

in every way that we are, though he is without sin" (Heb 4:15; cf. 7:26).

These references to Jesus' complete innocence, a unique and altogether exceptional case in a human life, excludes the notion of an Incarnation that would have consisted in assuming man's sinful condition. Nor, for that matter, did Jesus need to be saved from sin, [11] and in that sense he cannot be included among the "saved." Jesus Christ was always the perfect Savior, because he was totally exempt from sin.

Let us pause here to note the conformance between the soteriological and the ontological in Christ. This fact more adequately refutes the opinion that Christ would have demonstrated more total solidarity with his human brothers if he had been a sinner among sinners. First of all, if Jesus had admitted the existence of sin in himself he would have established a solidarity not only with sinners but with sin itself. And he would then have been in conflict with God, something that is totally incongruous with the person of the Son of God. In addition, since such solidarity with sinners would have had a soteriological purpose it could have been realized only within the context of the mission of salvation. But this mission demanded that the Savior be the innocent one who, in his very innocence and irreproachable holiness, assumed responsibility for the consequences of mankind's sins.

Impeccability means more than the mere absence of sin. It implies the impossibility of sinning. As such, it has not been made the object of a definition of faith, for it tends rather to be a theological statement on the holiness of Jesus.

The impeccability of Jesus has been generally accepted in Catholic theology, but there has been no agreement as to the reason why. Some scholars have drawn arguments from the beatific vision. According to Duns Scotus, Durandus, the Scotists and the nominalists, the human nature of Jesus, even though hypostatically united to the Son of God, was capable of sin, inasmuch as it enjoyed the exercise of free will. How-

---

[11] The *Epistle to the Hebrews* speaks of the one who could save Jesus *from death,* and who saved him from it by giving him a glorious victory over it (cf. Heb. 5:7). To "save from death" cannot be identified with "saving from sin."

ever, in their view, the beatific vision rendered Jesus' human nature impeccable, as is the case for the elect in heaven.

We have already pointed out why we cannot attribute the beatific vision to Jesus during his mortal life. The reasoning of the Scotists *et al* is invalid. On the other hand, the hypostatic unity of Christ necessarily postulates his impeccability. The divine person is the subject of all the intellectual and volitional activities of Jesus. Now, a divine person cannot perform a sinful act, that is, an act in conflict with God, for that would amount to a self-contradiction. He who is God cannot act against God. We must therefore admit that it was metaphysically impossible for Jesus to commit sin.

Obviously we are not speaking of an impossibility that regards only Jesus' human nature or that might be inherent in this nature. It stems from the divine person, the principle of Jesus' human activities. Impeccability, therefore, is not an exceptional quality of Christ's human nature. His human nature is like that of all other humans. Strictly speaking, it is not the humanity of Christ that must be called impeccable but Christ himself, the Son of God, in his human nature.

6. The Temptation of Jesus

The Gospel texts attest that Christ was not exempt from temptations. Even though the laconic accounts of the three temptations in the desert raise questions as to their historicity, they at least show how the sacred writers understood the conflict with Satan that characterized Christs's mission. Certain episodes, especially the one at Gethsemane, bring out deep interior struggles within Jesus' soul.

Exemption from sin does not, of itself, postulate exemption from temptation. Since Christ was like other men in all respects except sin, he was put to the test and tempted like the rest of us.

Certainly, we must affirm that Jesus was exempt from "concupiscence" which, though not sin in the strict sense, is a result of sin. According to the Council of Trent, "it is of sin and inclines to sin" (DS 1515). It stems from the imbalance in human nature that is a consequence of original sin, the disordered inclination to delight in evil. Jesus never experienced this inner disorder and never took secret pleasure in the evil proffered to him.

Granted that Jesus was exempt from concupiscence, can we conclude with certain scholars that Christ' temptations were entirely external? This conclusion has been suggested by theologians who wanted to defend the total integrity of Jesus' holiness and impeccability. According to this view temptations attacked Christ only externally. [12]

But what is a purely external temptation? Does not real temptation penetrate the consciousness and make its enticements felt?

The sign that Christ's temptations were not purely external is that they triggered deep, anguishing conflicts within his soul. Thus, the distress and fear that Mark mentions in connection with Gethsemane (Mk 44:33) tended to make Jesus flinch from his imminent Passion and render its acceptance very painful.

Christ's example helps to show that a deep inner conflict within a human soul does not necessarily imply moral disorder. At the time of his agony, Jesus was obliged to overcome his dread, his spontaneous revulsion against suffering. The struggle between his will and a lower, even violent and obsessive inclination is not in itself a sign of moral imperfection. For it occurred in Christ at the very moment he was meriting salvation for mankind.

To understand the meaning of Jesus' temptations, we must consider the redemptive finality of the Incarnation. The redemptive mission involved assuming responsibility for a sinful world in order to achieve victory over sin. This brought him a solidarity with human temptations and a deeper involvement in the war against evil that is waged in every human conscience. It was altogether normal that Christ should have been impelled to fight with all his psychological and moral resources against the seductive power of sin in order to conquer it.

---

[12] According to A. Michel, "these temptations were purely external." He adds that Jesus "permitted these temptations for our instruction ..., for our edification ... and finally for our consolation" (Article "Jesus-Christ," DTC 8, 1294-1295).

B. THE FREEDOM OF JESUS

1. *The Reality of this Freedom*

Jesus' impeccability did not deprive him of his freedom. We must affirm that he enjoyed freedom because it is an inherent attribute of the human will.

In the Gospel texts, Jesus is clearly a free man, master of his thoughts and actions. He himself emphasized his freedom in his Passion, in which ostensibly hostile circumstances were exerting inexorable pressures on him: "No one takes [my life] from me; I lay it down of my own free will" (Jn 10:18). And he added that the will of his Father did not rob him of his freedom but on the contrary confirmed it and demonstrated it: "... as it is in my power to lay [my life] down, so it is in my power to take it up again; and this is the command I have been given by my Father" (*ibid.*).

It was precisely in his redemptive sacrifice that Jesus exercised his freedom to the fullest. As the Council of Trent declares, Christ merited our justification (DS 1513, 1539, 1560). Now, merit requires freedom. It presupposes an individual is responsible for his actions, that he is not constrained to perform them, and that it is really within his power to do so by virtue of his own free decision.

The mystery of the Incarnation thus explicitly demands Christ's human freedom. In making the best possible use of his freedom out of obedience to his Father and in giving his life, Jesus made reparation for the evil use sinful men make of their freedom.

2. *Reconciling Jesus' Freedom with his Impeccability*

Reconciling freedom with impeccability poses a problem that we must clearly put into context. [13]

This problem has often been posed as relating to the Father's command. The dilemma was presented in these terms: either Jesus Christ was free and could therefore refuse to obey the Father's command to accept his Passion and death, and in that case he was capable of sinning, i.e., he was not im-

---

[13] Cf. A. Durand, "La liberté du Christ dans son rapport à l'impeccabilité," *NRT* 70 (1948) 811-822.

peccable. Or on the other hand the Father's command stripped him of his freedom. In view of this dilemma, many have tried to mitigate, limit, or entirely eliminate the Father's command. [14]

Actually, the real difficulty does not lie in harmonizing the Father's command with Christ's freedom. The command implies a moral obligation, but does not suppress Christ's freedom. On the contrary, it presupposes it. There was no reason to attenuate the Father's command. Christ really obeyed, and he did so freely. [15] The command and the freedom are coordinates.

The essential problem concerns Christ's impeccability in the strict sense. This impeccability may seem to suppress Christ's freedom from two points of view: first, it implies that Christ was predetermined, even before he acted, to a particular line of action; and secondly, it seems to exclude his use of the faculty to choose between good and evil.

However, these two basic affirmations are contestable. In reality, Christ's impeccability does not imply a prior determination to follow a given course of action. It merely excludes the possibility that he could sin. Besides, even where the faculty to choose between good and evil is excluded, authentic freedom can exist.

It is the nature of freedom that needs to be probed more deeply. If we consider the essence of freedom to be merely the faculty to choose between good and evil, it becomes impossible to reconcile freedom and impeccability. We are then reduced to presenting theories which sacrifice either impeccability or freedom.

In psychological experience, freedom is perceived essentially as the faculty to determine one's actions for oneself. It consists fundamentally in a self-mastery, a dominion that man exercises over his own behavior. It is the power to

---

[14] On these solutions, cf. P. Galtier, *De Incarnatione ac Redemptione*, Paris, 1947, 304-312.

[15] The existence of this freedom poses insurmountable problems for those who affirm the beatific vision. Cf. Michel, ("Jésus-Christ," *DTC* 8, 1303), who holds to the view that in this particular situation the influence of the intuitive vision was moderated in such a way as not to impede Christ's freedom, granted that this vision affected the mortal Christ only extrinsically and by way of a repercussion.

make decisions for oneself, without constraint either from external causes or inner necessities.

In God, freedom is defined by the absolute faculty to determine one's action for oneself. It cannot consist in the faculty of choosing between good and evil. God cannot act in any way whatsoever that would tend to evil. And yet he is perfectly free, more perfectly free than man. In this connection, let us call to mind the Pelagian controversy. In response to Julian of Eclane who admitted the existence of freedom only where there was a faculty for choosing, i.e., "the power to will the opposites," Augustine declared: "If no one is free unless he can will two things, that is to say, good and evil, then God is not free, for he cannot will evil. Is this the way you praise God, by stripping him of his freedom?" [16]

The essence of freedom, therefore, is not to be sought in the faculty to choose between good an evil. It consists in self-determination or the faculty to determine one's voluntary acts for oneself. This is the freedom of God, and at a lower level, it is also the freedom of man.

Admittedly, in man this faculty of self-determination finds expression through the choice between good and evil. Yet this faculty, which involves the possibility of choosing evil and of committing sin, is not a superior or perfect type of freedom and self-determination. Rather, it is an inferior, defective type, stemming from man's inherent imperfection. The faculty to choose to sin is obviously not a perfection of freedom but its limitation, as it were.

So, the saint is a human person who becomes increasingly free during his mortal life. As he progresses in his intimacy with God, he gradually loses the concrete faculty to choose evil, for evil entices him less and less. And yet he becomes increasingly free, because he tends more and more to make his decisions from the depths of his being, by surrendering himself ever more completely to God. By contrast, the inveterate sinner, in whom the faculty to choose evil is constantly growing, becomes increasingly the slave of his passions and becomes progressively less free.

---

[16] *Opus imperfectum contra Julianum,* I, 100, PL 45, 1116.

Nevertheless, the saint preserves the faculty to choose until he dies. But his example suggests to us what the suppression of the faculty to choose evil can be in its extreme form. This suppression coincides with a more authentic and deeper freedom. This ultimate outreach of freedom, which is beyond the grasp of ordinary men during their earthly lives, is precisely the freedom that is confirmed in Christ, by virtue of the hypostatic union.

Christ was perfectly free. He determined his own life for himself. He freely decided to obey his Father. And yet it was not possible for him to choose to disobey. His freedom consisted in his self-determination. Christ's impeccability, excluding the faculty to choose evil, was thus in perfect harmony with his freedom. Christ determined for himself to love the Father and to obey him.

In this explanation, we notice that the exclusion of the faculty to choose evil is not a deficiency or an obstacle to Christ's freedom. It is a perfection that makes his freedom more genuine. [17] From this we must conclude that Christ's impeccability, instead of being opposed to true freedom, made this freedom more perfect. Because he was impeccable, Christ was able to choose totally, inalienably to cleave to the Father's will.

A further comment will help clarify the perfection of Christ's freedom. The faculty to choose evil presupposes that evil can present itself to man as a positive good. Indeed, there is no perfection in seeing evil as a positive good. Christ could not have been marred by this imperfection. In his eyes evil always was what it really is, an evil and not a good. And for this reason he could never have willed evil: it is devoid of value, devoid of any claim to be desired.

Through the life of grace, Christ communicates to men a freedom analogous to his own. This is a superior freedom that tends increasingly to exclude the faculty to choose evil

---

[17] Cf. Durand, *ibid.*, 821: "Once we have understood that Christ enjoyed liberty in all its perfection, and that this perfection excluded any possibility of defection, that is to say, of choosing evil (the power to fall into sin which constitutes the blemish in the freedom of imperfect and sinful creatures), the problem of 'reconciling' freedom and impeccability is solved, solved because it has been overcome."

because evil tends to lose its charm and value. Along with this progressive diminution in the faculty to choose there is an emancipation from slavery to the passions and a corresponding increase in the faculty for self-determination, for cleaving to God's will.

CONCLUSION

THE SIGNIFICANCE OF THE INCARNATION OF THE SON OF GOD

In conclusion, we should like to review the answer to the question: Why is the Savior of mankind the Incarnate Son of God?

Certain non-Chalcedonian approaches to Christology present Jesus as the man in whom God revealed himself and acted. Such a view might give the impression that, for all practical purposes, the work of salvation would have been completely assured even by a Savior who was only a man and not a divine person. In other words, a "functional" Christ might appear to be equivalent to an ontological Christ. The efficacy of God's action would have been identical whether Jesus had been ontologically God or whether God had acted in the man Jesus. This would lead to the conclusion that the destiny of mankind would in no way have suffered if Jesus had been a human person, and that the only difference between this view and the teachings of traditional Christology would be in the realm of abstract formulas or concepts. In that event, an ontology that would inevitably remain deeply mysterious and subject to unending debate would not matter very much. The result for us would be the same. Only the functional would matter for us, that is to say, what Jesus did or what God did through him.

This alleged equivalence between a purely functional Christ and the Christ of traditional doctrine challenges us to explicate wherein the irreplaceable value of the Incanation of the Son of God consists.

1. *The Involvement of Divine Love*

The primordial significance of the Christology of the Son of God Incarnate resides in the depth of the involvement of divine love. As we have already pointed out, this involvement reached a high point in the sending of the Son by the Father. By giving his Son, the Father gave to mankind the most complete gift of his fatherly love. This gift is incomparably superior to a gift that would consist in the mission assigned to a mere man in whom he would act in a special, unique way. Between the Father who gives his own Son to mankind and a God who might perform his work of salvation within and through a privileged man, there is no equivalence.

Here we must note to what extent the ontological is involved in the functional and confers meaning on it. Only he who is ontologically the eternal Son of God can express in his Incarnation the most lofty gift of God's love to men. The fact that Jesus is this Son is a truth that far transcends the realm of abstractions or of conceptual elaborations. It is of the greatest importance to the life of all men, for it signifies the Father's gift of love.

This is made especially clear in the text in which St. Paul sets out to show that God is "on our side." "God who did not spare his own Son, but gave him up for us all, will be not also give all things with him?" (Rm 8:32). The involvement of the Father in the redemptive Incarnation brings all other graces along with it.

The importance of this consideration in the Christian's daily life has perhaps not always been recognized. It implies that in each grace the gift of the Father who delivered up his own Son is also present. This gift which was realized within the divine mystery of the relationship between the Father and the Son has continual repercussions in all the individual gifts that stem from it for men. It shows us how deeply the loftiest ontology is involved in the functional economy of grace.

Moreover, Paul adds, by way of a conclusion, that "nothing ... can ever come between us and the love of God made visible in Christ Jesus our Lord" (Rm 8:38-39). Thus the Father's supreme love can never be divorced from our concrete life. Efforts to present a purely human Christ would tend to separate us from this love, and to deprive mankind of the gift that the Father has given to men in the person of his Son. But it is impossible to be a Christian without this gift. Christian ontology can exist only through the ontology of Christ, the Son given by the Father.

This is also the doctrine professed in the Epistle to the Ephesians: "But God loves us with so much love that he was generous with his mercy: when we were dead through our sins, he brought us to life with Christ" (Ep 2: 4-5). The great love of God has taken concrete form in the gift of his Son, a gift that has radically transformed human life.

Likewise, if we do not recognize Jesus to be the eternal Son of God, we cannot understand the extraordinary degree to which "God is love," according to John (I Jn 4: 8). [1] This love was manifested in the sending of the only Son (cf. I Jn 4: 9; Jn 3: 16). The Johannine declarations attest that the functional cannot be separated from the ontological, not only because divine love would no longer retain its identity without the gift of the Son, but also because our own life depends totally on this gift: "God sent into the world his only Son so that we could have life through him" (I Jn 4: 9). This new life would lose its meaning if it were not a filial life, a sharing in the life of the Son.

The sending of the Son among men thus gives the involvement of divine love its full dimension, both as to its goal and to its origin. As source, it is the highest gift of the Father, and as goal it communicates divine life to mankind.

The comments of Paul and John stem from Jesus' own words as for instance in the parable of the homicidal vine-dressers (cf. Mk 12: 1 ff.). [2] For here the difference between

---

1 After noting that there is a definition of the being of God and that "God is in himself and has been from all eternity pure communication of himself and gift," C. Spicq adds: "God in himself is love, not as if he possessed an abstract quality, but — inasmuch as he is all vitality, all power, all diffusive goodness — he communicates himself totally to his. Son, he pours himself out into him, with infinite delight" (*Agapè dans le Nouveau Testament*, III, Paris 1959, 277).

2 Objections to the authenticity of this parable, and in particular to the son's mission, have recently been examined by M. Hubaut, "La parabole des

the beloved son and the servants reveals his immense superiority over them.

Jesus called attention to the great value of the gift the Father offers, a value that should inspire reflection. The purpose of the parable was to deter those who were plotting Jesus' death by showing how grave a crime it is to murder the Son. [3]

In this simple account of the sending of the son we discern an accent as poignant as the one that surfaces in Jesus' words: "Yes, God loved the world so much ..." (Jn 4:16). The parable puts the spotlight on the decisive act of salvation: the Father's sending of his beloved Son. Paul and John merely take an idea that is not in the least mythological and that has been proposed by Jesus in very concrete language comprehensible to anyone as well as to any cultural milieu. In fact, the parable clearly reveals the essential insufficiency of Christology that does not go beyond the "servant" stage.

We have only to probe the image of the beloved son sent by the master of the vineyard to discover Jesus' divine sonship and his consubstantiality with the Father. Far from being speculations provoked by philosophic concerns, these attributes of Christ are detailed to clarify the reason for the sending of the Son. That is the only way the Father's action can be understood. All the specifics of Christ's ontology must be understood in order to discern the quality of the divine love involved in the work of salvation.

2. The Revelation

The equivalence between the two Christologies we have been discussing might seem to be most obvious where Revelation is concerned. In this area, is it not what has been revealed that matters rather than the one who reveals? Could not God reveal himself quite as well in a Jesus who was

---

vignerons homicides: son authenticité, sa visée première" (*Revue Théologique de Louvain* 6, 1975, 50-61).

[3] In this sense, as Hubaut points out, "the Christological affirmation remains implicit, subordinated to Jesus' message: take care not to void the covenant by putting God's last messenger to death" (*ibid.*, 57). Nevertheless, the mention of the identity of the "beloved son" is essential. It is the high point of the parable.

simply a man as in a Christ who is the Son of the eternal Father? For even in the latter case, the revelation still comes through a man. And is not the message of salvation identical when it is transmitted by a man who receives it from God? Is it not sufficient that there be a man through whom God makes his words heard?

To the contrary, in the revelation of God as it has actually occurred, the personal identity of the Revealer is of capital importance. If Jesus had been merely the last of the prophets, this identity would have been much less significant. The essential contribution of the prophets to the Jewish religion consisted in the words they spoke in God's name. But the essential contribution of Jesus has been his coming in person to found a new religion. Attempts to reduce Christian Revelation to the type of Jewish Revelation are therefore totally inadequate.

During the era of the Old Covenant God intervened in history through human intermediaries, but he remained personally outside of this history. Through the New Covenant the Son of God entered human history in person, and he is called the Mediator in the transcendent sense as being both God and man. [4] The insertion of a divine person into human history is the unique event that confers a completely new character upon Revelation. [5]

This difference has been highlighted in the prologue to the Epistle to the Hebrews (1:2). When God spoke through the prophets, he did so in many ways and at various times. When he spoke to us "through his Son," he did so in a unique, non-repeatable way, in an era which was definitive because it was eschatological. The difference is not one of degree but of nature. The Revelation that was fulfilled in the Son of God dominates both space and time.

We encounter here again from the point of view of self-revelation the idea of the Father's supreme involvement ex-

---

[4] Cf. the author's article "Le Christ médiateur unique et universel," in *Studia Missionalia* 21 (1972) 303-320.

[5] Cf. R. Latourelle, "La spécificité de la révélation chrétienne," in *Studia Missionalia* 20 (1971) 51-53: "The revelatory function of Christ results directly from the Incarnation" (51). "Christianity is the only religion whose revelation is incarnated in a Person who presents himself as the living and absolute Truth" (53).

pressed elsewhere from the point of view of the redemptive sacrifice. Whereas in the oracles of the prophets God merely communicated his words, in his Son he gives his very self. As a result the self-revelation is the total communication of his divine being.

Not only is the subject of the revelation different in the New Covenant. There is also an essential difference in its object. The substance of the revelation is no longer simply a thought, a doctrine, an intention, but the divine person of the Son. When the revealer is God himself, he reveals who he is. That is also the reason why the revelation made by Christ is unique and definitive. Jesus expressed through human language and actions the Son that he truly is.

This explains why John in his Gospel thought he should first speak of the preexistence of the Word in order to point out the fundamental meaning and direction of the revelation. [6] This explains the difference between the Jewish and the Christian revelation of God: "... though the Law was given through Moses, grace and truth have come through Jesus Christ" (Jn 1:17). [7]

The object of the new revelation is God himself: "No one has ever seen God; it is God the only Son, who is (turned) toward the Father's heart, who has made him known" (Jn 1:18). [8] Only God can reveal God and make him visible.

---

[6] As F.M Braun points out, at the root of the theology of the Word there is the experience that relates to the person of Christ. For, according to Jesus' own words (cf. Jn 7:27-28; 8:14; 14:9-11), if we acknowledge only his earthly origin we are doomed never to know him (*Jean le Théologien, III, Sa Théologie*, I, *Le mystère de Jésus-Christ*, Paris, Gabalda, 1966, 24).

[7] This contrast is discussed by S.A. Panimolle in his study, *Il dono della legge e la grazia della verità* (*Gv 1,17*), Rome, Ave, 1973. He concludes: "Jesus of Nazareth is the Logos incarnate, the only Son of the Father. That is why it was possible for him to be the eschatological Revealer of the Father ..." (434).

[8] In this context, we must take note of the expression "God the only Son" which stresses the divinity of the author of the revelation. We go along with the *monogenès theos*, which is best attested to and seems to be the original lesson. Cf. B.A. Martin, "A Neglected Feature of the Christology of the Fourth Gospel," *NTS* 22 (1975) 37-41. After developing the arguments relating to this lesson, this author remarks that in John's Gospel the term "God" is applied three times to Jesus: as the preexisting Word (Jn 1:1), as the Word incarnate (Jn 1:18), and as the risen Christ (Jn 20:28).

It is a "God the only Son" who knows the Father in his innermost depths who has communicated to us the vision by which he penetrates deep into the Father's heart.

John the Evangelist acquired this manner of presenting the work of revelation from Jesus' own testimony about himself. His words: "To have seen me is to have seen the Father" (Jn 14:9) clearly express what many other words or actions of Jesus manifested in a more veiled way. It shows that man's supreme desire to know has been satisfied. What could not be realized earlier in Judaism because of the threat of death, namely, "to see God," was accomplished for the disciples thanks to the Incarnation.

In Johannine terminology, Jesus is the Word, he is the light of men (cf. Jn 1:9), the light of the world and the light of life (cf. Jn 8:12). He is the truth (cf. Jn 14:6). Word, Light, and Truth are identified in his incarnate divine person. [9] This identification shows how inseparable the person of Christ is from his mission of revelation.

3. The Meaning of Christ's Solidarity with Men

Christologies that limit themselves to defining Christ as a human person are attempting to bring him closer to men. They rest on the conviction that his solidarity with men is stronger when it is founded on a total equality with them in the human condition, claiming no superiority from some other source.

Actually such Christologies would tend to deprive Jesus of the quality that gives value to his solidarity with men. In his case, it is a God, a divine person, who becomes solidary with mankind by assuming a life like that of all other men. There is nothing exceptional in the fact that a man should share the condition of his human brothers. Why should anyone be surprised that a simple man should live like a man and be subject like all other men to the servitudes of the human condition?

He emphasizes that the term does not describe Christ's function, but indicates who he is by describing his person as such (*art. cit.*, 51).

[9] On the identification of Jesus with Truth in John's Gospel, cf. I. de la Potterie, *Gesù Verità*. This identity signifies that "the definitive Revelation has been fulfilled in him" (5).

However the case of the Son of God who comes down to our level is unique and exceptional. That is what we admire in Jesus. Although he is God, he spanned the distance that separates the Godhead from humanity, and he chose to be one of us. Everything that is really human in him takes on a special value in our eyes because his person is divine. We come to understand the "true man" in the same measure that we grasp that Christ is "true God."

That is the reason this solidarity transforms our human condition. By reason of the fact that a God has lived a human life just like ours and performed the most commonplace human actions, he elevated the dignity of this life and these actions to a divine level. Working, eating, drinking, confronting daily problems, suffering and dying have become God's actions. They have acquired this supreme value once and for all, regardless of their apparent banality. The Incarnation confers a transcendent dignity upon the activity of all human persons.

Far more important, the divine stature of Christ's personality enabled him to represent the whole of mankind in offering up his redemptive sacrifice. Whereas human solidarity gave him only the capacity to share in the lot of his brothers and sisters and to suffer with them, the infinite scope of his divine person qualified him to take upon himself the burden of the sufferings of all humans, to bear the weight of their sins, and obtain their universal salvation through his sacrifice. Not only did Jesus Christ suffer *along with* others, but he suffered *for* all.

Jesus has expressed this universal value of his sacrifice in these words: "For the Son of Man himself did not come to be served but so serve, and to give his life as a ransom for many" (Mk 10:45; Mt 20:28). How was it possible for him to make himself the ransom for many, that is to say, to offer himself for the liberation of all mankind? The reason is that he is "the Son of Man," a man who is at the same time a divine personage, the Son of God. This is the source of the maximal efficacy of his solidarity with humankind.

Lastly, this solidarity has assumed a lasting form in the historical development of the Church. In the promise: "And know that I am with you always, to the end of time" (Mt

28:20), the "I am" is the "I Am" of God who guarantees his fidelity to his covenant (cf. Ex 3:12-14).

Above all, in his interpersonal relations, Christ has remained present as the principle of love, the term of love, and the focus of union. He remains present in his disciples to inspire their charity, to make them love the way he has loved (cf. Jn 13:34; 15:12); he is present in all human persons receiving the love that is offered them (cf. Mt 25:40); and he is present in every union that is formed in his name: "For where two or three meet in my name, I shall be there in the midst of them" (Mt 18:20). It is in his person, as the incarnate Son of God, that he has become the universal center of convergence, and this he will remain until the end of the world.

4. *The Work of the Redemption*

Reducing Jesus to strictly human dimensions is to seriously improverish the work of the Redemption.

In particular, the theories that seek to explain Christ's action through the human influence of example and the stimulus of human love end up by considerably diminishing his salvific power. The contagion of example is necessarily limited to those who experience it firsthand. And we cannot forget that even today the great majority of mankind does not know the Jesus of the Gospels. If Jesus were purely and simply a man, there could be no question of claiming universal efficacy for his sacrifice. The number of those who have the opportunity to admire and imitate him is limited. If we insist on thinking of Jesus as simply a human person, we cannot explain the transformation he has wrought in the destiny of the whole human race.

We might point out that, in itself, the limiting of the sufferings of Calvary to the sufferings of a human person strips the drama of the Redemption of its true dimensions. It is no longer the Son of God who suffered for us, nor is it the Father who gave his only Son in sacrifice for us. In the Christological hymn of Philippians (2:6-11), the value of the sacrifice is seen to consist precisely in the fact that Someone who was by nature God became obedient even to death on a cross (cf. Ph 2:6-8). In the Epistle to the Hebrews the quality of his obedience is linked to his identity as Son: "Although he was Son, he learnt to obey through suffering" (Heb 5:8). If this divine person were not involved, we could not longer grasp the power of Christ's redemptive love.

Moreover, the efficacy of the work of the Redemption would have been so greatly diminished that Jesus would no longer deserve the title of Savior. Salvation would no longer correspond to what the first Christian community firmly believed it to be, as Peter expressed it: "For of all the names in the world given to men, this is the only one by which we can be saved" (Ac 4:12). Israel was saved by the name of Yahweh. Christians are to be saved by the name, that is to say, by the person of Christ, by a divine person who possesses the power to save mankind.

The granting of salvation involves the divine person from several points of view. It signifies the remission of sins: Christ exercises in his own name on earth power reserved to God alone. It involves a new creation, of such a nature that the one who is the Savior is at the same time the Creator at a superior level of being. It consists essentially in the communication of divine life. If Jesus were not God, he could not divinize mankind.

Christ consummated this redemptive work by sending the Holy Spirit, and this sending could only be the exercise of a divine power. As we well know, from Pentecost onward the manifestation of the gifts of the Holy Spirit has witnessed that Christ is Lord, possessing divine sovereignty and dominion over the unfolding of the life of God in the universe.

This quality of Lord, explicitly attributed to Christ in the first profession of faith (cf. I Co 12:3; Rm 10:9), assures him the central place in Christian prayer and worship. In the Eucharist, the command: "Do this as a memorial of me" (Lk 22:19) signifies that henceforth Jesus was to hold the place of God in worship, and that the divine presence was to consist in a special way in his presence as the incarnate Son of God.

Thus, the whole of the work of the Redemption would lose its substance if Christ were only a man and no more. Christian life would be as completely devalued as Jesus himself. The Eucharist would become unrecognizable. To use another Gospel expression, it is not from a mere man that

402

"fountains of living water" can flow, together with the abundance of the gifts of the Spirit (Jn 7:38).

5. God's Plan for a Filial Mankind

Only the incarnate Son of God could bring fulfillment to the divine plan for a filial mankind to be raised to the level of the divine sonship of the only Son and to share in his own intimacy with the Father.

We have stressed the relational character of the person. The person of the Son communicated his filial relationship to the humanity he assumed. By personalizing the human nature of Jesus, this divine person gave it a totally filial physiognomy. The Gospels present Jesus to us as a filial personality living by his relationship with the Father.

An exploration of Jesus' psychology leads us to the conclusion that the Son became humanly aware of his divine identity within the intimate contacts formed between the Father and himself. These contacts, made within the depths of his human soul and resulting from divine intervention, resembled the mystical contacts between the saints and God. However, their distinctive mark was their filial mysticism. Jesus discovered himself in his person of a Son through filial relations inspired in him by the One who wanted to be called "Abba."

The Son's human experience was filial in every respect. It was inspired in every detail as well and in the general orientation of his human behavior by the relational being of the Son constantly turned toward the Father. Christ's earthly life was a return toward the Father. Even as a child of twelve, according to the testimony of the Gospel concerning the development of his human consciousness, he expressed the dynamism of this return: "Did you not know that I must be in my Father's house?" (Lk 2:49).

The affirmation in John's Prologue: "In the beginning was the Word: the Word was toward God" (Jn 1:1) clearly indicates that the dynamism that from all eternity has impelled the Son toward the Father became incarnate in the dynamism of a temporal life, a life in which the Son turned all his human psychological energies toward the Father.

Besides, the relational being of the Son entered the human

community in order to communicate and share his filial relationship with the Father. He established filial contact between humans and the Father, sharing with them the privilege of calling the Father "Abba."

Jesus did not merely implant a filial functionalism or a simple attitude of filial love within the hearts of men. He engrafted in his brothers and sisters a truly dynamic filial ontology. His own hypostatic filial relationship, the filial reality that belonged uniquely to him, has become the foundation of the innermost existence of all human persons. In so doing he recreated mankind, conferring upon it a new reality that impels all humans toward the Father.

The filial quality of man stems from the quality of Son of God which is the definition of Jesus. Without the Incarnation of the Son of God the human community could certainly have developed certain filial sentiments. But it would not have been raised to the level of the most complete intimacy with the Father, and it could not have shared the eternal Son's own life of loving sonship. It is this Son who has constituted all men in their filial being and who has introduced them into the unity that binds him to the Father.

After forming a thoroughly filial human nature within himself, the Son formed and continues to form it in the human race as a whole as well as in each individual human person. By communicating his own divine sonship to men, he has endowed them with their noblest worth.

INDEX OF AUTHORS